FIXED INCOME MATHEMATICS

Analytical & Statistical Techniques

Third Edition

FRANK J. FABOZZI, CFA

IRWIN
Professional Publishing®
Chicago • London • Singapore

Times Mirror
Higher Education Group

Library of Congress Cataloging-in-Publication Data

Fabozzi, Frank J.
  Fixed income mathematics / Frank J. Fabozzi. —
3rd. ed.
      p.   cm.
  Rev. ed. of: Fixed income mathematics. Rev. ed. c1993.
  Includes index.
  ISBN 0-7863-1121-5
  1. Fixed-income securities—Mathematics.   2. Rate of return.
I. Fabozzi, Frank J.   Fixed income mathematics.   II. Title.
HG4650.F33   1997
332.63'2044—dc20   96–22266

Printed in the United States of America

1 2 3 4 5 6 7 8 9 0 *DO* 3 2 1 0 9 8 7 6

To my beautiful wife, Donna Marie
and
my son, Francesco Alfonso

CONTENTS

PREFACE

In the past decade, participants in the fixed-income markets have been introduced to new analytical frameworks for evaluating fixed-income securities and new fixed-income portfolio strategies. In discussing fixed-income securities and strategies, we often hear terms such as *duration, effective duration, convexity, negative convexity, option-adjusted spread, total return, PSA, CPR, spot rates, forward rates, yield volatility, binomial model, value-at-risk,* and *delta.* What do these concepts mean? Why are these concepts useful in fixed-income analysis? What are the dangers of using these concepts?

Fixed Income Mathematics: Analytical & Statistical Techniques not only explains these concepts, but also sets forth the foundation needed to understand them, their computation, their limitations, and their application to fixed-income portfolio management. It begins with the basic concepts of the mathematics of finance (the time value of money) and systematically builds on these, taking you through the state-of-the-art methodologies for evaluating fixed-income securities with embedded options, such as callable bonds, mortgage-backed securities (mortgage pass-through securities, collateralized mortgage obligations, and stripped mortgage-backed securities). The concepts are illustrated with numerical examples and graphs. The material is self-contained and requires only a basic knowledge of elementary algebra to understand.

Many of the chapters in this book are drawn from the lectures I delivered in my Fixed Income Seminar at Yale's School of Management and MIT's Sloan School of Management, my tutorials, and my presentations at various financial institutions in the United States, Europe, and Japan.

ACKNOWLEDGMENTS

Several individuals assisted me in various ways in this edition and the two previous editions. Andrew Kalotay and George Williams of Andrew Kalotay Associates assisted me in the preparation of parts of Chapter 17. Parts of Chapter 20 are adapted from work I coauthored with Scott Richard of Miller, Anderson & Sherrerd. David Canuel of Aeltus Investment Management provided the information for the real-world simulation in Chapter 22. Ardavan Nozari of Salomon Brothers, Inc., provided the data for one of the regression illustrations in Chapter 23.

Charles Basner of TIPS provided many helpful instructions that I used in developing the more efficient spreadsheet programs I wrote for several of the illustrations. His ideas saved me many days of programming.

Jan Mayle of TIPS and Dragomir Krgin provided me with information on the day count conventions discussed in Chapter 5. I am grateful to Dragomir for allowing me to reprint an exhibit in Chapter 5 that shows market conventions in major bond markets throughout the world.

I received comments on portions of this book from the following individuals: Scott Brody (Information Management Network), John Carlson (Fidelity), Ravi Dattatreya (Sumitomo Bank Capital Markets), Mark Dunetz (The Guardian Life Insurance Company), Joseph Guagliardo, Jr. (FNX), Eliot Jacobowitz (Information Management Network), Frank Jones (The Guardian

Life Insurance Company), Todd Middlebrook (Information Management Network), Mark Pitts (White Oak Capital Management), Edward Murphy (Merchants Mutual Insurance Company), Chuck Ramsey (Structured Capital Management), Frank Ramirez (Structured Capital Management), Scott Richard (Miller, Anderson & Sherrerd), Ken Spindel (Bear Stearns), David Yuen (Structured Capital Management), and Paul Zhao (TIAA).

Frank J. Fabozzi

1

⑥ INTRODUCTION

Before the 1980s, the analysis of fixed-income securities was relatively simple. In an economic environment that exhibited relatively stable interest rates, investors purchased fixed-income securities intending to hold them to maturity. Yield to maturity could be used as a proxy measure of their relative value. Risk was measured in terms of credit rating. When a fixed-income security was callable, a second measure—yield to call—was used to assess its relative value. For a callable bond, the long-standing rule of thumb for a conservative investor was to select the lower of the yield to maturity and the yield to call as the potential return.

Those days are gone. In today's environment, interest rates fluctuate substantially, and the shape of the yield curve shifts more frequently. Several factors have made the traditional approach to fixed-income analysis of limited value.

First, trading and portfolio strategies that require the sale of a fixed-income security prior to maturity mean that a measure such as the yield to maturity is meaningless. The same holds for the yield to call. And if a fixed-income security is not held to maturity, some measure of risk—to reflect its price volatility as interest rates change—is needed.

Second, investors recognize that the only way to achieve a return equal to the yield to maturity is to reinvest the coupon payments. More specifically, to achieve the yield to maturity that they once thought they had locked in by purchasing a fixed-income security, they must reinvest the coupon payments at an interest rate equal to the yield to maturity. The reduction in anticipated return actually occasioned by reinvesting the coupon payments at an interest rate less than the yield to maturity may not be trivial. The same is true for yield to call.

Third, the plain vanilla bond is being replaced with more complex fixed-income securities as investment bankers continue to design instruments to reduce the cost of debt for their clients. The securitization of mortgages introduces brand new instruments—mortgage pass-through securities, a wide range of collateralized mortgage obligation bond classes, and stripped mortgage-backed securities—that cannot be analyzed by using the traditional methodology. Many of these new fixed-income securities have options embedded in them. With the advancement of option theory have come frameworks for analyzing these securities with embedded options.

In their now classic work, *Inside the Yield Book*, Sidney Homer and Martin Leibowitz were the first to demonstrate clearly the limitations of the traditional yield measures (yield to maturity and yield to call).[1] They also document the characteristics of a bond that bear upon its price volatility as interest rates change.

A measure of bond price volatility, popularly known as *duration*, was developed separately as early as 1938 by Frederick Macaulay,[2] in 1945 by Paul Samuelson,[3] in 1946 by Sir John Hicks,[4] and in 1952 by F.M. Redington.[5] However, it was not until 1973 that the link between duration and price volatility was made by Michael Hopewell and George Kaufman.[6] A study by Lawrence Fisher and Roman Weil in 1971 shows the importance of duration for portfolio strategies.[7]

In 1984 a paper written by Stanley Diller with the assistance of his Financial Strategies Group staff when he was employed at Goldman Sachs (particularly Ravi Dattatreya) made two important contributions to our understanding of the price performance of a fixed-income security.[8] First, Diller demonstrated that yield and duration alone are not sufficient to assess the performance of a fixed-income security; a third measure, convexity, is necessary. Second, he linked option theory and fixed-income analysis, showing how the embedded option of a fixed-income security will affect the performance of the security. Since then, several works have been published that incorporate and extend the concepts developed by Diller.

There has also come greater recognition that it is not appropriate to value a fixed-income security by using one yield to discount all the cash flows. Instead, a fixed-income security should be viewed as a package of cash flows; each cash flow is effectively a zero-coupon instrument. A 10-year Treasury coupon security, for example, should be thought of as 20 cash flows—19 semiannual coupons and a payment equal to the final coupon payment plus the principal. These 20 cash flows should then be viewed as 20 zero-coupon instruments—the first 19 with a maturity value equal to the semiannual coupon payment and the last with a maturity value equal to the coupon payment plus the principal. The value of each zero-coupon instrument should be determined by discounting the maturity value at an appropriate discount rate derived from the Treasury yield curve (more specifically, from the theoretical Treasury spot rate curve).

1   Sidney Homer and Martin L. Leibowitz, *Inside the Yield Book* (Englewood Cliffs, N.J.: Prentice-Hall/New York Institute of Finance, 1972), pp. 164–167.
2   Frederick R. Macaulay, *Some Theoretical Problems Suggested by the Movement of Interest Rates, Bond Yields, and Stock Prices in the United States Since 1865* (New York: National Bureau of Economic Research, 1938).
3   Paul A. Samuelson, "The Effect of Interest Rate Increases on the Banking System," *American Economic Review* (March 1945), pp. 16–27.
4   John R. Hicks, *Value and Capital* (Oxford, England: Clarendon Press, 1946).
5   F. M. Redington, "Review of the Principle of Life Office Valuations," *Journal of the Institute of Actuaries* (1952), pp. 286–340.
6   Michael Hopewell and George G. Kaufman, "Bond Price Volatility and Years to Maturity," *American Economic Review* (September 1973).
7   Lawrence Fisher and Roman Weil, "Coping with the Risk of Interest Rate Fluctuations and Returns to Bondholders from Naive and Optimal Strategies," *Journal of Business* (October 1971), pp. 408–431.
8   Stanley Diller, *Parametric Analysis of Fixed Income Securities* (New York: Financial Strategies Group, Goldman Sachs & Co., June 1984). The paper is reprinted as Chapter 2 in Ravi E. Dattatreya (ed.), *Fixed Income Analytics* (Chicago: Probus Publishing, 1991).

Finally, the process of coupon stripping by dealers in the Treasury market, which began in 1982, has forced the price of Treasury securities to their theoretical value. Thus, an understanding of the Treasury yield curve is critical to the valuation of fixed-income securities.

OVERVIEW OF THE BOOK

The basic foundations of the mathematics of finance are presented in the three chapters of Part I. Chapter 2 explains how to compute the future value of an investment. Chapter 3 shows how to calculate the present value of cash flows to be received (or paid) in the future. The price of any financial asset is the present value of the cash flows expected, so it is essential to have a firm understanding of present value and its characteristics. The yield of any investment is explained in Chapter 4.

Bond pricing and yield measures are the subjects of Part II. Chapter 5 extends the present value concept to the traditional analysis of bonds, showing how their value is determined. Conventional yield measures—yield to maturity and yield to call—which are simply applications of the yield measure reviewed in Chapter 4 are explained in Chapter 6. Chapter 7 brings the Treasury yield curve into the analysis of fixed-income securities. This chapter explains the Treasury yield curve and then discusses the concept of spot rates and forward rates and how these rates can be determined. The use of spot rates to value fixed-income securities is explained.

Part III covers return analysis. The potential sources of monetary return by investing in a bond are explained in Chapter 8. The conventional yield measures discussed in Chapter 6 are then critically evaluated in terms of whether they properly account for each of these sources. After highlighting the deficiencies of the conventional yield measures, Chapter 9 describes a better measure of potential return—total return—that does take into consideration all sources of potential dollar return, even if a bond is expected to be sold prior to the maturity date. Chapter 10 shows how to calculate the historical return for a portfolio.

The price volatility of option-free bonds (i.e., bonds without embedded options) is covered in Part IV. Price volatility properties of bonds, as well as the characteristics of bonds that affect their price volatility, are illustrated in Chapter 11. Two measures of bond price volatility—price value of a basis point and yield value of a price change—are explained in Chapter 12. The most common measure of price volatility, duration, is the subject of Chapter 13. Chapter 14 demonstrates the importance of convexity in explaining the potential price performance of a bond and how to calculate convexity. Chapter 15 explains how to incorporate the effect of a change in the yield curve on the duration of a portfolio.

Part V explains how to analyze bonds with embedded options. This involves determining their fair or theoretical value and their price volatility. Since the value and price volatility of a bond with an embedded option will depend on the value of the embedded option, it is necessary to understand the investment characteristics of options. This coverage is provided in Chapter 16. Chapter 17 then explains how to value bonds with an embedded option. The valuation model used is the binomial model. A product of a valuation model is the option-adjusted spread. This concept is explained in Chapter 17. Also introduced in Chapter 17 are the concepts of effective duration and convexity.

Examples of fixed-income securities with embedded call options are mortgage-backed securities (mortgage pass-through securities, collateralized mortgage obligations, and stripped mortgage-backed securities). Part VI applies the framework in Part V to the valuation of these securities. Chapter 18 explains determination of the cash flow and the concept of prepayment risk for mortgages. Chapter 19 provides a brief review of mortgage-backed securities and then illustrates how the current market convention—the PSA benchmark—is used to construct the estimated monthly cash flow of a mortgage pass-through security. Also explained is the prepayment convention for home equity loans. Two models for valuing mortgage-backed securities—static cash flow model and the Monte Carlo simulation model—are explained in Chapter 20. The concepts of option-adjusted spread and effective duration and convexity as applied to mortgage-backed securities are also explained in this chapter.

The four chapters in Part VII explain the statistical and management science techniques commonly used in fixed-income portfolio management. Chapter 21 reviews basic probability theory and its applications. The concepts explained include the expected value, the standard deviation (variance), and the normal distribution. This chapter also illustrates the various ways that interest-rate volatility is measured by market participants. Monte Carlo simulation is the subject of Chapter 22. Regression analysis, a statistical technique for estimating relationships, is covered in Chapter 23. In the last chapter, Chapter 24, optimization techniques are described.

I

⑥ TIME VALUE OF MONEY

2

⑥ FUTURE VALUE

The notion that money has a time value is one of the most basic concepts in financial analysis. Money has a time value because of the opportunities for investing money at some interest rate. In the three chapters of Part I of this book, we review the three fundamental concepts involved in understanding the time value of money. First, we explain how to determine the future value of an investment. In the next chapter, we explain the procedure for determining how much money must be invested today (called the present value) in order to realize a specific amount in the future. Chapter 3 shows how to compute the yield on any investment.

FUTURE VALUE OF AN INVESTMENT

Suppose an investor places $1,000 in a bank account and the bank agrees to pay interest of 7% a year. At the end of 1 year, the account will contain $1,070, that is, $1,000 of the original principal plus $70 of interest. Suppose that the investor decides to let the $1,070 remain in the bank account for another year and that the bank continues paying interest of 7% a year. The amount in the bank account at the end of the second year will equal $1,144.90, determined as follows:

Principal at beginning of year 2	$1,070.00
Interest for year 2 ($1,070 × .07)	74.90
Total in bank account	$1,144.90

In terms of our original $1,000 investment, the $1,144.90 represents the following:

Original investment at beginning of year 1	$1,000.00
Interest for year 1 ($1,000 × .07)	70.00
Interest for year 2 based on the original investment	70.00
Interest for year 2 earned on the interest from year 1 ($70 × .07)	4.90
Total	$1,144.90

The interest of $4.90 in year 2 above the $70 interest earned on the original principal of $1,000 is interest earned on interest.

After 8 years, the $1,000 investment—if allowed to accumulate tax-free at an annual interest rate of 7%—will be $1,718.19, as shown below:

Original investment at beginning of year 1	$1,000.00
At the end of year 1 ($1,000.00 × 1.07)	$1,070.00
At the end of year 2 ($1,070.00 × 1.07)	$1,144.90
At the end of year 3 ($1,144.90 × 1.07)	$1,225.04
At the end of year 4 ($1,225.04 × 1.07)	$1,310.79
At the end of year 5 ($1,310.79 × 1.07)	$1,402.55
At the end of year 6 ($1,402.55 × 1.07)	$1,500.73
At the end of year 7 ($1,500.73 × 1.07)	$1,605.78
At the end of year 8 ($1,605.78 × 1.07)	$1,718.19

After 8 years, $1,000 will grow to $1,718.19 if allowed to accumulate tax-free at an annual interest rate of 7%. We refer to the amount at the end of 8 years as the *future value*.

Notice that the total interest at the end of 8 years is $718.19. The total interest represents $560 of interest earned on the original principal ($70 × 8) plus $158.19 ($718.19 – $560) earned by the reinvestment of the interest.

Computing the Future Value of an Investment

To compute the amount that $1,000 will grow to at the end of 8 years if interest is earned at an annual rate of 7%, $1,000 can be multiplied by 1.07 eight times, as shown below:

$$\$1,000 \, (1.07) \, (1.07) \, (1.07) \, (1.07) \, (1.07) \, (1.07) \, (1.07) \, (1.07)$$
$$= \$1,718.19.$$

A shorthand notation for this calculation is

$$\$1,000 \, (1.07)^8 = \$1,718.19.$$

To generalize the formula, suppose $1,000 is invested for N periods at an annual interest rate of i (expressed as a decimal). Then, the future value N years from now can be expressed as follows:

$$\$1,000 \, (1 + i)^N.$$

For example, if $1,000 is invested for 4 years at an annual interest rate of 10% ($i = .10$), then the future value will be $1,464.10:

$$\$1,000 \, (1.10)^4$$
$$= \$1,000 \, (1.4641)$$
$$= \$1,464.10.$$

The expression $(1 + i)^N$ is the amount to which $1 will grow at the end of N years if an annual interest rate of i is earned. This expression is called the *future value of $1*. The future value of $1 multiplied by the original principal yields the future value of the original principal.

For example, we just demonstrated that the future value of $1,000 invested for 4 years at an annual interest rate of 10% would be $1,464.10. The future value of $1 is $1.4641. Therefore, if instead of $1,000, $50,000 is invested, the future value would be

$$\$50,000 \, (1.4641) = \$73,205.$$

We can generalize the formula for the future value as follows:

$$FV = P \, (1 + i)^N$$

where

   FV = Future value ($);
   P = Original principal ($);
   i = Interest rate (in decimal form);
   N = Number of years.

The following five illustrations show how to apply the future value formula.

Illustration 2-1   A pension fund manager invests $10 million in a financial instrument that promises to pay 8.7% per year for 5 years. The future value of the $10 million investment is $15,175,665, as shown below:

P = $10,000,000;
i = .087;
N = 5.

$$FV = \$10,000,000 \, (1.087)^5$$
$$= \$10,000,000 \, (1.5175665)$$
$$= \$15,175,665.$$

Illustration 2-2   A life insurance company receives a premium of $10 million, which it invests for 5 years. The investment promises to pay an annual interest rate of 9.25%. The future value of $10 million at the end of 5 years is $15,563,500, as shown below:

P = $10,000,000;
i = .0925;
N = 5.

$$FV = \$10,000,000 \, (1.0925)^5$$
$$= \$10,000,000 \, (1.5563500)$$
$$= \$15,563,500.$$

Illustration 2-3   Suppose that a life insurance company has guaranteed a payment of $14 million to a pension fund 4 years from now. If the life insurance company receives a premium of $11 million and can invest the entire premium for 4 years at an annual interest rate of 6.5%, will it have sufficient funds from this investment to meet the $14 million obligation?

The future value of the $11 million investment at the end of 4 years is $14,151,130, as shown below:

$P = \$11,000,000;$
$i = .065;$
$N = 4.$

$$FV = \$11,000,000\ (1.065)^4$$
$$= \$11,000,000\ (1.2864664)$$
$$= \$14,151,130.$$

Since the future value is expected to be $14,151,130, the life insurance company will have sufficient funds from this investment to satisfy the $14 million obligation to the pension fund.

Illustration 2-4   The portfolio manager of a tax-exempt fund is considering investing $400,000 in an instrument that pays an annual interest rate of 5.7% for 4 years. At the end of 4 years, the portfolio manager plans to reinvest the proceeds for 3 more years and expects that, for the 3-year period, an annual interest rate of 7.2% can be earned. The future value of this investment is $615,098, as shown below.

Future value of the $400,000 investment for 4 years at 5.7%:

$P = \$400,000;$
$i = .057;$
$N = 4.$

$$FV = \$400,000\ (1.057)^4$$
$$= \$400,000\ (1.248245)$$
$$= \$499,298.$$

Future value of $499,298 reinvested for 3 years at 7.2%:

$P = \$499,298;$
$i = .072;$
$N = 3.$

$$FV = \$499,298\ (1.072)^3$$
$$= \$499,298\ (1.231925)$$
$$= \$615,098.$$

Illustration 2-5   Suppose that the portfolio manager in the previous illustration has the opportunity to invest the $400,000 for 7 years in an instrument that promises to pay an annual interest rate of 6.15%. Is this alternative a more attractive investment than the one analyzed in the previous illustration?

The future value of $400,000 invested for 7 years at 6.15% is $607,435:

$P = \$400,000;$
$i = .0615;$
$N = 7.$

$$FV = \$400,000\ (1.0615)^7$$
$$= \$400,000\ (1.518588)$$
$$= \$607,435.$$

Assuming that both investments have the same default risk, the investment in the previous illustration will provide a greater future value at the end of 7 years *if* the expectation of the portfolio manager—concerning the annual interest rate at which the rolled-over funds can be reinvested—is realized.

Fractional Periods

In our illustrations, we have computed the future value for whole years. The future value formula, however, is the same if an investment is made for part of a year.

For example, suppose that $100,000 is invested for 7 years and three months. Since 3 months is .25 of 1 year, N in the future value formula is 7.25. Assuming an annual interest rate of 5%, the future value of $100,000 invested for 7 years and 3 months is $142,437, as shown below:

P = $100,000;
i = .05;
N = 7.25.

$$FV = \$100,000 \ (1.05)^{7.25}$$
$$= \$100,000 \ (1.424369)$$
$$= \$142,437.$$

Compounding More Than One Time Per Year

An investment may pay interest more than one time per year. For example, interest may be paid semiannually, quarterly, monthly, weekly, or daily. The future value formula handles interest payments that are made more than once per year by adjusting the annual interest rate and the exponent. The annual interest rate is adjusted by dividing by the number of times that interest is paid per year. The exponent, which represents the number of years, is adjusted by multiplying the number of years by the number of times that interest is paid per year.

Mathematically, we can express the future value when interest is paid m times per year as follows:

$$FV = P \ (1 + i)^n,$$

where

i = *Annual* interest rate divided by m;
n = Number of interest payments ($= N \times m$).

Illustration 2-6   Suppose that a portfolio manager invests $1 million in an investment that promises to pay an annual interest rate of 6.4% for 6 years. Interest on this investment is paid semiannually. The future value is $1,459,340, as shown below:

P = $1,000,000;
m = 2;
i = .032 (= .064/2);
N = 6;
n = 12 (6 × 2).

$$FV = \$1,000,000 \ (1.032)^{12}$$
$$= \$1,000,000 \ (1.459340)$$
$$= \$1,459,340.$$

If interest were paid only once per year, the future value would be $1,450,941 instead of $1,459,340. The higher future value when interest is paid semiannually reflects the more frequent opportunity for reinvesting the interest paid.

Illustration 2-7   Suppose that in the previous illustration, interest is paid quarterly rather than semiannually. The future value is $1,463,690, as shown below:

$P = \$1,000,000;$
$m = 4;$
$i = .016 \ (= .064/4);$
$N = 6;$
$n = 24 \ (6 \times 4).$

$$FV = \$1,000,000 \ (1.016)^{24}$$
$$= \$1,000,000 \ (1.4563690)$$
$$= \$1,463,690.$$

The future value is greater than if interest were paid semiannually.

FUTURE VALUE OF AN ORDINARY ANNUITY

Suppose that an investor expects to receive $10,000 a year from some investment for each of the next 5 years starting 1 year from now. Each time the investor receives the $10,000 he plans to invest it. Let's assume that the investor can earn an annual interest rate of 6% each time $10,000 is invested. How much money will the investor have at the end of 5 years?

Our future value formula makes it simple to determine how much each $10,000 investment will grow to. This calculation is shown below and is illustrated graphically in Exhibit 2-1.

Future value of the first $10,000, received 1 year from now:

$P = \$10,000;$
$i = .06;$
$N = 4.$

Notice that N is 4 since the first payment of $10,000 will be invested from the beginning of year 2 (or end of year 1) until the end of year 5.

$$FV \ of \ first \ \$10,000 = \$10,000(1.06)^{4}$$
$$= \$10,000 \ (1.262470)$$
$$= \$12,624.70.$$

Future value of the second $10,000, received 2 years from now:

$P = \$10,000;$
$i = .06;$
$N = 3.$

E X H I B I T 2–1

Future Value of an Ordinary Annuity of $10,000 Per Year for 5 Years

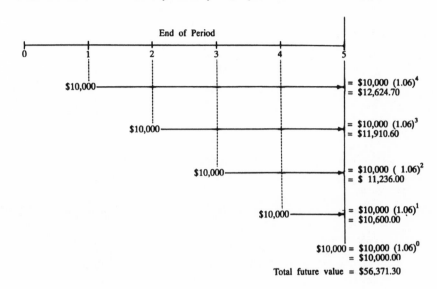

$$FV \ of \ second \ \$10,000 = \$10,000(1.06)^3$$
$$= \$10,000 \ (1.191060)$$
$$= \$11,910.60.$$

Future value of the third $10,000, received 3 years from now:

$P = \$10,000;$
$i = .06;$
$N = 2.$

$$FV \ of \ third \ \$10,000 = \$10,000(1.06)^2$$
$$= \$10,000 \ (1.123600)$$
$$= \$11,236.00.$$

Future value of the fourth $10,000, received 4 years from now:

$P = \$10,000;$
$i = .06;$
$N = 1.$

$$FV \text{ of fourth } \$10,000 = \$10,000(1.06)^1$$
$$= \$10,000 \ (1.06)$$
$$= \$10,600.00.$$

Future value of the last $10,000, received 5 years from now:

$P = \$10,000;$
$i = .06;$
$N = 0.$

$$FV \text{ of fifth } \$10,000 = \$10,000(1.06)^0$$
$$= \$10,000 \ (1.00)$$
$$= \$10,000.00.$$

Notice that since the last payment is received at the end of the fifth year, it will not be invested. Therefore, its future value will be simply $10,000.

If we total all the future values, we obtain

Future value of first $10,000	$12,624.70
Future value of second $10,000	11,910.60
Future value of third $10,000	11,236.00
Future value of fourth $10,000	10,600.00
Future value of fifth $10,000	10,000.00
Total future value	$56,371.30

The total future value of $56,371.30 is composed of the five payments of $10,000, or $50,000, plus $6,371.30 of interest earned by investing the $10,000 annual payments.

When the same amount of money is received (or paid) periodically, it is referred to as an *annuity*. When the first receipt (or payment) occurs one period from now, it is referred to as an *ordinary annuity*.

Computing the Future Value of an Annuity

In Chapter 9, you will need to know how to compute the future value of an ordinary annuity. Of course, the procedure we just followed—whereby we computed the future value of each investment—can be used. Fortunately, there is a formula that can be used to speed up this computation. The formula is

$$FV = A\left[\frac{(1+i)^N - 1}{i}\right],$$

where

A = Amount of the annuity ($);
i = Annual interest rate (in decimal form).

The term in the brackets is the *future value of an ordinary annuity of $1 per year*. Multiplying the future value of an ordinary annuity of $1 by the amount of the annuity produces the future value of an ordinary annuity.

Using the previous example in which $10,000 is invested each year for the next 5 years, starting 1 year from now, we would have

A = $10,000;
i = .06;
N = 5;

therefore,

$$FV = \$10,000 \left[\frac{(1.06)^5 - 1}{.06} \right]$$

$$= \$10,000 \left[\frac{1.3382256 - 1}{.06} \right]$$

$$= \$10,000 \, (5.63710)$$

$$= \$56,371.$$

This value agrees with our earlier calculation.

Illustration 2-8   Suppose that a portfolio manager purchases $5 million of par value of a 10-year bond that promises to pay 8% interest per year.[1] The price of the bond is $5 million. The interest payment is made once per year by the issuer; the first annual interest payment will be made 1 year from now. How much will the portfolio manager have if she (1) holds the bond until it matures 10 years from now and (2) can reinvest the annual interest payments at an annual interest rate of 6.7%?

The amount that the portfolio manager will have at the end of 10 years will be equal to

1. The $5 million when the bond matures;

2. 10 annual interest payments of $400,000 (.08 × $5 million);

3. The interest earned by investing the annual interest payments.

We can determine the sum of (2) and (3) by applying the formula for the future value of an ordinary annuity. In this illustration, the annuity is $400,000 per year (.08 × $5,000,000). Therefore,

A = $400,000;
i = .067;
N = 10.

$$FV = \$400,000 \left[\frac{(1.067)^{10} - 1}{.067} \right]$$

$$= \$400,000 \left[\frac{1.912688 - 1}{.067} \right]$$

$$= \$400,000 \, (13.62221)$$

$$= \$5,448,884.$$

---

1   Eurodollar bonds, for example, pay coupon interest once per year.

The future value of the ordinary annuity of $400,000 per year for 10 years invested at 6.7% is $5,448,884. Since $4,000,000 of this future value represents the total annual interest payments made by the issuer and invested by the portfolio manager, $1,448,884 ($5,448,884 − $4,000,000) must be the interest earned by reinvesting the annual interest payments. Therefore, the total amount that the portfolio manager will have at the end of 10 years by making the investment will be

Par (maturity) value	$ 5,000,000
Interest payments	4,000,000
Interest on reinvestment of interest payments	1,448,884
Total	$10,448,884

As you will see in Chapter 9, it will be necessary to determine the total future amount at the end of some investment horizon to assess the relative performance of a bond.

Future Value of an Ordinary Annuity When Payments Occur More Than Once Per Year

We can easily generalize the future value of an ordinary annuity formula to handle situations in which payments are made more than one time per year. For example, instead of assuming that an investor receives and then invests $10,000 per year for 5 years, starting 1 year from now, suppose that the investor receives $5,000 every 6 months for 5 years, starting 6 months from now.

The general formula for the future value of an ordinary annuity when payments occur m times per year is

$$FV = A \left[\frac{(1+i)^n - 1}{i} \right],$$

where

  A = Amount of the annuity ($);
  i = Annual interest rate divided by m (in decimal form);
  $n = N \times m$.

The value in the brackets is the *future value of an ordinary annuity of $1 per period.*

Illustration 2-9   Let's rework the analysis for the bond in Illustration 2-8 assuming that the interest is paid every 6 months and that the first payment is to be received and invested 6 months from now. The interest payment every 6 months is $200,000. The future value of the 20 semiannual interest payments of $200,000 to be received plus the interest earned by investing the interest payments is found as follows:

  A = $200,000;
  m = 2;
  i = .0335 (.067/2);
  n = 20 (10 × 2).

$$FV = \$200,000 \left[\frac{(1.0335)^{20} - 1}{.0335} \right]$$

$$= \$200,000 \left[\frac{1.932901 - 1}{.0335} \right]$$

$$= \$200,000 \, [27.84779]$$

$$= \$5,569,558.$$

Since the interest payments are equal to $4,000,000, the interest earned on the interest payments invested is $1,569,558. Because of the more frequent reinvestment of the interest payments received, the interest of $1,569,558 earned by investing the interest payments exceeds the interest earned if interest is paid only one time per year, that is, $1,448,884 (see Illustration 2-8).

The total amount that the portfolio manager will have at the end of 10 years by making the investment will be

Par (maturity) value	$ 5,000,000
Interest payments	4,000,000
Interest on reinvestment of interest payments	1,569,558
Total	$10,569,558

SUMMARY

In this chapter we have explained how to compute the future value of an investment. The formulas that we introduced are summarized in Exhibit 2-2.

Summary of Formulas for Future Value Computations

1. Future value of an investment made for N years:

$$FV = P \, (1 + i)^N,$$

where

  FV = Future value ($);
  P = Original principal ($);
  i = Interest rate (in decimal form);
  N = Number of years.

2. Future value of an investment made for n periods:

$$FV = P \, (1 + i)^n$$

where

  i = *Annual* interest rate divided by m;
  n = Number of periods ($=N \times m$);
  m = Number of payments per year.

3. Future value of an ordinary annuity for N years:

$$FV = A \left[\frac{(1 + i)^N - 1}{i} \right],$$

where

  A = Amount of the annuity ($);
  i = Annual interest rate (in decimal form).

4. Future value of an ordinary annuity for n periods:

$$FV = A \left[\frac{(1 + i)^n - 1}{i} \right],$$

where

  A = Amount of the annuity ($);
  i = Annual interest rate divided by m (in decimal form);
  n = Number of periods ($N \times m$);
  m = Number of payments per year.

CHAPTER

3

⑥ PRESENT VALUE

In the previous chapter, we illustrated how to compute the future value of an investment. In this chapter, we show how to work the process in reverse; that is, given the future value of an investment, we show how to determine the amount of money that must be invested today in order to realize the future value. The amount of money that must be invested today is called the *present value*. Since, as we shall explain later in this chapter, the price of *any* financial instrument is the present value of its expected cash flows, it is necessary to understand present value in order to be able to price a fixed-income instrument.

PRESENT VALUE OF A SINGLE AMOUNT TO BE RECEIVED IN THE FUTURE

Recall from the previous chapter that the future value of a sum invested for N years can be expressed as

$$FV = P (1 + i)^N,$$

where

FV = Future value ($);
P = Original principal ($);
i = Interest rate (in decimal form);
N = Number of years;
$(1 + i)^N$ = Future value of $1 invested at i for N years.

How do we determine the amount of money that must be invested today, earning an interest rate of i for N years, in order to produce a specific future value? This is done by solving the future value formula for P, the original principal:

$$P = FV\left[\frac{1}{(1+i)^N}\right].$$

Instead of using P in the formula, we shall denote the present value as PV. Therefore, the present value formula can be rewritten as

$$PV = FV\left[\frac{1}{(1+i)^N}\right].$$

The term in the brackets is equal to the present value of $1; that is, it indicates how much must be set aside today, earning an interest rate of i, in order to have $1 N years from now.

The process of computing the present value is also referred to as *discounting*. Therefore, the present value is sometimes referred to as the *discounted value*, and the interest rate is referred to as the *discount rate*.

The following four illustrations demonstrate how to compute the present value.

Illustration 3-1 A pension fund manager must satisfy a liability of $9 million 6 years from now. Assuming that an annual interest rate of 7.5% can be earned on any sum invested today, the pension fund manager must invest $5,831,654 today in order to have $9 million 6 years from now, as shown below:

$FV = \$9,000,000$;
$i = .075$;
$N = 6$.

$$PV = \$9,000,000\left[\frac{1}{(1.075)^6}\right]$$
$$= \$9,000,000\left[\frac{1}{1.543302}\right]$$
$$= \$9,000,000\,(.647961)$$
$$= \$5,831,654.$$

Illustration 3-2 Suppose now that the pension fund manager could earn 8.3% instead of 7.5%; then the present value of the $9 million to be paid 6 years from now would be $5,577,912, as shown below:

$FV = \$9,000,000$;
$i = .083$;
$N = 6$.

$$PV = \$9,000,000\left[\frac{1}{(1.083)^6}\right]$$
$$= \$9,000,000\left[\frac{1}{1.613507}\right]$$
$$= \$9,000,000(.619768)$$
$$= \$5,577,912.$$

Illustration 3-3 Suppose a money manager has the opportunity to purchase a financial instrument that promises to pay $800,000 in 4 years. The price of the financial instrument is $572,000. Should the money manager invest in this financial instrument if she wants a 7.8% annual interest rate?

To answer this, the money manager must determine the present value of the $800,000 to be received 4 years from now. The present value is $592,400, as shown below:

$FV = \$800,000;$
  $i = .078;$
  $N = 4.$

$$PV = \$800,000 \left[\frac{1}{(1.078)^4} \right]$$

$$= \$800,000 \left[\frac{1}{1.350439} \right]$$

$$= \$800,000(.740500)$$

$$= \$592,400.$$

As the price of the financial instrument is $572,000, the money manager will realize more than a 7.8% annual interest rate if the financial instrument is purchased and the issuer pays $800,000 in 4 years. In the next chapter, we'll show how to compute the annual interest rate that the money manager would realize.

Another way of looking at the problem faced by this money manager is to ask how much the $572,000 would grow to in 4 years if invested at 7.8%. Using the formula for the future value of an investment, we find that the future value is $772,451, as shown below:

$P = \$572,000;$
  $i = .078;$
  $N = 4.$

$$FV = \$572,000(1.078)^4$$

$$= \$572,000(1.350439)$$

$$= \$772,451.$$

A $572,000 investment at 7.8% would grow to only $772,451. Yet, an investment of $572,000 in the particular financial instrument produces $800,000 in 4 years. Consequently, the financial instrument offers more than a 7.8% annual interest rate. The present value of $592,400 tells the money manager that as long as she pays no more than $592,400, an annual interest rate of at least 7.8% will be earned from this investment.

Illustration 3-4 Instead of promising $800,000 in 4 years, suppose that the financial instrument in the previous illustration promises to pay $800,000 in 5 years. Assume that the money manager still wants an annual interest rate of 7.8%. Is the investment still attractive if it is selling for $572,000?

As shown below, the present value of the $800,000 in 5 years is $549,536:

$FV = \$800,000;$
  $i = .078;$
  $N = 5.$

$$PV = \$800,000 \left[\frac{1}{(1.078)^5} \right]$$

$$= \$800,000 \left[\frac{1}{1.455733} \right]$$

$$= \$800,000(.686920)$$

$$= \$549,536.$$

Here the present value is less than the price of $572,000, so the financial instrument offers an annual interest rate that is less than 7.8%.

PRESENT VALUE FOR A FRACTIONAL PERIOD

If a future value is to be received or paid over a fractional part of a year, the number of years is adjusted accordingly. For example, if $1,000 is to be received 9 years and 3 months from now and the interest rate is 7%, the present value is determined as follows:

$FV = \$1,000;$
  $i = .07;$
  $N = 9.25$ years (3 months is .25 years)

$$PV = \$1,000 \left[\frac{1}{(1.07)^{9.25}} \right]$$

$$= \$1,000 \left[\frac{1}{1.86982} \right]$$

$$= \$1,000(.53481)$$

$$= \$534.81.$$

PROPERTIES OF PRESENT VALUE

There are two properties of present value that you should recognize.

First, for a given future value at a specified time in the future, the higher the interest rate (or discount rate) is, the lower the present value . To see this, compare the present value in Illustration 3-1 to that in Illustration 3-2. When the annual interest rate increased from 7.5% to 8.3%, the present value of the $9 million needed 6 years from now decreased from $5,831,654 to $5,577,912. The reason that the present value decreases as the interest rate increases should be easy to understand. The higher the interest rate that can be earned on any sum invested today, the less has to be invested today to realize a specified future value.

The second property of the present value is that for a given interest rate (discount rate), the farther into the future the future value will be received, the lower the present value is. This is demonstrated in Illustrations 3-3 and 3-4. When the amount of $800,000 is to be received 4 years from now, the present value is $592,400; if the $800,000 is to be received 5 years from now, the present value declines to $549,536. The reason is that the farther into the future a given future value is to be received, the more time there is for interest to accumulate. The result is that fewer dollars have to be invested.

PRESENT VALUE OF A SERIES OF FUTURE VALUES

In most applications in investment management and asset/liability management, a financial instrument will offer a series of future values, or a financial institution will have multiple liabilities in the future. To determine the present value of a series of future values, the present value of each future value must first be computed. Then, the present values are added to obtain the present value of the series of future values. This procedure is demonstrated in the following three illustrations.

Illustration 3-5   A pension fund manager knows that the following liabilities must be satisfied:

Years from Now	Liability
1	$200,000
2	340,000
3	500,000
4	580,000

Suppose that the pension fund manager wants to invest a sum of money that will satisfy this liability stream. Let's assume that any amount that can be invested today can earn an annual interest rate of 8.5%. How much must be invested to satisfy this liability stream?

The answer is the present value of the liability stream. Consequently, the present value of each liability must be calculated and the results must be totaled, as shown below.

Years from Now	Future Value of Liability ($)	Present Value of $1 at 8.5%	Present Value of Liability
1	$200,000	0.921659	$184,332
2	340,000	0.849455	288,815
3	500,000	0.782908	391,454
4	580,000	0.721574	418,513
		Total present value =	$1,283,114

The present value of $1,283,114 means that if this sum is invested today at an annual interest rate of 8.5%, it will provide sufficient funds to satisfy the liability stream.

For those who must be convinced that this is true, let's look at what would happen if $1,283,114 were invested at 8.5% in a bank account, and at the end of each year enough money is withdrawn from the bank account to satisfy the annual liability.

(1) Year	(2) Amount at Beginning of Year ($)	(3) Interest at 8.5% [.085 × (2)]	(4) Amount Withdrawn to Pay Liability	(5) Amount at End of Year [(2) + (3) − (4)]
1	$1,283,114	$109,065	$200,000	$1,192,179
2	1,192,179	101,335	340,000	953,514
3	953,514	81,049	500,000	534,563
4	534,563	45,437	580,000	0

As these computations show, the $1,283,114 investment will provide enough money to pay the liability stream. At the end of the fourth year (after the last liability is paid), there is no money left in the account.

Illustration 3-6   An investor is considering the purchase of a financial instrument that promises to make the following payments:

Years from Now	Promised Payment by Issuer
1	$ 100
2	100
3	100
4	100
5	1,100

This financial instrument is selling for $1,243.83. Assume that the investor wants a 6.25% annual interest rate on this investment. Should the investor purchase this investment?

To answer this question, the investor first must compute the present value of the future amounts that are expected to be received, as follows:

Years from now	Future Value of Payment	Present Value of $1 at 6.25%	Present Value of Payment
1	$ 100	0.9412	$ 94.12
2	100	0.8858	88.58
3	100	0.8337	83.37
4	100	0.7847	78.47
5	1,100	0.7385	812.35
		Total present value =	$1,156.89

The present value of the series of future values promised by the issuer of this financial instrument is less than the price of $1,243.83, so the investor would earn an annual interest rate of less than 6.25%. Thus, the financial instrument is unattractive.

PRESENT VALUE OF AN ORDINARY ANNUITY

When the same amount of money is received or paid each year, the series is referred to as an *annuity*. When the first payment is received or paid 1 year from now, the annuity is called an *ordinary annuity*. When the first payment or receipt is immediate, the annuity is called an *annuity due*. In all the applications discussed in this book, we deal with ordinary annuities.

Of course, one way to compute the present value of an ordinary annuity is to follow the procedure explained in the previous section: compute the present value of each future value and then total the present values. Fortunately, there is a formula that can be employed to compute—in one step—the present value of an ordinary annuity:

$$PV = A\left[\frac{1 - \left[\frac{1}{(1+i)^N}\right]}{i}\right],$$

where

A = Amount of the annuity ($).

The term in the large brackets is the *present value of an ordinary annuity of $1 for N years.*
Two illustrations will show how to apply this formula.

Illustration 3-7   An investor has the opportunity to purchase a financial instrument that promises to pay $500 a year for the next 20 years, beginning 1 year from now. The financial instrument is being offered for a price of $5,300. The investor seeks an annual interest rate of 5.5% on this investment. Should the investor purchase this financial instrument?

Since the first payment is to be received 1 year from now, the financial instrument is offering a 20-year annuity of $500 per year. The present value of this ordinary annuity is calculated as follows:

A = $500;
i = .055;
N = 20.

$$PV = \$500\left[\frac{1 - \left[\frac{1}{(1.055)^{20}}\right]}{.055}\right]$$

$$= \$500\left[\frac{1 - \left[\frac{1}{2.917757}\right]}{.055}\right]$$

$$= \$500\left[\frac{1 - .342729}{.055}\right]$$

$$= \$500(11.950382)$$

$$= \$5,975.19.$$

Since the present value of an ordinary annuity of $500 per year when discounted at 5.5% exceeds the price of the financial instrument ($5,300), this financial instrument offers an annual interest rate in excess of 5.5%. Therefore, it is an attractive investment for this investor.

Illustration 3-8   In Illustration 3-6 we computed the present value of a financial instrument that offers $100 a year for 4 years and $1,100 at the end of the fifth year. This payment series is equivalent to an ordinary annuity of $100 a year for 5 years *plus* a future value payment of $1,000 in 5 years. Viewing the payments of the financial instrument in this way, let's compute the present value.

The present value of an ordinary annuity of $100 per year for 5 years at an annual interest rate of 6.25% is

A = $100;
i = .0625;
N = 20.

$$PV = \$100 \left[\frac{1 - \left[\frac{1}{(1.0625)^5} \right]}{.0625} \right]$$

$$= \$100 \left[\frac{1 - \left[\frac{1}{1.354081} \right]}{.0625} \right]$$

$$= \$100 \left[\frac{1 - .738508}{.0625} \right]$$

$$= \$100(4.1838)$$

$$= \$418.38 .$$

The present value of the $1,000 to be received 5 years from now is $738.51, as shown below:

FV = $1,000;
i = .0625;
N = 5

$$PV = \$1,000 \left[\frac{1}{(1.0625)^5} \right]$$

$$= \$1,000 \left[\frac{1}{1.354081} \right]$$

$$= \$1,000(.738508)$$

$$= \$738.51 .$$

The present value of the series offered by this financial instrument is then

Present value of ordinary annuity of $100 for 5 years at 6.25%	$ 418.38
Present value of $1,000 in 5 years at 6.25%	738.51
Total present value	$1,156.89

This agrees with the computation in Illustration 3-6.

Perpetual Annuity: Special Case

So far we have shown how to compute the present value of an ordinary annuity over a specific time period. Suppose, instead, that the annuity will last forever. This is called a *perpetual annuity*. The formula for a perpetual annuity is[1]

$$PV = \frac{A}{i}.$$

Illustration 3-9   An investor can purchase for $1,000 a financial instrument that promises to pay $80 per year forever. The investor wants an annual interest rate of 10% from this investment. Is this investment attractive to the investor?

The present value of the $80 perpetual annuity is equal to $800, as shown below:

$A = \$80;$
$i = .10$

$$PV = \frac{\$80}{.10}$$
$$= \$800$$

Since the $1,000 price for the financial instrument is greater than the present value of the perpetual annuity ($800), the investment offers an annual interest rate that is less than 10%; therefore, it is not an attractive investment, given the minimum annual interest rate required by the investor.

PRESENT VALUE WHEN THE FREQUENCY IS MORE THAN ONCE PER YEAR

In the computations of present value, we have assumed that the future value is to be received or paid once each year. In practice, the future value may be received or paid more than once per year. In this situation, the formulas for the present value given earlier in this chapter must be modified in two ways. First, the annual interest rate is divided by the frequency per year.[2] For example, if the future values are received or paid semiannually, the annual interest rate is divided by 2; if quarterly, the annual interest rate is divided by 4. Second, the periods when the future value will be received or paid must be adjusted by multiplying the number of years by the frequency per year.

The general formula for the present value of a future sum is

$$PV = FV\left[\frac{1}{(1+i)^n}\right],$$

where

i = Periodic interest rate [annual interest rate (in decimal form) divided by m];
n = Number of periods [number of years (N) times m];
m = Frequency of receipt or payment of the future value.

---

1   The formula is derived from the formula for the present value of an ordinary annuity. As the number of years gets very large, the value of $1/(1+i)^N$ approaches zero. The numerator in the large brackets is then equal to 1, producing the formula for the present value of a perpetual annuity.

2   Technically, this is not the proper way for adjusting the annual interest rate. For example, an 8% annual interest rate is not equal to a quarterly interest rate of 2%. However, in the computation of the yield on bonds, the market has adopted a convention that embodies this approach. This will be made clearer in the next two chapters.

Illustration 3-10   An investor is considering the purchase of a financial instrument that promises to make the following payments every 3 months (quarterly):

Period (3 months)	Promised Payments
1	$1,000
2	1,200
3	1,500
4	1,700
5	1,800
6	2,000

If the investor seeks an annual interest rate of 12% from this investment, what is the most that the investor should pay for it?

The most that the investor should pay in order to earn an annual interest rate of at least 12% is the present value of the future payments promised. As shown below, the present value is $8,212.79.

Periods from Now	Future Value of Payment	Present Value of $1 at 3.0%*	Present Value of Payment
1	$1,000	.97087	$ 970.87
2	1,200	.94260	1,131.12
3	1,500	.91514	1,372.71
4	1,700	.88849	1,510.43
5	1,800	.86261	1,552.70
6	2,000	.83748	1,674.96

Total present value = $8,212.79

*.12 annual interest rate divided by 4.

When the present value of an ordinary annuity is sought, the general formula is

$$PV = A \left[\frac{1 - \left[\frac{1}{(1 + i)^n} \right]}{i} \right],$$

where

A = Amount of the annuity ($ *per period*).

Illustration 3-11   In Illustration 3-6, we computed the present value of the following series of future amounts, assuming an annual interest rate of 6.25%:

Years from Now	Promised Payment by Issuer
1	$ 100
2	100
3	100
4	100
5	1,100

Instead of annual payments, let's assume that the payments are made by the issuer every 6 months, in the following way:

6-month Periods from Now	Promised Payment by Issuer
1	$ 50
2	50
3	50
4	50
5	50
6	50
7	50
8	50
9	50
10	1,050

This is equivalent to an ordinary annuity of $50 per 6-month period for 10 6-month periods and $1,000 to be paid 10 6-month periods from now. Notice that the $1,000 is treated on the same time-period basis as the annuity.

The present value of the ordinary annuity, for

$A = \$50$;
$m = 2$ (that is, payments every 6 months);
$\quad i = .03125$ (.0625 annual interest rate divided by 2);
$\quad n = 10$ (5 years times 2)

is

$$PV = \$50\left[\frac{1 - \left[\frac{1}{(1.03125)^{10}}\right]}{.03125}\right]$$

$$= \$50\left[\frac{1 - \left[\frac{1}{1.360315}\right]}{.03125}\right]$$

$$= \$50\left[\frac{1 - .735124}{.03125}\right]$$

$$= \$50(8.4760)$$

$$= \$423.80.$$

The present value of the $1,000 to be received after 10 6-month periods, for

$FV = \$1,000$;
$\quad m = 2$ (that is, payments every 6 months);
$\quad i = .03125$ (.0625 annual interest rate divided by 2);
$\quad n = 10$ (5 years times 2)

is

$$PV = \$1,000 \left[\frac{1}{(1.03125)^{10}} \right]$$

$$= \$1,000 \left[\frac{1}{1.360315} \right]$$

$$= \$1,000(.735124)$$

$$= \$735.12.$$

The present value of the future value series offered by the financial instrument is then:

Present value of ordinary annuity of $50 for 10 6-month periods at 3.125%	$ 423.80
Present value of $1,000 after 10 6-month periods at 3.125%	735.12
Total present value	$1,158.92

Notice that because the payments are made more often, the present value of the future payments has increased from $1,156.89 to $1,158.92.

Illustration 3-12   Suppose a banker agrees to make a $100,000 30-year loan to an individual to purchase a home. Under the terms of the loan, the monthly payments to be made by the individual will all be the same. The annual interest rate that the banker charges for the loan is 12%. How much must the fixed monthly payment be in order for the banker to realize an annual interest rate of 12%?

We can employ the formula for the present value of an ordinary annuity to determine the fixed monthly payment. The banker wants to receive an annuity of some fixed monthly amount such that the present value of that ordinary annuity, at an annual interest rate of 12%, is $100,000. In the formula for the present value of an ordinary annuity, the number of monthly payments is 360 (30 years times 12) and the interest rate is 1% (12% divided by 12). Therefore, we know the following:

$$\$100,000 = A \left[\frac{1 - \left[\frac{1}{(1.01)^{360}} \right]}{.01} \right].$$

The unknown is A, the monthly annuity or monthly loan payment. We can solve for A as follows:

$$\$100,000 = A \left[\frac{1 - \left[\frac{1}{35.949641} \right]}{.01} \right]$$

$$= A \left[\frac{1 - .0278167}{.01} \right]$$

$$= A (97.21833).$$

Solving for A,

$$A = \left[\frac{\$100,000}{97.21833} \right] = \$1,028.61.$$

Therefore, the fixed monthly payment must be $1,028.61.

Unequal Discount Rates

Throughout this chapter we have assumed that the same required yield or discount rate should be used to calculate the present value of each payment to be received. This assumption is unwarranted. As we explain in Chapter 7, there is a reason why each payment to be received should be discounted at a unique rate. The present value of a series of payments is then the sum of the present value of each payment where each payment is discounted at a unique rate.

Illustration 3-13   Let's consider Illustration 3-6 where the financial instrument makes the following five payments: $100 for 4 years and $1,100 in the fifth year. When each payment is discounted at a 6.25% annual interest rate, the total present value is $1,156.89. Suppose, instead, that the required yield for each year is as shown below:

Years from Now	Promised Payment by Issuer ($)	Required Yield (%)
1	$ 100	4.80%
2	100	5.25
3	100	5.50
4	100	6.00
5	1,100	6.25

The present value of each promised payment is shown below. Each payment is discounted at the required yield.

Years from Now	Promised Payment by Issuer ($)	Required Yield (%)	Present Value of $1	Present Value of Payment ($)
1	$ 100	4.80%	.954198	$ 95.4198
2	100	5.25	.902726	90.2725
3	100	5.50	.851614	85.1613
4	100	6.00	.792094	79.2093
5	1,100	6.25	.738508	812.3590

Total present value = $1,162.4219

The present value of the cash flows is $1,162.42

PRICING ANY FINANCIAL INSTRUMENT

The price of any financial instrument is equal to the present value of the *expected* cash flows from investing in the financial instrument. Determining the price, therefore, requires the following input:

   1. Estimation of the expected cash flows;

2. Determination of the appropriate interest rate or discount rate so that the present value of the cash flows can be computed.

The cash flow in any period is simply the difference between the cash inflow and the cash outflow from investing in the financial instrument. The expected cash flows of some financial instruments are simple to compute; for others, the task is not as simple. The determination of the interest rate or discount rate reflects the required yield for financial instruments with *comparable* risk.

SUMMARY

In this chapter we explained how to compute the present value of amounts to be received in the future or payments to be made in the future. A summary of the formulas used in this chapter to compute present values is presented in Exhibit 3-1.

EXHIBIT 3-1

Summary of Formulas for Computing Present Value

1. Present value of a future value N years from now:

$$PV = FV\left[\frac{1}{(1+i)^N}\right],$$

where

PV = Present value($);
FV = Future value($);
$\ \ i$ = Interest rate(in decimal form);
N = Number of years.

2. Present value of a future value n periods from now:

$$PV = FV\left[\frac{1}{(1+i)^n}\right],$$

where

$\ i$ = Periodic interest rate [annual interest rate (in decimal form) divided by m];
n = Number of periods [number of years (N) times m];
m = Frequency of receipt or payment of the future value.

3. Present value of an ordinary annuity for N years:

$$PV = A\left[\frac{1-\left[\dfrac{1}{(1+i)^N}\right]}{i}\right],$$

where

A = Amount of the annuity ($).

4. Present value of an ordinary annuity for n periods:

$$PV = A\left[\frac{1-\left[\dfrac{1}{(1+i)^n}\right]}{i}\right],$$

where

A = Amount of the annuity (in dollars) per period;
$\ i$ = Periodic interest rate [annual interest rate (in decimal form) divided by m].

5. Present value of a perpetual annuity:

$$PV = \frac{A}{i}.$$

4

⑥ YIELD (INTERNAL RATE OF RETURN)

In the previous chapter we showed how to use present value to determine whether a financial instrument provides a minimum annual interest rate specified by an investor. For example, if the present value of the promised future value payments of some financial instrument selling for $944.14 is $1,039.57 when discounted at 9%, then the investment offers an annual interest rate greater than 9%. But how much greater? What yield will the investor earn by buying the financial instrument for $944.14? The purpose of this chapter is to explain how to compute the yield on any investment.

COMPUTING THE YIELD ON ANY INVESTMENT

The yield on any investment is computed by determining the interest rate that will make the present value of the cash flow from the investment equal to its price. Mathematically, the yield, y, on any investment is the interest rate that will make the following relationship hold:

$$p = \frac{C_1}{(1+y)^1} + \frac{C_2}{(1+y)^2} + \frac{C_3}{(1+y)^3} + \cdots + \frac{C_N}{(1+y)^N},$$

where

p = Price;
C_t = Cash flow in year t;
N = Number of years.

The individual terms summed to produce the price are the present values of the cash flow. The yield calculated from the above relationship is also called the *internal rate of return*.

Alternatively, using the capital Greek letter sigma to denote summation, the above expression can be rewritten as

EXHIBIT 4–1

Step-by-Step Summary of Yield Computation for Any Investment

Objective	Find the interest rate that will make the present value of the cash flow equal to the price of the investment.
Step 1	Select an interest rate.
Step 2	Compute the present value of each cash flow by using the interest rate selected in Step 1.
Step 3	Total the present value of the cash flows found in Step 2.
Step 4	Compare the total present value found in Step 3 with the price of the investment. Then,
	if the total present value of the cash flows found in Step 3 is equal to the price of the investment, the interest rate selected in Step 1 is the yield.
	if the total present value of the cash flows found in Step 3 is more than the price of the investment, the interest rate used is not the yield. Go back to Step 1 and use a higher interest rate.
	if the total present value of the cash flows found in Step 3 is less than the price of the investment, the interest rate used is not the yield. Go back to Step 1 and use a lower interest rate.

$$p = \sum_{t=1}^{N} \frac{C_t}{(1+y)^t}.$$

Solving for the yield (y) requires a trial-and-error procedure. The objective is to find the interest rate that will make the present value of the cash flows equal to the price. Exhibit 4-1 explains the trial-and-error procedure. The following two illustrations demonstrate how it is carried out.

Illustration 4-1   A financial instrument offers the following annual payments:

Years from Now	Promised Annual Payments (Cash Flow to Investor; $)
1	$2,000
2	2,000
3	2,500
4	4,000

Suppose that the price of this financial instrument is $7,704. What is the yield or internal rate of return offered by this financial instrument?

To compute the yield, we must try different interest rates until we find one that makes the present value of the cash flows equal to $7,704 (its price). Trying an annual interest rate of 10% gives the following present value:

Years from Now	Promised Annual Payments (Cash Flow to Investor; $)	Present Value of Cash Flow at 10% ($)
1	$2,000	$1,818
2	2,000	1,652
3	2,500	1,878
4	4,000	2,732
		Total present value = $8,080

The present value computed using a 10% interest rate exceeds the price of $7,704, so a higher interest rate must be tried. If a 14% interest rate is tried, the present value is $7,348, as shown below:

Years from Now	Promised Annual Payments (Cash Flow to Investor; $)	Present Value of Cash Flow at 14% ($)
1	$2,000	$1,754
2	2,000	1,538
3	2,500	1,688
4	4,000	2,368
		Total present value = $7,348

At 14%, the present value of the cash flows is less than the $7,704 price of the financial instrument. Therefore, a lower interest rate must be tried. The present value at a 12% interest rate is shown below:

Years from Now	Promised Annual Payments (Cash Flow to Investor; $)	Present Value of Cash Flow at 12% ($)
1	$2,000	$1,786
2	2,000	1,594
3	2,500	1,780
4	4,000	2,544
		Total present value = $7,704

The present value of the cash flows is now equal to the price of the financial instrument when a 12% interest rate is used. Therefore, the yield is 12%.

Although the formula for the yield is based on annual cash flows, the formula can be generalized to any number of periodic payments in a year. The generalized formula for determining the yield is

$$p = \frac{C_1}{(1+y)^1} + \frac{C_2}{(1+y)^2} + \frac{C_3}{(1+y)^3} + \cdots + \frac{C_n}{(1+y)^n},$$

where

C_t = Cash flow in period t;

n = Number of periods.

In shorthand notation, this can be expressed as

$$p = \sum_{t=1}^{n} \frac{C_t}{(1+y)^t}.$$

Keep in mind that the yield computed is now the yield for the period. That is, if the cash flows are semiannual, the yield is a semiannual yield. If the cash flows are monthly, the yield is a monthly yield. The annual interest rate must be computed by multiplying the yield for the period by the appropriate factor (m).

Illustration 4-2   In Illustration 3-11 of the previous chapter, an investor considered purchasing a financial instrument that promised the following *semiannual* cash flows:

10 payments of $50 every 6 months;

$1,000 10 6-month periods from now.

Suppose the price of this financial instrument is $1,243.88. At the 6.5% annual interest rate sought by the investor, the present value of the cash flows is equal to $1,158.92; thus, the financial instrument would not be an attractive investment for this investor. What yield is this financial instrument offering?

The yield can be computed by a trial-and-error procedure, as summarized in the table below:

Annual Interest Rate (%)	Semi-annual Interest Rate (%)	Present Value of 10 6-Month Payments of $50 ($)*	Present Value of $1,000 10 6-Month Periods from Now($)**	Total Present Value ($)
6.000%	3.000%	$426.51	$744.09	$1,160.60
5.500	2.750	432.00	762.40	1,194.40
5.000	2.500	437.60	781.20	1,218.80
4.500	2.225	443.31	800.51	1,243.83

*$50 × present value of an ordinary annuity of $1 for 10 periods.

**$1,000 × present value of $1 10 periods from now.

As can be seen from the calculation, when a semiannual interest rate of 2.250% is used to find the present value of the cash flows, the present value is equal to the price of $1,243.83. Hence, 2.250% is the 6-month yield. Doubling this yield gives the annual interest rate of 4.5%. This agrees with our earlier conclusion: this financial instrument is unattractive because it offers a yield that is less than the 6.5% annual interest rate required by the investor.

Illustration 4-3   Suppose that the financial instrument analyzed in the previous illustration is selling for $944.14 instead of $1,243.83. What is the yield offered on this financial instrument at this lower price?

The table below shows the calculation of the yield:

Annual Interest Rate (%)	Semi-annual Interest Rate (%)	Present Value of 10 6-month Payments of $50 ($)*	Present Value of $1,000, 10 6-month Periods from Now ($)**	Total Present Value ($)
9.000%	4.500%	$395.64	$643.93	$1,039.57
9.500	4.750	390.82	628.72	1,019.54
10.000	5.000	386.09	613.91	1,000.00
10.500	5.250	381.44	599.49	980.93
11.000	5.500	376.88	585.43	962.31
11.500	5.750	372.40	571.74	944.14

*$50 × present value of an ordinary annuity of $1 for 10 periods.
**$1,000 × present value of $1 10 periods from now.

An interest rate of 5.75% equates the present value of the cash flows to the price of the financial instrument; hence, 5.75% is the 6-month yield, and 11.50% is the annual interest rate.

Illustration 4-4   A 30-year mortgage for $50,000 is originated today. The mortgage requires that the homeowner (borrower) pay $349.60 each month for 360 months. The manager of a mortgage portfolio has the opportunity to purchase this mortgage today for $43,449. What is the yield offered for this series of monthly mortgage payments?

The computations below show that the monthly yield is .75% (.0075):

Annual Interest Rate (%)	Monthly Interest Rate (%)	Present Value of 360 Monthly Payments of $349.60 ($)*
7.50%	.6250%	$50,000
8.00	.6667	47,643
8.50	.7083	45,469
9.00	.7500	43,449

*$349.60 × present value of an ordinary annuity of $1 for 360 periods.

Since the monthly yield is .7500%, the annual interest rate is 9.0%.

Illustration 4-5   Issuers of financial instruments must determine the cost of the funds they obtain. The cost of funds, referred to as the *all-in-cost of funds*, is just the interest rate that will equate the present value of the cash payments that the issuer must pay the security holders to the net proceeds received at the time of issuance. That is, the all-in-cost of funds is the internal rate of return.

Suppose that an issuer agrees to make the following payments to security holders every 6 months:

30 payments every 6 months of $1 million;

$20 million, 30 6-month periods from now.

At the time of issuance, the issuer receives net proceeds of $19,696,024. The all-in-cost of funds for this issue is 5.10% semiannually, as shown below:

Annual Interest Rate (%)	Semi-annual Interest Rate (%)	Present Value of 30 6-Month Payments of $1 Million ($)*	Present Value of $20 Million, 30 6-Month Periods from Now ($)**	Total Present Value ($)
10.000%	5.000%	$15,372,451	$4,627,549	$20,000,000
10.100	5.050	15,285,221	4,561,927	19,847,148
10.200	5.100	15,198,759	4,497,265	19,696,024

*$1 million × present value of an ordinary annuity of $1 for 30 periods.

**$20 million × present value of $1 30 periods from now.

YIELD CALCULATION WHEN THERE IS ONLY ONE CASH FLOW

There is a special case when it is unnecessary to go through the time-consuming trial-and-error procedure to determine the yield. This occurs when there is only one cash flow provided by the investment. We'll introduce the formula by means of an illustration.

Illustration 4-6 A financial instrument that can be purchased for $6,805.82 promises to pay $10,000 in 5 years. The yield is the interest rate that will make $6,805.82 grow to $10,000 in 5 years. That is, we are looking for the value of y that will satisfy the following relationship:

$$\$10,000 = \$6,805.82 \, (1 + y)^5.$$

We can solve this equation as follows. Divide both sides by $6,805.82:

$$\frac{\$10,000}{\$6,805.82} = (1+y)^5$$
$$1.46933 = (1+y)^5.$$

Take the fifth root of both sides:

$$(1.46933)^{1/5} = (1+y)$$
$$(1.46933)^{.20} = (1+y)$$
$$1.0800 = (1+y)$$

Subtract 1 from both sides:

$$1.0800 - 1 = y.$$
$$.08 = y.$$

Hence, the yield on this investment is 8%.

It is not necessary to go through all the steps in Illustration 4-6 to compute the yield. The following formula is consistent with those steps:

$$y = (\text{Future value per dollar invested})^{1/n} - 1,$$

where

n = Number of periods until the cash flow will be received;

$$\frac{\text{Future value}}{\text{per dollar invested}} = \frac{\text{Cash flow from investment}}{\text{Amount invested (or price)}}.$$

Illustration 4-7   An investment offers a payment 20 years from now of \$84,957. The price of the investment is \$20,000. The yield for this investment is 7.50%, as shown below:

$n = 20$;

$$\text{Future value per dollar invested} = \frac{\$84,957}{\$20,000} = 4.24785.$$

$$y = (4.24785)^{1/20} - 1$$
$$= 1.07499 - 1$$
$$= .074999 \; or \; 7.5\%.$$

Illustration 4-8   In Illustration 2-8, we computed how many dollars would be available to a portfolio manager if he invests \$5 million (the par value) in a bond that matures in 10 years and promises to pay an annual interest rate of 8%. The interest is assumed to be paid once per year, and these payments are assumed to be reinvested at an annual interest rate of 6.7%. We calculated that at the end of 10 years, the portfolio manager would have \$10,448,884, consisting of \$5 million in par value, \$4 million in annual interest payments, and the balance, \$1,448,884, from interest earned on the reinvestment of the annual interest payments.

The yield on this investment based on the portfolio manager's expectations can be computed by finding the yield that will make a \$5 million investment grow to \$10,448,884 in 10 years. Since we have reduced the problem to that of an investment that provides the portfolio manager with one cash flow, the yield can be found as follows:

$n = 10 \, (= N)$;

$$\text{Future value per dollar invested} = \frac{\$10,448,884}{\$5,000,000} = 2.08978.$$

$$y = (2.08978)^{1/10} - 1$$
$$= 1.07649 - 1$$
$$= .07649 \; or \; 7.65\%$$

ANNUALIZING YIELDS

So far throughout this book, we have annualized interest rates by simply multiplying by the frequency of payments per year. We called the resulting rate the annual interest rate. For example, if we computed a semiannual yield, we annualized it by multiplying by 2. Alternatively, if we had an annual interest rate and wanted to use a semiannual interest rate, we divided by 2.

This single procedure given for computing the annual interest rate, given a periodic (weekly, monthly, quarterly, semiannual, etc.) interest rate is not correct. To see why, suppose that \$100 is invested for 1 year at an annual interest rate of 8%. At the end of 1 year, the interest is $8. Suppose, instead, that $100 is invested for 1 year at an annual interest rate of 8%, but interest is paid semiannually at 4% (one-half the annual interest rate). The interest at the end of 1 year is found by first calculating the future value of $100 at the end of 1 year:

$$\$100\ (1.04)^2$$
$$= \$100\ (1.0816)$$
$$= \$108.16$$

Interest is therefore $8.16 on a $100 investment. The interest rate or yield on the $100 investment is therefore 8.16% ($8.16/$100). The 8.16% is called the *effective annual yield.*

Investors who are familiar with certificates of deposit offered by banks and thrifts should recognize the difference between the annual interest rate and effective annual yield. Typically, both of these interest rates are quoted for a certificate of deposit, the higher interest rate being the effective annual yield.

To obtain the effective annual yield associated with a periodic interest rate, the following formula can be used:

$$\text{Effective annual yield} = (1 + \text{Periodic interest rate})^m - 1,$$

where

m = Frequency of payments per year.

For example, in the previous example, the periodic yield is 4%, and the frequency of payments is twice per year. Therefore,

$$\text{Effective annual yield} = (1.04)^2 - 1$$
$$= 1.0816 - 1$$
$$= .0816\ or\ 8.16\%.$$

If interest is paid quarterly, then the periodic interest rate is 2% (8%/4), and the effective annual yield is 8.24%, as shown below:

$$\text{Effective annual yield} = (1.02)^4 - 1$$
$$= 1.0824 - 1$$
$$= .0824\ or\ 8.24\%.$$

We can also determine the periodic interest rate that will produce a given annual interest rate. For example, suppose we want to know what quarterly interest rate would produce an effective annual yield of 12%. The following formula can be used:

$$\text{Periodic interest rate} = (1 + \text{Effective annual yield})^{1/m} - 1.$$

Applying this formula to determine the quarterly interest rate to produce an effective annual yield of 12%, we find

$$\text{Periodic interest rate} = (1.12)^{1/4} - 1$$
$$= 1.0287 - 1$$
$$= .0287\ or\ 2.87\%.$$

SUMMARY

In this chapter we explained how to compute the yield on any investment, given the expected cash flows and the price. The yield is the interest rate that will make the present value of the cash flows equal to the price of the financial instrument. The yield computed in this manner is also called the internal rate of return. We also demonstrated how to compute the effective annual yield of an investment. A summary of the formulas introduced in this chapter is provided in Exhibit 4-2.

EXHIBIT 4-2

Summary of Yield (Internal Rate of Return) Formulas

1. Yield (or internal rate of return) on any investment from which the cash flows are received annually is the interest rate y that will make the following relationship hold:

$$p = \frac{C_1}{(1+y)^1} + \frac{C_2}{(1+y)^2} + \frac{C_3}{(1+y)^3} + \cdots + \frac{C_N}{(1+y)^N}$$

or

$$p = \sum_{t=1}^{N} \frac{C_t}{(1+y)^t},$$

where

p = Price;
C_t = Cash flow in year t;
y = Yield;
N = Number of years.

2. Yield (or internal rate of return) on any investment from which the cash flows are received periodically is the interest rate y that will make the following relationship hold:

$$p = \frac{C_1}{(1+y)^1} + \frac{C_2}{(1+y)^2} + \frac{C_3}{(1+y)^3} + \cdots + \frac{C_n}{(1+y)^n}$$

or

$$p = \sum_{t=1}^{n} \frac{C_t}{(1+y)^t},$$

where

C_t = Cash flow in period t;
n = Number of periods.

3. Yield (internal rate of return) on an investment in which there is only one cash flow received n periods from now:

$$y = (\text{Future value per dollar invested})^{1/n} - 1,$$

where

n = Number of periods when cash flow will be received;

$$\frac{\text{Future value}}{\text{per dollar invested}} = \frac{\text{Cash flow from investment}}{\text{Amount invested (or price)}}.$$

4. Effective annual yield associated with a periodic interest rate:

$$\text{Effective annual yield} = (1 + \text{Periodic interest rate})^m - 1,$$

where

m = Frequency of payments per year.

5. Periodic interest rate consistent with an effective annual yield:

$$\text{Periodic interest rate} = (1 + \text{Effective annual yield})^{1/m} - 1.$$

⑥ BOND PRICING AND YIELD MEASURES FOR OPTION-FREE BONDS

5

⑥ THE PRICE OF A BOND

In Chapter 3 we explained that the price of any financial instrument is equal to the present value of the expected cash flows. The interest rate or discount rate used to compute the present value depends on the yield offered on comparable securities in the market. In this chapter we explain how to compute the price of an option-free bond (i.e., a bond that is not callable or putable). Options and the valuation of securities with embedded options are discussed in later chapters.

DETERMINING THE CASH FLOWS

The first step in determining the price of a bond is to determine its cash flows. The cash flows of a noncallable bond consist of (1) periodic coupon interest payments to the maturity date and (2) the par (or maturity) value at maturity. While the periodic coupon payments can be made over any time period during the year (weekly, monthly, quarterly, semiannually, or annually), most bonds issued in the United States pay coupon interest semiannually.

In our illustrations, we shall assume that the coupon interest is paid semiannually. To simplify the analysis, we also assume that the next coupon payment for the bond will be made exactly 6 months from now. Later in the chapter we generalize the pricing model to allow for a coupon payment that is more or less than 6 months from now.

Consequently, the cash flows for an option-free bond consist of an annuity (that is, the fixed coupon interest paid every 6 months) and the par or maturity value. For example, a 20-year bond with a 9% coupon rate (4.5% each 6 months) and a par or maturity value of $1,000 has the following cash flows:

$$\text{Semiannual coupon interest} = \$1,000 \times .045$$
$$= \$45;$$
$$\text{Maturity value} = \$1,000.$$

Therefore, there are 40 semiannual cash flows of $45, and a $1,000 cash flow 40 6-month periods from now.

Notice the treatment of the par value. It is *not* treated as if it is received 20 years from now. Instead, it is treated on a consistent basis with the coupon payments, which are semiannual.

DETERMINING THE REQUIRED YIELD

The interest rate or discount rate that an investor wants from investing in a bond is called the *required yield*. The required yield is determined by investigating the yields offered on comparable bonds in the market. By comparable, we mean noncallable bonds of the same credit quality and the same maturity.[1]

The required yield is typically specified as an annual interest rate. When the cash flows are semiannual, the convention is to use one-half the annual interest rate as the periodic interest rate with which to discount the cash flows. As explained at the end of the previous chapter, a periodic interest rate that is one-half the annual yield will produce an effective annual yield that is greater than the annual interest rate.

PRICING A BOND

Given the cash flows of a bond and the required yield, we have all the necessary data to price the bond. The price of a bond is the present value of the cash flows, which can be determined by adding

1. The present value of the semiannual coupon payments.
2. The present value of the par or maturity value.

In general, the price of a bond can be computed using the formula:

$$p = \frac{c}{(1+i)^1} + \frac{c}{(1+i)^2} + \frac{c}{(1+i)^3} + \cdots + \frac{c}{(1+i)^n} + \frac{M}{(1+i)^n},$$

where

p = Price ($);
c = Semiannual coupon payment ($);
i = Periodic interest rate (required yield/2) (in decimal form);
n = Number of periods (number of years × 2);
M = Maturity value.

Since the semiannual coupon payments are equivalent to an ordinary annuity, the present value of the coupon payments, that is, the present value of

---

1 In Chapter 13, we introduce a measure of interest rate risk known as duration. Instead of talking in terms of a bond with the same maturity as being comparable, the analysis can be recast in terms of the same duration.

$$p = \frac{c}{(1+i)^1} + \frac{c}{(1+i)^2} + \frac{c}{(1+i)^3} + \cdots + \frac{c}{(1+i)^n},$$

can be expressed

$$c\left[\frac{1 - \left[\dfrac{1}{(1+i)^n}\right]}{i}\right].$$

This formula is the same as the formula for the present value of an ordinary annuity for n periods introduced in Chapter 3 (see Exhibit 3-1). Instead of using A to represent the annuity, we have used c, the semiannual coupon payment.

Illustration 5-1   Compute the price of a 9% coupon bond with 20 years to maturity and a par value of $1,000 if the required yield is 12%.

The cash flows for this bond are as follows:

1. 40 semiannual coupon payments of $45;

2. $1,000, 40 6-month periods from now.

The semiannual or periodic interest rate is 6%.

The present value of the 40 semiannual coupon payments of $45 discounted at 6% is $677.08, as shown below:

$c = \$45;$
$n = 40;$
$i = .06.$

$$\$45\left[\frac{1 - \left[\dfrac{1}{(1.06)^{40}}\right]}{.06}\right]$$

$$= \$45\left[\frac{1 - \left[\dfrac{1}{10.28572}\right]}{.06}\right]$$

$$= \$45(15.04630)$$

$$= \$677.08.$$

The present value of the par or maturity value 40 *6-month periods from now* discounted at 6% is $97.22, as shown below:

$M = \$1,000;$
$n = 40;$
$i = .06.$

$$\$1,000\left[\frac{1}{(1.06)^{40}}\right]$$

$$= \$1,000 \left[\frac{1}{10.28572} \right]$$
$$= \$1,000(.097222)$$
$$= \$97.22.$$

The price of the bond is then equal to the sum of the two present values:

Present value of coupon payments	$677.08
Present value of par (maturity) value	97.22
Price	$774.30

Illustration 5-2 Compute the price of the bond in Illustration 5-1, assuming that the required yield is 7%.

The cash flows are unchanged, but the periodic interest rate is now 3.5% (7%/2).

The present value of the 40 semiannual coupon payments of $45 discounted at 3.5% is $960.98, as shown below:

$c = \$45;$
$n = 40;$
$i = .035.$

$$\$45 \left[\frac{1 - \left[\frac{1}{(1.035)^{40}} \right]}{.035} \right]$$

$$= \$45 \left[\frac{1 - \left[\frac{1}{3.95926} \right]}{.035} \right]$$

$$= \$45 \left[\frac{1 - .252572}{.035} \right]$$

$$= \$45(21.35509)$$

$$= \$960.98.$$

The present value of the par or maturity value of $1,000 40 *6-month periods from now* discounted at 3.5% is $252.57, as shown below:

$M = \$1,000;$
$n = 40;$
$i = .035.$

$$\$1,000 \left[\frac{1}{(1.035)^{40}} \right]$$

$$= \$1,000 \left[\frac{1}{3.95926} \right]$$

$$= \$1,000(.252572)$$

$$= \$252.57.$$

The price of the bond is then equal to the sum of the two present values:

Present value of coupon payments	$ 960.98
Present value of par (maturity) value	252.57
Price	$1,213.55

Illustration 5-3   Compute the price of the bond in Illustration 5-1, assuming that there are 16 years to maturity rather than 20 years. (Assume that the required yield is still 12%.)

The cash flows for this bond are as follows:

1. 32 semiannual coupon payments of $45;

2. $1,000, 32 6-month periods from now.

The semiannual or periodic interest rate is 6%.

The present value of the 32 semiannual coupon payments of $45 discounted at 6% is

$c = \$45;$
$n = 32;$
$i = .06.$

$$\$45 \left[\frac{1 - \left[\frac{1}{(1.06)^{32}} \right]}{.06} \right]$$

$$= \$45 \left[\frac{1 - \left[\frac{1}{6.45339} \right]}{.06} \right]$$

$$= \$45 \left[\frac{1 - .154957}{.06} \right]$$

$$= \$45(14.08404)$$

$$= \$633.78.$$

The present value of the par or maturity value 32 *6-month periods from now* discounted at 6% is:

$M = \$1,000;$
$n = 32;$
$i = .06.$

$$\$1,000 \left[\frac{1}{(1.06)^{32}} \right]$$

$$= \$1,000 \left[\frac{1}{6.45339} \right]$$

$$= \$1,000(.154957)$$

$$= \$154.96.$$

The price of the bond is then equal to the sum of the two present values:

Present value of coupon payments	$633.78
Present value of par (maturity) value	154.96
Price	$788.74

Illustration 5-4   Compute the price of a 14-year bond with a 9% coupon rate assuming that the required yield is 7%.

The cash flows for this bond are as follows:

1. 28 semiannual coupon payments of $45;

2. $1,000, 28 6-month periods from now.

The periodic interest rate is 3.5%.

The present value of the 28 semiannual coupon payments when discounted at 3.5% is

c = $45;
n = 28;
i = .035.

$$\$45\left[\frac{1-\left[\frac{1}{(1.035)^{28}}\right]}{.035}\right]$$

$$\$45\left[\frac{1-\left[\frac{1}{(2.62017)}\right]}{.035}\right]$$

$$= \$45(17.66700)$$
$$= \$795.02.$$

The present value of the par or maturity value *28 6-month periods from now* discounted at 3.5% is

M = $1,000;
n = 32;
i = .035.

$$\$1,000\left[\frac{1}{(1.035)^{28}}\right]$$

$$= \$1,000\left[\frac{1}{2.62017}\right]$$

$$= \$1,000(.381654)$$
$$= \$381.65.$$

The price of the bond is then equal to the sum of the two present values:

Present value of coupon payments	$ 795.02
Present value of par (maturity) value	381.65
Price	$1,176.67

RELATIONSHIP BETWEEN REQUIRED YIELD AND PRICE AT A GIVEN TIME

The price of a bond changes in the direction opposite from the change in the required yield. The reason is that the price of the bond is the present value of the cash flows. As the required yield increases, the present value of the cash flows decreases; hence, the price decreases. The opposite is true when the required yield decreases: the present value of the cash flows increases and, therefore, the price of the bond increases.

We can see this by comparing the price of the 20-year, 9% coupon bond that we priced in Illustrations 5-1 and 5-2. When the required yield is 12%, the price of the bond is $774.30. If, instead, the required yield is 7%, the price of the bond is $1,213.55. Exhibit 5-1 shows the price of the bond for required yields from 5% to 14% for the 20-year, 9% coupon bond.

If we graph the price/yield relationship for any option-free bond, we will find it has the "bowed" shape shown in Exhibit 5-2. This shape is referred to as *convex*. The convexity of the price/yield relationship has important implications for the investment properties of a bond. In Chapter 12 we examine this relationship more closely.

E X H I B I T 5-1

Price/Yield Relationship for a 20-Year, 9% Coupon Bond

Required Yield (%)	Present Value of 40 Coupon Payments ($)*	Present Value of Par Value in 40 Periods ($)**	Price of Bond ($)
5%	$1,129.62	$372.43	$1,502.05
6	1,040.16	306.56	1,346.72
7	960.98	252.57	1,213.55
8	890.67	208.29	1,098.96
9	828.07	171.93	1,000.00
10	772.16	142.05	914.21
11	722.08	117.46	839.54
12	677.08	97.22	774.30
13	636.55	80.54	717.09
14	599.93	66.78	666.71

*Computed as follows:

$$\$45 \left[\frac{1 - \left[\frac{1}{(1+i)^{40}} \right]}{i} \right],$$

where i is one-half the required yield.

**Computed as follows:

$$\$1,000 \left[\frac{1}{(1+i)^{40}} \right],$$

where i is one-half the required yield.

EXHIBIT 5–2

Price/Yield Relationship for an Option-Free Bond

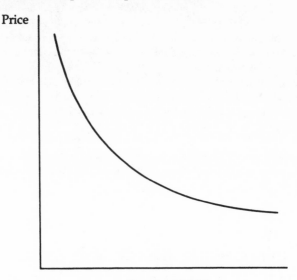

RELATIONSHIPS AMONG COUPON RATE, REQUIRED
YIELD, AND PRICE

For a bond issue, the coupon rate and the term to maturity are fixed. Consequently, as yields in the marketplace change, the only variable that can change to compensate for the new yield required in the market is the price of the bond. As we saw in the previous section, as the required yield increases (decreases), the price of the bond decreases (increases).

Generally, a bond's coupon rate at the time of issuance is set at approximately the prevailing yield in the market.[2] The price of the bond will then be approximately equal to its par value. For example, in Exhibit 5-1, we see that when the required yield is equal to the coupon rate, the price of the bond is its par value ($1,000). Consequently, we have the following properties:

When the coupon rate equals the required yield, then the price equals the par value.

When the price equals the par value, then the coupon rate equals the required yield.

When yields in the marketplace rise above the coupon rate at *a particular time,* the price of the bond has to adjust so that the investor can realize additional interest income. This adjustment happens when the bond's price falls below the par value. The difference between

---

2 The exception is an original-issue deep-discount bond such as a zero-coupon bond. We'll discuss zero-coupon bonds later in this chapter.

the par value and the price is a capital gain and represents a form of interest income to the investor to compensate for the coupon rate being lower than the required yield.

When a bond sells below its par value, it is said to be selling at a *discount*. We can see this in Exhibit 5-1. When the required yield is greater than the coupon rate of 9%, the price of the bond is always less than the par value ($1,000). Consequently, we have the following properties:

When the coupon rate is less than the required yield,
then the price is less than the par value.

When the price is less than the par value, then the coupon rate
is less than the required yield.

Finally, when the required yield in the market is below the coupon rate, the bond must sell above its par value. This occurs because investors who would have the opportunity to purchase the bond at par would be getting a coupon rate in excess of what the market would require. Because its yield is attractive, investors would bid up the price of the bond to a price that offers the required yield in the market.

A bond whose price is above its par value is said to be selling at a *premium*. Exhibit 5-1 shows that for a required yield less than the coupon rate of 9%, the price of the bond is higher than its par value. Consequently, we have the following properties:

When the coupon rate is higher than the required yield,
then the price is higher than the par value.

When the price is higher than the par value, then the coupon rate
is higher than the required yield.

TIME PATH OF A BOND

If the required yield is unchanged between the time a bond is purchased and the maturity date, what will happen to the price of the bond? For a bond selling at par value, the coupon rate is equal to the required yield. As the bond moves closer to maturity, the bond will continue to sell at par value. Thus, the price of a bond selling at par will remain at par as the bond moves toward the maturity date.

The price of a bond will *not* remain constant for a bond selling at a premium or a discount. This can be seen for a discount bond by comparing the price found in Illustration 5-1 to that found in Illustration 5-3. In both illustrations the bond has a 9% coupon rate and the required yield is 12%. In Illustration 5-1, the maturity of the bond is 20 years, while in Illustration 5-3 the maturity is 16 years. With 20 years to maturity, the price of the bond is $774.30. Four years later, when the bond has 16 years remaining to maturity, the price of the bond increases to $788.74. For all discount bonds the following is true: as a bond moves toward maturity, its price will increase if *the required yield* does not change.

Exhibit 5-3 shows the price of the 20-year, 9% coupon bond as it moves toward maturity, assuming that the required yield remains at 12%. The price of the bond is decomposed into the present value of the coupon payments and the present value of the par value. Notice that as the bond moves toward maturity, there are fewer coupon payments to be received by the bondholder. The present value of the coupon payments decreases. Since the maturity date is closer, however, the present value of the par value increases. The increase in the present value of the par value

E X H I B I T 5–3

Time Path of the Price of a Discount Bond:
20-Year, 9% Coupon, 12% Required Yield

Years Remaining to Maturity	Present Value of Coupon Payments of $45 at 6% ($)	Present Value of Par Value at 6% ($)	Price of Bond ($)
20	$677.08	$ 97.22	$ 774.30
18	657.94	122.74	780.68
16	633.78	154.96	788.74
14	603.28	195.63	798.91
12	564.77	256.98	811.75
10	516.15	311.80	827.95
8	454.77	393.65	848.42
6	377.27	496.97	874.24
4	279.44	627.41	906.85
2	155.93	792.09	948.02
1	82.50	890.00	972.50
0	0.00	1,000.00	1,000.00

is greater than the decline in the present value of the coupon payments, resulting in a price increase. Exhibit 5-4 graphs the time path of a bond selling at a discount.

For a bond selling at a premium, the price of the bond declines as it moves toward maturity. Illustrations 5-2 and 5-4 show this property for a 9% coupon bond for which the required yield is 7%. When the bond has 20 years to maturity, its price is $1,213.55. Six years later, when the bond has 14 years remaining to maturity, the price of the bond declines to $1,176.67.

The time path of the 20-year, 9% coupon bond selling to yield 7% is shown in Exhibit 5-5. As the bond moves toward maturity, the present value of the coupon payments decreases, and the present value of the par value increases. Unlike a bond selling at a discount, the increase in the present value of the par value is not sufficient to offset the decline in the present value of the coupon payments. As a result, the price of a bond selling at a premium decreases over time if the required yield does not change. A graphical depiction of the time path of any premium bond is presented in Exhibit 5-6.

ANALYSIS OF BOND PRICE CHANGES

A money manager will be concerned with investigating the expected performance of a bond over an investment horizon, given certain assumptions about the future direction of interest rates. We'll demonstrate how this is done in Chapter 9. Doing so requires that we know how to analyze the way a bond's price will change under a specified set of assumptions.

The price of a bond can change for one or more of the following three reasons:

1. A change in the required yield due to changes in the credit quality of the issuer;

Time Path of a Discount Bond, Assuming No Change in Required Yield

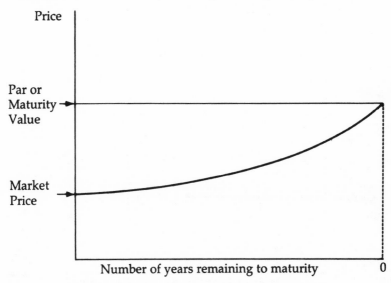

**Time Path of the Price of a Premium Bond: 20-Year, 9% Coupon,
7% Required Yield**

Years Remaining to Maturity	Present Value of Coupon Payments of $45 at 3.5% ($)	Present Value of Par Value at 3.5% ($)	Price of Bond ($)
20	$960.98	$ 252.57	$1,213.55
18	913.07	289.83	1,202.90
16	858.10	332.59	1,190.69
14	795.02	381.65	1,176.67
12	722.63	437.96	1,160.59
10	639.56	502.57	1,142.13
8	544.24	576.71	1,120.95
6	434.85	661.78	1,096.63
4	309.33	759.41	1,068.74
2	165.29	871.44	1,036.73
1	85.49	933.51	1,019.00
0	0.00	1,000.00	1,000.00

E X H I B I T 5–6

Time Path of a Premium Bond, Assuming No Change in Required Yield

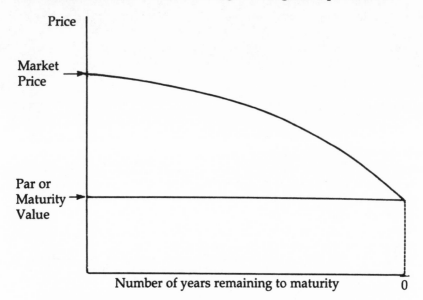

2. A change in the maturity of the bond as it moves toward maturity without any change in the required yield (that is, the time path of the bond);
3. A change in the required yield due to a change in the yield on comparable bonds (that is, a change in the yield required by the market).

Predicting the change in an issue's credit quality before that change is recognized by the market is one of the challenges of investment management. For purposes of our illustrations below, let's suppose that the issue's credit quality is unchanged, so that we can focus on the last two reasons.

It is informative to separate the effect of the change in price due to the time path of a bond from that of the change due to a change in the required yield. The next two illustrations show how this is done.

Illustration 5-5   Suppose that a money manager purchases a 20-year, 9% coupon bond at a price of $774.30 to yield 12%. The money manager expects to hold this bond for 4 years, at which time the money manager believes that the required yield on comparable 16-year bonds will be 8%. On the basis of these expectations, we can investigate what will happen to the price of the bond 4 years from now.

After this bond is held for 4 years, it becomes a 16-year bond. If the required yield for a 16-year bond is 8%, the price of the bond 4 years from now will be $1,089.37.[3] The price of this bond is therefore expected to increase by $315.07 ($1,089.37 − $744.30). Not all of the price change, however, is due to the decline in market yield. If the required yield remains at 12%, the price of the bond in 4 years will have increased to $788.74, an increase of $14.44 ($788.74 − $744.30). Therefore, we can decompose the expected price change after 4 years as follows:

Price change due to the time path of a discount bond	$ 14.44
Price change due to the change in the required yield	300.63
Total price change	$315.07

Illustration 5-6 Suppose that a money manager is considering the purchase of a 20-year, 9% coupon bond selling at $1,213.55 to yield 7%. If the money manager purchases this bond, she expects to hold it for 6 years, at which time she expects that the required yield on 14-year bonds may be 11%. What would be the price performance of this bond based on the money manager's expectations?

The price of a 14-year, 9% coupon bond if an 11% required yield is assumed is $858.79.[4] If the required yield remained at 7%, however, the price of a 14-year bond with a coupon rate of 9% would be $1,176.67 (see Exhibit 5-5). The price change can be broken down as follows:

Price change due to the time path of a discount bond	− $ 36.88
Price change due to the change in the required yield	− 317.88
Total price change	− $354.76

THE PRICE OF A ZERO-COUPON BOND

So far we have determined the price of coupon-bearing bonds. There are bonds that do not make any periodic coupon payments. Instead, the investor realizes interest by the amount of the difference between the maturity value and the purchase price.

The pricing of a zero-coupon bond is no different from the pricing of a coupon bond: its price is the present value of the expected cash flows. In the case of a zero-coupon bond, the only cash flow is the maturity value. Therefore, the formula for the price of a zero-coupon bond that matures N years from now is

$$p = M\left[\frac{1}{(1+i)^n}\right],$$

where

---

3 The price is determined as follows:

Present value of 32 coupon payments at 4%	$ 804.31
Present value of par (maturity) value at 4%	285.06
Price	$1,089.37

4 The price is determined as follows:

Present value of 28 coupon payments at 5.5%	$635.47
Present value of par (maturity) value at 5.5%	223.32
Price	$858.79

p = Price;
M = Maturity value;
  i = Periodic interest rate (annual interest rate/2);
  n = $2 \times N$, where
  N = Number of years.

Pay particular attention to the number of periods used in the pricing of a zero-coupon bond. Although an issue may mature in N years, the number of 6-month periods is used in the exponent, and the periodic interest rate is the required yield divided by 2. The reason is that the pricing of a zero-coupon bond must be made consistent with the pricing of a coupon bond. Recall that with a coupon bond the present value of the maturity value is computed using twice the number of years to maturity. Therefore, we handle the maturity value for the zero-coupon bond the same way.

Illustration 5-7   Compute the price of a zero-coupon bond that matures 10 years from now if the maturity value is $1,000 and the required yield is 8.6%.

The price is determined as follows:

M = $1,000;
  i = .043 (.086/2);
N = 10;
n = 20 (2 ×10).

$$p = \$1,000 \left[\frac{1}{(1.043)^{20}} \right]$$

$$= \$1,000 \left[\frac{1}{2.321059} \right]$$

$$= \$1,000(.43083)$$

$$= \$430.83.$$

Illustration 5-8   Compute the price of a 7-year, zero-coupon bond with a maturity value of $100,000 if the required yield is 9.8%.

The price is $51,185.06, as shown below:

M = $100,000;
  i = .049 (.098/2);
N = 7;
n = 14 (2×7).

$$p = \$100,000 \left[\frac{1}{(1.049)^{14}} \right]$$

$$= \$100,000 \left[\frac{1}{1.953695} \right]$$

$$= \$100,000(.5118506)$$

$$= \$51,185.06.$$

PRICE QUOTATIONS

In all but our last illustration, we have assumed that the maturity or par value of the bond is $1,000. A bond can have a maturity or par value of any amount. Consequently, traders quote bond prices as a percentage of par value.

A bond selling at par is quoted as 100, meaning 100% of its par value. A bond selling at a discount will be selling for less than 100; a bond selling at a premium will be selling for more than 100. The following examples illustrate how a price quote is converted into a dollar price.

(1) Price quote	(2) Converted to a decimal [(1)/100]	(3) Par value	(4) Dollar price [(2)×(3)]
95	.9500000	$ 1,000	$ 950.00
95 ½	.9550000	100,000	95,500.00
98 ¼	.9825000	5,000	4,912.50
80 ⅛	.8012500	10,000	8,012.50
74 $\frac{1}{32}$	.7403125	1,000,000	740,312.50
100	1.0000000	10,000	10,000.00
103	1.0300000	1,000	1,030.00
106 ¾	1.0675000	500,000	533,750.00
108 ⅜	1.0837500	25,000	27,093.75
111 $\frac{11}{32}$	1.1134375	100,000	111,343.75

For some securities a unique market convention has been adopted for quoting prices. For example, for Treasury notes and bonds, a quote of "95-5," "95.5," or "95:05" means 95% plus 5/32, the number following the hyphen, decimal, or colon representing the number of 32nds. So for a $100,000 par value Treasury note or bond, a quote of 95-5 or 95.5 or 95:05 indicates a dollar price of $95,156.25, as shown below:

$$95 \tfrac{5}{32}\% = 95.15625\% = .9515625;$$

then,

$$\$100,000 \times .9515625 = \$95,156.25.$$

Corporate and municipal bonds are frequently quoted in eighths rather than 32nds.

DETERMINING THE PRICE WHEN THE SETTLEMENT DATE FALLS BETWEEN COUPON PERIODS

Our illustrations have assumed that the next coupon payment is 6 months away. This means that settlement occurs on the day after a coupon date. Typically, an investor purchases a bond between coupon dates, so that the next coupon payment is less than 6 months away. To compute the price, we have to answer three questions:

1. How many days are there until the next coupon payment?

2. How should we determine the present value of cash flows received over fractional periods?

3. How much must the buyer compensate the seller for the coupon interest earned by the seller for the fraction of the period that the bond was held?

The first question is the "day count" question. The second is the "compounding" question. The last question asks how accrued interest is determined.

Day Count Conventions

Market conventions for the number of days in a coupon period and the number of days in a year differ by type of bond issuer (i.e., government, government-related entity, local government, and corporate) and by country. The following notation is typically used to denote a day count convention:

Number of days in a month/Number of days in a year

In practice, there are six day count conventions:[5]

1. Actual/actual (in period);
2. Actual/365;
3. Actual/365 (366 in leap year);
4. Actual/360;
5. 30/360;
6. 30E/360.

In calculation of the actual number of days, only one of the two bracketing dates in question is included. For example, the actual number of days between August 20 and August 24 is 4 days.

The last two day count conventions, 30/360 and 30E/360, require some explanation. We use the notation following to explain them:

Let

D1/M1/Y1 = The day (D1), month (M1), and year (Y1) of the first date;
D2/M2/Y2 = The day (D2), month (M2), and year (Y2) of the second date.

30/360 Day Count

The number of days between two dates assumes 30-day months, according to the following rules for the number of days between the dates D1/M1/Y1 and D2/M2/Y2:

- If D1 is 31, change to 30.
- If D2 is 31 and D1 is 30 or 31, change D2 to 30; otherwise leave at 31.
- Then, the number of days between the two dates is

$$(Y2 - Y1) \times 360 + (M2 - M1) \times 30 + (D2 - D1).$$

---

5 Dragomir Krgin, *Price/Yield Calculations for Periodic Payment Fixed Income Securities*, undated manuscript, p. 16.

For example, there are 29 days between May 1 and May 30 and 30 days between May 1 and May 31.

30E/360 Day Count
The number of days between two dates assumes 30-day months, according to the following rules for the number of days between dates D1/M1/Y1 and D2/M2/Y2:

* If D1 is 31, change D1 to 30.
* If D2 is 31, change D2 to 30.
* Then, the number of days between the two dates is

$$(Y2 - Y1) \times 360 + (M2 - M1) \times 30 + (D2 - D1).$$

Just as in the 30/360 day count convention, the number of days between May 1 and May 30 is 29 days. However, unlike the previous day count convention, the number of days between May 1 and May 31 is not 30 days but 29 days. This is because D2 in this case is 31, and therefore D2 is changed to 30.

The various day count conventions in major bond markets throughout the world, as well as the frequency of coupon payments, are listed in Exhibit 5-7.

Application to U.S. Treasury Bonds
In the U.S. Treasury coupon securities market, the day count convention used is to determine the actual number of days between two dates and the actual number of days in a year. This is referred to as the "actual/actual" day count convention. For example, consider a Treasury bond whose previous coupon payment was March 1 and whose next coupon payment is on September 1. Suppose this bond is purchased with a settlement date of July 17. The actual number of days between July 17 (the settlement date) and September 1 (the date of the next coupon payment) is 46 days, as shown below:

July 17 to July 31	14 days
August	31 days
September 1	1 day
	46 days

The number of days in the coupon period is the actual number of days between March 1 and September 1, which is 184 days.

Application to Federal Agency, Corporate, and Municipal Securities
In contrast to the "actual/actual" day count convention for coupon-bearing Treasury securities, for corporate and municipal bonds and agency securities, the day count convention is "30/360." That is, each month is assumed to have 30 days and each year, 360 days. For example, suppose that the security in our previous example is not a coupon-bearing Treasury security but instead either a coupon-bearing corporate bond, municipal bond, or agency security. The number of days between July 17 and September 1 is as shown below:

July 17 to July 31	13 days
August	30 days
September 1	1 day
	44 days

E X H I B I T 5–7

Coupon Frequency, Day Count Conventions, and Ex-Dividend Trading Practices in Major Bond Markets Throughout the World

Market	Coupon Payments	Day Count	Ex-Dividend Trading
U.S. Government	Semiannual	Actual/Actual (in period)	N
U.S. Corporate	Semiannual	30/360	N
U.S. Government Agency	Annual	30/360	N
	Semiannual		N
	Quarterly		N
U.S. Municipal	Semiannual	30/360	N
U.K. Government	Semiannual	Actual/365	Y
Australian Government	Semiannual	Actual/Actual (in period)	Y
New Zealand Government	Semiannual	Actual/Actual (in period)	Y
Canadian Government	Semiannual	Actual/Actual (in period)	N
German Government	Annual	30E/360	Y
Swiss Government	Annual	30E/360	N
Dutch Government	Annual	30E/360	Y
Eurobond	Annual	30E/360	N
Italian Government	Annual	30E/360	N
French Government	Annual	Actual/Actual (in period)	N
Danish Government	Annual	30E/360	Y
Swedish Government	Annual	30E/360	Y
Spanish Government	Semiannual	Actual/Actual (in period)	N
Belgian Government	Annual	30E/360	N
Irish Government	Annual	Actual/365	Y
Austrian Government	Annual	30E/365	Y
Norwegian Government	Annual	Actual/365	Y

Source: Dragomir Krgin, *Price/Yield Calculations for Periodic Payment Fixed Income Securities*, undated manuscript, Appendix A, p. 18.

Basic financial calendars provide the day count between settlement and the next coupon payment. Most money managers, however, use software programs that will furnish this information.

Compounding

Once the number of days between the settlement date and the next coupon date is determined, the present value formula must be modified to take into account that the cash flows will not be received 6 months (one full period) from now. The "street" convention is to compute the price as follows:

1. Determine the number of days in the coupon period.

2. Compute the ratio:

$$w = \frac{\text{Number of days between settlement and next coupon payment}}{\text{Number of days in the coupon period}}$$

For a corporate bond, municipal bond, or agency security, the number of days in the coupon period will be 180, since a year is assumed to have 360 days. For a coupon-bearing Treasury security, the number of days is the actual number of days. The number of days in the coupon period is called the *basis*.

3. For a bond with n coupon payments remaining to maturity, the price is:

$$p = \frac{c}{(1+i)^w} + \frac{c}{(1+i)^{1+w}} + \frac{c}{(1+i)^{2+w}} + \cdots$$
$$+ \frac{c}{(1+i)^{n-1+w}} + \frac{M}{(1+i)^{n-1+w}}$$

where

p = Price ($);
c = *Semiannual* coupon payment ($);
i = Periodic interest rate (required yield divided by 2) (in decimal form);
n = Number of coupon payments remaining;
M = Maturity value.

The period (exponent) in the formula for determining the present value can be expressed generally as $t - 1 + w$. For example, for the first cash flow, the period is $1 - 1 + w$, or simply w. For the second cash flow it is $2 - 1 + w$, or simply $1 + w$. If the bond has 20 coupon payments remaining, the period is $20 - 1 + w$, or simply $19 + w$.

Illustration 5-9   Suppose that a corporate bond with a coupon rate of 10% maturing March 1, 2003, is purchased with a settlement date of July 17, 1997. What would the price of this bond be if it is priced to yield 6.5%?

The next coupon payment will be made on September 1, 1997. Since the bond is a corporate bond, the 30/360 day count convention is that there are 44 days between the settlement date and the next coupon date. The number of days in the coupon period is 180 days. Therefore,

$$w = \frac{44}{180} = .24444.$$

The number of coupon payments remaining, n, is 12. The semiannual interest rate is 3.25% (6.5%/2). Calculation of the price is shown in Exhibit 5-8.

The price of this corporate bond is $120.0281. The price calculated in this way is called the *full price* or *dirty price* because it reflects the portion of the coupon interest that the buyer will receive but that the seller has earned.

EXHIBIT 5-8

Calculation of Full (Dirty) Price When a Bond Is Purchased Between Coupon Payments

Period	Cash Flow per $100 of Par ($)	Present Value of $1 at 3.25% ($)	Present Value of Cash Flow ($)
0.24444	$ 5.00	$0.992212	$ 4.961060
1.24444	5.00	0.960980	4.804902
2.24444	5.00	0.930731	4.653658
3.24444	5.00	0.901435	4.507175
4.24444	5.00	0.873060	4.365303
5.24444	5.00	0.845579	4.227896
6.24444	5.00	0.818963	4.094815
7.24444	5.00	0.793184	3.965922
8.24444	5.00	0.768217	3.841087
9.24444	5.00	0.744036	3.720181
10.24444	5.00	0.720616	3.603081
11.24444	105.00	0.697933	73.283000
			Total $120.028100

Accrued Interest

The buyer must compensate the seller for the portion of the next coupon interest payment the seller has earned but will not receive from the issuer because the issuer will send the next coupon payment to the buyer. This amount is called *accrued interest*. Interest accrues on a bond from and including the date of the previous coupon up to but *excluding* a date called the *value date*. The value date is usually, but not always, the same as the settlement date. Unlike the settlement date, the value date is not constrained to fall on a business day.[6]

Calculation of accrued interest assumes the coupon payment takes place on the scheduled date, even if in practice it will be delayed because the scheduled date is a nonbusiness day. In the formulas below we use the settlement date rather than the value date.

The accrued interest is calculated as follows:

$$AI = c \left\{ \frac{\text{Number of days from last coupon payment to settlement date}}{\text{Number of days in coupon period}} \right\},$$

---

6 The term "value date" is not used consistently across markets—the definition in the text is that used by the Association of International Bond Dealers (AIBD). In some markets the interest accrues up to and *including* a date that is called the value date. The "dated date" is the date from which accrued interest is calculated on a newly issued security.

where

AI = Accrued interest ($);
c = Semiannual coupon payment ($).

Accrued interest is not computed for all bonds. No accrued interest is computed for bonds in default and income bonds. A bond that trades without accrued interest is said to be traded "flat."

Illustration 5-10   Let's continue with the hypothetical corporate bond in Illustration 5-9. Since the number of days between settlement (July 17, 1997) and the next coupon payment (September 1, 2003) is 44 days and the number of days in the coupon period is 180, the number of days from the last coupon payment date (March 1, 1997) to the settlement date is 136 (180 − 44). The accrued interest per $100 of par value is

$$AI - \$5 \left(\frac{136}{180} \right) = \$3.777778.$$

Illustration 5-11   If the bond in the previous illustration were a Treasury bond rather than a corporate bond, the accrued interest would be computed as follows. The number of days in the coupon period is based on the actual number of days. Between March 1 and September 1 the actual number of days is 184. The actual number of days between March 1 and July 17 is 138. Accrued interest per $100 of par value is then

$$AI = \$5 \left(\frac{138}{184} \right) = \$3.75.$$

Cum-Dividend and Ex-Dividend Trading

When the buyer receives the next coupon, the bond is said to be traded *cum-dividend* (or *cum-coupon*), and the buyer pays the seller accrued interest. If the buyer forgoes the next coupon, the bond is said to be traded *ex-dividend* (or *ex-coupon*), and the seller pays the buyer accrued interest. In some markets (the U.S. is one) bonds are always traded cum-dividend. In other markets, bonds are traded ex-dividend for a certain period before the coupon date. The last column in Exhibit 5-7 shows the practices in major bond markets throughout the world.

PRICE BUYER PAYS AND PRICE QUOTES

The full or dirty price includes the accrued interest that the seller is entitled to receive. For example, in the calculation of the full price in Exhibit 5-8, the next coupon payment of $5 is included as part of the cash flow. The *clean price* or *flat price* is the dirty price of the bond minus the accrued interest; that is,

Clean price = Dirty price − Accrued interest

The price that the buyer pays the seller is the dirty price. It is important to note that in calculation of the dirty price, the next coupon payment is a discounted value, but in calculation of accrued interest it is an undiscounted value. Because of this market practice, if a bond is selling at par and the settlement date is not a coupon date, the yield will be slightly less than the coupon rate. Only when the settlement date and coupon date coincide is the yield equal to the coupon rate for a bond selling at par.

In the U.S. market, the convention is to quote a bond's clean or flat price. The buyer, however, pays the seller the dirty price. In some non-U.S. markets, the dirty price is quoted.

TAX TREATMENT OF ORIGINAL-ISSUE DISCOUNT COUPON

A bond purchased at a price less than its redemption value at maturity is said to be bought at a discount. The tax treatment of the discount depends upon whether the discount represents original-issue discount or market discount. One application of the principles presented in this chapter is calculation of the numbers that must be reported under the current tax law for a bond classified as having an original-issue discount.[7]

When bonds are issued, they may be sold at a price that is less than their redemption value at maturity. The difference between the redemption value and the original issue price is called the *original-issue discount*. Zero-coupon bonds are examples of bonds that have an original-issue discount. Under the current tax law, each year a portion of the original-issue discount must be accrued and included in the taxpayer's gross income. There is a corresponding increase in the adjusted basis of the bond.[8]

The amount of the original-issue discount amortized is based on the *constant-yield method* (also called the *effective or scientific method*) and is included in gross income based on the number of days in the tax year that bond is held. With this method for determining the amount of the original-issue discount to be included in gross income, the interest for the year is first determined by multiplying the adjusted issue price (essentially, the adjusted basis the bond would have in the hands of the first holder of the bond) by the yield to maturity at issuance. From this interest, the coupon interest is subtracted. The difference is the amount of the original-issue discount amortized for the year. The same amount is then added to the adjusted basis.

To illustrate the tax rules for original-issue discount bonds, consider a bond with a 4% coupon rate (interest paid semiannually), maturing in 5 years, that was issued for $7,683 and has a redemption value of $10,000. The yield to maturity for this hypothetical bond is 10%. The original-issue discount is $2,317 ($10,000 − $7,683). Suppose that the bond was purchased by an investor on the day it was issued, January 1, 19X1. The constant-yield method is used to determine the amortization and the adjusted basis. The procedure is as follows. Every 6 months, the investor of this hypothetical bond is assumed to realize for tax purposes interest income (including accrued original-issue discount) equal to 5% of the adjusted issue price. The 5% represents one-half of the 10% yield to maturity. The original issue price is the purchase price of $7,683. In the first 6 months the bond is held, the investor realizes for tax purposes interest

---

7 For a further discussion of the tax treatment for original-issue discount bonds, market discount bonds, and premium bonds, see Frank J. Fabozzi, *Bond Portfolio Management* (New Hope, PA: Frank J. Fabozzi Associates, 1996), Chapter 9.
8 In the tax code, a bond's original basis in the hands of a taxpayer is the total cost on the date of acquisition. The adjusted basis of a capital asset is its original basis minus the amortization of a discount or premium.

equal to 5% of $7,683, or $384. The coupon payment for the first 6-month period that the bond is held is $200. Therefore, $184 ($384 – $200) is assumed to be realized (although not received) by the investor. Thus, the amount of the original-issue discount from holding this bond for 6 months is $200 in coupon interest plus the $184 of the original-issue discount amortized. The adjusted issue price for the bond at the end of the first 6 months will equal the original-issue price of $7,683 plus the amount of the original-issue discount amortized, $184. Thus, the adjusted issue price is $7,867. The bondholder's adjusted basis in the bond (used in calculating gain or loss from sale) will also be increased by the amount of accrued original issue discount. This way, the increase in the value of the bond (as it approaches maturity) that is included in income as accrued original-issue discount is not taxed again as capital gain.

Let's carry this out for one more 6-month period. If the bond is held for another 6 months, the amount of interest that the investor is expected to realize for tax purposes is 5% of the adjusted issue price. Since the adjusted issue price at the beginning of the second 6-month period is $7,867, the interest is $393. The coupon interest for the second 6 months is $200. Therefore, the amount of the original-issue discount amortized for the second 6-month period is $193 ($393 – $200). The $393 reported for holding the bond for the second 6 months is $200 in coupon interest and $193 in accrued interest of the original-issue discount. The adjusted issue price at the end of the second 6-month period is $8,060—the previous adjusted issue price of $7,867 plus $193. If this bond, which was assumed to be purchased on January 1, 19X1, were sold on December 31, 19X1 (i.e., within the same year), interest income would be $777, consisting of $400 of coupon interest and $377 of the original-issue discount amortized. If this bond were sold on December 31, 19X1 for $8,200, there would be a capital gain of $140, the difference between the sale proceeds of $8,200 and the adjusted basis of $8,060.[9]

Exhibit 5-9 shows the amount of the original-issue discount that must be reported as gross income for each 6-month period that the bond is held and the adjusted issue price at the end of the period. Notice that accrual is lower in the earlier years, generally increasing over the life of the bond on a compounding basis.

Holders of original-issue discount tax-exempt bonds need to accrue the original-issue discount by using the constant-yield method as well. However, the amount of the original-issue discount amortized is not included as part of gross income because all interest is exempt from federal income taxes. As with taxable bonds, the amount of original-issue discount accrued on a tax-exempt bond is added to its adjusted basis.

The original-issue discount rules do not apply to noninterest-bearing obligations such as Treasury bills and many other taxable short-term obligations with no more than 1 year to maturity. When these obligations are held by investors who report for tax purposes on a cash rather than an accrual basis, the discount is not recognized until the obligation is redeemed or sold.

The original-issue discount is treated as zero if the discount is less than one-fourth of 1% of the redemption value at maturity multiplied by the number of complete years to maturity.

---

9 Because it is assumed that the investor purchased the bond at the original issuance, the bondholder's adjusted basis equals the bond's adjusted issue price. Had the bondholder purchased the bond in the secondary market, the bondholder's adjusted basis might have been greater or less than the bond's adjusted issue price.

E X H I B I T   5–9

Amortization Schedule for an Original-Issue Discount Bond

Characteristics of hypothetical bond

Coupon = 4%	Years to maturity = 5
Interest payments = Semiannual	Yield to maturity = 10%
Issue price = $7,683	Original-issue discount = $2,317
Redemption value = $10,000	Basis at time of purchase = $7,683

Amortization based on constant-yield method

For the Period

Period Held (years)	Adjusted Issue Price ($)*	Gross Income Reported ($)**	Coupon Interest ($)	Original-Issue Discount Amortized ($)***
0.5	$ 7,867	$384	$200	$184
1.0	8,060	393	200	193
1.5	8,263	403	200	203
2.0	8,476	413	200	213
2.5	8,700	424	200	224
3.0	8,935	435	200	235
3.5	9,182	447	200	247
4.0	9,441	459	200	259
4.5	9,713	472	200	272
5.0	10,000	486	200	286

*Adjusted issue price at the end of the period. The adjusted issue price is found by adding the original-issue discount amortized for the period to the previous period's adjusted issue price.

**The gross income reported is equal to the coupon interest for the period plus the original-issue discount amortized for the period.

***By the constant-yield method, it is found as follows: (adjusted issue price at the end of the previous period × 0.05) – $200.

For example, suppose a bond maturing in 20 years is initially sold for $990 for each $1,000 of redemption value at maturity. The discount is $10. The redemption value multiplied by the number of years to maturity is $20,000. The original-issue discount is 0.0005 of $20,000. Since it is less than one-fourth of 1% (0.0025), the original-issue discount is treated as zero; that is, the investor does not have to amortize the discount and report it as gross income.

SUMMARY

In this chapter we have shown how to determine the price of an option-free bond. The price is simply the present value of the bond's expected cash flows, where the discount rate is equal to the yield offered on comparable bonds. For an option-free bond, the cash flows are the coupon payments and the par value or maturity value. For a zero-coupon bond, there are no coupon payments: the price is equal to the present value of the maturity value, where the number of periods used to compute the present value is double the number of years. Exhibit 5-10 summarizes the pricing formulas presented in this chapter.

The higher (lower) the required yield, the lower (higher) the price of a bond. Therefore, a bond's price changes in the direction opposite from the change in the required yield. When the coupon rate is equal to the required yield, the bond will sell at its par value. When the coupon rate is less (higher) than the required yield, the bond will sell for less (more) than its par value. A bond selling below (above) its par value is said to be selling at a discount (premium).

Over time, the price of a bond will change. Assuming the credit quality of the issuer is unchanged, the price change can be broken down into an amount attributed to a change in the required yield and an amount attributed to the time path of the bond.

When a bond is purchased between coupon payments, the buyer must pay the seller accrued interest. To calculate the accrued interest, the following must be determined: (1) number of days between the previous coupon payment and the next coupon payment and (2) present value of the coupons. The conventions for determining these vary by market sector and from country to country. The payment made by the buyer to the seller is called the dirty price. The price quoted in the U.S. is the clean price or flat price, which is equal to the dirty price minus the accrued interest.

Summary of Pricing Formulas

1. Price of an option-free bond when next coupon payment is 6 months away:

$$p = \frac{c}{(1+i)^1} + \frac{c}{(1+i)^2} + \frac{c}{(1+i)^3} + \cdots + \frac{c}{(1+i)^n} + \frac{M}{(1+i)^n}$$

where

p = Price ($);
c = Semiannual coupon payment ($);
i = Periodic interest rate (required yield/2) (in decimal form);
n = Number of periods (number of years times 2);
M = Maturity value.

2. Present value of the coupon payments:

$$c \; \frac{1 - \left[\dfrac{1}{(1+i)^n}\right]}{i}.$$

3. Price of a zero-coupon bond:

$$p = M\left[\frac{1}{(1+i)^n}\right],$$

where

$n = 2 \times N$;
N = Number of years.

4. Price of a bond purchased between coupon payments with n coupon payments remaining:

$$p = \frac{c}{(1+i)^w} + \frac{c}{(1+i)^{1+w}} + \frac{c}{(1+i)^{2+w}}$$
$$+ \cdots + \frac{c}{(1+i)^{n-1+w}} + \frac{M}{(1+i)^{n-1+w}},$$

where

i = Periodic interest rate (required yield/2) (in decimal form);

$w = \dfrac{\text{Number of days between settlement and next coupon payment}}{\text{Number of days in the coupon period}}$;

n = Number of coupon payments remaining.

5. Accrued interest:

$$AI = c\left\{\frac{\text{Number of days from last coupon payment to settlement date}}{\text{Number of days in the coupon period}}\right\},$$

where

AI = Accrued interest ($).

6. Dirty price = Full price = Present value of the bond's cash flows.

7. Clean price = Flat price = Dirty price − Accrued interest.

6

⑥ CONVENTIONAL YIELD MEASURES FOR BONDS

In the previous chapter, we explained how to compute the price of a bond, given the required yield. In this chapter, we show how to compute various yield measures for a bond, given its price. We focus largely on four conventional yield measures commonly quoted by dealers and traders: (1) current yield, (2) yield to maturity, (3) yield to call, and (4) yield to put. While our focus in Part II is on option-free bonds, it is convenient to introduce yield measures for callable and putable bonds here. In Chapter 8, we evaluate these yield measures; in Chapter 9 we suggest a yield measure that is more useful for determining the potential return by investing in a bond.

CURRENT YIELD

The current yield relates the *annual* coupon interest to the market price. The formula for the current yield is

$$\text{Current yield} = \frac{\text{Annual dollar coupon interest}}{\text{Price}}.$$

Illustration 6-1 The current yield for an 18-year, 6% coupon bond selling for $700.89 is 8.56%, as shown below:

$$\text{Annual dollar coupon interest} = \$1,000 \times .06$$
$$= \$60$$

$$\text{Current yield} = \frac{\$60}{\$700.89} = .0856 \text{ or } 8.56\%.$$

Illustration 6-2 The current yield for a 19-year, 11% coupon bond selling for $1,233.64 is 8.92%, as shown below:

$$\text{Annual dollar coupon interest} = \$1,000 \times .11$$
$$= \$110$$

$$\text{Current yield} = \frac{\$110}{\$1,233.64} = .0892 \; or \; 8.92\%.$$

The current yield considers only the coupon interest and no other source of return that will affect an investor's yield. For example, in Illustration 6-1, no consideration is given to the capital gain that the investor will realize when the bond matures; in Illustration 6-2, no recognition is given to the capital loss that the investor will realize when the bond matures.

YIELD TO MATURITY

In Chapter 4 we explained how to compute the yield or internal rate of return on any investment. The yield is the interest rate that will make the present value of the cash flows equal to the price (or initial investment). The yield to maturity is computed in the same way as the yield; the cash flows are those that the investor would realize by holding the bond to maturity. For a semiannual-pay bond whose next coupon payment will be received 6 months from now, the yield to maturity is computed by solving the following relationship for y:

$$p = \frac{c}{(1+y)^1} + \frac{c}{(1+y)^2} + \frac{c}{(1+y)^3} + \cdots + \frac{c}{(1+y)^n} + \frac{M}{(1+y)^n},$$

where

p = Price (\$);
c = *Semiannual* coupon interest (\$);
y = One-half the yield to maturity;
n = Number of periods (number of years $\times 2$) ;
M = Maturity value (\$).

For a semiannual-pay bond, doubling the interest rate or discount rate (y) gives the yield to maturity.

Using the Greek letter sigma to denote summation, we can express this relationship as follows:

$$p = \sum_{t=1}^{n} \frac{c}{(1+y)^t} + \frac{M}{(1+y)^n} .$$

The yield to maturity considers not only the current coupon income but any capital gain or loss that the investor will realize by *holding the bond to maturity*. The yield to maturity also considers the timing of the cash flows.

Recall from Chapter 4 that computation of the yield requires a trial-and-error procedure. The next two illustrations show how to compute the yield to maturity for a bond.

Illustration 6-3   In Illustration 6-1 we computed the current yield for an 18-year, 6% coupon bond selling for \$700.89. The maturity or par value for this bond is \$1,000. The yield to maturity for this bond is 9.5%, as shown below:

Cash flows for the bond are

1. 36 coupon payments of $30 every 6 months;
2. $1,000, 36 6-month periods from now.

To get y, different interest rates must be tried until one is found that makes the present value of the cash flows equal to the price of $700.89. Since the coupon rate on the bond is 6% and the bond is selling at a discount, the yield must be greater than 6%. Exhibit 6-1 shows the present value of the cash flows of the bond for periodic interest rates from 3.25% to 4.75% (corresponding to annual interest rates from 6.50% to 9.50%, respectively). As can be seen from this exhibit, at the interest rate of 4.75%, the present value of the cash flows is $700.89. Therefore, y is 4.75%, and the yield to maturity is 9.50%.

Illustration 6-4   In Illustration 6-2 we computed the current yield for a 19-year, 11% coupon bond selling for $1,233.64. The maturity or par value for this bond is $1,000. The yield to maturity for this bond is 8.50%, as shown below:

EXHIBIT 6-1

Computation of Yield to Maturity for an 18-Year, 6% Coupon Bond Selling at $700.89

Objective: Find—by trial and error—the semiannual interest rate that will make the present value of the following cash flows equal to $700.89:

36 coupon payments of $30 every 6 months;
$1,000, 36 6-month periods from now.

Annual Interest Rate (%)	Semi-annual Rate (%)	Present Value of 36 Payments of $30 ($)*	Present Value of $1,000, 36 Periods from Now ($)**	Present Value of Cash Flows ($)
6.50%	3.25%	$631.20	$316.20	$947.40
7.00	3.50	608.71	289.83	898.54
7.50	3.75	587.42	265.72	853.14
8.00	4.00	567.25	243.67	810.92
8.50	4.25	548.12	223.49	771.61
9.00	4.50	529.98	205.03	735.01
9.50	4.75	512.76	188.13	700.89

$$* \$30 \left[\frac{1 - \left[\frac{1}{(1 + \text{Semiannual interest rate})^{36}} \right]}{\text{Semiannual interest rate}} \right]$$

$$** \$1,000 \left[\frac{1}{1 + \text{Semiannual interest rate})^{36}} \right]$$

Cash flows for the bond are

1. 38 coupon payments of $55 every 6 months;
2. $1,000, 38 6-month periods from now.

We are looking for the interest rate y that will make the present value of the cash flows equal to $1,233.64 (the price of the bond). Since the bond is selling at a premium and the coupon rate is 11%, the yield must be less than 11%. Exhibit 6-2 shows the present value of the cash flows of the bond for periodic interest rates from 3.00% to 4.25% (corresponding to annual interest rates from 6.0% to 8.50%, respectively). The present value of the cash flows is equal to the price when a 4.25% interest rate is used. The value for y is therefore 4.25%. Doubling 4.25% produces the yield to maturity of 8.50%.

Yield to Maturity for a Zero-Coupon Bond

In Chapter 4 we explained that when there is only one cash flow, it is much easier to compute the yield on an investment. A zero-coupon bond is characterized by a single cash flow resulting from the investment. Consequently, the following formula, presented in Chapter 4 (Exhibit 4-2), can be applied to compute the yield to maturity for a zero-coupon bond:

EXHIBIT 6-2

Computation of Yield to Maturity for a 19-Year, 11% Coupon Bond Selling at $1,233.64

Objective: Find—by trial and error—the semiannual interest rate that will make the present value of the following cash flows equal to $1,233.64:

38 coupon payments of $55 every 6 months;
$1,000, 38 6-month periods from now.

Annual Interest Rate (%)	Semi-annual Rate (%)	Present Value of 38 Payments of $55 ($)*	Present Value of $1,000, 38 Periods from Now ($)**	Present Value of Cash Flows ($)
6.00%	3.00%	$1,237.09	$325.23	$1,562.32
6.50	3.25	1,190.36	296.60	1,486.96
7.00	3.50	1,146.26	270.56	1,416.82
7.50	3.75	1,104.60	246.86	1,351.46
8.00	4.00	1,065.23	225.29	1,290.52
8.50	4.25	1,028.00	205.64	1,233.64

$$* \quad \$55 \left[\frac{1 - \left[\frac{1}{(1 + \text{Semiannual interest rate})^{38}} \right]}{\text{Semiannual interest rate}} \right].$$

$$** \quad \$1,000 \left[\frac{1}{(1 + \text{Semiannual interest rate})^{38}} \right].$$

$$y = (\text{Future value per dollar invested})^{1/n} - 1,$$

where

y = One-half the yield to maturity;

$$\text{Future value per dollar invested} = \frac{\text{Maturity value}}{\text{Price}}.$$

Once again, doubling y gives the yield to maturity. *Remember that the number of periods used in the formula is double the number of years.*

Illustration 6-5   The yield to maturity for a zero-coupon bond selling for $274.78 with a maturity value of $1,000, maturing in 15 years, is 8.8%, as computed below:

$\text{Future value per dollar invested} = \dfrac{\$1,000.00}{\$274.78}$;

$n = 30 \ (15 \times 2)$;

$$
\begin{aligned}
y &= (3.639275)^{1/30} - 1 \\
&= (3.639275)^{.033333} - 1 \\
&= 1.044 - 1 \\
&= .044 \text{ or } 4.4\% \ .
\end{aligned}
$$

Doubling 4.4% gives the yield to maturity of 8.8%.

Computing the Yield to Maturity When the Settlement Date Falls Between Coupon Payments

In the last chapter we explained how to determine the price that the buyer pays the seller when a bond is purchased between coupon payments. The amount paid is the dirty or full price. The yield to maturity for a bond when settlement falls between coupon dates is the interest rate that will make the present value of the cash flows equal to the dirty price. That is, for a semiannual-pay bond with n coupon payments remaining, we must solve the following relationship for y:

$$
\begin{aligned}
tp = {} & \frac{c}{(1+y)^w} + \frac{c}{(1+y)^{1+w}} + \frac{c}{(1+y)^{2+w}} \\
& + \cdots + \frac{c}{(1+y)^{n-1+w}} + \frac{M}{(1+y)^{n-1+w}},
\end{aligned}
$$

where

tp = Dirty price ($);

c = *Semiannual* coupon payment ($);

y = One-half the yield to maturity;

$w = \dfrac{\text{Number of days between settlement and the next coupon payment}}{\text{Number of days in the coupon period}}$;

n = Number of coupon payments remaining;

M = Maturity value.

Doubling y gives the yield to maturity.

Using the Greek letter sigma to denote summation, the formula can be expressed as follows:

$$tp = \sum_{t=1}^{n} \frac{c}{(1+y)^{t-1+w}} + \frac{M}{(1+y)^{n-1+w}}.$$

Illustration 6-6   Suppose that a 10% coupon corporate bond maturing on March 1, 2003, has a dirty price of $118.778. The settlement date is July 17, 1997. The cash flows for this bond per $100 of par value, and the corresponding periods they will be received, are:

Period	Cash Flow
.24444 through 10.2444	$ 5.00
11.24444	$105.00

The semiannual interest rate that will make the present value of the cash flows equal to the dirty price of $118.778 is 3.3735%. Doubling the semiannual interest rate gives a yield to maturity of 6.747%.

Illustration 6-7   If the bond in Illustration 6-6 were a Treasury bond rather than a corporate bond, the cash flows for the bond would be as follows:

Number of days from settlement to next coupon payment = 46;
Number of days in coupon period = 184;

$$w = \frac{46}{184} = .25.$$

The cash flows for this bond per $100 of par value and the corresponding periods they will be received are as follows:

Period	Cash Flow
.25 through 10.25	$ 5.00
11.25	105.00

Suppose the dirty price is $118.75. The interest rate that will make the present value of the cash flows equal to $118.75 is 3.374%. The yield to maturity is then 6.748%.

Relationships Among Coupon Rate, Current Yield, and Yield to Maturity

These relationships pertain among coupon rate, current yield, and yield to maturity:

Bond Selling at	Relationship
Par	Coupon rate = Current yield = Yield to maturity
Discount	Coupon rate < Current yield < Yield to maturity
Premium	Coupon rate > Current yield > Yield to maturity

The relationships for discount and premium bonds can be verified from the illustrations presented earlier in this chapter.

Problem with the Annualizing Procedure

As we pointed out in Chapter 4, multiplying a semiannual interest rate by 2 will produce an underestimate of the effective annual yield. The proper way to annualize the semiannual yield is by applying the following formula presented in Chapter 4 (see Exhibit 4-2):

$$\text{Effective annual yield} = (1 + \text{Periodic interest rate})^m - 1,$$

where

m = Number of payments per year.

For a semiannual-pay bond, the formula can be modified as follows:

$$\text{Effective annual yield} = (1 + \text{Semiannual interest rate})^2 - 1$$

or

$$\text{Effective annual yield} = (1 + y)^2 - 1.$$

For example, in Illustration 6-3, the semiannual interest rate is 4.75%, and the effective annual yield is 9.73%, as shown below:

$$
\begin{aligned}
\text{Effective annual yield} &= (1.0475)^2 - 1 \\
&= 1.0973 - 1 \\
&= .0973 \; or \; 9.73\%
\end{aligned}
$$

Although the proper way to annualize a semiannual interest rate is given in the formula above, the convention adopted in the bond market is to double the semiannual interest rate. The yield to maturity computed in this manner—doubling the semiannual yield—is called a *bond equivalent yield*. In fact, this convention is carried over to yield calculations for other types of fixed income securities.[1]

Yield on a Eurobond

While the practice in the United States is to pay interest semiannually, in the Eurobond market interest is paid annually. This practice is also followed in the domestic bond market of some countries. The calculation of the yield to maturity for an annual-pay bond is the same as for a semiannual-pay bond: it is the interest rate that makes the present value of the cash flow equal to the dirty price.

---

1 For example, in Chapter 20, we discuss the yield calculation for mortgage pass-through securities. The periodic interest rate is computed on a monthly basis. To compute an annual yield, the practice is first to compute an effective semiannual yield as follows:

$$\text{Effective semiannual yield} = (1 + \text{Monthly interest rate})^6 - 1.$$

Then the effective semiannual yield is doubled.

EXHIBIT 6–3

Computation of Yield to Maturity for a Eurobond with 10 Years to Maturity, a Coupon Rate of 9.125%, and a Price of $993.33 (Par $1,000)

Objective: Find—by trial and error—the annual interest rate that makes the present value of the following cash flows equal to $993.33:

10 coupon payments of $91.25;
$1,000, 10 years from now.

Annual Interest Rate (%)	Present Value of 10 Payments of $91.25 ($)	Present Value of $1,000, 10 Years from Now ($)*	Present Value of Cash Flows ($)**
9.18%	$581.00	$415.50	$996.50
9.19	580.75	415.12	995.86
9.20	580.49	414.74	995.23
9.21	580.24	414.36	994.60
9.22	579.98	413.98	993.96
9.23	579.73	413.60	993.33

$$* \$91.25 \left[\frac{1 - \left[\frac{1}{(1 + \text{Annual interest rate})^{10}} \right]}{\text{Annual interest rate}} \right]$$

$$** \$1,000 \left[\frac{1}{(1 + \text{Annual interest rate})^{10}} \right]$$

Illustration 6-8   Suppose that a Eurobond with a coupon rate of 9.125% and 10 years to maturity is selling for $993.33 per $1,000 par value. The yield to maturity for this bond is 9.23%, as shown in Exhibit 6-3.

An adjustment is required to make a direct comparison between the yield to maturity on a U.S. bond issue and that on a Eurodollar bond issue. Given the yield to maturity on a Eurodollar bond issue, its yield to maturity on a bond equivalent basis is computed as follows:

$$\text{Yield to maturity on a bond equivalent basis} = 2[(1 + \text{Yield to maturity})^{1/2} - 1].$$

Illustration 6-9   For the Eurobond in the previous illustration whose yield to maturity is 9.23%, the yield to maturity on a bond equivalent basis is:

$$2\,[(1.0923)^{1/2} - 1] = 0.0903 = 9.03\%.$$

Notice that the yield to maturity on a bond equivalent basis will always be less than the yield to maturity on an annual-pay bond.

Alternatively, to convert the yield to maturity on a bond equivalent basis of a U.S. bond issue to an annual-pay basis so that it can be compared to the yield to maturity of a Eurodollar bond, the following formula can be used:

Yield to maturity on an annual–pay basis

$$=\left[\left(\frac{\text{Yield to maturity on a bond equivalent basis}}{2}\right)^2 - 1\right].$$

Illustration 6-10 Suppose an investor wants to compare the yield to maturity of a 10-year, 9.125% coupon Eurobond and the yield to maturity of a 10-year, 9% coupon U.S. bond issue. Suppose that the price of the Eurobond is $993.33 and the U.S. bond issue is $990.31. From Illustration 6-8, we know that the yield to maturity is 9.23% and from Illustration 6-9, we know that the yield to maturity on a bond equivalent basis is 9.03%. For the U.S. bond issue, the yield to maturity on a bond equivalent basis is 9.15%, if the price is $990.31. To convert this yield to an annual-pay basis, the previous formula is used:

$$\left[1+\left(\frac{0.0915}{2}\right)^2 - 1\right] = 0.0936 = 9.36\%.$$

Notice that the yield to maturity on an annual basis is always greater than the yield to maturity on a bond equivalent basis.

Below we have a comparison for our two hypothetical bonds:

Issue	Coupon Rate (%)	Price ($)	Yield on a Bond Equivalent Basis (%)	Yield on an Annualized Basis (%)
Eurobond	9.125%	$993.33	9.03%	9.23%
U.S.	9.000	990.31	9.15	9.36

The summary shows that the yield on the U.S. bond issue is higher than the yield on the Eurobond issue whether calculated on a bond equivalent basis or an annual basis. An improper comparison of the unadjusted yield—9.23% for the Eurobond issue and 9.15% for the U.S. bond issue—would give a different conclusion.

YIELD TO CALL

Many issues have a provision allowing the issuer an option to buy back all or part of the issue prior to the stated maturity date. The right of the issuer to retire the issue prior to the stated maturity date is referred to as a *call option* and the bond is said to be a *callable bond*. If an issuer exercises this right, the issuer is said to "call the bond." The price which the issuer must pay to retire the issue is referred to as the *call price*. Typically, there is not one call price but a call schedule which sets forth a call price based on when the issuer can exercise the call option.

When a bond is issued, typically the issuer may not call the bond for a number of years. That is, the issue is said to have a *deferred call*. The date at which the bond may first be called is referred to as the *first call date*.

Generally, the call schedule is such that the call price at the first call date is a premium over the par value and scaled down to the par value over time. The date at which the issue is first callable at par value is referred to as the *first par call date*. For example, the Becton Dickinson & Co. 8.70s due January 15, 2025 were issued on January 10, 1995. The first call date is January 15, 2005. Thus, at issuance this corporate bond had a 10-year deferred call. The call schedule for this issue is as follows:

If Redeemed During the 12 months beginning January 15	Call Price ($)
2005	$103.949
2006	103.554
2007	103.159
2008	102.764
2009	102.369
2010	101.975
2011	101.580
2012	101.185
2013	100.790
2014	100.395
2015 and thereafter	100.000

The first par call date for this issue is January 15, 2015.

When a bond is callable, an investor can calculate a yield to an assumed call date. The yield to call is the interest rate that makes the present value of the cash flows to the assumed call date equal to the dirty price of the bond. Mathematically, the yield to an assumed call date for a bond on which the next coupon payment will be due 6 months from now can be expressed as follows:

$$p = \frac{c}{(1+y)^1} + \frac{c}{(1+y)^2} + \frac{c}{(1+y)^3} + \cdots + \frac{c}{(1+y)^{n*}} + \frac{CP}{(1+y)^{n*}},$$

where

p = Price ($);
c = *Semiannual* coupon interest ($);
y = one-half the yield to call (in decimal form);
$n*$ = Number of periods until assumed call date (number of years $\times$ 2);
CP = Call price at assumed call date from the call schedule.

For a semiannual-pay bond, doubling the interest rate (y) gives the yield to call.

Alternatively, the yield to call can be expressed as follows:

$$p = \sum_{t=1}^{n*} \frac{c}{(1+y)^t} + \frac{CP}{(1+y)^{n*}}.$$

Two commonly used call dates are the first call date and the first par call date. To calculate the yield to the first call date, the value for CP used in the formula is the call price on the first call date as given in the call schedule. In computing the yield to the first par call date, the par value is used for CP in the formula.

The next two illustrations show how to calculate the yield to the first call date.

Illustration 6-11   In Illustrations 6-1 and 6-3 we computed the current yield and yield to maturity for an 18-year, 6% coupon bond selling for $700.89. Suppose that this bond is first callable in 5 years at $1,030. The cash flows for this bond if it is called at the first call date are

1. 10 coupon payments of $30 every 6 months;
2. $1,030, 10 6-month periods from now.

The value for y that we seek is the one that will make the present values of the cash flows equal to $700.89. From Exhibit 6-4 it can be seen that when y is 7.6%, the present value of the cash flows is $700.11, which is close enough to $700.89 for our purposes. Therefore, the yield to the first call date on a bond equivalent basis is 15.2% (double the periodic interest rate of 7.6%).

Illustration 6-12   In Illustrations 6-2 and 6-4 we computed the current yield and yield to maturity for a 19-year, 11% coupon bond selling for $1,233.64. Suppose that this bond is first

EXHIBIT 6-4

Computation of Yield to the First Call Date for an 18-Year, 6% Coupon Bond, Callable in 5 Years (First Call Date) at $1,030, Selling at $700.89

Objective: Find—by trial and error—the semiannual interest rate that will make the present value of the following cash flows equal to $700.89:

10 coupon payments of $30 every 6 months;
$1,030, 10 6-month periods from now.

Annual Interest Rate (%)	Semi- annual Rate (%)	Present Value of 10 Payments of $30 ($)*	Present Value of $1,030, 10 Periods from Now ($)**	Present Value of Cash Flows ($)
11.20%	5.60%	$225.05	$597.31	$822.36
11.70	5.85	222.38	583.35	805.73
12.20	6.10	219.76	569.75	789.51
12.70	6.35	217.19	556.50	773.69
13.20	6.60	214.66	543.58	758.24
13.70	6.85	212.18	531.00	743.18
14.20	7.10	209.74	518.73	728.47
14.70	7.35	207.34	506.78	714.12
15.20	7.60	204.99	495.12	700.11

* $30 $\left[\dfrac{1 - \left[\dfrac{1}{(1 + \text{Semiannual interest rate})^{10}}\right]}{\text{Semiannual interest rate}}\right]$

** $1,030 $\left[\dfrac{1}{(1 + \text{Semiannual interest rate})^{10}}\right]$

Computation of Yield to the First Call Date for a 19-Year, 11% Coupon Bond, Callable in 6 Years (First Call Date) at $1,055, Selling at $1,233.64

Objective: Find—by trial and error—the semiannual interest rate that will make the present value of the following cash flows equal to $1,233.64:

12 coupon payments of $55 every 6 months;
$1,055, 12 6-month periods from now.

Annual Interest Rate (%)	Semi- Annual Rate (%)	Present Value of 12 Payments of $55 ($)*	Present Value of $1,055, 12 Periods from Now ($)**	Present Value of Cash Flows ($)
5.10%	2.55%	$562.47	$779.87	$1,342.34
5.60	2.80	554.06	757.42	1,311.48
6.10	3.05	545.84	735.66	1,281.50
6.60	3.30	537.79	714.58	1,252.37
7.10	3.55	529.92	694.15	1,224.07
7.60	3.80	522.22	674.35	1,196.57

$$* \$55 \left[\frac{1 - \left[\dfrac{1}{(1 + \text{Semiannual interest rate})^{12}} \right]}{\text{Semiannual interest rate}} \right]$$

$$** \$1,055 \left[\frac{1}{(1 + \text{Semiannual interest rate})^{12}} \right]$$

callable in 6 years at $1,055. If the bond is called on the first call date, the cash flows for this bond would be

1. 12 coupon payments of $55 every 6 months;
2. $1,055, 12 6-month periods from now.

Exhibit 6-5 shows the present value of the cash flows for several interest rates. The interest rate that equates the present value of the cash flows to the price of $1,233.64 is approximately 3.55%. Therefore, the yield to the first call date on a bond equivalent basis is 7.1%.

YIELD TO PUT

A call provision grants the issuer the right to change the maturity of the bond. An issue with a *put provision* grants the bondholder the right to sell the issue back to the issuer at par value on designated dates. Consequently, a bond with a put provision gives the bondholder the right to change the maturity of the bond. A bond with this provision is called a *putable bond*. There may be one put price or a schedule of put prices. Most putable bonds have just one put price.

For a putable bond, a yield to put can be calculated for any possible put date. The formula for the yield to put for any assumed put date is

$$p = \frac{c}{(1+y)^1} + \frac{c}{(1+y)^2} + \frac{c}{(1+y)^3} + \cdots + \frac{c}{(1+y)^{n*}} + \frac{PP}{(1+y)^{n*}},$$

where

p = Price (\$);
c = *Semiannual* coupon interest (\$);
y = one-half the yield to put (in decimal form);
$n*$ = Number of periods until assumed put date (number of years $\times$ 2);
PP = put price at assumed put date.

Doubling y gives the yield to put on a bond equivalent basis.

Alternatively, the yield to put can be expressed as follows:

$$p = \sum_{t=1}^{n*} \frac{c}{(1+y)^t} + \frac{PP}{(1+y)^{n*}}.$$

YIELD TO WORST

A bond issue may be callable and/or putable. Thus, in addition to the yield to maturity, a bond can have a yield to call for all possible call dates and a yield to put for all possible put dates. Some practitioners calculate the *yield to worst* for a bond. This is the smallest yield measure of all the possible yields that can be computed for the issue.

PORTFOLIO YIELD

There are two conventions that have been adopted by practitioners to calculate a portfolio yield: (1) weighted average portfolio yield and (2) internal rate of return.

Weighted Average Portfolio Yield

Probably the most common—and most flawed—method for calculating a portfolio yield is to calculate the weighted average of the yield of all the securities in the portfolio. The yield is weighted by the proportion of the portfolio that a security makes up. In general, if we let

w_i = Market value of security i relative to the total market value of the portfolio;
y_i = Yield on security i;
K = Number of securities in the portfolio;

then, the weighted average portfolio yield is

$$w_1 y_1 + w_2 y_2 + w_3 y_3 + \cdots + w_K y_K.$$

Illustration 6-13   Consider the following three-bond portfolio:

Bond	Coupon Rate (%)	Maturity (years)	Par Value ($)	Market Value ($)	Yield to Maturity (%)
A	7.0%	5	$10,000,000	$ 9,209,000	9.0%
B	10.5	7	20,000,000	20,000,000	10.5
C	6.0	3	30,000,000	28,050,000	8.5

In this illustration, the total market value of the portfolio is $57,259,000, K is equal to 3, and

$$w_1 = 9,209,000/57,259,000 = .161 \qquad y_1 = .090$$
$$w_2 = 20,000,000/57,259,000 = .349 \qquad y_2 = .105$$
$$w_3 = 28,050,000/57,259,000 = .490 \qquad y_3 = .085$$

The weighted average portfolio yield is then

$$.161\,(.090) + .349\,(.105) + .490\,(.085) = .0928 = 9.28\%.$$

While it is the most commonly used measure of portfolio yield, the average yield measure provides little insight into the potential yield of a portfolio. To see this, consider a portfolio consisting of only two bonds: a 6-month bond offering a yield to maturity of 11%, and a 30-year bond offering a yield to maturity of 8%. Suppose that 99% of the portfolio is invested in the 6-month bond and 1%, in the 30-year bond. The weighted average yield for this portfolio would be 10.97%. But what does this yield mean? How can it be used within any asset/liability framework? The portfolio is basically a 6-month portfolio even though it has a 30-year bond. Would a manager of a depository institution feel confident offering a 2-year CD with a yield of 9%? This would suggest a spread of 197 basis points above the yield on the portfolio, based on the weighted average portfolio yield. This would be an imprudent policy because the yield on this portfolio over the next 2 years will depend on interest rates 6 months from now.

Portfolio Internal Rate of Return

Another measure used to calculate a portfolio yield is the internal rate of the portfolio's cash flow. It is computed by first determining the cash flows for all the securities in the portfolio, and then finding the interest rate that will make the present value of the cash flows equal to the market value of the portfolio.[2]

Illustration 6-14 To illustrate how to calculate a portfolio's internal rate of return, we will use the three bonds in Illustration 6-11. To simplify the illustration, it is assumed that the coupon payment date is the same for each bond.

The portfolio's total market value is $57,259,000. The cash flows for each bond in the portfolio and for the whole portfolio are given in Exhibit 6-6. To determine the yield (internal rate of return) for this three-bond portfolio, the interest rate that makes the present value of the

---

2 In Chapter 13 we discuss the concept of duration. A good approximation to the yield for a portfolio can be obtained by using duration to weight the yield to maturity of the individual bonds in the portfolio.

E X H I B I T   6–6

Cash Flows for a Three-Bond Portfolio

Period Cash Flow Received	Bond A ($)	Bond B ($)	Bond C ($)	Portfolio ($)
1	$ 350,000	$ 1,050,000	$ 900,000	$ 2,300,000
2	350,000	1,050,000	900,000	2,300,000
3	350,000	1,050,000	900,000	2,300,000
4	350,000	1,050,000	900,000	2,300,000
5	350,000	1,050,000	900,000	2,300,000
6	350,000	1,050,000	30,900,000	32,300,000
7	350,000	1,050,000	—	1,400,000
8	350,000	1,050,000	—	1,400,000
9	350,000	1,050,000	—	1,400,000
10	10,350,000	1,050,000	—	11,400,000
11	—	1,050,000	—	1,050,000
12	—	1,050,000	—	1,050,000
13	—	1,050,000	—	1,050,000
14	—	21,050,000	—	21,050,000

cash flows shown in the last column of Exhibit 6-6 equal to $57,259,000 (the total market value of the portfolio) must be found. If an interest rate of 4.77% is used, the present value of the cash flows will equal $57,259,000. Doubling 4.77% gives 9.54%, which is the yield on the portfolio on a bond equivalent basis.

The portfolio internal rate of return, while superior to the weighted average portfolio yield, suffers from the same problems as yield measures in general, discussed in subsequent chapters.

DISCOUNTED MARGIN FOR FLOATING-RATE SECURITIES

A *floating-rate security* is one in which the coupon rate is reset at designated dates according to a predetermined formula. The formula for a simple floating-rate security is

Floating-rate security = Reference rate + Index spread.

The *reference rate* is the underlying interest rate or interest rate index. Two common reference rates are LIBOR and Treasury rates. The *index spread* is the additional amount that the issuer agrees to pay over the reference rate. Typically, the index spread is positive. For some floating-rate securities, there is a negative index spread. That is, the investor will receive by contract a rate less than the reference rate.

Since the future values of the reference rate are unknown today, it is not possible to determine what the cash flows will be. Consequently, it is not possible to calculate the yield to maturity.

A measure commonly used to gauge the potential return of a floating-rate security is the *discounted margin*. This measure estimates the average spread or margin over the reference rate the investor can expect to earn over the life of the security if the reference rate does not change from its current level. The procedure for calculating the discounted margin is as follows:

1. Determine the cash flows assuming that the reference rate does not change over the life of the security.

2. Select a margin.

3. Discount the cash flows found in (1) by the current value of the reference rate plus the margin selected in (2).

4. Compare the present value of the cash flows as calculated in (3) to the price. If the present value is equal to the security's price, the discounted margin is the margin assumed in (2). If the present value is not equal to the security's price, go back to (2) and try a different margin.

For a security selling at par, the discounted margin is simply the spread over the index.

Illustration 6-15   To illustrate the calculation, suppose that a 6-year floating-rate security selling for $99.3098 pays the reference rate plus 80 basis points (the index spread). The coupon rate is reset every 6 months. Assume that the current value of the reference rate is 10%.

Exhibit 6-7 shows the calculation of the discounted margin for this security. The second column shows the current value of the reference rate. The third column sets forth the cash flows for the security. The cash flow for the first 11 periods is equal to one-half the value of the reference rate (5%) plus the semiannual spread of 40 basis points multiplied by 100. In the twelfth 6-month period, the cash flow is $5.4 plus the maturity value of $100. The top row of the last five columns shows the assumed margin. The rows below the assumed margin show the present value of each cash flow. The last row gives the total present value of the cash flows.

For the five assumed yield spreads, the present value is equal to the price of the floating-rate security ($99.3098) when the assumed margin is 96 basis points. Therefore, the discounted margin on a semiannual basis is 48 basis points and 96 basis points on an annual basis. (Notice that the discounted margin is 80 basis points, the same as the index spread, when the security is selling at par.)

There are two drawbacks of the discounted margin as a measure of the potential return from investing in a floating-rate security. First, the measure assumes that the value of the reference rate will not change over the life of the security. Second, if the floating-rate security has a cap or floor, this is not taken into consideration.

SUMMARY

In this chapter we have explained five conventional yield measures: (1) current yield, (2) yield to maturity, (3) yield to call, (4) yield to put, and (5) yield to worst. Two measures of portfolio yield—weighted average portfolio yield and internal rate of return—were explained. The discounted margin is the spread measure used for a floating-rate security. Exhibit 6-8 summarizes the formulas presented in this chapter to calculate these yield measures. The shortcomings of these measures for evaluating the potential return from owning a bond are explained in the next chapter.

E X H I B I T 6–7

Calculation of the Discounted Margin for a Floating-Rate Security

Floating-rate security: Maturity = 6 years
Coupon rate = Reference rate + 80 basis points
Resets every 6 months
Maturity value = $100

			Present Value of Cash Flow: Assumed Annual Spread (in basis points)				
Period	Reference Rate (%)	Cash Flow ($)*	80	84	88	96	100
1	10%	$ 5.4	$ 5.1233	$ 5.1224	$ 5.1214	$ 5.1195	$ 5.1185
2	10	5.4	4.8609	4.8590	4.8572	4.8535	4.8516
3	10	5.4	4.6118	4.6092	4.6066	4.6013	4.5987
4	10	5.4	4.3755	4.3722	4.3689	4.3623	4.3590
5	10	5.4	4.1514	4.1474	4.1435	4.1356	4.1317
6	10	5.4	3.9387	3.9342	3.9297	3.9208	3.9163
7	10	5.4	3.7369	3.7319	3.7270	3.7171	3.7122
8	10	5.4	3.5454	3.5401	3.5347	3.5240	3.5186
9	10	5.4	3.3638	3.3580	3.3523	3.3409	3.3352
10	10	5.4	3.1914	3.1854	3.1794	3.1673	3.1613
11	10	5.4	3.0279	3.0216	3.0153	3.0028	2.9965
12	10	105.4	56.0729	55.9454	55.8182	55.5647	55.4385
		Present value =	$100.0000	$99.8269	$99.6541	$99.3098	$99.1381

* For periods 1–11: Cash flow = 100 (Reference rate + Assumed margin) (.5).
For period 12: Cash flow = 100 (Reference Rate + Assumed margin) (.5) + 100.

EXHIBIT 6-8

Summary of Formulas for Conventional Yield Measures

1. Current yield:

$$\text{Current yield} = \frac{\text{Annual dollar coupon interest}}{\text{Price}}.$$

2. Yield to maturity for a bond with a coupon payment due 6 months from now—solve for y:

$$p = \frac{c}{(1+y)^1} + \frac{c}{(1+y)^2} + \frac{c}{(1+y)^3} + \cdots + \frac{c}{(1+y)^n} + \frac{M}{(1+y)^n}$$

or

$$p = \sum_{t=1}^{n} \frac{c}{(1+y)^t} + \frac{M}{(1+y)^n},$$

where

p = Price;
c = Semiannual coupon interest (\$);
y = One-half the yield to maturity (in decimal form);
n = Number of periods (number of years $\times$ 2);
M = Maturity value (\$).

For a semiannual-pay bond,

$$\text{Yield to maturity} = 2 \times y.$$

3. Yield to maturity for a zero-coupon bond:

$$y = (\text{Future value per dollar invested})^{1/n} - 1,$$

where

y = One-half the yield to maturity (in decimal form);

$$\text{Future value per dollar invested} = \frac{\text{Maturity value}}{\text{Price}}$$

Yield to maturity = $2 \times y$.

4. Yield to maturity when the settlement date is between coupon payments—solve for y:

$$tp = \frac{c}{(1+y)^w} + \frac{c}{(1+y)^{1+w}} + \frac{c}{(1+y)^{2+w}}$$

$$+ \cdots + \frac{c}{(1+y)^{n-1+w}} + \frac{M}{(1+y)^{n-1+w}},$$

Continued

EXHIBIT 6-8

Continued

or

$$tp = \sum_{t=1}^{n} \frac{c}{(1+y)^{t-1+w}} + \frac{M}{(1+y)^{n-1+w}},$$

where

tp = Dirty price ($);
c = *Semiannual* coupon payment ($);
y = One-half the yield to maturity (in decimal form);
$w = \dfrac{\text{Number of days between settlement and the next coupon payment}}{\text{Number of days in the coupon period}}$.
n = Number of coupon payments remaining;
M = Maturity value.

Yield to maturity = $2 \times y$.

5. Yield to call—solve for y:

$$p = \frac{c}{(1+y)^1} + \frac{c}{(1+y)^2} + \frac{c}{(1+y)^3} + \cdots + \frac{c}{(1+y)^{n*}} + \frac{CP}{(1+y)^{n*}}$$

or

$$p = \sum_{t=1}^{n*} \frac{c}{(1+y)^t} + \frac{CP}{(1+y)^{n*}},$$

where

p = Price ($);
c = *Semiannual* coupon interest ($);
y = one-half the yield to call (in decimal form);
$n*$ = Number of periods until assumed call date (number of years $\times$ 2);
CP = Call price at assumed call date from the call schedule.

Yield to call = $2 \times y$.

6. Yield to put—solve for y:

$$p = \frac{c}{(1+y)^1} + \frac{c}{(1+y)^2} + \frac{c}{(1+y)^3} + \cdots + \frac{c}{(1+y)^{n*}} + \frac{PP}{(1+y)^{n*}}$$

or

Continued

EXHIBIT 6-8

Concluded

$$p = \sum_{t=1}^{n^*} \frac{c}{(1+y)^t} + \frac{PP}{(1+y)^{n^*}},$$

where

p = Price (\$);
c = *Semiannual* coupon interest (\$);
y = one-half the yield to put (in decimal form);
n^* = Number of periods until assumed put date (number of years × 2);
PP = Put price at assumed put date.

Yield to put = $2 \times y$.

7. Weighted average portfolio yield:

$$w_1 y_1 + w_2 y_2 + w_3 y_3 + \cdots + w_K y_K,$$

where

w_i = Market value of security i relative to the total market value of the portfolio;
y_i = Yield on security i;
K = Number of securities in the portfolio.

7

⑥ THE YIELD CURVE, SPOT RATE CURVE, AND FORWARD RATES

Up to this point, we know the basic principles for pricing a bond and the various yield measures. One of the assumptions made in the illustrations of how to price a bond is that the cash flow for each period should be discounted at the same interest rate or yield. In this chapter, we modify this assumption and explain how the appropriate interest rate that should be used to discount the cash flow for each period is determined. The process begins with the Treasury yield curve. From the Treasury yield curve, two important interest rates are derived: (1) spot rates and (2) forward rates. These are the rates that should be used to value bonds.

A BOND IS A PACKAGE OF ZERO-COUPON INSTRUMENTS

Modern financial theory tells us that a "bond is not a bond." Well, if it is not a bond, what is it? A bond should be viewed as a package of cash flows, with each cash flow viewed as a zero-coupon instrument, with the maturity date the date that the cash flow will be paid and the maturity value equal to the cash flow. This means that a 30-year, 8% coupon Treasury bond with a par value of $100,000 should be viewed as a package of 60 zero-coupon instruments: 59 zero-coupon instruments maturing every 6 months for the next 29.5 years, with a maturity value equal to the semiannual coupon of $4,000, and one zero-coupon instrument that matures 30 years from now, with a maturity value equal to $104,000 (the semiannual coupon plus $100,000).

If a bond is viewed as a package of zero-coupon instruments, how then should a bond be valued? The value of a bond is the total value of all the zero-coupon instruments. The value of each zero-coupon instrument is determined in turn by discounting its maturity value at a rate that is unique to that zero-coupon instrument. But what is the yield that should be used to value each zero-coupon instrument? The minimum yield is the yield that the U.S. Treasury would have to pay if it issued a zero-coupon bond with the maturity of the cash flow analyzed.

Of course, the U.S. Treasury does not issue zero-coupon bonds. While there are stripped Treasury securities created by dealers, the yield offered on these securities is not the same as what the U.S. Treasury would have to pay if it issued zero-coupon bonds; stripped Treasuries have less liquidity. Fortunately, we can use arbitrage arguments to calculate from the yield curve theoretical zero-coupon rates that the Treasury would have to pay.

THE YIELD CURVE

The graphical depiction of the relationship between the yield to maturity on securities of the same credit risk and different maturity is called the *yield curve*. The yield curve is constructed from the maturity and observed yield of Treasury securities because Treasuries reflect the pure effect of maturity alone on yield, given that market participants do not perceive government securities to have any credit risk. When market participants refer to the "yield curve," they usually mean the Treasury yield curve. This is also true in the bond markets of other countries; the reference is to risk-free government securities.

Exhibit 7-1 shows four yield curves that have been observed in the U.S. Treasury market (and occur in other major government bond markets). In the yield curve in panel (a), the yield increases with maturity. This shape is commonly referred to as an *upward sloping* or *normal yield curve*. The yield curve in panel (b) is a *downward sloping* or an *inverted yield curve*,

EXHIBIT 7-1

Four Hypothetical Yield Curves

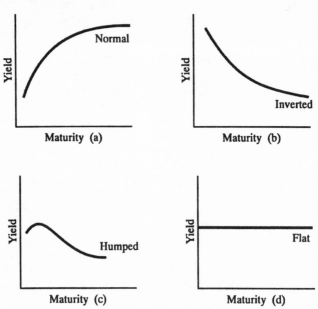

because yield decreases with maturity. In a *humped yield curve*, depicted in panel (c) of the exhibit, the yield curve initially is upward sloping, but after a certain maturity it becomes downward sloping. Finally, a *flat yield curve* is one where the yield is the same regardless of the maturity. A flat yield curve is shown in panel (d).

Several theories have been proposed to explain the shape of the yield curve, although discussion of these theories is beyond the scope of this book.[1] Analysis of the yield curve in this chapter is based on what is called the *pure expectations theory of interest rates*. According to the pure expectations theory, the only factor that affects the shape of the yield curve is the market expectation about future interest rates.

THE SPOT RATE CURVE

The Treasury yield curve shows the relationship between the yield on Treasury securities (Treasury bills and coupon securities) and maturity. According to the pure expectations theory and arbitrage arguments, we can determine the theoretical relationship between the yield on zero-coupon Treasury securities and maturity. This relationship is called the *Treasury spot rate curve*. The yield on a zero-coupon instrument is called a *spot rate*.

To illustrate how to construct a theoretical spot rate curve from the yield offered on Treasury securities, we use the 20 hypothetical Treasury securities shown in Exhibit 7-2.

The basic principle is that the value of a Treasury coupon security should be equal to the value of a package of zero-coupon Treasury securities. Consider first the 6-month Treasury bill in Exhibit 7-2. Because a Treasury bill is a zero-coupon instrument, its yield of 8% is equal to the spot rate. Similarly, for the 1-year Treasury, the yield of 8.3% is the 1-year spot rate. Given these two spot rates, we can compute the spot rate for a 1.5-year zero-coupon Treasury. The value or price of a 1.5-year zero-coupon Treasury should equal the present value of the three cash flows from the 1.5-year coupon Treasury, where the yield used for discounting is the spot rate corresponding to the cash flow. Using $100 as par, the cash flow for the 1.5-year coupon Treasury is as follows:

0.5 year	$.085 \times \$100 \times .5$	=	$4.25
1.0 year	$.085 \times \$100 \times .5$	=	$4.25
1.5 years	$.085 \times \$100 \times .5 + 100$	=	$104.25

The present value of the cash flow is then

$$\frac{4.25}{(1+z_1)^1} + \frac{4.25}{(1+z_2)^2} + \frac{104.25}{(1+z_3)^3},$$

where

z_1 = One-half the 6-month theoretical spot rate;
z_2 = One-half the 1-year theoretical spot rate;
z_3 = One-half the 1.5-year theoretical spot rate.

---

[1]   The interested reader is referred to Chapter 9 of Frank J. Fabozzi, *Bond Markets, Analysis and Strategies* (Englewood Cliffs, NJ: Prentice Hall, 1996 for a discussion of these theories.

E X H I B I T   7–2

Maturity and Yield to Maturity for 20 Hypothetical Treasury Securities

Maturity (years)	Coupon	Yield to Maturity	Price ($)
.50	.0000	.080	$ 96.15
1.00	.0000	.083	92.19
1.50	.0850	.089	99.45
2.00	.0900	.092	99.64
2.50	.1100	.094	103.49
3.00	.0950	.097	99.49
3.50	.1000	.100	100.00
4.00	.1000	.104	98.72
4.50	.1150	.106	103.16
5.00	.0875	.108	92.24
5.50	.1050	.109	98.38
6.00	.1100	.112	99.14
6.50	.0850	.114	86.94
7.00	.0825	.116	84.24
7.50	.1100	.118	96.09
8.00	.0650	.119	72.62
8.50	.0875	.120	82.97
9.00	.1300	.122	104.30
9.50	.1150	.124	95.06
10.00	.1250	.125	100.00

Because the 6-month spot rate and 1-year spot rate are 8.0% and 8.3%, respectively, then

$$z_1 = .04 \text{ and } z_2 = .0415.$$

Therefore the present value of the 1.5-year coupon Treasury security is

$$\frac{4.25}{(1.0400)^1} + \frac{4.25}{(1.0415)^2} + \frac{104.25}{(1 + z_3)^3} .$$

As the price of the 1.5-year coupon Treasury security is $99.45, the following relationship must hold:

$$99.45 = \frac{4.25}{(1.0400)^1} + \frac{4.25}{(1.0415)^2} + \frac{104.25}{(1 + z_3)^3} .$$

We can now solve for the theoretical 1.5-year spot as follows:

$$99.45 = 4.08654 + 3.91805 + \frac{104.25}{(1 + z_3)^3}.$$

$$91.4451 = \frac{104.25}{(1 + z_3)^3}$$

$$(1+z_3)^3 = 1.140024$$

$$z_3 = .04465.$$

Doubling this yield, we obtain the bond equivalent yield of .0893 or 8.93%, which is the theoretical 1.5-year spot rate.

Given the theoretical 1.5-year spot rate, we can obtain the theoretical 2-year spot rate. The cash flow for the 2-year coupon Treasury in Exhibit 7-2 is given below:

0.5 year	$.090 \times \$100 \times .5$	=	$4.50
1.0 year	$.090 \times \$100 \times .5$	=	$4.50
1.5 years	$.090 \times \$100 \times .5$	=	$4.50
2.0 years	$.090 \times \$100 \times .5 + 100$	=	$104.50

The present value of the cash flow is as follows:

$$\frac{4.50}{(1 + z_1)^1} + \frac{4.50}{(1 + z_2)^2} + \frac{4.50}{(1 + z_3)^3} + \frac{4.50}{(1 + z_4)^4},$$

where

z_4 = one-half the 2-year theoretical spot rate.

The 6-month spot rate, 1-year spot rate, and 1.5-year spot rate are 8.0%, 8.3%, and 8.93%, respectively, so

$$z_1 = .04, z_2 = .0415 \text{ and } z_3 = .04465.$$

Therefore the present value of the 2-year coupon Treasury security is

$$\frac{4.50}{(1.0400)^1} + \frac{4.50}{(1.0415)^2} + \frac{4.50}{(1.04465)^3} + \frac{104.50}{(1 + z_4)^4}.$$

Because the price of the 2-year coupon Treasury security is $99.64, the following relationship must hold:

$$99.64 = \frac{4.50}{(1.0400)^1} + \frac{4.50}{(1.0415)^2} + \frac{4.50}{(1.04465)^3} + \frac{104.50}{(1 + z_4)^4}.$$

We can now solve for the theoretical 2-year spot rate as follows:

$$99.64 = 4.32692 + 4.14853 + 3.94730 + \frac{104.50}{(1 + z_4)^4}$$

$$87.21725 = \frac{104.50}{(1 + z_4)^4}$$

$$(1 + z_4)^4 = 1.198158$$

$$z_4 = .046235.$$

Doubling this yield, we obtain the theoretical 2-year spot rate bond equivalent yield of 9.247%.

We can then use the theoretical 2-year spot rate and the 2.5-year coupon Treasury in Exhibit 7-2 to compute the 2.5-year theoretical spot rate. In general, to compute the theoretical spot rate for the nth 6-month period, the following equation must be solved:

$$P_n = \frac{c^*}{(1 + z_1)^1} + \frac{c^*}{(1 + z_2)^2} + \frac{c^*}{(1 + z_3)^3} + \ldots + \frac{c^* + 100}{(1 + z_n)^n},$$

where

P_n = Price of the coupon Treasury with n periods to maturity (per \$100 of par value);

c^* = *Semiannual* coupon interest for the coupon Treasury with n periods to maturity per \$100 of par value;

z_t for $t = 1, 2, \cdots, n-1$ are the theoretical spot rates that are known.

This expression can be rewritten as follows:

$$P_n = c^* \sum_{t=1}^{n-1} \frac{1}{(1 + z_t)^t} + \frac{c^* + 100}{(1 + z_n)^n}.$$

Solving for z_n, we get:

$$z_n = \left[\frac{c^* + 100}{P_n - c^* \sum_{t=1}^{n-1} \frac{1}{(1 + z_t)^t}} \right]^{1/n} - 1.$$

Doubling z_n gives the theoretical spot rate on a bond equivalent basis.

The equation above is used to determine the theoretical spot rates for each hypothetical Treasury security shown in Exhibit 7-2. The theoretical spot rates are presented in Exhibit 7-3. *It is this yield/maturity structure that would be used to construct the theoretical spot rate curve that is referred to as the term structure of interest rates.* The methodology described above for deriving the spot rate curve is called *bootstrapping*.

In practice, the Treasury securities used to determine the spot rates are the "on-the-run Treasury securities." These are the most recently auctioned Treasury securities. Currently, the U.S. Department of the Treasury auctions 3-month and 6-month Treasury bills every Monday and the 1-year (52-week bill) Treasury bill is auctioned the third week of every month. Coupon securities with maturities of 2, 3, 5, 10, and 30 years are auctioned on a regular basis.[2] Two- and 5-year notes are auctioned each month. At the beginning of the second month of each calendar quarter (February, May, August, and November), the Treasury auctions 3-year, 10-year, and 30-year securities.

The preference for using the on-the-run Treasury securities is twofold. First, seasoned Treasury coupon securities that are not the most recently auctioned Treasury coupon securities (called "off-the-run" Treasuries) may trade at a substantial premium or discount from par. Consequently, their price, and hence yield, reflects any favorable or unfavorable tax treatment of the discount or premium from par. The on-the-run Treasury coupon securities trade close to

---

2 At one time, the Treasury issued 7-year notes and 20-year bonds. Until 1985, the Treasury issued 30-year bonds that were callable within 5 years of maturity.

EXHIBIT 7-3

Theoretical Spot Rates

Maturity (years)	Yield to Maturity	Theoretical Spot Rate
.50	.0800	.08000
1.00	.0830	.08300
1.50	.0890	.08930
2.00	.0920	.09247
2.50	.0940	.09468
3.00	.0970	.09787
3.50	.1000	.10129
4.00	.1040	.10592
4.50	.1060	.10850
5.00	.1080	.11021
5.50	.1090	.11175
6.00	.1120	.11584
6.50	.1140	.11744
7.00	.1160	.11991
7.50	.1180	.12405
8.00	.1190	.12278
8.50	.1200	.12546
9.00	.1220	.13152
9.50	.1240	.13377
10.00	.1250	.13623

par so that their prices are not biased by tax considerations. Second, on-the-run issues trade with greater liquidity than off-the-run issues. Consequently, the latter have a liquidity premium built into their yield.[3]

Thus, unlike in our illustration where all 6-month points on the yield curve are used to begin the analysis, beyond 1 year only 2-, 3-, 5-, 10-, and 30-year maturities are available in practice. To obtain the yield for any maturity between two maturity dates, a simple linear interpolation is used. The resulting yield curve that is then used to generate the spot rate curve via bootstrapping is called the *par yield curve*.

---

3 Some practitioners prefer to use all Treasury issues—on-the-run and off-the-run issues—to estimate the spot rates. Those who do so believe that there is information contained in all Treasury issues and this information is not used when only the on-the-run issues are used. Complicated statistical techniques are used when all Treasury issues are used to estimate the spot rates. For a further discussion, see Richard W. McEnally and James V. Jordan, "The Term Structure of Interest Rates," in Frank J. Fabozzi (ed.), *The Handbook of Fixed Income Securities* (Burr Ridge, IL: Irwin Professional Publishing, 1995), Chapter 37.

PRICING A BOND

Given the cash flows of a bond and the Treasury spot rate curve, we can determine the price of a Treasury security by discounting each cash flow by the corresponding spot rate and adding up the present value of the cash flows. For example, consider an 8.8% coupon Treasury bond with 25 years to maturity. Exhibit 7-4 shows the cash flow for this bond per $100 of par value. Also shown in the exhibit are the assumed Treasury spot rates. The price of this Treasury bond is $96.6133.

Suppose instead that the 25-year bond is an option-free corporate bond rather than a Treasury bond. The corporate bond would trade at a lower price than the Treasury bond. The appropriate spot rate at which each cash flow will be discounted is the Treasury spot rate plus a premium to reflect the credit risk associated with investing in a corporate bond. For example, if an appropriate premium is 100 basis points, discounting the cash flows in Exhibit 7-4 by the assumed Treasury spot rate plus 100 basis points would give a price of $88.5473. While by that description we assume that the premium is the same for each period, a spot rate default spread curve can be developed and used to determine the spot rate at which to discount each cash flow.[4]

DRAWBACK OF TRADITIONAL YIELD SPREAD ANALYSIS

Traditional analysis of the yield premium for a non-Treasury bond involves calculating the difference between the yield to maturity (or yield to call) of the bond in question and the yield to maturity of a comparable-maturity coupon Treasury. The latter is obtained from the Treasury yield curve. For example, consider the following two 8.8% coupon, 25-year bonds:

Issue	Price ($)	Yield to Maturity (%)
Treasury	$96.6133	9.15%
Corporate	87.0798	10.24

The yield spread for these two bonds as traditionally computed is 109 basis points (10.24% minus 9.15%). The drawbacks of this convention, however, are (1) for both bonds, the yield fails to take into consideration the yield curve or spot rate curve; and (2) in the case of callable and/or putable bonds, expected interest rate volatility may alter the cash flow of a bond. In this chapter, we focus only on the first problem: failure to consider the spot rate curve, which can be met by calculating a measure called *zero-volatility spread* or *static spread*. We will deal with the second problem in Chapter 17.

Zero-Volatility Spread

In traditional yield spread analysis, the investor compares the yield to maturity of a particular bond with the yield to maturity of a similar maturity on-the-run Treasury security. This means that the yield to maturity of both a 25-year zero-coupon corporate bond and a 25-year, 8.8% coupon corporate bond would be compared to the on-the-run 25-year Treasury security. Such

---

4   See Robert Litterman and Thomas Iben, "Corporate Bond Valuation and the Term Structure of Credit Spreads,"
    Journal of Portfolio Management (Spring 1991), pp. 52–64.

E X H I B I T   7–4

Calculation of Price of a 25-Year, 8.8% Coupon Bond Using Treasury Spot Rates

Period	Cash Flow ($)	Treasury Spot Rate (%)	Present Value ($)
1	$4.4	7.00000%	$4.2512
2	4.4	7.04999	4.1055
3	4.4	7.09998	3.9628
4	4.4	7.12498	3.8251
5	4.4	7.13998	3.6922
6	4.4	7.16665	3.5622
7	4.4	7.19997	3.4351
8	4.4	7.26240	3.3077
9	4.4	7.33315	3.1820
10	4.4	7.38977	3.0611
11	4.4	7.44517	2.9434
12	4.4	7.49135	2.8302
13	4.4	7.53810	2.7200
14	4.4	7.57819	2.6141
15	4.4	7.61959	2.5112
16	4.4	7.66205	2.4111
17	4.4	7.70538	2.3139
18	4.4	7.74391	2.2207
19	4.4	7.78888	2.1291
20	4.4	7.83434	2.0404
21	4.4	8.22300	1.8879
22	4.4	8.33333	1.7923
23	4.4	8.40000	1.7080
24	4.4	8.50000	1.6204
25	4.4	8.54230	1.5465
26	4.4	8.72345	1.4500
27	4.4	8.90000	1.3581
28	4.4	9.00000	1.2829
29	4.4	9.01450	1.2252
30	4.4	9.23000	1.1367
31	4.4	9.39000	1.0611
32	4.4	9.44840	1.0045
33	4.4	9.50000	0.9514
34	4.4	9.50000	0.9083
35	4.4	9.50000	0.8671
36	4.4	9.50000	0.8278

Continued

E X H I B I T 7–4

Concluded

Period	Cash Flow ($)	Treasury Spot Rate (%)	Present Value ($)
37	4.4	9.55000	0.7833
38	4.4	9.56000	0.7462
39	4.4	9.58000	0.7095
40	4.4	9.58000	0.6671
41	4.4	9.60000	0.6436
42	4.4	9.70000	0.6020
43	4.4	9.80000	0.5625
44	4.4	9.90000	0.5251
45	4.4	10.00000	0.4897
46	4.4	10.10000	0.4563
47	4.4	10.30000	0.4154
48	4.4	10.50000	0.3774
49	4.4	10.60000	0.3503
50	104.4	10.80000	7.5278

Theoretical price = $96.6133

a comparison makes little sense, since the cash flow characteristics of the two corporate bonds will not be the same as that of the benchmark Treasury.

The proper way to compare non-Treasury bonds of the same maturity but with different coupon rates is to compare them to a portfolio of Treasury securities that have the same cash flows. For example, consider the 8.8%, 25-year corporate bond selling for $87.0798. The cash flow per $100 par value for this corporate bond, assuming that interest rates do not change (that is, assuming interest rates are static) is 49 6-month payments of $4.40 and a payment in 25 years (at the end of 50 6-month periods) of $104.40. A portfolio that will replicate this cash flow would include 50 zero-coupon Treasury securities with maturities coinciding with the amounts and timing of the cash flows of the corporate bond.

The corporate bond's value is equal to the present value of all of its cash flows. Assuming the cash flows are riskless, the value will equal the present value of the replicating portfolio of Treasury securities. In turn, these cash flows are valued at the Treasury spot rates. The price of the risk-free 8.8%, 25-year bond assuming the Treasury spot rate curve shown in Exhibit 7-4, is $96.6133. The corporate bond's price is $87.0798, less than that package of zero-coupon Treasury securities, because investors in fact require a yield premium for the risk associated with holding a corporate bond rather than a riskless package of Treasury securities.

The *zero-volatility spread* or *static spread* is a measure of the spread that the investor would realize over the entire Treasury spot rate curve if the bond is held to maturity. It is not a spread off one point on the Treasury yield curve, as is the traditional yield spread. The zero-volatility spread, which is found by trial-and-error, is the spread that makes the present value of the cash flows from the corporate bond, when discounted at the Treasury spot rate plus the spread, equal to the corporate bond's price.

To illustrate the trial-and-error procedure, let's use the corporate bond in the previous illustration. Select some spread, say, 100 basis points, and add that to each Treasury spot rate shown in the third column in Exhibit 7-4. For example, the 14-year (period 28) spot rate becomes 10.0% (9% plus 1%). The spot rate plus 100 basis points is then used to calculate the present value of $88.5473. Because the present value is not equal to the corporate bond's price, which we know to be $87.0798, the zero-volatility spread is not 100 basis points. If a spread of 110 basis points is tried, that results in a present value of $87.8031; again, because this is not equal to the corporate bond's price, 110 basis points is not the static spread. The last column of Exhibit 7-5 shows the present value when a 120-basis-point spread is tried. Here the present value is equal to the corporate bond price, $87.0798. Therefore 120 basis points is the static spread, in comparison with the traditional yield spread of 109 basis points.

Exhibit 7-6 shows the static spread and the traditional yield spread for bonds with various maturities and prices, assuming the Treasury spot rates shown in Exhibit 7-4. Notice that the shorter the maturity of the bond, the less the zero-volatility spread differs from the traditional yield spread. The magnitude of the difference between the traditional yield spread and the zero-volatility spread also depends on the shape of the yield curve. The steeper the yield curve, the more the difference for a given coupon and maturity.

The difference between the traditional yield spread and the zero-volatility spread will be considerably greater for sinking fund bonds and mortgage-backed securities in a steep yield curve environment.

FORWARD RATES

We have seen how the theoretical spot rate curve can be constructed from the yield curve. But there may be more information contained in the yield curve. Specifically, can we use the yield curve to infer the market's expectations of future interest rates? Let's explore this possibility.

Suppose an investor with a 1-year investment horizon is considering two alternatives:

Alternative 1. Buy a 1-year Treasury bill.
Alternative 2. Buy a 6-month Treasury bill, and when it matures in 6 months buy
                  another 6-month Treasury bill.

The investor will be indifferent between the two alternatives if they produce the same yield or the same number of dollars per dollar invested over the 1-year investment horizon. The investor knows the spot rate on the 6-month Treasury bill and the 1-year Treasury bill, but not what yield will be available on a 6-month Treasury bill purchased 6 months from now. The yield on a 6-month Treasury bill 6 months from now is called the *forward rate*. Given the spot rate for the 6-month Treasury bill and the 1-year Treasury bill rate, it is possible to determine the forward rate on a 6-month Treasury bill that will make investors indifferent to the two alternatives.

By investing in the 1-year Treasury bill, the investor will receive the maturity value at the end of 1 year. Suppose that the maturity value of the 1-year Treasury bill is $100. The price (cost) of the 1-year Treasury bill would be as follows:

EXHIBIT 7-5

Calculation of the Zero-Volatility Spread for a 25-Year, 8.8% Coupon Corporate Bond

Period	Cash Flow ($)	Treasury Spot Rate (%)	Present Value if Spread Used Is		
			100 BP	110 BP	120 BP
1	$4.4	7.00000%	$4.2308	$4.2287	$4.2267
2	4.4	7.04999	4.0661	4.0622	4.0583
3	4.4	7.09998	3.9059	3.9003	3.8947
4	4.4	7.12498	3.7521	3.7449	3.7377
5	4.4	7.13998	3.6043	3.5957	3.5871
6	4.4	7.16665	3.4607	3.4508	3.4408
7	4.4	7.19997	3.3212	3.3101	3.2990
8	4.4	7.26240	3.1828	3.1706	3.1584
9	4.4	7.33315	3.0472	3.0340	3.0210
10	4.4	7.38977	2.9174	2.9034	2.8895
11	4.4	7.44517	2.7917	2.7770	2.7624
12	4.4	7.49135	2.6715	2.6562	2.6409
13	4.4	7.53810	2.5552	2.5394	2.5236
14	4.4	7.57819	2.4440	2.4277	2.4115
15	4.4	7.61959	2.3366	2.3198	2.3032
16	4.4	7.66205	2.2327	2.2157	2.1988
17	4.4	7.70538	2.1325	2.1152	2.0981
18	4.4	7.74391	2.0368	2.0193	2.0020
19	4.4	7.78888	1.9435	1.9259	1.9085
20	4.4	7.83434	1.8536	1.8359	1.8184
21	4.4	8.22300	1.7072	1.6902	1.6733
22	4.4	8.33333	1.6131	1.5963	1.5796
23	4.4	8.40000	1.5300	1.5132	1.4967
24	4.4	8.50000	1.4446	1.4282	1.4119
25	4.4	8.54230	1.3722	1.3559	1.3398
26	4.4	8.72345	1.2806	1.2648	1.2492
27	4.4	8.90000	1.1938	1.1785	1.1635
28	4.4	9.00000	1.1224	1.1075	1.0929
29	4.4	9.01450	1.0668	1.0522	1.0378
30	4.4	9.23000	0.9852	0.9712	0.9575
31	4.4	9.39000	0.9154	0.9020	0.8888
32	4.4	9.44840	0.8625	0.8495	0.8367
33	4.4	9.50000	0.8131	0.8004	0.7880
34	4.4	9.50000	0.7725	0.7601	0.7480
35	4.4	9.50000	0.7340	0.7219	0.7100
36	4.4	9.50000	0.6974	0.6855	0.6739

Continued

E X H I B I T 7–5

Concluded

Period	Cash Flow ($)	Treasury Spot Rate (%)	Present Value if Spread Used Is		
			100 BP	110 BP	120 BP
37	4.4	9.55000	0.6568	0.6453	0.6341
38	4.4	9.56000	0.6227	0.6116	0.6007
39	4.4	9.58000	0.5893	0.5785	0.5679
40	4.4	9.58000	0.5597	0.5492	0.5389
41	4.4	9.60000	0.5295	0.5193	0.5093
42	4.4	9.70000	0.4929	0.4832	0.4737
43	4.4	9.80000	0.4585	0.4492	0.4401
44	4.4	9.90000	0.4260	0.4172	0.4086
45	4.4	10.00000	0.3955	0.3871	0.3789
46	4.4	10.10000	0.3668	0.3588	0.3511
47	4.4	10.30000	0.3323	0.3250	0.3179
48	4.4	10.50000	0.3006	0.2939	0.2873
49	4.4	10.60000	0.2778	0.2714	0.2652
50	104.4	10.80000	5.9416	5.8030	5.6677
		Total present value =	$88.5473	$87.8031	$87.0798

$$\frac{100}{(1+z_2)^2},$$

where z_2 is one-half the bond equivalent yield of the theoretical 1-year spot rate.

Suppose that the investor purchases a 6-month Treasury bill for P dollars. At the end of 6 months, the value of this investment would be

$$P(1+z_1),$$

where z_1 is one-half the bond equivalent yield of the theoretical 6-month spot rate.

Let f be one-half the forward rate on a 6-month Treasury bill available 6 months from now. Then the future dollars available at the end of 1 year from the P dollars invested would be given by

$$P(1+z_1)(1+f).$$

Suppose that today we want to know how many P dollars the investor must invest in order to get $100 in 1 year. This can be found as follows:

$$P(1+z_1)(1+f) = 100.$$

Solving for P, we get

$$P = \frac{100}{(1+z_1)(1+f)}.$$

E X H I B I T   7–6

Comparison of Traditional Yield Spread and Zero-Volatility Spread for Various Bonds*

Bond	Price ($)	Yield to Maturity (%)	Spread (in basis points) Traditional	Zero volatility	Difference
		25-year, 8.8% coupon bond			
Treasury	$ 96.6133	9.15%	—	—	—
A	88.5473	10.06	91	100	9
B	87.8031	10.15	100	110	10
C	87.0798	10.24	109	120	11
		15-year, 8.8% coupon bond			
Treasury	$101.9603	8.57%	—	—	—
D	94.1928	9.54	97	100	3
E	93.4639	9.63	106	110	4
F	92.7433	9.73	116	120	4
		10-year, 8.8% coupon bond			
Treasury	$107.4906	7.71%	—	—	—
G	100.6137	8.71	100	100	0
H	99.9585	8.81	110	110	0
I	99.3088	8.91	120	120	0
		5-year, 8.8% coupon bond			
Treasury	$105.9555	7.36%	—	—	—
J	101.7919	8.35	99	100	1
K	101.3867	8.45	109	110	1
L	100.9836	8.55%	119	120	1

*Assumes Treasury spot rate curve given in Exhibit 7–4.

The investor will be indifferent between the two alternatives if the same dollar investment is made and $100 is received from both investments at the end of 1 year. That is, the investor will be indifferent if

$$\frac{100}{(1 + z_2)^2} = \frac{100}{(1 + z_1)(1 + f)} \ .$$

Solving for f, we get

$$f = \frac{(1 + z_2)^2}{(1 + z_1)} - 1.$$

Doubling f gives the bond equivalent yield for the 6-month forward rate.

To illustrate application of this equation, we will use the theoretical spot rates shown in Exhibit 7-3. Because we use the theoretical spot rates to compute the forward rate, the resulting forward rate is called the *implied forward rate*. We know that

6-month bill rate = .080; therefore z_1 = .0400;
1-year bill rate = .083; therefore z_2 = .0415

Substituting into the equation, we have

$$f = \frac{(1.0415)^2}{1.0400} - 1$$

$$= .043.$$

The forward rate on a 6-month security, quoted on a bond equivalent basis, is 8.60% (.043 × 2).

We can confirm these results. The price of a 1-year Treasury bill with a $100 maturity value is

$$\frac{100}{(1.0415)^2} = 92.19.$$

If 92.19 is invested for 6 months at the 6-month spot rate of 8%, the amount at the end of 6 months would be

$$92.19(1.0400) = 95.8776.$$

If 95.8776 is reinvested for another 6 months in a 6-month Treasury offering 4.3% for 6 months (8.6% annually), the amount at the end of 1 year is

$$95.8876(1.043) = 100.$$

Each alternative has the same $100 payoff if the 6-month Treasury bill yield 6 months from now is 4.3% (8.6% on a bond equivalent basis). This means that if investors are guaranteed a 4.3% yield (8.6% bond equivalent basis) on a 6-month Treasury bill 6 months from now, they will be indifferent between the two alternatives.

While we have calculated only the implied 6-month forward rate 6 months from now, we can follow the same methodology to determine the implied forward rate 6 months from now for an investment for a period longer than 6 months. That is, we can use the yield curve or, more specifically, the spot rate curve generated from the yield curve to construct an implied forward rate 6 months from now for 1-year investments, 1.5-year investments, 2-year investments, 2.5-year investments, and so on.

We can even take this one step farther. It is not necessary to limit ourselves to implied forward rates 6 months from now. The yield curve can be used to calculate the implied forward rate for any time into the future for any investment horizon. As examples, the following can be calculated:

- The 2-year implied forward rate 5 years from now;
- The 6-year implied forward rate 10 years from now;
- The 7-year implied forward rate 3 years from now.

How is this done? To demonstrate how, we must introduce some notation. We will continue to let f represent the forward rate. But now we must identify two aspects of the forward rate. First, we want to denote when the forward rate begins. Second, we want to denote the length of time of the forward rate. To identify these two aspects of the forward rate, we use the following notation:

$_nf_t$ = The forward rate n periods from now for t periods.

Remember that for our bond examples each period is equal to 6 months. Consider first the earlier example of the 6-month forward rate 6 months from now. In this case, because we are looking at a forward rate 6 months from now, this is equal to one period from now. Thus n is 1. The length of the forward rate is 6 months, so t is equal to 1. Consequently, the 6-month forward rate 6 months from now is denoted by $_1f_1$. The 6-month forward rates are then expressed as follows:

$_2f_1$ = 6-month forward rate 1 year (two periods) from now;
$_3f_1$ = 6-month forward rate 1.5 years (three periods) from now;
$_4f_1$ = 6-month forward rate 2 years (four periods) from now, etc.

For forward rates 4 years (eight periods) from now, we would have the following:

$_8f_1$ = 6-month forward rate 4 years (eight periods) from now;
$_8f_2$ = 1-year (two period) forward rate 4 years (eight periods) from now;
$_8f_3$ = 1.5-year forward rate 4 years (eight periods) from now, etc.

Now let's see how the spot rates can be used to calculate the implied forward rate. We assume in the illustration that there are zero-coupon Treasury securities available.[5] Suppose that an investor with a 5-year investment horizon is considering two alternatives:

Alternative 1.   Buy a 5-year (ten period) zero-coupon Treasury security
Alternative 2.   Buy a 3-year (6 period) zero-coupon Treasury security, and when it matures in 3 years buy a 2-year Treasury security.

The investor will be indifferent between the two alternatives if they produce the same yield or the same number of dollars per dollar invested over the 5-year investment horizon. The spot rates on the 5-year Treasury security and the 3-year Treasury security are known, but the yield available on a 2-year Treasury security purchased 3 years from now is not known. That is, the investor does not know the 2-year forward rate 3 years from now. In terms of our notation that unknown is $_6f_4$.

The price of the 5-year zero-coupon Treasury security with a maturity value of $100 would be

$$\frac{100}{(1 + z_{10})^{10}},$$

where z_{10} is one-half the bond equivalent yield of the theoretical 5-year spot rate.

Suppose that the investor purchases a 3-year zero-coupon Treasury security for P dollars. At the end of 3 years, the value of this investment would be

---

5   The existence of zero-coupon Treasury securities is not necessary for determination of the implied forward rates. The assumption just simplifies the presentation.

$$P(1 + z_6)^6,$$

where z_6 is one-half the bond equivalent yield of the theoretical 3-year spot rate. Let $_6f_4$ be the semiannual 2-year forward rate 3 years from now. Then the future dollars available at the end of 5 years from the P dollars invested are

$$P(1 + z_6)^6 (1 + _6f_4)^4 .$$

Suppose that today we want to know how many P dollars the investor must invest in order to get \$100, 1 year from now. This can be found as follows:

$$P(1 + z_6)^6 (1 + _6f_4)^4 = 100.$$

Solving for P,

$$P = \frac{100}{(1 + z_6)^6 (1 + _6f_4)^4} .$$

Investors will be indifferent between the two alternatives if they make the same dollar investment and receive \$100 at the end of 5 years from both alternatives. That is, the investor will be indifferent if

$$\frac{100}{(1 + z_{10})^{10}} = \frac{100}{(1 + z_6)^6 (1 + _6f_4)^4} .$$

Solving for $_6f_4$, we get

$$_6f_4 = \left[\frac{(1 + z_{10})^{10}}{(1 + z_6)^6} \right]^{1/4} - 1.$$

Doubling $_6f_4$ gives the bond equivalent yield for the 2-year forward rate 3 years from now.

To illustrate this, we use the theoretical spot rates shown in Exhibit 7.3. We know that

3-year spot rate = .09787; therefore z_6 = .048935;
5-year spot rate = .11021; therefore z_{10} = .055105.

Substituting into the equation, we have

$$_6f_4 = \left[\frac{(1.055105)^{10}}{(1.048935)^6} \right]^{1/4} - 1$$

$$= \left[\frac{(1.709845)^{10}}{(1.331961)^6} \right]^{1/4} - 1$$

$$= .0644.$$

The implied forward rate on a 2-year Treasury security 3 years from now, quoted on a bond equivalent basis, is calculated as 12.88% (.0644 × 2). Let's confirm our results. The price of a 5-year zero-coupon Treasury security with a \$100 maturity value is

$$\frac{100}{(1.055105)^{10}} = 58.48.$$

If \$58.48 is invested for 3 years at the 3-year spot rate of 9.787%, the amount at the end of 6 periods will be

$$\$58.48 \ (1.048935)^6 = \$77.8931.$$

If \$77.8931 is reinvested for another 2 years (four periods) at 6.44% (12.88% annually), the amount at the end of the fifth year will be

$$\$77.8931 \ (1.0644)^4 = \$100.$$

Each alternative does have the same \$100 payoff if the 2-year Treasury rate 3 years from now is 6.44% (12.88% on a bond equivalent basis).

In general, the formula for the implied forward rate is:

$$_n f_t = \left[\frac{(1 + z_{n+t})^{n+t}}{(1 + z_n)^n} \right]^{1/t} - 1,$$

where z_n is a semiannual spot rate. Doubling $_n f_t$ gives the implied forward rate on a bond equivalent basis.

To illustrate application of the general equation, consider the earlier example where we sought the 6-month forward rate 6 months from now. That is, we sought $_1 f_1$. Because n is equal to 1 and t is equal to 1,

$$_1 f_1 = \left[\frac{(1 + z_{1+1})^{1+1}}{(1 + z_1)^1} \right]^{1/1} - 1$$

or

$$= \frac{(1 + z_2)^2}{(1 + z_1)^1} - 1.$$

This agrees with our earlier equation for a 1-period spot rate 1 period from now.

Relationship Between Long Spot Rates and Short-Term Implied Forward Rates

Suppose our investor purchases a 5-year zero-coupon Treasury security for \$58.48 with a maturity value of \$100. The investor instead could buy a 6-month Treasury bill and reinvest the proceeds every 6 months for 5 years. The number of dollars that will be realized will depend on the 6-month forward rates. If the investor could actually reinvest the proceeds maturing every 6 months at the implied 6-month forward rates, let's see how many dollars would accumulate at the end of 5 years. The implied 6-month forward rates were calculated for the yield curve given in Exhibit 7-2. The semiannual implied forward rates from Exhibit 7-3 are

$_1 f_1 = .043000;$
$_2 f_1 = .050980;$
$_3 f_1 = .051005;$

$_4f_1 = .051770;$
$_5f_1 = .056945;$
$_6f_1 = .060965;$
$_7f_1 = .069310;$
$_8f_1 = .064625;$
$_9f_1 = .062830.$

By investing the $58.48 at the 6-month spot rate of 4% (8% on a bond equivalent basis) and reinvesting at the forward rates above, the number of dollars accumulated at the end of 5 years will be

$$54.48(1.04)(1.043)(1.05098)(1.051005)(1.05177)(1.056945)$$
$$\times (1.060965)(1.06931)(1.064625)(1.06283) = \$100.$$

Therefore, we see that if the implied forward rates are realized, the $54.48 investment will produce the same number of dollars as an investment in a 5-year zero-coupon Treasury security at the 5-year spot rate. From this illustration, we can see that the 5-year spot rate is related to the current 6-month spot rate and the implied 6-month forward rates.

In general the relationship among a t-period spot rate, the current 6-month spot rate, and the implied 6-month forward rates is as follows:

$$z_t = [(1 + z_1)(1 + {}_1f_1)(1 + {}_2f_1)(1 + {}_3f_1) \cdots (1 + {}_tf_1)]^{\frac{1}{t}} - 1.$$

For example, the 5-year spot rate $(2 \times z_{10})$ can be computed from the current 6-month rate (z_1) of 4% and the nine 6-month implied forward rates. This is demonstrated below:

$$z_{10} = [(1.04)(1.043)(1.05098)(1.051005)(1.05177)(1.056945)$$
$$\times (1.060965)(1.06931)(1.064625)(1.06283)]^{1/10} - 1$$
$$= 0.055105.$$

The 5-year spot rate is then 11.021%, which agrees with the value in Exhibit 7-3.

Valuing Cash Flows and Bonds Using Implied Forward Rates

Since spot rates and implied forward rates are related, then it makes no difference whether spot rates or implied forward rates are used to determine the present value of a cash flow. In general, the present value of a cash flow c in period t using implied forward rates is

$$\frac{c}{(1 + z_1)(1 + {}_1f_1)(1 + {}_2f_1) \cdots (1 + {}_tf_1)}.$$

The general formula for using implied forward rates to value an n-period maturity bond whose semiannual cash flow is denoted by c and maturity value is denoted by M is

$$Price = \frac{c}{(1 + z_t)} + \frac{c}{(1 + z_1)(1 + f_1)} + \frac{c}{(1 + z_1)(1 + {}_1f_1)(1 + {}_2f_1)}$$
$$+ \cdots + \frac{c + M}{(1 + z_1)(1 + {}_1f_1)(1 + {}_2f_1) \cdots (1 + {}_nf_1)}.$$

Oftentimes, vendors of analytical systems will state how they value cash flows. Some state that spot rates are used while others state that (implied) forward rates are used. The results from the discounting process will be the same.

Forward Rate as a Hedgeable Rate

A natural question about implied forward rates is how well they do at predicting future interest rates. Studies have demonstrated that forward rates do not do a good job in predicting future interest rates.[6] Then, why the big deal about understanding implied forward rates? As we demonstrated in our illustration of how to select between two alternative investments, the reason is that the implied forward rates indicate how an investor's expectations must differ from the rate built into bond prices in order to make the correct decision.

In our illustration, the 6-month forward rate may not be realized. That is irrelevant. The fact is that the 6-month forward rate indicated to the investor that if his expectation about the 6-month rate 6 months from now is less than 4.3% (the implied forward rate in our illustration), he would be better off with Alternative 1.

For this reason, some market participants prefer not to talk about implied forward rates as being market consensus rates. Instead, they refer to implied forward rates as being *hedgeable rates*. For example, by buying the 1-year security, the investor is able to hedge the 6-month rate 6 months from now.

SUMMARY

A bond should be viewed as a package of cash flows, with each cash flow representing nothing more than a zero-coupon instrument. The price of a bond is then the total value of all of the zero-coupon instruments. To determine the value of each cash flow/zero-coupon instrument, the starting point is the theoretical rate on Treasury zero-coupon instruments.

The yield curve shows the relationship between the yield on Treasury securities and maturity. From the yield curve, the theoretical Treasury spot rate curve can be derived through arbitrage arguments. The theoretical spot rates (or equivalently zero-coupon rates) are then used to calculate the value of a Treasury security. A non-Treasury security is valued by adding to the Treasury spot rate curve a premium to reflect credit and liquidity risks.

Traditional yield spread analysis fails to take into account (1) the yield curve or spot rate curve, and (2) any options embedded in the bond. We consider the first problem in this chapter and the second problem later on in this book. The zero-volatility spread measures the spread over the Treasury spot rate curve assuming that interest rates will not change in the future.

Implied forward rates can be obtained from spot rates. Spot rates are therefore related to implied forward rates and it makes not difference if spot rates or implied forward rates are used to value a cash flow or a bond. While implied forward rates are poor predictors of future interest rates they are, however, used by investors in making investment decisions since they represent rates that can be locked in today.

---

6 Eugene F. Fama, "Forward Rates as Predictors of Future Spot Rates," *Journal of Financial Economics,* Vol. 3, No. 4, 1976, pp. 361–377.

III

⑥ RETURN ANALYSIS

8

⑥ POTENTIAL SOURCES OF DOLLAR RETURN

To make an intelligent decision about the attractiveness of a bond, an investor must be able to measure the potential yield from owning it. This requires an understanding of the potential sources of dollar return from investing in a bond and then converting the total dollar return from all sources into a yield measure that can be used to compare different bonds.

The purpose of this chapter is threefold: (1) to explain the potential sources of dollar return, (2) to examine the characteristics of a bond that affect its dollar return, and (3) to analyze whether the conventional measures of yield discussed in Chapter 6 appropriately account for the potential sources of dollar return. In the next chapter, we present a measure of yield that is more useful to an investor in assessing the potential performance of bonds.

POTENTIAL SOURCES OF DOLLAR RETURN

The dollar return a bond investor expects to receive takes the form of the periodic interest payments made by the issuer (that is, the coupon interest payments) and any capital appreciation realized when the bond is sold. For example, suppose that an investor buys a 20-year, 7% coupon bond with a par value of $1,000 for $816. Holding this bond until it matures, the investor will receive 40 coupon interest payments of $35, one every 6 months; then at the end of 20 years he will receive $1,000 for the bond he purchased for $816. This will result in a capital gain of $184. In other words, an investor who buys this bond and holds it to maturity expects a return in the form of 40 semiannual coupon interest payments of $35 and a capital gain of $184.

There is, however, another potential source for a bond's dollar return that may not be recognized by many investors. That source is the interest income that can be realized by reinvesting the coupon interest payments. For example, an investor receiving the first $35 coupon interest payment from the bond issuer must do something with that money. If the money is invested in another instrument for the next 19.5 years, this reinvestment will add to the return from holding the bond. This is also true for the second coupon interest payment of $35, which can be invested for 19 years; and so on for subsequent coupon interest payments. This potential source of return is referred to as the *interest-on-interest* component of a bond's dollar return. In fact, for certain bonds, the interest-on-interest component can represent more than 80% of a bond's potential dollar return.

CONVENTIONAL MEASURES AND THE THREE POTENTIAL SOURCES OF A BOND'S DOLLAR RETURN

To summarize, an investor who purchases a bond can expect to receive a dollar return from one or more of the following sources:

1. The periodic interest payments made by the issuer (that is, the coupon interest payments);

2. Any capital gain (or capital loss, which reduces the dollar return) when the bond matures or is sold;

3. Income from reinvestment of the periodic interest payments (the interest-on-interest component).

Any measure of a bond's potential yield should consider all three of these potential sources of return. Do the three conventional bond measures (current yield, yield to maturity, and yield to call) take into account these three potential sources of return?

Current yield considers only the coupon interest payments. No consideration is given to any capital gain (or loss) or interest on interest.

Yield to maturity takes into account coupon interest and any capital gain (or loss). It also considers the interest-on-interest component, although implicit in this computation is an assumption that the coupon payments can be reinvested at the computed yield to maturity. The yield to maturity, therefore, is a *promised* yield. That is, the promised yield to maturity will be realized if (1) the bond is held to maturity and (2) the coupon interest payments are reinvested at the yield to maturity. If either (1) or (2) does not occur, the actual yield realized by an investor will be greater than or less than the yield to maturity.

For example, for our 20-year, 7% coupon bond selling at $816, the yield to maturity is 9%. Thus, if an investor buys this bond, holds it to maturity and reinvests each semiannual coupon payment at 9% until the maturity date, the promised yield to maturity of 9% at the time of the purchase will be realized. We'll demonstrate this in the next section.

Although the yield to maturity does consider the interest-on-interest component of a bond's potential dollar return, the assumption that the coupon interest payments can be reinvested at the yield to maturity is not very realistic. For example, in 1981 an investor could have purchased a long-term investment grade coupon bond offering a yield to maturity of 16%. To realize that promised yield, each coupon payment had to be reinvested at a rate of interest equal to 16%. In recent years, however, yields on investment grade bonds have been nowhere near this rate. Thus, it is unlikely that a 16% yield would be realized by the investor holding the bond to maturity.

The yield to call also takes into account all three potential sources of return. In this case, the assumption is that the coupon payments can be reinvested at the yield to call. This yield measure therefore suffers from the same drawback concerning the reinvestment rate of the coupon interest payments.

COMPUTATION OF THE INTEREST-ON-INTEREST COMPONENT OF A BOND'S DOLLAR RETURN

The interest-on-interest component can represent a substantial portion of a bond's potential return. In this section we explain how to determine the contribution of the interest-on-interest component.

The portion of the potential total dollar return from coupon interest and interest on interest can be computed by using the formula for the future value of an annuity (see Exhibit 2-2 of Chapter 2):

$$FV = A \left[\frac{(1 + i)^n - 1}{i} \right],$$

where

A = Amount of the annuity ($);
i = Annual interest rate divided by m (in decimal form);
m = Number of payments per year;
n = Number of periods.

For purposes of computing the coupon interest and interest on interest for a bond paying interest semiannually,

A = Semiannual coupon interest ($);
i = Semiannual reinvestment rate (in decimal form);
m = 2;
n = Double the number of years to maturity.

Letting

c = *Semiannual* coupon interest ($)

and

r = *Semiannual* reinvestment rate (in decimal form),

we can rewrite the formula for the future value of an annuity for computing the coupon interest plus interest on interest, as

$$\begin{array}{c} \text{Coupon interest} \\ \text{plus} \\ \text{interest on interest} \end{array} = c \left[\frac{(1 + r)^n - 1}{r} \right].$$

The total coupon interest is found by multiplying the semiannual coupon interest by the number of periods; that is,

$$\text{Total coupon interest} = n \times c.$$

The interest-on-interest component is then the difference between the coupon interest plus interest on interest and the total coupon interest. Mathematically, this can be expressed as

$$\text{Interest on interest} = c \left[\frac{(1 + r)^n - 1}{r} \right] - n \times c.$$

The reinvestment rate assumed for the yield to maturity is the yield to maturity.

The three illustrations that follow demonstrate the application of these formulas, as well as the importance of the interest-on-interest component as a source of potential return from a bond.

Illustration 8-1   Suppose that an investor is considering purchasing a 7-year issue selling at par ($1,000) and having a coupon rate of 9%. Since this bond is selling at par, the yield to maturity is 9%.

Remember that a yield to maturity of 9% as conventionally computed means a 4.5% semiannual yield.[1] If an investor is promised a yield of 4.5% for 14 6-month periods (7 years) on a $1,000 investment, the amount at the end of 14 6-month periods would be[2]

$$\$1,000\,(1.045)^{14} = \$1,852.$$

Since the investment is $1,000, the total dollar return that the investor expects is $852.

Let's look at the total dollar return from holding this bond to maturity. The total dollar return comes from two sources:

1. Coupon interest of $45 every 6 months for 7 years;

2. Interest earned from reinvesting the semiannual coupon interest payments at 4.5%.

Since the bond is selling at par, no capital gain will be realized by holding the bond to maturity. For this bond,

$c = \$45;$
$m = 2;$
$r = .045\ (= .09/2);$
$n = 14\ (= 7 \times 2).$

$$\begin{array}{l}\text{Coupon interest}\\ \quad\text{plus}\\ \text{interest on interest}\end{array} = \$45\left[\frac{(1.045)^{14} - 1}{.045}\right]$$

$$= \$45\left[\frac{1.8519 - 1}{.045}\right]$$

$$= \$45(18.9321)$$

$$= \$852.$$

Notice that the total dollar return for this bond is the same as the return that we computed for an investment of $1,000 for 14 6-month periods at 4.5%.

The total coupon interest is $14 \times \$45 = \$630$.

The interest-on-interest component is then $222, as shown below:

$$\text{Interest on interest} = \$45\left[\frac{(1.045)^{14} - 1}{.045}\right] - 14\ (\$45)$$

---

1   See Chapter 6.
2   This is just an application of the future value of $1 formula, see Chapter 2.

$$= \$852 - \$630$$
$$= \$222.$$

Interest on interest as a percentage of total dollar return is

$$\frac{\$222}{\$852} = 26\%.$$

For this 7-year, 9% coupon bond selling at par to offer a yield to maturity of 9%, 26% of this bond's total dollar return must come from reinvesting the coupon payments at a simple annual interest rate of 9%.

Illustration 8-2   Suppose that an investor is considering a 20-year, 7% coupon bond selling for $816. The yield to maturity for this bond is 9%.

First, let's consider how much the total dollar return should be for an investment of $816 for 40 6-month periods if the semiannual yield is 4.5%. The total future amount would be $4,746, because

$$\$816 \, (1.045)^{40} = \$4,746.$$

Since the investment is $816, the total dollar return should be $3,930.

Now let's look at the $816 investment in the bond. The total dollar return from holding this bond to maturity comes from all three sources:

1. Coupon interest of $35 every 6 months for 20 years;

2. Interest earned from reinvesting the semiannual coupon interest payments at 4.5%;

3. A capital gain of $184 (= $1,000 − $816).

For this bond,

$c = \$35;$
$m = 2;$
$r = .045 \ (= .09/2);$
$n = 40 \ (= 20 \times 2).$

$$\begin{array}{l} \text{Coupon interest} \\ \text{plus} \\ \text{interest on interest} \end{array} = \$35 \left[\frac{(1.045)^{40} - 1}{.045} \right]$$

$$= \$35 \left[\frac{5.8164 - 1}{.045} \right]$$

$$= \$35(107.031)$$

$$= \$3,746.$$

The total coupon interest is $40 \times \$35 = \$1,400$.

The interest-on-interest component is then $2,346, as shown by the following calculation

$$\text{Interest on interest} = \$35 \left[\frac{(1.045)^{40} - 1}{.045} \right] - 40 \, (\$35)$$

$$= \$3,746 - \$1,400$$
$$= \$2,346.$$

The total dollar return is then

Total coupon interest	$1,400
Interest on interest	2,346
Capital gain	184
Total	$3,930

Once again, the total dollar return is the same as the return that would be expected from investing $816 for 40 6-month periods at 4.5%.

The percentage breakdown of the total dollar return is

Total coupon interest	35%
Interest on interest	60%
Capital gain	5%

Hence, for this bond, the interest-on-interest component must represent 60% of total dollar return if the investor is to realize a 9% yield to maturity.

Illustration 8-3   The two previous illustrations have shown the computation of the interest-on-interest component for a bond selling at par (Illustration 8-1) and a bond selling at a discount (Illustration 8-2), both with a yield to maturity of 9%. Now let's consider a bond selling at a premium with a yield to maturity of 9%. Suppose an investor is considering a 12% coupon bond with 25 years to maturity selling for $1,296. The yield to maturity is 9%.

The total dollar return from holding this bond to maturity is composed of

1. Coupon interest of $60 every 6 months for 25 years;

2. Interest earned from reinvesting the semiannual coupon interest payments at 4.5%;

3. A capital loss of $296 (= $1,000 – $1,296).

For this premium bond,

$c = \$60;$
$m = 2;$
$r = .045 \ (= .09/2);$
$n = 50 \ (= 25 \times 2).$

$$\begin{array}{l} \text{Coupon interest} \\ \text{plus} \\ \text{interest on interest} \end{array} = \$60 \left[\frac{(1.045)^{50} - 1}{.045} \right]$$

$$= \$60 \left[\frac{9.0326 - 1}{.045} \right]$$

$$= \$60(178.503)$$

$$= \$10,710.$$

The total coupon interest is $50 \times \$60 = \$3,000$.

The interest-on-interest component is then $7,710, as shown below:

$$\text{Interest on interest} = \$60 \left[\frac{(1.045)^{50} - 1}{.045} \right] - 50 \, (\$60)$$

$$= \$10,710 - \$3,000$$

$$= \$7,710.$$

The total dollar return is then

Total coupon interest	$3,000
Interest on interest	7,710
Capital loss	(296)
Total	$10,414

The percentage breakdown of the total dollar return is

Total coupon interest	29%
Interest on interest	74%
Capital loss	-3%

For this long-term bond selling at a premium, the interest on interest represents 74% of the total dollar return necessary to produce a 9% yield to maturity.

To see that the total dollar return from investing in this bond agrees with an investment of $1,296 for 50 6-month periods at 4.5%, the future value is

$$\$1,296 \, (1.045)^{50} = \$11,706.$$

Subtracting from the future value the investment of $1,296 gives the total dollar return of $10,410. (The difference between $10,414 and $10,410 is due to rounding.)

BOND CHARACTERISTICS THAT AFFECT THE IMPORTANCE OF THE INTEREST-ON-INTEREST COMPONENT

There are two characteristics of a bond that determine the importance of the interest-on-interest component: (1) maturity and (2) coupon.

The Effect of Maturity

For a given yield to maturity and a given coupon rate, the longer the maturity of a bond is, the greater is the interest-on-interest component as a percentage of the total dollar return. The following three illustrations demonstrate this characteristic.

Illustration 8-4   Consider a 20-year, 9% coupon bond selling at par for a yield to maturity of 9%. Using the formulas presented in the previous section, the total dollar return would be $4,816, broken down as follows:

Total coupon interest	$1,800
Interest on interest	3,016
Total	$4,816

Comparing this bond with the 7-year, 9% coupon bond selling at 9% in Illustration 8-1, we find

	Total Dollar Return		% Dollar Return	
	7-year	20-year	7-year	20-year
Total coupon interest	$630	$1,800	74%	37%
Interest on interest	222	3,016	26	63
Total	$852	$4,816	100%	100%

The interest-on-interest component is 26% of the total dollar return on the 7-year bond but 63% of the total dollar return for the 20-year bond.

Illustration 8-5   Consider a 5-year, 7% coupon bond selling for $921, thereby offering a yield to maturity of 9%. The breakdown of the total dollar return is

Total coupon interest	$350
Interest on interest	80
Capital gain	79
Total	$509

A comparison of this bond with the 20-year, 7% coupon bond analyzed in Illustration 8-2 is given below:

	Total Dollar Return		% Dollar Return	
	5-year	20-year	5-year	20-year
Total coupon interest	$350	$1,400	69%	35%
Interest on interest	80	2,346	16	60
Capital gain	79	184	15	5
Total	$509	$3,930	100%	100%

Only 16% of the bond's total dollar return needed to produce a 9% yield to maturity comes from the reinvestment of coupon interest for the 5-year bond, compared to 60% for the 20-year bond.

Illustration 8-6   For a 7-year, 12% coupon bond selling at $1,153 with a yield to maturity of 9%, the total dollar return is as follows:

Total coupon interest	$840
Interest on interest	296
Capital loss	(153)
Total	$983

In Illustration 8-3, the total dollar return breakdown for a 25-year, 12% coupon bond priced to give a yield to maturity of 9% was computed. A comparison of the bond in this illustration with the one in Illustration 8-3 is given below:

	Total Dollar Return		% Dollar Return	
	7-year	25-year	7-year	25-year
Total coupon interest	$840	$ 3,000	85%	29%
Interest on interest	296	7,710	30	74
Capital loss	(153)	(296)	–5	–3
Total	$983	$10,414	100%	100%

For the longer-term bond, the interest-on-interest component is 74% of the potential total dollar return, compared with 30% for the 7-year bond.

The Effect of Coupon Rate

For a given maturity and a given yield to maturity, the higher the coupon rate is, the more dependent the bond's total dollar return necessary to produce some yield to maturity is on the reinvestment of coupon interest. This means that holding maturity and yield to maturity constant, premium bonds will be more dependent on the interest-on-interest component than bonds selling at par. Discount bonds will be less dependent on the interest-on-interest component than bonds selling at par. These statements are verified in the illustrations below.

Illustration 8-7   Let's compare the total dollar return breakdown of the 20-year, 9% coupon bond selling at par to offer a yield to maturity of 9% (Illustration 8-4) with a 20-year, 5% coupon bond selling at $632 to offer a yield to maturity of 9%. The breakdown of the total dollar return and the percentage return for each bond, which demonstrates that a lower coupon (discount) bond is less dependent on the interest-on-interest component than the higher coupon (par) bond, is summarized below:

	Total Dollar Return		% Dollar Return	
	5% Coupon *(discount)*	9% Coupon *(par)*	5% Coupon *(discount)*	9% Coupon *(par)*
Total coupon interest	$1,000	$1,800	33%	37%
Interest on interest	1,676	3,016	55	63
Capital gain	368	0	12	0
Total	$3,044	$4,816	100%	100%

Illustration 8-8   Comparison of a 7-year, 9% coupon bond selling at par to offer a yield to maturity of 9% with a 7-year, 14% coupon bond selling at $1,256 to offer a yield to maturity of 9%, summarized below, shows that a bond selling at par is less dependent on the reinvestment of coupon interest than a premium bond:

	Total Dollar Return		% Dollar Return	
	9% Coupon (par)	14% Coupon (premium)	9% Coupon (par)	4% Coupon (premium)
Total coupon interest	$630	$ 980	74%	92%
Interest on interest	222	345	26	32
Capital gain	0	(256)	0	–24
Total	$852	$1,069	100%	100%

For zero-coupon bonds, none of the bond's total dollar return is made up of interest on interest. The reason, of course, is that no coupon interest is paid.

TAX CONSIDERATIONS

Thus far, we have ignored the impact of federal income taxes on the total dollar return of a bond if it is held to maturity. There are taxes on interest income and any capital gain. There may or may not be a preferential tax treatment for the capital gain. Incorporating tax consequences into the total dollar return calculation is fairly straightforward.

Taxation of coupon income has three adverse effects. First it reduces the amount of the coupon income by 1 minus the tax rate. Mathematically,

$$\text{After-tax semiannual coupon} = c(1 - T_c),$$

where

T_c = Tax rate on coupon income;
c = Semiannual coupon interest ($).

The total coupon income over the life of the bond is also reduced and can be expressed as follows:

$$\text{After-tax total coupon income} = c(1 - T_c)\, n,$$

where

n = Number of periods to maturity.

Illustration 8-9   Consider a 30-year bond with a coupon rate of 4.2% and a par value of $1,000. Suppose that the tax rate on interest income is 35%. The pretax semiannual coupon is $21. The after-tax semiannual coupon income is

$$\$21(1 - 0.35) = \$13.65.$$

The total after-tax total coupon income is

$$\$21(1 - 0.35)60 = \$819.$$

The second adverse effect of taxation of the coupon income is that there are less dollars to reinvest each period. Consequently, the interest on interest is reduced. The third adverse effect is that the interest earned on the interest income is reduced since it is taxed.

The total after-tax income from coupon interest and interest on interest is found as follows:

$$\begin{matrix} \text{After–tax coupon} \\ \text{income plus} \\ \text{interest on interest} \end{matrix} = c \left[\frac{[(1 + r(1 - T_c)]^n - 1}{r} \right],$$

where

r = Semiannual reinvestment rate assumed;

c, n, and T_c are as defined earlier.

Illustration 8-10   Consider once again the 4.2%, 30-year bond in the previous illustration. If the reinvestment rate is assumed to be 6% and the tax rate is 35%, then the total income from coupon interest and interest on interest is

$$\$21 \left[\frac{[1 + 0.03(1 - 0.35)]^{60} - 1}{0.03} \right] = \$1,530.$$

The after-tax coupon interest on interest is found by subtracting from the after-tax interest plus interest on interest the after-tax coupon interest. Mathematically, this is expressed as follows:

After-tax interest on interest

$$= c \left[\frac{[(1 + r(1 - T_c)]^n - 1}{r} \right] - c(1 - T_c)n.$$

Illustration 8-11   Since the total after-tax coupon interest is $819, this means that the after-tax interest on interest is $711 ($1,530 – $819).

The effect of taxes on coupon income and interest on interest for a 4.2%, 30-year bond selling at par is shown below:

Source	Tax Not Considered	35% Tax Rate
Total coupon interest	$1,260	$ 819
Interest on interest	2,164	711
Total	$3,424	$1,530

Notice that while the total coupon interest is reduced proportionately by the tax rate, the interest on interest is reduced more than proportionately. That is, the total coupon income after reduction for a 35% tax rate is 65% of the total coupon payments ignoring taxes. This is not so for the interest on interest. Interest on interest after taxes declines by 67%.

The effect of taxes on any capital gain must be considered.[3] The capital gain is found by multiplying 1 minus the tax rate by the capital gain. The applicable tax rate depends on whether the capital gain qualifies for preferential tax treatment. In general, the after-tax capital gain is found as follows:

---

3 See Chapter 5 for a discussion of the tax treatment of original-issue discount. For a discussion of the tax treatment of bonds purchased at a discount, see Frank J. Fabozzi, *Bond Portfolio Management* (New Hope, PA: Frank J. Fabozzi Associates, 1996), Chapter 9.

Capital gain after taxes = $g(1 - T_g)$,

where

g = Capital gain ($);
T_g = Applicable tax rate on the capital gain.

Illustration 8-12   Suppose that our 30-year, 4.2% coupon bond is purchased at $750. The capital gain is $250. Assume that the capital gain is taxed at a preferential tax rate of 20%. Then at the maturity date, the amount after the 20% capital gains tax rate will be $20.

The total dollar return to maturity for this bond assuming a reinvestment rate of 6% and that coupon income is taxed at 35% is as follows:

	Taxes not considered		Taxes considered	
Source	($)	(%)	($)	(%)
Total coupon payments	$126.0000	34.3%	$ 81.9000	47.3%
Interest on interest	216.4132	58.9	71.1139	41.1
Capital gain	25.0000	6.8	20.0000	11.6
Total future dollars	$342.4132	100.0%	$173.0139	100.0%

Notice that the relative importance of each source has changed once taxes are considered.

SUMMARY AND INVESTMENT IMPLICATIONS

In this chapter we have explained the three potential sources of dollar return from investing in a bond: (1) coupon interest, (2) interest on interest, and (3) capital gain (or loss). The shortcomings of the three conventional yield measures with respect to each of these sources are explained. The yield to maturity considers all three sources, but it assumes that all coupon interest can be reinvested at the yield to maturity. The yield to call assumes that the coupon interest can be reinvested at the yield to call.

The formulas for computing the interest-on-interest component are presented and applied. The formulas are summarized in Exhibit 8-1. For some bonds, particularly high-coupon, long-term bonds, the interest-on-interest component can be well in excess of 80% of the total dollar return necessary to generate the promised yield to maturity. The longer the term of a coupon bond, all other factors constant, the greater is the interest-on-interest component needed to realize the promised yield to maturity. Lower-coupon bonds, all other factors constant, are less dependent on the reinvestment of coupon interest than higher-coupon bonds. For zero-coupon bonds, none of the bond's total dollar return necessary to generate the yield to maturity at the time of purchase is dependent on the reinvestment of coupon interest. Tax considerations can be taken into account. Taxes change the relative contribution of each source of dollar return.

This chapter has focused on bonds that pay interest semiannually. The same principles apply to fixed income instruments with more frequent cash flow payments, such as mortgage-backed securities. The interest-on-interest component becomes even more important for such securities.

EXHIBIT 8-1

Summary of Formulas for Computing the Interest-on-Interest Components of a Bond's Total Dollar Return

1. Coupon interest plus interest on interest ignoring taxes:

$$\begin{array}{c}\text{Coupon interest}\\\text{plus}\\\text{interest on interest}\end{array} = c\left[\frac{(1+r)^n - 1}{r}\right],$$

where

c = Semiannual coupon interest ($);
r = Semiannual reinvestment rate (in decimal form);
n = Number of periods to maturity.

The reinvestment rate assumed for the yield to maturity is the yield to maturity.

2. Total coupon interest ignoring taxes:

$$\text{Total coupon interest} = n \times c.$$

3. Interest on interest ignoring taxes:

$$\text{Interest on interest} = c\left[\frac{(1+r)^n - 1}{r}\right] - n \times c.$$

4. After-tax total coupon income:

$$\text{After-tax total coupon income} = c(1 - T_c)n,$$

where

T_c = Tax rate on coupon income;
c = Semiannual coupon interest ($);
n = Number of periods to maturity.

5. After-tax coupon income plus interest on interest:

$$\begin{array}{c}\text{After–tax coupon}\\\text{income plus}\\\text{interest on interest}\end{array} = c\left[\frac{[(1 + r(1 - T_c)]^n - 1}{r}\right],$$

where

r = Semiannual reinvestment rate assumed.

6. After-tax interest on interest:

$$\begin{array}{c}\text{After-tax interest on interest}\\[4pt]= c\left[\frac{[(1 + r(1 - T_c)]^n - 1}{r}\right] - c(1 - T_c)n.\end{array}$$

Continued

EXHIBIT 8–1

Concluded

7. Capital gain after taxes:

$$\text{Capital gain after taxes} = g\,(1 - T_g),$$

where

    g = Capital gain ($);

    T_g = Applicable tax rate on the capital gain.

9

⑥ TOTAL RETURN

In the previous chapter, we explained the three potential sources of dollar return from investing in a bond. We also demonstrated the importance of the interest-on-interest component as a source of dollar return. In this chapter, we present a yield measure that is more meaningful than the commonly used yield to maturity and yield to call for assessing the potential performance of a bond or a portfolio. This yield measure is called the *total return*.[1]

ANOTHER LOOK AT THE DRAWBACKS OF THE YIELD TO MATURITY AND YIELD TO CALL

Yield to Maturity

In the previous chapter, we explained that the yield to maturity is a *promised* yield. The promised yield assumes:

1. The bond is held to maturity;
2. All coupon interest payments are reinvested at the yield to maturity.

We focused on the second assumption in the previous chapter, where we showed that the interest-on-interest component for a bond may constitute a substantial portion of the bond's promised total dollar return. Failure to reinvest the coupon interest payments at a rate of interest at least equal to the yield to maturity will produce a yield less than the yield to maturity. This risk is called *reinvestment risk*.

---

1 Bond market participants also refer to this yield measure as horizon return, or realized compound yield. The term realized compound yield was first used by Sidney Homer and Martin Leibowitz in *Inside the Yield Book* (Prentice-Hall/New York Institute of Finance, 1972).

Rather than assume that the coupon interest payments are reinvested at a rate of interest equal to the yield to maturity, nothing prevents an investor from making an explicit assumption about the reinvestment rate on the basis of different expectations. The total return is a measure of yield that incorporates an explicit assumption about the reinvestment rate.

Let's take a careful look now at the first assumption. An investor need not hold a bond until maturity. Suppose, for example, that an investor who has a 5-year investment horizon is considering four bonds:

Bond	Coupon (%)	Maturity (years)	Yield to Maturity (%)
A	5%	3	9.0%
B	6	20	8.6
C	11	15	9.2
D	8	5	8.0

Assuming that all four bonds are of the same credit quality, which one is the most attractive to this investor? An investor who selects bond C because it offers the highest yield to maturity is failing to recognize that the bond must be sold after 5 years at a price that will depend on the yield required in the market for 10-year, 11% coupon bonds at the time. Hence, there could be a capital gain or capital loss that will make the return higher or lower than the yield to maturity promised now. Moreover, the higher coupon on bond C relative to the other three bonds means that more of this bond's return will be dependent on reinvestment of coupon interest payments.

Bond A offers the second highest yield to maturity. On the surface, it seems to be particularly attractive because it eliminates the problem in the bond C purchase of realizing a possible capital loss when the bond must be sold prior to the maturity date. Moreover, the reinvestment risk seems to be less than for the other three bonds because the coupon rate is the lowest. The investor would not be eliminating the reinvestment risk, however, because after 3 years the proceeds received at maturity must be reinvested for 2 more years. The yield that the investor will realize then will depend on the interest rates 3 years from now, when the investor must reinvest the proceeds.

Which is the best bond? The yield to maturity doesn't seem to be helping us answer this question. The answer depends on the expectations of the investor. Specifically, it depends on the interest rate at which the coupon interest payments can be reinvested until the end of the investor's investment horizon. Also, for bonds with a maturity greater than the investment horizon, it depends on the investor's expectations about interest rates at the end of the investment horizon. Consequently, any of these bonds could be the best investment vehicle on the basis of some reinvestment rate and some future interest rate at the end of the investment horizon. The total return measure takes these expectations into account.

Yield to Call

The yield to call is subject to the same problems as the yield to maturity. First, it assumes that the bond will be held until the first call date. Second, it assumes that the coupon interest payments will be reinvested at the yield to call. If an investor's investment horizon is shorter than the time to the first call date, there remains the potential of having to sell the bond below its acquisition cost. If, on the other hand, the investment horizon is longer than the time to the first call date, there is the problem of reinvesting the proceeds when the bond is called until the end of the investment horizon. Consequently, the yield to call doesn't tell us very much. The total return, however, can accommodate the analysis of callable bonds.

COMPUTING THE TOTAL RETURN FOR A BOND HELD TO MATURITY

The idea underlying the total return is simple. The objective is to compute the total future amount that will result from an investment. The total return is the interest rate that will make the initial investment in the bond grow to the computed total future amount. To illustrate the computation, we first show how the total return is computed, assuming a bond is held to the maturity date.

For an assumed reinvestment rate, the dollar return that will be available at maturity can be computed from the coupon interest payments and the interest-on-interest component. In the previous chapter we explained how to do this. In addition, at maturity the investor will receive the par value. The total return is then the interest rate that will make the amount invested in the bond (that is, the current market price plus accrued interest) equal to the total future amount available at the maturity date.

More formally, the steps for computing the total return for a bond *held to maturity* are now given.

Step 1   Compute the total future amount that will be received from the investment. This is the sum of the amount that will be received from the coupon payments, interest on interest based on the coupon payments and the assumed reinvestment rate, and the par value. The coupon payments plus the interest on interest can be computed by using the formula presented in the previous chapter:

$$\text{Coupon interest plus interest on interest} = c \left[\frac{(1 + r)^n - 1}{r} \right],$$

where

c = Semiannual coupon interest (\$);
r = Semiannual reinvestment rate (in decimal form);
n = Number of periods to maturity.

In the case of the yield to maturity, the reinvestment rate is assumed to be one-half the yield to maturity. In computing the total return, the reinvestment rate is set equal to one-half the simple annual interest that the investor assumes can be earned by reinvesting the coupon interest payments.

Notice that the total future amount is different from the total dollar return that we have used in showing the importance of the interest-on-interest component in the previous chapter. The total dollar return includes only the capital gain (or capital loss if there is one), not the entire par value, which is used to compute the total future amount. That is,

Total dollar return = Total future amount − Price of bond.

Step 2   To obtain the semiannual total return, use the following formula:

$$\left[\frac{\text{Total future amount}}{\text{Price of bond}}\right]^{1/n} - 1.$$

This formula is an application of the yield discussed in Chapter 4 for an investment that has only one cash flow.

Step 3   Since interest is assumed to be paid semiannually, double the interest rate found in Step 2. The resulting interest rate is the total return on a bond equivalent basis. The total return can also be computed by compounding the semiannual rate as follows:

$$(1 + \text{Semiannual total return})^2 - 1.$$

The total return calculated in this manner is said to be on an *effective rate basis*.

The four illustrations that follow show how to compute the total return for a bond held to maturity.

Illustration 9-1   The total return for a 7-year, 9% coupon bond selling at par, assuming a reinvestment rate of 5% (simple annual interest rate), is 8.1%, as shown in Exhibit 9-1. Since this bond is selling at par, its yield to maturity is 9%, yet its total return is only 8.1%. The total return is less than the yield to maturity because the coupon interest payments are assumed to be reinvested at 5% rather than 9%.

Illustration 9-2   The computation of the total return for the bond in the previous illustration, assuming a reinvestment rate of 9%, is shown in Exhibit 9-2. The total return is 9%. In this case, the total return is equal to the yield to maturity because the coupon interest payments are assumed to be reinvested at 9%.

Illustration 9-3   The total return for a 20-year, 7% coupon bond selling for $816, assuming a reinvestment rate of 6% (simple annual interest rate), is 7.62%, as shown in Exhibit 9-3. The yield to maturity is 9%. The total return is less than the yield to maturity because the coupon interest payments are assumed to be reinvested at 6% rather than 9%.

Illustration 9-4   The total return for the bond in the previous illustration is 10.04% if the reinvestment rate is 11%. The computations are shown in Exhibit 9-4. Since the reinvestment rate is greater than the yield to maturity, the total return is greater than the yield to maturity of 9%.

EXHIBIT 9–1

Computation of the Total Return for a 7-Year, 9% Bond Selling at Par and Held to Maturity: Reinvestment Rate = 5%

Step 1   The total future amount from this bond includes:

1. Coupon interest of $45 every 6 months for 7 years,
2. Interest earned from reinvesting the semiannual coupon interest payments at 2.5% (one-half the assumed annual reinvestment rate);
3. The par value of $1,000.

The coupon interest plus interest on interest can be found as follows:

$c = \$45;$
$m = 2;$
$r = .025\ (=.05/2);$
$n = 14\ (= 7 \times 2).$

$$\begin{array}{l}\text{Coupon interest} \\ \text{plus} \\ \text{interest on interest}\end{array} = \$45 \left[\frac{(1.025)^{14} - 1}{.025} \right]$$

$$= \$45 \left[\frac{1.4130 - 1}{.025} \right]$$

$$= \$45(16.5189)$$

$$= \$743.35.$$

Total future amount:

Coupon interest plus interest on interest	$ 743.35
Par value	1,000.00
Total	$1,743.35

Step 2   Compute the following:

$$\left[\frac{\$1,743.35}{\$1,000.00} \right]^{1/14} - 1$$

$$= (1.74335)^{.07143} - 1$$

$$= 1.0405 - 1$$

$$= .0405\ or\ 4.05\%.$$

Step 3   Doubling 4.05% gives a total return of 8.1%.

EXHIBIT 9-2

Computation of the Total Return for a 7-Year, 9% Bond Selling at Par and Held to Maturity: Reinvestment Rate = 9%

Step 1   The total future amount for this bond includes:

1. Coupon interest of $45 every 6 months for 7 years;
2. Interest earned from reinvesting the semiannual coupon interest payments at 4.5% (one-half the assumed annual reinvestment rate);
3. The par value of $1,000.

The coupon interest plus interest on interest can be found as follows:

c = $45;
m = 2;
r = .045 (=.09/2);
n = 14 (= 7 × 2).

$$\begin{array}{l} \text{Coupon interest} \\ \qquad \text{plus} \\ \text{interest on interest} \end{array} = \$45\left[\frac{(1.045)^{14} - 1}{.045}\right]$$

$$= \$45\left[\frac{1.8519 - 1}{.045}\right]$$

$$= \$45(18.9321)$$

$$= \$851.94.$$

Total future amount:

Coupon interest plus interest on interest	$ 851.94
Par value	1,000.00
Total	$1,851.94

Step 2   Compute the following:

$$\left[\frac{\$1,851.94}{\$1,000.00}\right]^{1/14} - 1$$

$$= (1.85194)^{.07143} - 1$$

$$= 1.0450 - 1$$

$$= .0450 \; or \; 4.50\%.$$

Step 3   Doubling 4.50% gives a total return of 9.0%.

EXHIBIT 9-3

Computation of the Total Return for a 20-Year, 7% Bond Selling for $816 and Held to Maturity: Reinvestment Rate = 6%

Step 1   The total future amount from this bond includes:

1. Coupon interest of $35 every 6 months for 20 years;
2. Interest earned from reinvesting the semiannual coupon interest payments at 3% (one-half the assumed annual reinvestment rate);
3. The par value of $1,000.

The coupon interest plus interest on interest can be found as follows:

c = $35;
m = 2;
r = .03 (= .06/2);
n = 40 (= 20 × 2).

$$
\begin{array}{l}
\text{Coupon interest}\\
\text{plus}\\
\text{interest on interest}
\end{array}
= \$35 \left[\frac{(1.03)^{40} - 1}{.03} \right]
$$

$$
= \$35 \left[\frac{3.2620 - 1}{.03} \right]
$$

$$
= \$35(74.4013)
$$

$$
= \$2,639.04.
$$

Total future amount:

Coupon interest plus interest on interest	$2,639.04
Par value	1,000.00
Total	$3,639.04

Step 2   Compute the following:

$$
\left[\frac{\$3,639.04}{\$816} \right]^{1/40} - 1
$$

$$
= (4.45961)^{.025} - 1
$$

$$
= 1.0381 - 1
$$

$$
= .0381 \text{ or } 3.81\%.
$$

Step 3   Doubling 3.81% gives a total return of 7.62%.

EXHIBIT 9–4

Computation of the Total Return for a 20-Year, 7% Bond Selling for $816 and Held to Maturity: Reinvestment Rate = 11%

Step 1   The total future amount from this bond includes:

1. Coupon interest of $35 every 6 months for 20 years;
2. Interest earned from reinvesting the semiannual coupon interest payments at 5.5% (one-half the assumed annual reinvestment rate);
3. The par value of $1,000.

The coupon interest plus interest on interest can be found as follows:

$c = \$35;$
$m = 2;$
$r = .055 \ (= .11/2);$
$n = 40 \ (= 20 \times 2).$

$$\begin{matrix} \text{Coupon interest} \\ \text{plus} \\ \text{interest on interest} \end{matrix} = \$35 \left[\frac{(1.055)^{40} - 1}{.055} \right]$$

$$= \$35 \left[\frac{8.5133 - 1}{.055} \right]$$

$$= \$35(136.6056)$$

$$= \$4,781.20.$$

Total future amount:

Coupon interest plus interest on interest	$4,781.20
Par value	1,000.00
Total	$5,781.20

Step 2   Compute the following:

$$\left[\frac{\$5,781.20}{\$816} \right]^{1/40} - 1$$

$$= (7.08480)^{.025} - 1$$

$$= 1.0502 - 1$$

$$= .0502 \ or \ 5.02\%.$$

Step 3   Doubling 5.02% gives a total return of 10.04%.

COMPUTING THE TOTAL RETURN FOR A BOND TO BE SOLD PRIOR TO MATURITY

The total return as calculated above suffers from the same problem as the yield to maturity in that it assumes holding the bond until maturity. Fortunately, it is quite simple to modify the calculation of the total return to determine the potential yield from holding it until the end of a predetermined investment horizon. We need make only one adjustment to the three steps given above to calculate the total return.

In Step 1, the total future amount is calculated on the basis of (1) the coupon interest payments until the end of the investment horizon, (2) the interest on interest from reinvesting the coupon interest payments until the end of the investment horizon, and (3) the expected price of the bond at the end of the investment horizon.

How does one know the expected price of the bond at the end of the investment horizon? The expected price depends on the investor's expectations about what interest rates will be at the end of the investment horizon. Given the expected yield that the bond will be selling for at the end of the investment horizon and the remaining time to maturity of the bond, the expected price can easily be determined from the formula for the price of a bond given in Chapter 5 (see Exhibit 5-10):

$$p = \frac{c}{(1+i)^1} + \frac{c}{(1+i)^2} + \frac{c}{(1+i)^3} + \cdots + \frac{c}{(1+i)^n} + \frac{M}{(1+i)^n},$$

where

p = Price ($);
c = Semiannual coupon payment ($);
i = *Semiannual* required yield (in decimal form);
n = Number of periods (number of years $\times$ 2);
M = Maturity value.

In applying this formula, it is important to remember that n is the number of periods remaining to maturity *at the end of the investment horizon.* For example, if the investment horizon is 5 years and the number of years to maturity at the present time is 20 years, there would remain 15 years to maturity at the end of the investment horizon. In this case, n would be 30.

The present value of the coupon interest payments in the price formula can be computed by using the formula (see Chapter 5, Exhibit 5-10):

$$c \left[\frac{1 - \left[\frac{1}{(1+i)^n} \right]}{i} \right].$$

Illustration 9-5   Suppose that an investor with a 5-year investment horizon is considering purchasing a 7-year, 9% coupon bond selling at par. The investor expects that the coupon interest payments can be reinvested at an annual interest rate of 9.4% and that at the end of the investment horizon 2-year bonds will be selling to offer a yield to maturity of 11.2%. As shown in Exhibit 9-5, the total return for this bond is 8.54%. The yield to maturity for this bond is 9%.

EXHIBIT 9–5

Computation of the Total Return for a 7-Year, 9% Bond Selling at Par and Held for 5 Years: Reinvestment Rate = 9.4%

Step 1   The total future amount from this bond includes:

1. Coupon interest of $45 every 6 months for 5 years (the investment horizon);
2. Interest earned from reinvesting the semiannual coupon interest payments at 4.7% (one-half the a;ssumed annual reinvestment rate) until the end of the investment horizon;
3. The expected price of the bond at the end of 5 years.

The coupon interest plus interest on interest can be found as follows:

$c = \$45;$
$m = 2;$
$r = .047 \ (= .094/2);$
$n = 10 \ (= 5 \times 2).$

$$\begin{array}{l} \text{Coupon interest} \\ \text{plus} \\ \text{interest on interest} \end{array} = \$45 \left[\frac{(1.047)^{10} - 1}{.047} \right]$$

$$= \$45 \left[\frac{1.5830 - 1}{.047} \right]$$

$$= \$45 \ (12.4032)$$

$$= \$588.14.$$

The expected price of the bond 5 years from now is determined as follows:

(a)   Present value of coupon interest payments, assuming the required yield to maturity at the end of the investment horizon is 11.2%:

$c = \$45;$
$i = .056 \ (= .112/2);$
$n = 4 \ (= \text{remaining years to maturity} \times 2).$

$$PV = \$45 \left[\frac{1 - \left[\frac{1}{(1.056)^4} \right]}{.056} \right]$$

$$= \$45 \left[\frac{1 - .8042}{.056} \right]$$

$$= \$45(3.4964)$$

$$= \$157.34.$$

Continued

EXHIBIT 9-5

Concluded

(b)   Present value of the maturity value:

$$\frac{\$1,000}{(1.056)^4} = \$804.16.$$

$$\text{Expected price} = \$157.34 + \$804.16$$
$$= \$961.50.$$

Total future amount:

Coupon interest plus interest on interest	$558.14
Expected price	961.50
Total	$1,519.64

Step 2   Compute the following:

$$\left[\frac{\$1,519.64}{\$1,000.00}\right]^{\!1/10} - 1$$
$$= (1.51964)^{.10} - 1$$
$$= 1.0427 - 1$$
$$= .0427 \ or \ 4.27\%.$$

Step 3   Doubling 4.27% gives a total return of 8.54%.

Illustration 9-6   Suppose that an investor with a 3-year investment horizon is considering purchasing a 20-year, 8% coupon bond for $828.40. The investor expects that the coupon interest payments can be reinvested at an annual interest rate of 6% and that at the end of the investment horizon 17-year bonds will be selling to offer a yield to maturity of 7%. The total return for this bond is 17.16%. (The computations are shown in Exhibit 9-6.) The yield to maturity for this bond is 10%.

Illustration 9-7   Suppose that an investor has a 6-year investment horizon. The investor is considering a 13-year, 9% coupon bond selling at par. The investor's expectations are as follows:

1. The first four semiannual coupon payments can be reinvested from the time of receipt to the end of the investment horizon at an annual interest rate of 8%;

2. The last eight semiannual coupon payments can be reinvested from the time of receipt to the end of the investment horizon at a 10% annual interest rate;

3. The required yield to maturity on 7-year bonds at the end of the investment horizon is 10.6%.

Based on these three assumptions, the total return is 8.14%. The calculations are shown in Exhibit 9-7.

EXHIBIT 9–6

Computation of the Total Return for a 20-Year, 8% Bond Selling for $828.40 and Held for 3 Years: Reinvestment Rate = 6%

Step 1   The total future amount from this bond includes:

1. Coupon interest of $40 every 6 months for 3 years (the investment horizon);

2. Interest earned from reinvesting the semiannual coupon interest payments at 3% (one-half the assumed annual reinvestment rate);

3. The expected price of the bond at the end of 3 years.

The coupon interest plus interest on interest can be found as follows:

$c = \$40$;
$m = 2$;
$r = .03 \, (= .06/2)$;
$n = 6 \, (= 3 \times 2)$.

$$
\begin{array}{c}
\text{Coupon interest} \\
\text{plus} \\
\text{interest on interest}
\end{array} = \$40 \left[\frac{(1.03)^6 - 1}{.03} \right]
$$

$$
= \$45 \left[\frac{1.1941 - 1}{.03} \right]
$$

$$
= \$40 \, (6.4684)
$$

$$
= \$258.74.
$$

The expected price of the bond 3 years from now is determined as follows:

(a) Present value of coupon interest payments, assuming the required yield to maturity at the end of the investment horizon is 7%:

$c = \$40$;
$i = .035 \, (= .07/2)$;
$n = 34 \, (= \text{Remaining years to maturity} \times 2)$.

$$
PV = \$40 \left[\frac{1 - \left[\dfrac{1}{(1.035)^{34}} \right]}{.035} \right]
$$

$$
= \$40 \left[\frac{1 - .3105}{.035} \right]
$$

$$
= \$40 \, (19.7007)
$$

$$
= \$788.03.
$$

(b) Present value of the maturity value:

$$
\frac{\$1,000}{(1.035)^{34}} = \$310.48
$$

Continued

EXHIBIT 9—6

Concluded

$$\text{Expected price} = \$788.03 + \$310.48$$
$$= \$1,098.51.$$

Total future amount:

Coupon interest plus interest on interest	$ 258.74
Expected price	1,098.51
Total	$1,357.25

Step 2   Compute the following:

$$\left[\frac{\$1,357.25}{\$828.40}\right]^{\frac{1}{6}} - 1$$
$$= (1.63840)^{.16667} - 1$$
$$= 1.0858 - 1$$
$$= .0858 \text{ or } 8.58\%.$$

Step 3   Doubling 8.58% gives a total return of 17.16%.

EXHIBIT 9-7

Computation of the Total Return for a 13-Year, 9% Bond Selling at Par and Held for 6 Years: Two Different Reinvestment Rates

Step 1   The total future amount from this bond includes:

1. Coupon interest of $45 every 6 months for 6 years (the investment horizon);

2. Interest earned from reinvesting the first four semiannual coupon interest payments at 4% (one-half the assumed annual reinvestment rate) until the end of the investment horizon;

3. Interest earned from reinvesting the last eight semiannual coupon interest payments at 5% (one-half the assumed annual reinvestment rate) until the end of the reinvestment horizon;

4. The expected price of the bond at the end of 6 years.

The coupon interest plus interest on interest for the first four coupon payments can be found as follows:

$c = \$45;$
$m = 2;$

Continued

EXHIBIT 9-7

Continued

$r = .04 (= .08/2)$;
$n = 4$.

$$\begin{array}{c} \text{Coupon interest} \\ \text{plus} \\ \text{interest on interest} \end{array} = \$45 \left[\frac{(1.04)^4 - 1}{.04} \right]$$

$$= \$45 \left[\frac{1.1699 - 1}{.04} \right]$$

$$= \$45(4.2465)$$

$$= \$191.09.$$

This gives the coupon interest plus interest on interest as of the end of the second year (four periods). Reinvesting at 4% until the end of the investment horizon, 4 years or eight 6-month periods later, $191.09 will grow to

$$\$191.09 \ (1.04)^8 = \$261.52.$$

The coupon interest plus interest on interest for the last eight coupon payments can be found as follows:

$c = \$45$;
$m = 2$;
$r = .05 (= .10/2)$;
$n = 8$.

$$\begin{array}{c} \text{Coupon interest} \\ \text{plus} \\ \text{Interest on interest} \end{array} = \$45 \left[\frac{(1.05)^8 - 1}{.05} \right]$$

$$= \$45 \left[\frac{1.47746 - 1}{.05} \right]$$

$$= \$45 \ (9.5491)$$

$$= \$429.71.$$

The coupon interest and interest on interest from all 12 coupon interest payments is $691.23 ($261.52 + $429.71).

The expected price of the bond 6 years from now is determined as follows:

(a) Present value of coupon interest payments, assuming the required yield to maturity at the end of the investment horizon is 10.6%:

$c = \$45$;
$i = .053 (= .106/2)$;
$n = 14 (= \text{Remaining years to maturity} \times 2)$

Continued

EXHIBIT 9-7
Concluded

$$PV = \$45 \left[\frac{1 - \left[\frac{1}{(1.053)^{14}} \right]}{.053} \right]$$

$$= \$45 \left[\frac{1 - .4853}{.053} \right]$$

$$= \$45 \, (9.7115)$$

$$= \$437.02.$$

(b) Present value of the maturity value:

$$\frac{\$1,000}{(1.053)^{14}} = \$485.29.$$

$$\text{Expected price} = \$437.02 + \$485.29$$
$$= \$922.31.$$

Total future amount:

Coupon interest plus interest on interest	$ 691.23
Expected price	922.31
Total	$1,613.54

Step 2 Compute the following:

$$\left[\frac{\$1,613.54}{\$1,000.00} \right]^{1/12} - 1$$

$$= (1.61354)^{.08333} - 1$$
$$= 1.0407 - 1$$
$$= .0407 \; or \; 4.07\%.$$

Step 3 Doubling 4.07% gives a total return of 8.14%.

ANALYZING CALLABLE BONDS WITH THE TOTAL RETURN

The total return can be used to assess the potential return from holding a callable bond. If the first call date falls within the investment horizon, the proceeds from the coupon interest payments plus the interest on interest and the proceeds from calling the issue (the call price) will be available at the first call date. These proceeds can then be reinvested until the end of the investment horizon. Given the total future amount at the end of the investment horizon, the total return can then be computed. The next illustration shows how this is done.

Illustration 9-8   An investor is considering bond C, which we presented earlier in this chapter: 11% coupon, 15 years to maturity and 9.2% yield to maturity. The price for this bond is $1,144.88. Suppose that this bond is callable in 3 years at $1,055. The yield to call for this bond is 7.48%. Since the yield to call is less than the yield to maturity, this investor might use the 7.48% to assess the relative attractiveness of this bond. However, suppose that this investor's investment horizon is 5 years (a period extending beyond the first call date but shorter than the maturity of the bond). Also assume that this investor believes that any proceeds can be reinvested at a 6% annual interest rate (3% semiannually).

Exhibit 9-8 shows the computation of the total return on the assumption that the bond is called in 3 years. The total return is 6.66%. This investor's reinvestment assumption and the investment horizon make this the appropriate yield to use in assessing the attractiveness of this bond compared to other bonds that are purchase candidates.

EXHIBIT 9-8

Computation of the Total Return for a 15-Year, 11% Bond Selling for $1,144.88, Callable in 3 Years at $1,055 and Held for 3 Years: Reinvestment Rate = 6%

Step 1   The total future amount from this bond includes:

1. Coupon interest of $55 every 6 months for 3 years (to the first call date);
2. Interest earned from reinvesting the first 6 semiannual coupon interest payments at 3% (one-half the assumed annual reinvestment rate) until the first call date;
3. Proceeds from reinvesting the call price plus (1) and (2) above for 2 years at 3% until the end of the investment horizon.

The coupon interest plus interest on interest for the first six coupon payments can be found as follows:

$$c = \$55;$$
$$m = 2;$$
$$r = .03 \ (= .06/2);$$
$$n = 6.$$

$$\begin{array}{c} \text{Coupon interest} \\ \text{plus} \\ \text{interest on interest} \end{array} = \$55 \left[\frac{(1.03)^6 - 1}{.03} \right]$$

$$= \$55 \left[\frac{1.1941 - 1}{.03} \right]$$

$$= \$55 \ (6.4683)$$

$$= \$355.76.$$

This gives the coupon interest plus interest on interest as of the end of the third year (six periods) when the bond is called. Adding the call price of $1,055 gives the total proceeds that must be

Continued

EXHIBIT 9–8

Concluded

---

reinvested at 3% until the end of the investment horizon, for 2 years or 4 periods.

$$\text{Proceeds to be reinvested} = \$355.76 + \$1,055$$
$$= \$1,410.76.$$

Reinvesting $1,410.76 for 4 periods at 3%:

$$\$1,410.76 \ (1.03)^4 = \$1,587.82.$$

Therefore, the total future amount is $1,587.82.

Step 2   Compute the following:

$$\left[\frac{\$1,587.82}{\$1,144.88} \right]^{1/10}$$
$$= (1.38689)^{.10} - 1$$
$$= 1.0304 - 1$$
$$= .0333 \ or \ 3.33\%.$$

Step 3   Doubling 3.33% gives a total return of 6.66%.

AFTER-TAX TOTAL RETURN TO MATURITY

In the previous chapter we discussed the effect of taxes on total dollar contributions. Given the total future dollars at maturity after accounting for taxes, the after-tax total return to maturity (on a semiannual basis) can be calculated as follows:

$$\left(\frac{\text{After–tax total dollar return at maturity}}{\text{Price of bond}} \right)^{1/n} - 1,$$

where n is the number of periods to maturity. The semiannual rate can then be annualized on a bond equivalent basis or on an effective rate basis.

Illustration 9-9   In Illustration 8-11 of the previous chapter, the after-tax total dollar return at maturity for a 4.2%, 30-year bond selling at $750 assuming a 35% tax rate on coupon income, 20% capital gains tax rate, and 6% reinvestment rate was shown to be $1,530. The after-tax total return to maturity (on a semiannual basis) is

$$\left(\frac{\$1,530}{\$750} \right)^{1/60} - 1 = .0201 = 2.01\%.$$

The bond equivalent after-tax total return to maturity is 4.02%. On an effective rate basis the after-tax total return to maturity is 4.07%.

The after-tax total return to maturity is a more appropriate measure for comparing the potential return from holding a taxable bond and the same maturity municipal bond to the maturity date. For a municipal bond, the coupon payments will not be taxed; however, the capital gain will be.

Effective Par Rate

In the early 1970s, Martin Leibowitz introduced the concept of an *effective par rate* to benchmark a bond's after-tax total return to new issue par bonds.[2] Specifically, the effective par rate is the coupon or yield to maturity of a par bond that gives the same after-tax total return of a given bond.

The steps to calculate the effective par rate are now given.

Step 1   Calculate the after-tax total dollars per dollar invested.

Step 2   Based on the assumed reinvestment rate used to calculate the after-tax total dollars, calculate the semiannual after-tax reinvestment rate as follows:

$$\text{Semiannual after-tax reinvestment rate} = r\,(1 - T),$$

where

$r = Semiannual$ reinvestment rate assumed;

$T = $ Tax rate.

Step 3   Given the semiannual after-tax reinvestment rate in Step 2, determine the total future dollars per \$100 of par value for an annuity of \$1 for the number of years equal to the maturity of the bond analyzed. This can be found by using the following formula:

$$\frac{[1 - r\,(1 - T)]^n - 1}{100\,r\,(1 - T)}.$$

Step 4   Divide the amount found in Step 3 by the amount in Step 1. This amount is the semiannual after-tax coupon payment required to make a par bond produce the same after-tax total future dollars as our given bond.

Step 5   Divide the amount in Step 4 by 1 minus the tax rate. This gives the amount of the semiannual coupon payment necessary to produce the amount in Step 4 after taxes.

Step 6   Multiply the amount in Step 5 by 2 to get the annual coupon on a par bond required to generate the same after-tax total dollar return as the given bond.

Step 7   Divide the amount in Step 6 by 100 to get the effective par rate.

---

2   Martin L. Leibowitz, "Integrating Tax Effects into Bond Portfolio Management," *The Bankers Magazine* (Spring 1975).

Illustration 9-10   Consider once again the 4.2%, 30-year bond selling at $750.

Step 1. Since the after-tax total dollars is $173.0139 and the purchase price is $75, the after-tax total dollars per dollar invested is $2.306851.

Step 2. Since the reinvestment rate is 6% and the tax rate on reinvestment income is 35%, the semiannual after-tax reinvestment rate is

$$0.03 \ (1 - .35) = 1.95\%.$$

Step 3. The total future dollars of an annuity of $1 for 60 periods per $100 par assuming a 1.95% semiannual after-tax reinvestment rate is

$$\frac{(1 + 0.0195)^{60} - 1}{\$100 \ (0.0195)} = \$1.120981.$$

Step 4. Divide $2.306851 by $1.120981. The result is 2.0578. This means that each semiannual coupon payment must net $2.0578 after taxes.

Step 5. Divide 2.0578 by 1 minus 35%. This gives 3.1658.

Step 6. Multiplying 3.1658 by 2 gives 6.33.

Step 7. The effective par rate is found by dividing 6.33 by 100. Therefore, the effective par rate is 6.33%.

The effective par rate can be used to compare newly issued par bonds with secondary market issues that have different degrees of taxation embedded within the price. If the new issue has a coupon rate that is less than the effective par rate, then the investor would be better off with the seasoned issue. If the new issue has a coupon rate that is greater than the effective par rate, then the new issue would give a greater after-tax total return than the seasoned issue.

SCENARIO ANALYSIS

Because the total return depends on the reinvestment rate and the yield at the end of the investment horizon, portfolio managers assess performance over a wide range of scenarios for these two variables. This approach is referred to as *scenario analysis*.

Illustration 9-11   Suppose a portfolio manager is considering the purchase of bond A, a 20-year, 9% noncallable bond selling at $109.896 per $100 of par value. The yield to maturity for this bond is 8%. Assume also that the portfolio manager's investment horizon is 3 years and that the portfolio manager believes the reinvestment rate range can vary from 3% to 6.5% and the yield at the end of the investment horizon from 5% to 12%.

The top panel of Exhibit 9-9 shows the total future dollars at the end of 3 years under various scenarios. The bottom panel shows the total return (based on the effective annualizing of the 6-month total return). The portfolio manager knows that the maximum and minimum total return will be 14.64% and –.2%, respectively, and the scenarios under which each will be realized. If the portfolio manager faces 3-year liabilities guaranteeing, say, 6%, the major

EXHIBIT 9–9

Scenario Analysis for Bond A

Bond A = 9% coupon, 20-year noncallable bond;
Price = $109.896;
Yield to maturity = 8.00%;
Investment horizon = 3 years.

			Yield at End of Horizon				
5.00%	6.00%	7.00%	8.00%	9.00%	10.00%	11.00%	12.00%
			Horizon Price				
145.448	131.698	119.701	109.206	100.000	91.9035	84.763	78.4478

Reinv. Rate (%)	Total Future Dollars							
	5.00%	6.00%	7.00%	8.00%	9.00%	10.00%	11.00%	12.00%
3.0%	173.481	159.731	147.734	137.239	128.033	119.937	112.796	106.481
3.5	173.657	159.907	147.910	137.415	128.209	120.113	112.972	106.657
4.0	173.834	160.084	148.087	137.592	128.387	120.290	113.150	106.834
4.5	174.013	160.263	148.266	137.771	128.565	120.469	113.328	107.013
5.0	174.192	160.443	148.445	137.950	128.745	120.648	113.508	107.193
5.5	174.373	160.623	148.626	138.131	128.926	120.829	113.689	107.374
6.0	174.555	160.806	148.809	138.313	129.108	121.011	113.871	107.556
6.5	174.739	160.989	148.992	138.497	129.291	121.195	114.054	107.739

Reinv. Rate (%)	Total Return (Effective Rate)							
	5.00%	6.00%	7.00%	8.00%	9.00%	10.00%	11.00%	12.00%
3.0%	16.44	13.28	10.37	7.69	5.22	2.96	0.87	−1.05
3.5	16.48	13.32	10.41	7.73	5.27	3.01	0.92	−0.99
4.0	16.52	13.36	10.45	7.78	5.32	3.06	0.98	−0.94
4.5	16.56	13.40	10.50	7.83	5.37	3.11	1.03	−0.88
5.0	16.60	13.44	10.54	7.87	5.42	3.16	1.08	−0.83
5.5	16.64	13.49	10.59	7.92	5.47	3.21	1.14	−0.77
6.0	16.68	13.53	10.63	7.97	5.52	3.26	1.19	−0.72
6.5	16.72	13.57	10.68	8.02	5.57	3.32	1.25	−0.66

consideration is scenarios that will produce a 3-year total return of less than 6%. These scenarios can be determined from Exhibit 9-9.

Illustration 9-12   Suppose that the same portfolio manager owns bond B, a 14-year noncallable bond with a coupon rate of 7.25% and a current price of $94.553 per $100 par value. The yield to maturity is 7.9%. Exhibit 9-10 reports the total future dollars and total return over a 3-year investment horizon under the same scenarios as Exhibit 9-9. A portfolio manager considering swapping from bond B to bond A would compare the relative performance of the two bonds as reported in Exhibits 9-9 and 9-10. Exhibit 9-11 shows the difference between the performance of the two bonds in basis points. This comparative analysis assumes that the two bonds are of the same investment quality and ignores the financial accounting and tax consequences associated with the disposal of bond B to acquire bond A.

APPLICATION TO CHEAPEST TO DELIVER FOR FUTURES CONTRACT

The total return framework is used in the analysis of Treasury bond futures contracts traded on the Chicago Board of Trade (CBT). The underlying instrument for a Treasury bond futures contract is $100,000 par value of a *hypothetical* 20-year, 8% coupon bond.

The seller (short) of a Treasury bond future who decides to make delivery rather than liquidate his position by buying back the contract prior to the settlement date must deliver some Treasury bond. But what Treasury bond? The CBT allows the seller to deliver one of several Treasury bonds that the CBT declares is acceptable for delivery. The specific bonds that the seller may deliver are published by the CBT prior to the initial trading of a futures contract with a specific settlement date.

To make delivery equitable to both parties, the CBT has introduced *conversion factors* for determining the invoice price of each acceptable deliverable Treasury issue against the Treasury bond futures contract. The conversion factor is determined by the CBT before a contract with a specific settlement date begins trading. The conversion factor is constant throughout the trading period of the futures contract.

In selecting the issue to be delivered, the short will select from all the deliverable issues the one that will give the largest total return from a *cash and carry trade*. A cash and carry trade is one in which a cash bond that is acceptable for delivery is purchased and simultaneously the Treasury bond futures contract is sold. The bond purchased can be delivered to satisfy the short futures position. Thus, by buying the Treasury bond that is acceptable for delivery and selling the futures, an investor has effectively sold the bond at the delivery price (i.e., converted price).

A total return can be calculated for this trade. The total return is determined by

1. The price plus accrued interest of the Treasury bond that could be purchased;
2. The converted price plus the accrued interest that will be received upon delivery of that Treasury bond to satisfy the short futures position;
3. The coupon payments that will be received between today and the delivery date;
4. The reinvestment income that will be realized on the coupon payments between the time received and the delivery date.

EXHIBIT 9–10

Scenario Analysis for Bond B

Bond B = 7.25% coupon, 14-year noncallable bond;
Price = $94.553;
Yield to maturity = 7.90%;
Investment horizon = 3 years.

				Yield at End of Horizon				
5.00%	6.00%	7.00%	8.00%	9.00%	10.00%	11.00%	12.00%

				Horizon Price				
118.861	109.961	101.896	94.5808	87.9386	81.9009	76.4066	71.4012

Reinv. Rate (%)	5.00%	6.00%	7.00%	8.00%	9.00%	10.00%	11.00%	12.00%
				Total Future Dollars				
3.0%	141.443	132.543	124.478	117.163	110.521	104.483	98.989	93.983
3.5	141.585	132.685	124.620	117.305	110.663	104.625	99.131	94.125
4.0	141.728	132.828	124.763	117.448	110.806	104.768	99.273	94.268
4.5	141.872	132.971	124.907	117.592	110.949	104.912	99.417	94.412
5.0	142.017	133.116	125.051	117.736	111.094	105.056	99.562	94.557
5.5	142.162	133.262	125.197	117.882	111.240	105.202	99.708	94.703
6.0	142.309	133.409	125.344	118.029	111.387	105.349	99.855	94.849
6.5	142.457	133.556	125.492	118.176	111.534	105.497	100.002	94.997

Reinv. Rate (%)	5.00%	6.00%	7.00%	8.00%	9.00%	10.00%	11.00%	12.00%
				Total Return (Effective Rate)				
3.0%	14.37	11.92	9.60	7.41	5.34	3.38	1.54	−0.20
3.5	14.41	11.96	9.64	7.45	5.38	3.43	1.59	−0.15
4.0	14.44	12.00	9.68	7.50	5.43	3.48	1.64	−0.10
4.5	14.48	12.04	9.72	7.54	5.48	3.53	1.69	−0.05
5.0	14.52	12.08	9.77	7.58	5.52	3.57	1.74	0.00
5.5	14.56	12.12	9.81	7.63	5.57	3.62	1.79	0.05
6.0	14.60	12.16	9.85	7.67	5.61	3.67	1.84	0.10
6.5	14.64	12.20	9.90	7.72	5.66	3.72	1.89	0.16

EXHIBIT 9-11

Scenario Analysis Showing the Relative Performance of Bonds A and B

Reinv.	Total Return for Bond A – Total Return for Bond B in Basis Points							
Rate	Yield at End of Horizon							
(%)	5.00%	6.00%	7.00%	8.00%	9.00%	10.00%	11.00%	12.00%
3.0%	207	136	77	28	−12	−43	−67	−85
3.5	207	136	77	28	−11	−42	−66	−84
4.0	207	136	77	28	−11	−42	−66	−84
4.5	207	136	77	29	−11	−42	−66	−83
5.0	207	137	78	29	−10	−41	−65	−83
5.5	208	137	78	29	−10	−41	−65	−82
6.0	208	137	78	30	−10	−41	−64	−82
6.5	208	137	78	30	−9	−40	−64	−81

The first three elements are known. The last element will depend on the reinvestment rate that can be earned. While the reinvestment rate is unknown, typically this is a small part of the total return and not much is lost by assuming that the reinvestment rate can be predicted with certainty.

The general formula for the annualized total return is as follows:

$$\text{Annualized total return} = \frac{\text{Dollar return}}{\text{Dollar investment}} \times \frac{360}{\text{Days}},$$

where

Dollar return = Converted price plus accrued interest received
− Purchase price plus accrued interest
+ Coupon income + Reinvestment income;
Dollar investment = Dollar amount invested in the trade;
Days = Number of days from the settlement date on the bond until the futures delivery date.

The dollar amount invested in the trade is not simply the purchase price of the Treasury issue plus accrued interest that had to be paid at the inception of the cash and carry trade. The reason is that part of the investment is recovered by the coupon income plus reinvestment income. In practice, the dollar investment is calculated as follows:

Dollar investment = Days_1 (Purchase price plus accrued interest)
− Days_2 (Coupon payment received + Reinvestment income),

where

Days$_1$ = Number of days from the settlement date on the bond until the futures
delivery date;

Days$_2$ = Number of days between interim coupon payment and the futures delivery
date.

The annualized total return calculated for an acceptable Treasury issue is more popularly referred to as the *implied repo rate*. Market participants will seek to maximize the implied repo rate; that is, they will use the acceptable Treasury issue that gives the largest total return in the cash and carry trade. The issue that satisfies this criterion is referred to as the *cheapest-to-deliver issue*. It plays a key role in the pricing of this futures contract.

SUMMARY AND IMPLICATIONS

In this chapter we have presented an alternative yield measure, the total return, that investors can use to assess the relative attractiveness of bonds over some investment horizon. The total return takes into consideration the investor's (1) investment horizon, (2) expected reinvestment rate over the investment horizon, and (3) expected yield for the bond at the end of the investment horizon. We show how multiple reinvestment rates can be incorporated into the analysis and how callable bonds can be evaluated using the total return framework.

The total return is applicable as well to evaluating mortgage-backed securities and floating-rate securities. The total return can handle the situation where a taxable bond is included in a taxable portfolio so that only a portion of the coupon interest payments can be reinvested. This permits a comparison of taxable and tax-exempt bonds in a taxable portfolio, which is more meaningful than the common procedure of multiplying the taxable yield by one minus the marginal tax rate. The evaluation of a bond swap, the sale of a bond in a portfolio for another bond, should be conducted using the total return framework.

One objection to the total return is that it requires the investor to make assumptions about reinvestment rates and future yields, as well as to think in terms of an investment horizon. It is more convenient for some to simply use a meaningless measure such as the yield to maturity or yield to call. If an investor is managing money, however, expectations are part of the game. It is not difficult to use the total return framework to analyze the performance of a bond assuming different interest rate scenarios and investment horizons. This is called scenario analysis.

CHAPTER

10

⑥ MEASURING HISTORICAL PERFORMANCE

In the previous two chapters we looked at the potential dollar sources of return from investing and the potential total return. Our focus in this chapter is measurement of the historical performance of a bond portfolio. Performance measurement involves the calculation of the total return realized by a portfolio manager over some evaluation period.

PORTFOLIO PERIOD RETURN

Let's begin with the basic concept. The dollar return realized on a portfolio for any evaluation period (i.e., a year, month, or week) is equal to the sum of

1. The difference between the market value of the portfolio at the end of the evaluation period and the market value at the beginning of the evaluation period, and

2. Any distributions made from the portfolio.

It is important that any capital or income distributions from the portfolio to a client or beneficiary of the portfolio be included.

The rate of return, or simply return, expresses the dollar return in terms of the amount of the market value at the beginning of the evaluation period. Thus, the return can be viewed as the amount (expressed as a fraction of the initial portfolio value) that can be withdrawn at the end of the evaluation period while maintaining the initial market value of the portfolio intact.

In equation form, the *portfolio period return* realized can be expressed as follows:

$$R_p = \frac{V_1 - V_0 + D}{V_0},$$

where

R_p = Portfolio period return;

V_1 = Portfolio market value at the end of the evaluation period;
V_0 = Portfolio market value at the beginning of the evaluation period;
D = Cash distributions from the portfolio to the client during the evaluation period.

Illustration 10-1   Assume the following information for an external manager for a pension plan sponsor: the portfolio's market values at the beginning and end of the evaluation period are $100 million and $112 million, respectively, and during the evaluation period $5 million are distributed to the plan sponsor from investment income. Thus

V_1 = \$112,000,000;
V_0 = \$100,000,000;
D = \$5,000,000.

$$R_p = \frac{\$112,000,000 - \$100,000,000 + \$5,000,000}{\$100,000,000}$$
$$= .17 = 17\%.$$

Assumptions in Calculating the Return

There are three assumptions in calculating the portfolio period return. First, it assumes that cash inflows into the portfolio from interest income that occur during the evaluation period but are not distributed are reinvested in the portfolio. For example, suppose that during the evaluation period $7 million are received from interest income. This amount is reflected in the market value of the portfolio at the end of the period.

The second assumption is that if there are distributions from the portfolio, they occur at the end of the evaluation period or are held in the form of cash until the end of the evaluation period. In our example, $5 million are distributed to the plan sponsor. But when did that distribution actually occur? To understand why the timing of the distribution is important, consider two extreme cases: (1) the distribution is made at the end of the evaluation period, as assumed in the portfolio period return calculation, and (2) the distribution is made at the beginning of the evaluation period. In the first case, the manager had the use of the $5 million to invest for the entire evaluation period. By contrast, in the second case, the manager loses the opportunity to invest the funds until the end of the evaluation period. Consequently, the timing of the distribution will affect the return, but this is not considered in the portfolio period return calculation.

The third assumption is that there is no cash paid into the portfolio by the client. For example, suppose that some time during the evaluation period, the plan sponsor gives an additional $8 million to the manager to invest. Consequently, the market value of the portfolio at the end of the evaluation period, $112 million in our example, would reflect the contribution of $8 million. The portfolio period return calculation does not reflect that the ending market value of the portfolio is affected by the cash paid in by the sponsor. Moreover, the timing of this cash inflow will affect the calculated return.

Thus, while the portfolio period return calculation can be determined for an evaluation period of any length of time such as 1 day, 1 month, or 5 years, from a practical point of view, the assumptions discussed above limit its application. The longer the evaluation period the more likely it is that the assumptions will be violated. For example, it is highly likely that there may be more than one distribution to the client and more than one contribution from the client if the evaluation period is 5 years. Thus, a return calculation made over a long period of time, if longer than a few months, would not be very reliable because of the assumption underlying the calculations that all cash payments and inflows are made and received at the end of the period.

Subperiod Returns

Not only does the violation of the assumptions make it difficult to compare the returns of two managers over some evaluation period, but it is also not useful for evaluating performance over different periods. For example, the portfolio period return will not give reliable information to compare the performance of a 1-month evaluation period and a 3-year evaluation period. To make such a comparison, the return must be expressed per unit of time, for example, per year.

The way to handle these practical issues is to calculate the return for a short unit of time such as a month or a quarter. We call the return so calculated the *subperiod return*. The subperiod return is calculated in the same way as the portfolio period return. To get the return for the evaluation period, the subperiod returns are then averaged. So, for example, if the evaluation period is 1 year and 12 monthly returns are calculated, the monthly returns are the subperiod returns and they are averaged to get the 1-year return. If a 3-year return is sought and 12 quarterly returns can be calculated, quarterly returns are the subperiod returns and they are averaged to get the 3-year return. The 3-year return can then be converted into an annual return by the straightforward procedure described later.

AVERAGING SUBPERIOD RETURNS

There are three methodologies that have been used in practice to calculate the average of the subperiod returns: (1) the arithmetic average rate of return, (2) the time-weighted rate of return (also called the geometric rate of return), and (3) the dollar-weighted return.

Arithmetic Average Rate of Return

The *arithmetic average rate of return* is an unweighted average of the subperiod returns. The general formula is

$$R_A = \frac{R_{p1} + R_{p2} + \cdots + R_{pN}}{N},$$

where

R_A = Arithmetic average rate of return;
R_{Pk} = Portfolio return for subperiod k, $k = 1, \ldots, N$;
N = Number of subperiods in the evaluation period.

Illustration 10-2   Suppose the portfolio subperiod returns were 12%, 25%, –15%, and –2% in months January, February, March, and April, respectively. The arithmetic average monthly return is 5%, as shown below:

$N = 4;$
$R_{P1} = .12;$
$R_{P2} = .25;$
$R_{P3} = -.15;$
$R_{P3} = -.02.$

$$R_A = \frac{.12 + .25 + (-.15) + (-0.2)}{4} = .05 = 5\%.$$

There is a major problem with using the arithmetic average rate of return. To see this problem, suppose the initial market value of a portfolio is $140 million and the market values at the end of the next 2 months are $280 million and $140 million, and assume that there are no distributions or cash inflows from the client for either month. The subperiod return for the first month (R_{P1}) is 100% and the subperiod return for the second month (R_{P2}) is –50%. The arithmetic average rate of return is then 25%. Not a bad return! But think about this number. The portfolio's initial market value was $140 million. Its market value at the end of 2 months is $140 million. The return over this 2-month evaluation period is zero. Yet, the arithmetic average rate of return says it is a whopping 25%.

Thus, it is improper to interpret the arithmetic average rate of return as a measure of the average return over an evaluation period. The proper interpretation is as follows: *it is the average value of the withdrawals (expressed as a fraction of the initial portfolio market value) that can be made at the end of each subperiod while keeping the initial portfolio market value intact.* In Illustration 10-2, in which the average monthly return is 5%, the investor can withdraw 12% of the initial portfolio market value at the end of the first month, can withdraw 25% of the initial portfolio market value at the end of the second month, must add 15% of the initial portfolio market value at the end of the third month, and must add 2% of the initial portfolio market value at the end of the fourth month. In our example of the limitation of the average arithmetic return, the average monthly return of 25% means that 100% of the initial portfolio market value ($140 million) can be withdrawn at the end of the first month and 50% must be added at the end of the second month.

Time-Weighted Rate of Return

The *time-weighted rate of return* measures the compounded rate of growth of the initial portfolio market value during the evaluation period, assuming that all cash distributions are reinvested in the portfolio. It is also commonly referred to as the *geometric rate of return* since it is computed by taking the geometric average of the portfolio subperiod returns. The general formula is

$$R_T = \left[(1 + R_{p1})(1 + R_{p2}) \cdots (1 + R_{pN}) \right]^{1/N} - 1,$$

where R_T is the time-weighted rate of return and R_{Pk} and N are as defined earlier.

Illustration 10-3   Assume that the portfolio returns were 12%, 25%, –15%, and –2% in January, February, March, and April, as in Illustration 10-2. Then the time-weighted rate of return is

$$R_T = [(1 + .12)(1 + .25)(1 + (-.15))(1 + (-.02))]^{1/4} - 1$$

$$= [(1.12)(1.25)(.85)(.98)]^{1/4} - 1 = 0.0392 = 3.92\%.$$

Since the time-weighted rate of return is 3.92% per month, $1 invested in the portfolio at the beginning of January would have grown at a rate of 3.92% per month during the 4-month evaluation period.

The time-weighted rate of return in the example where the first month's return is 100% followed by a return of 50% in the second month is 0%, as expected, as shown below:

$$R_T = [(1 + 1.00)(1 + (-.50))]^{1/2} - 1$$

$$= [(2.00)(.50)]^{1/2} - 1 = 0\%.$$

In general, the arithmetic and time-weighted average returns will give different values for the portfolio return over some evaluation period. This is because in computing the arithmetic average rate of return, the amount invested is assumed to be maintained (through additions or withdrawals) at its initial portfolio market value. The time-weighted return, on the other hand, is the return on a portfolio that varies in size because of the assumption that all proceeds are reinvested.

In general, the arithmetic average rate of return will exceed the time-weighted average rate of return. The exception is in the special situation where all the subperiod returns are the same, in which case the averages are identical. The magnitude of the difference between the two averages is smaller the less the variation in the subperiod returns over the evaluation period. For example, suppose that the evaluation period is 4 months and that the four monthly returns are as follows:

$$R_{P1} = .04, \quad R_{P2} = .06, \quad R_{P3} = .02, \quad \text{and } R_{P4} = -.02.$$

The average arithmetic rate of return is 2.5% and the time-weighted average rate of return is 2.46%—not much of a difference. In our earlier example in which we calculated an average rate of return of 25% but a time-weighted average rate of return of 0%, the large discrepancy is due to the substantial variation in the two monthly returns.

Dollar-Weighted Rate of Return

The *dollar-weighted rate of return* is computed by finding the interest rate that will make the present value of the cash flows from all the subperiods in the evaluation period plus the terminal market value of the portfolio equal to the initial market value of the portfolio. The cash flow for each subperiod reflects the difference between the cash inflows due to investment income (i.e., coupon interest) and the contribution(s) made by the client to the portfolio, and the cash outflows reflecting distributions to the client. Notice that it is not necessary to know the market value of the portfolio for each subperiod to determine the dollar-weighted rate of return.

The dollar-weighted rate of return is simply an internal rate of return calculation; hence it is also called the *internal rate of return*. The general formula for the dollar-weighted return is

$$V_0 = \frac{C_1}{(1+R_D)} + \frac{C_2}{(1+R_D)^2} + \cdots + \frac{C_N + V_N}{(1+R_D)^n},$$

where

R_D = Dollar-weighted rate of return;
V_0 = Initial market value of the portfolio;
V_N = Terminal market value of the portfolio;
C_k = Cash flow for the portfolio (cash inflows minus cash outflows) for subperiod k, with $k = 1, \ldots N$.

Illustration 10-4   Consider a portfolio with a market value of $100,000 at the beginning of July; capital withdrawals of $5,000 at the end of months July, August, and September; no cash inflows from the client in any month; and a market value at the end of September of $110,000. Then

V_0 = $100,000;
$N = 3$;
$C_1 = C_2 = C_3 = \$5,000$;
$V_3 = \$110,000$;
R_D = the interest rate that satisfies the following equation:

$$\$100,000 = \frac{\$5,000}{(1+R_D)} + \frac{\$5,000}{(1+R_D)^2} + \frac{\$5,000 + \$110,000}{(1+R_D)^3}.$$

It can be verified that the interest rate that satisfies the above expression is 8.1%. This, then, is the dollar-weighted return.

The dollar-weighted rate of return and the time-weighted rate of return will produce the same result if no withdrawals or contributions occur over the evaluation period and all investment income is reinvested. The problem with the dollar-weighted rate of return is that it is affected by factors that are beyond the control of the manager. Specifically, any contributions made by the client or withdrawals that the client requires will affect the calculated return. This makes it difficult to compare the performance of two managers.

To see this, suppose that a pension plan sponsor engaged two managers, A and B, with $10 million given to A to manage and $200 million given to B. Suppose that (1) both managers invest in identical portfolios (that is, the two portfolios have the same securities and are held in the same proportion), (2) for the following 2 months the rate of return on the two portfolios is 20% for month 1 and 50% for month 2, and (3) the amount received in investment income is in cash. Also assume that the plan sponsor does not make an additional contribution to the portfolio of either manager. Under these assumptions, it is clear that the performance of both managers would be identical. Suppose, however, that the plan sponsor withdraws $4 million from the amount given to manager A at the beginning of month 2. This means that manager A could not invest the entire amount at the end of month 1 and capture the 50% increase in the portfolio value. Manager A's net cash flow would be as follows: (1) in month 1 the net cash flow would be –$2 million since $2 million is realized in investment income and $4 million is withdrawn by the plan sponsor. The dollar-weighted rate of return is then calculated as follows:

$$\$10 = \frac{-\$2}{(1 + R_D)} + \frac{\$12}{(1 + R_D)^2} \Rightarrow R_D = 0\%.$$

For Manager B, the cash inflow for month 1 is $40 million ($200 million times 20%) and the portfolio value at the end of month 2 is $360 million ($240 million × 1.5). The dollar-weighted rate of return is:

$$\$200 = \frac{\$40}{(1 + R_D)} + \frac{\$330}{(1 + R_D)^2} \Rightarrow R_D = 38.8\%.$$

These are quite different results for two managers we agreed had identical performance. The withdrawal by the plan sponsor and the size of the withdrawal relative to the portfolio value had a significant affect on the calculated return. Notice also that even if the plan sponsor had withdrawn $4 million from the amount given to manager B at the beginning of month 2, this would not have had as significant an impact. The problem would also have occurred if we assumed that the return in month 2 is –50% and that instead of manager A realizing a withdrawal of $4 million, the plan sponsor contributed $4 million.

Despite this limitation, the dollar-weighted rate of return does provide information. It indicates information about the growth of the fund which a client will find useful. This growth, however, is not attributable to the performance of the manager because of contributions and withdrawals.

ANNUALIZING RETURNS

The evaluation period may be less than or greater than 1 year. Typically, return measures are reported as an average annual return. This requires the annualization of the subperiod returns. The subperiod returns are typically calculated for a period of less than 1 year for the reasons described earlier. The subperiod returns are then annualized using the following formula:

Annual return = (1 + Average period return)$^{\text{Number of periods in year}}$ – 1.

So, for example, suppose the evaluation period is 3 years and a monthly period return is calculated. Suppose further that the average monthly return is 2%. Then the annual return would be

Annual return = $(1.02)^{12} - 1 = 26.8\%$.

Suppose instead that the period used to calculate returns is quarterly and the average quarterly return is 3%. Then the annual return would be

Annual return = $(1.03)^4 - 1 = 12.6\%$.

AIMR PERFORMANCE PRESENTATION STANDARDS

As just demonstrated, there are subtle issues in calculating the return over the evaluation period. There are also industry concerns as to how managers should present results to clients and how managers should disclose performance data and records to prospects from whom they are seeking to obtain funds to manage.

In 1993, Committee for Performance Presentation Standards (CPPS) of the Association for Investment Management and Research (AIMR) adopted standards that represent "a set of guiding ethical principles intended to promote full disclosure and fair representation by investment managers in reporting their investment results."[1] A secondary objective of the standards is to ensure uniformity in the presentation of results so it is easier for clients to compare the performance of managers. The standards set forth how returns should be calculated.

In our illustrations of the various ways to measure portfolio return, we used the same length of time for the subperiod (e.g., a month or a quarter). The subperiod returns were averaged with the preferred method being geometric averaging. The AIMR standards require that the return measure minimize the effect of contributions and withdrawals so that cash flows beyond the control of the manager are minimized. If the subperiod return is calculated daily, the impact of contributions and withdrawals will be minimized. The time-weighted return measure can then be calculated from the daily returns.

From a practical point of view, the problem is that calculating a daily return requires that the market value of the portfolio be determined at the end of each day. While this does not present a problem for a mutual fund that must calculate the net asset value of the portfolio each business day, it is a time-consuming administrative problem for other managers. Moreover, there are fixed-income sectors in which the determination of daily prices would be difficult (e.g., esoteric derivative mortgage-backed securities and structured notes).

An alternative to the time-weighted rate of return has been suggested. This is the dollar-weighted rate of return, which as we noted earlier is less desirable in comparing the performance of managers because of the affect of withdrawals and contributions beyond the control of the manager. The advantage of this method from an operational perspective is that market values do not have to be calculated daily. The effect of withdrawals and contributions is minimized if they are small relative to the length of the subperiod. However, if the cash flow is over 10% at any time, the AIMR standards require that the portfolio be revalued on that date.[2]

Once the subperiod returns in an evaluation period are calculated, they are compounded. The AIMR standards specify that for evaluation periods of less than 1 year returns should *not* be annualized. Thus, if the evaluation period is 7 montshs and the subperiod returns are calculated monthly, the 7-month return should be reported by calculating the compounded 7-month return instead.

SUMMARY

Performance measurement involves the calculation of the return realized by a manager over some evaluation period. The rate of return expresses the dollar return in terms of the amount of the initial investment (i.e, the initial market value of the portfolio). There are three methodolo-

1   *Performance Presentation Standards: 1993* (Charlottesville, VA: Association for Investment Management and Research, 1993).
2   For a further discussion of the implementation of the AIMR Standards, see Deborah H. Miller, "How to Calculate the Numbers According to the Standards," in *Performance Reporting for Investment Managers: Applying the AIMR Performance Presentation Standards* (Charlottesville, VA: Association for Investment Management and Research, 1991).

gies that have been used in practice to calculate the average of the subperiod returns: (1) the arithmetic average rate of return, (2) the time-weighted (or geometric) rate of return, and (3) the dollar-weighted return.

The arithmetic average rate of return is the average value of the withdrawals (expressed as a fraction of the initial portfolio market value) that can be made at the end of each period while keeping the initial portfolio market value intact. The time-weighted rate of return measures the compounded rate of growth of the initial portfolio over the evaluation period, assuming that all cash distributions are reinvested in the portfolio. The dollar-weighted rate of return is computed by finding the interest rate that will make the present value of the cash flows from all the subperiods in the evaluation period plus the terminal market value of the portfolio equal to the initial market value of the portfolio.

The dollar-weighted rate of return is an internal rate of return calculation and will produce the same result as the time-weighted rate of return if (1) no withdrawals or contributions occur over the evaluation period and (2) all dividends are reinvested. Because the dollar-weighted rate of return too is affected by factors that are beyond the control of the manager (i.e., any contributions made by the client or withdrawals that the client requires), it is difficult to compare the performance of managers.

The AIMR has adopted standards for the presentation and disclosure of performance results and provides guidelines for calculating the historical return.

The formulas for the measures presented in this chapter are summarized in Exhibit 10-1.

EXHIBIT 10–1

Summary of Formulas for Measuring Historical Returns

1. Portfolio Period Return and Subperiod Return

$$R_p = \frac{V_1 - V_0 + D}{V_0},$$

where

    R_p = Portfolio period return;
    V_1 = Portfolio market value at the end of the evaluation period;
    V_0 = Portfolio market value at the beginning of the evaluation period;
    D = Cash distributions from the portfolio to the client during the evaluation period.

2. Arithmetic average rate of return:

$$R_A = \frac{R_{P1} + R_{P2} + \cdots + R_{PN}}{N}$$

where

    R_A = Arithmetic average rate of return;
    R_{Pk} = Portfolio return for subperiod k, with k = 1, . . . , N;
    N = Number of subperiods in the evaluation period.

3. Time-weighted rate of return

$$R_T = \left[(1 + R_{P1})(1 + R_{P2}) \cdots (1 + R_{PN}) \right]^{1/N} - 1,$$

where

    R_T = Time-weighted rate of return;
    R_{Pk} = Portfolio return for subperiod k, k = 1, . . . ·, N;
    N = Number of subperiods in the evaluation period.

4. Dollar-weighted rate of return:

$$V_0 = \frac{C_1}{(1 + R_D)} + \frac{C_2}{(1 + R_D)^2} + \cdots + \frac{C_N + V_N}{(1 + R_D)^n},$$

where

    R_D = Dollar-weighted rate of return;
    V_0 = Initial market value of the portfolio;
    V_N = Terminal market value of the portfolio;
    C_k = Cash flow for the portfolio (cash inflows minus cash outflows) for subperiod k, with k = 1, 2, . . . , N.

5. Annualizing returns:

$$\text{Annual return} = (1 + \text{Average period return})^{\text{Number of periods in year}} - 1.$$

IV

PRICE VOLATILITY FOR OPTION-FREE BONDS

CHAPTER

11

⑥ PRICE VOLATILITY PROPERTIES OF OPTION-FREE BONDS

To implement effective portfolio trading and risk-control strategies, it is necessary to understand the price volatility characteristics of bonds. The four chapters in this section of the book focus on bond price volatility. In this chapter, general price volatility properties of option-free bonds are discussed, as well as bond characteristics that determine price volatility.

A CLOSER LOOK AT THE PRICE/YIELD RELATIONSHIP FOR OPTION-FREE BONDS

In Chapter 2 we demonstrated a fundamental principle of all option-free bonds (a bond that does not have an embedded option): *the price of a bond changes in the opposite direction of the change in the required yield for the bond.* This principle follows from the fact that the price of an option-free bond is equal to the present value of its expected cash flows. An increase (decrease) in the required return decreases (increases) the present value of its expected cash flows, and therefore, the bond's price.

Exhibit 11-1 illustrates this property for 12 hypothetical bonds: three bonds with the same coupon rate but different maturities (5, 15, and 30 years), and four bonds with the same maturity but different coupon rates (0%, 8%, 10%, and 14%). These 12 bonds are used in this and the following three chapters to demonstrate the bond price volatility of option-free bonds and measures of bond price volatility.

For each bond in Exhibit 11-1 the price of the bond (with par equal to 100) is shown for 13 yield levels. The top panel shows the price for yield levels from 10% to 13%; the bottom panel, the price for yield levels from 7% to 10%.

If the price/yield relationship for any of the 12 bonds in Exhibit 11-1 is graphed, the shape of the graph would be as shown in Exhibit 11-2. As the required yield rises, the price of the option-free bond declines. However, the relationship is not linear (that is, it is not a straight line). The price/yield relationship for all option-free bonds takes this nonlinear shape, referred to as *convex.*

EXHIBIT 11-1
Price/Yield Relationship for 12 Hypothetical Bonds

Coupon (%)	Term (years)	Yield Level							
		10.00%	10.01%	10.10%	10.50%	11.00%	12.00%	13.00%
.00%	5	$ 61.39	$ 61.36	$ 61.10	$ 59.95	$ 58.54	$ 55.84	$ 53.27
.00	15	23.14	23.10	22.81	21.54	20.06	17.41	15.12
.00	30	5.35	5.34	5.20	4.64	4.03	3.03	2.29
8.00	5	92.28	92.24	91.91	90.46	88.69	85.28	82.03
8.00	15	84.63	84.56	83.95	81.32	78.20	72.47	67.35
8.00	30	81.07	80.99	80.29	77.30	73.83	67.68	62.42
10.00	5	100.00	99.96	99.61	98.09	96.23	92.64	89.22
10.00	15	100.00	99.92	99.24	96.26	92.73	86.24	80.41
10.00	30	100.00	99.91	99.06	95.46	91.28	83.84	77.45
14.00	5	115.44	115.40	115.02	113.35	111.31	107.36	103.59
14.00	15	130.74	130.65	129.81	126.15	121.80	113.76	106.53
14.00	30	137.86	137.73	136.60	131.79	126.17	116.16	107.52

EXHIBIT 11-1
Concluded

					Yield Level			
Coupon (%)	Term (years)	10.00%	9.99%	9.90%	9.50%	9.00%	8.00%	7.00%
.00%	5	$ 61.39	$ 61.42	$ 61.68	$ 62.87	$ 64.39	$ 67.56	$ 70.89
.00	15	23.14	23.17	23.47	24.85	26.70	30.83	35.63
.00	30	5.35	5.37	5.51	6.18	7.13	9.51	12.69
8.00	5	92.28	92.32	92.65	94.14	96.04	100.00	104.16
8.00	15	84.63	84.70	85.31	88.13	91.86	100.00	109.20
8.00	30	81.07	81.15	81.87	85.19	89.68	100.00	112.47
10.00	5	100.00	100.04	100.39	101.95	103.96	108.11	112.47
10.00	15	100.00	100.08	100.77	103.96	108.14	117.29	127.57
10.00	30	100.00	100.09	100.95	104.94	110.32	122.62	137.42
14.00	5	115.44	115.49	115.87	117.59	119.78	124.33	129.11
14.00	15	130.74	130.84	131.69	135.60	140.72	151.88	164.37
14.00	30	137.86	137.99	139.13	144.44	151.60	167.87	187.31

EXHIBIT 11–2

Shape of Price/Yield Relationship for an Option-Free Bond

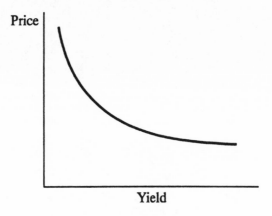

While all option-free bonds will have the convex shape shown in Exhibit 11-2, the curvature of every option-free bond will be different. As we will see in this chapter and the following three, it is this convex shape that holds the key to assessing the performance of a bond and a portfolio of bonds.

It is important to keep in mind that the price/yield relationship that we have discussed refers to an instantaneous change in the yield. As we explained in Chapter 2, assuming no change in the perceived credit risk of the issuer as a bond moves toward maturity, there are two factors that influence the price of any option-free bond. First, the bond's price will change as the required yield changes, as we know. Second, for discount and premium bonds the bond's price will change even if yields remain the same. In particular, the price of a discount bond will increase as it moves toward maturity, reaching par value at the maturity date; for a premium bond, the bond's price will decrease as it moves closer to maturity, finally declining to the par value at the maturity date.

THE PRICE VOLATILITY CHARACTERISTICS OF OPTION-FREE BONDS

To investigate bond price volatility in terms of percentage price change, let's assume that the prevailing yield in the market is 10% for all 12 bonds. The dollar price change per $100 of par value for various changes in yield is shown in Exhibit 11-3. Exhibit 11-4 shows the corresponding percentage change in each bond's price. The percentage price change shown in Exhibit 11-4 is found by dividing the dollar price change in Exhibit 11-3 by the price of the bond at a 10% yield, as shown in Exhibit 11-1.

For example, consider the 8%, 15-year bond. The price for this bond if the required yield is 10% is $84.63. If the required yield increases 100 basis points to 11%, the price of this bond would fall to $78.20. The dollar price change per $100 of par value is – $6.43, as shown in Exhibit 11-3. The percentage price change is then

EXHIBIT 11-3

Dollar Price Change per $100 of Par Value as Yield Changes for 12 Hypothetical Bonds

		Change in Basis Points from 10%					
		1	10	50	100	200	300
		New Yield Level					
Coupon (%)	Term (years)	10.01%	10.10%	10.50%	11.00%	12.00%	13.00%
.00%	5	$ -.03	$ -.26	$ -1.15	$ -1.41	$ -2.70	$ -2.57
.00	15	-.03	-.33	-1.59	-3.07	-5.73	-8.02
.00	30	-.02	-.15	-.71	-1.33	-2.32	-3.07
8.00	5	-.04	-.37	-1.81	-3.58	-7.00	-10.25
8.00	15	-.07	-.68	-3.31	-6.43	-12.16	-17.27
8.00	30	-.08	-.78	-3.78	-7.25	-13.39	-18.65
10.00	5	-.04	-.39	-1.91	-3.77	-7.36	-10.78
10.00	15	-.08	-.76	-3.74	-7.27	-13.76	-19.59
10.00	30	-.09	-.94	-4.54	-8.72	-16.16	-22.55
14.00	5	-.04	-.42	-2.09	-4.14	-8.08	-11.85
14.00	15	-.09	-.94	-4.59	-8.94	-16.98	-24.22
14.00	30	-.13	-1.25	-6.07	-11.68	-21.70	-30.34

EXHIBIT 11-3
Concluded

| | | Change in Basis Points from 10% | | | | | |
| | | −1 | −10 | −50 | −100 | −200 | −300 |
Coupon (%)	Term (years)	9.99%	9.90%	9.50%	9.00%	8.00%	7.00%
				New Yield Level			
.00%	5	$ .03	$ .29	$ 1.48	$ 3.00	$ 6.17	$ 9.50
.00	15	.03	.33	1.72	3.56	7.69	12.49
.00	30	.02	.16	.82	1.78	4.15	7.34
8.00	5	.04	.37	1.86	3.77	7.72	11.88
8.00	15	.07	.69	3.51	7.23	15.37	24.57
8.00	30	.08	.79	4.12	8.61	18.93	31.40
10.00	5	.04	.39	1.95	3.96	8.11	12.47
10.00	15	.08	.77	3.96	8.14	17.29	27.59
10.00	30	.09	.95	4.94	10.32	22.62	37.42
14.00	5	.04	.42	2.14	4.34	8.89	13.66
14.00	15	.09	.95	4.85	9.98	21.13	33.63
14.00	30	.13	1.27	6.58	13.74	30.01	49.45

EXHIBIT 11-4

Percentage Price Change as Yield Changes for 12 Hypothetical Bonds

Coupon (%)	Term (years)	1	10	50	100	200	300
				Change in Basis Points from 10%			
		10.01%	10.10%	10.50%	11.00%	12.00%	13.00%
				New Yield Level			
.00%	5	-.05%	-.47%	-2.35%	-4.64%	-9.04%	-13.22%
.00	15	-.14	-1.42	-6.89	-13.28	-24.75	-34.66
.00	30	-.29	-2.82	-13.30	-24.80	-43.38	-57.30
8.00	5	-.04	-.40	-1.97	-3.88	-7.58	-11.11
8.00	15	-.08	-.80	-3.91	-7.60	-14.37	-20.41
8.00	30	-.10	-.96	-4.66	-8.94	-16.52	-23.01
10.00	5	-.04	-.39	-1.91	-3.77	-7.36	-10.78
10.00	15	-.08	-.76	-3.74	-7.27	-13.76	-19.59
10.00	30	-.09	-.94	-4.54	-8.72	-16.16	-22.55
14.00	5	-.04	-.37	-1.81	-3.58	-7.00	-10.26
14.00	15	-.07	-.72	-3.51	-6.84	-12.99	-18.52
14.00	30	-.09	-.91	-4.40	-8.48	-15.74	-22.01

EXHIBIT 11–4

Concluded

Coupon (%)	Term (years)	Change in Basis Points from 10%					
		−1	−10	−50	−100	−200	−300
		New Yield Level					
		9.99%	9.90%	9.50%	9.00%	8.00%	7.00%
.00%	5	.05%	.48%	2.41%	4.89%	10.04%	15.48%
.00	15	.14	1.44	7.41	15.40	33.25	53.98
.00	30	.29	2.90	15.38	33.16	77.57	137.10
8.00	5	.04	.40	2.02	4.08	8.37	12.87
8.00	15	.08	.81	4.14	8.54	18.16	29.03
8.00	30	.10	.98	5.08	10.62	23.35	38.73
10.00	5	.04	.39	1.95	3.96	8.11	12.47
10.00	15	.08	.77	3.96	8.14	17.29	27.59
10.00	30	.09	.95	4.94	10.32	22.62	37.42
14.00	5	.04	.37	1.86	3.76	7.70	11.84
14.00	15	.07	.73	3.71	7.63	16.16	25.72
14.00	30	.09	.92	4.78	9.96	21.77	35.87

$$\frac{\$78.20 - \$84.63}{\$84.63} = -.076 \text{ or } -7.60\%.$$

This is shown in Exhibit 11-4.

An examination of Exhibits 11-3 and 11-4 reveals the following four properties about price volatility of option-free bonds.

Property 1: Price Volatility Is Not the Same for All Bonds   Although the prices of all option-free bonds move in the opposite direction of the change in yield, for a given change in the yield, the price change is not the same for all bonds. A natural question is what characteristics of a bond determine its price volatility. We'll focus on this question in the next section.

Property 2: Price Volatility Is Approximately Symmetric for Small Yield Changes
For very small changes in yield, the percentage price change for a given bond is roughly the same, whether the yield increases or decreases. For example, look at the top panel of both Exhibits 11-3 and 11-4. For a 10-basis-point change in the required yield, the 10%, 30-year bond's price would decrease by $0.94 per $100 of par value or 0.94% of the initial price. Now in the bottom panel of the two exhibits, note that the 10%, 30-year bond's price would increase by $0.95 per $100 of par value or 0.95% of the initial price for a 10-basis-point decrease in the required yield.

Property 3: Price Volatility Is Not Symmetric for Large Yield Changes   For large changes in yield, the percentage price change is not the same for an increase in yield as it is for a decrease in yield. Once again, look at the 10%, 30-year coupon bond. Note that if the required yield increases by 300 basis points (from 10% to 13%), the price decline per $100 of par value would be $22.55 or 22.55% of the initial price; for a 300-basis-point decrease in the yield, the price increase per $100 of par value would be $37.42 or 37.42% of the initial price.

Property 4: For Large Yield Changes Price Increases Are Greater Than Price Decreases   For a given large change in yield, the price increase is greater than the price decrease. This can be seen in Exhibits 11-3 and 11-4 by comparing the upper panel (which shows price volatility for increases in yield) to the lower panel (which shows price volatility for decreases in yield). For each bond, the price change is larger in the lower panel than in the upper panel for a given large change in yield.

The reason for this property lies in the convex shape of the price/yield relationship. This is illustrated graphically in Exhibit 11-5. Suppose the initial required yield is Y in Exhibit 11-5. The corresponding initial price is P. Consider large equal basis point changes in the initial yield. Y_1 and Y_2 indicate the lower and higher yields, respectively; the corresponding prices are denoted P_1 and P_2. The vertical distance from the yield axis to the price/yield relationship represents the price. The distance between P_1 and P measures the price increase if the yield decreases; the distance between P and P_2 measures the price decrease if the yield increases. The diagram clarifies that the price increase will be greater than the price decrease for an equal change in basis points.

This will always be true when the curve is convex, and because all option-free bonds have a convex price/yield relationship, this property will always hold for option-free bonds. Exhibit

EXHIBIT 11–5

Illustration of Property 4

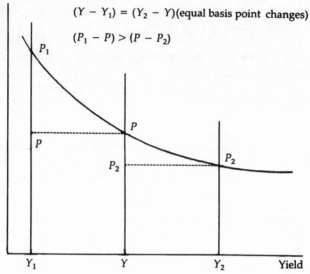

EXHIBIT 11–6

The Impact of Less Convexity on Property 4

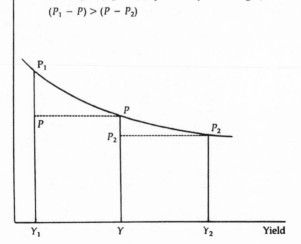

11-6 shows a less convex price/yield relationship than is shown in Exhibit 11-5. While the property still holds, the price gain when the yield falls is not that much greater than the price loss for an equal basis point increase in the yield.

An implication of Property 4 is that if an investor owns a bond (that is, is long a bond), the price appreciation that will be realized if the yield decreases is greater than the capital loss that will be realized if the yield rises by the same number of basis points. For an investor who is short a bond, the reverse is true: the potential capital loss is greater than the potential capital gain if the yield changes by a given number of basis points.

CHARACTERISTICS OF A BOND THAT AFFECT ITS PRICE VOLATILITY

Property 1 states that price volatility is not the same for each bond. There are two characteristics of an option-free bond that determine its price volatility: (1) coupon and (2) term to maturity.

Characteristic 1: Price Volatility Is Greater, the Lower the Coupon Rate[1]   For a given term to maturity and initial yield, the price volatility of a bond is greater the lower the coupon rate. This characteristic can be seen by comparing the 0%, 8%, 10%, and 14% coupon bonds with the same maturity. For example, if the yield for all the 30-year bonds is 10% and the yield rises to 12% (i.e., a 200-basis-point increase), the 0% coupon bond will fall by 43.38% while the 14%, 30-year bond will fall by a smaller percentage, 15.74%.[2]

The investment implication is that bonds selling at a deep discount will have greater price volatility than bonds selling near or above par. Zero-coupon bonds will have the greatest price volatility for a given maturity.

Characteristic 2: Price Volatility Increases with Maturity   For a given coupon rate and initial yield, the longer the term to maturity the greater the price volatility. This can be seen in Exhibit 11-4 by comparing the 5-year bonds to the 30-year bonds with the same coupon. For example, if the yield increases 200 basis points from 10% to 12%, the 10%, 30-year bond's price will fall by 16.16%, while that of the 5-year bond will fall by only 7.36%.

The investment implication is that an investor expecting interest rates to fall, all other factors constant, should hold bonds with long maturities in the portfolio. To reduce a portfolio's price volatility in anticipation of a rise in interest rates, bonds with short maturities should be held in the portfolio.

The Effect of the Yield Level on Price Volatility

So far, we have described how the characteristics of a bond affect its price volatility. But we cannot ignore the fact that credit considerations cause different bonds to trade at different yields, even if they have the same coupon and maturity. How, then, holding other factors constant, does

---

1   This property does not necessarily hold for long-term deep discount coupon bonds.
2   Notice that while the percentage price change is greater, the lower the coupon rate, the dollar price change is smaller, the lower the coupon rate.

EXHIBIT 11-7

Price Change for a 100-Basis-Point Change in Yield for 10%, 15-Year Bonds Trading at Different Yield Levels

Yield Level (%)	Initial Price ($)	New Price ($)*	Price Decline ($)	Percent Decline (%)
7%	$127.57	$117.29	$10.28	8.1%
8	117.29	108.14	9.15	7.8
9	108.14	100.00	8.14	7.5
10	100.00	92.73	7.27	7.3
11	92.73	86.24	6.49	7.0
12	86.24	80.41	5.83	6.8
13	80.41	75.18	5.23	6.5

* As a result of a 100-basis-point increase in yield.

the yield to maturity affect a bond's price volatility? As it turns out, the higher the yield to maturity that a bond trades at, the lower the price volatility.

To see this, compare a 10%, 15-year bond trading at various yield levels as shown in Exhibit 11-7. The first column shows the yield level each bond is trading at and the second column the initial price. The third column indicates the bond's price if yields change by 100 basis points. The fourth and fifth columns show the dollar price change and the percentage price change, respectively. As can be seen from these last two columns, the higher the initial yield, the less the price volatility.

This can also be seen in Exhibit 11-8. When the yield level is high (Y_H in the exhibit), a given change in yield will not produce as large a change in the price of a bond as when the yield level is low (Y_L in the exhibit).

An implication of this is that, for a given change in yields, price volatility is greater when yield levels in the market are high, and price volatility is lower when yield levels are low. For example, in the early 1980s when yields on long-term Treasury bonds were in the neighborhood of 14%, a yield change of 10 basis points produced a greater price change than in 1992 when long-term Treasury yields were 7.5%. Also, another implication is that high-yield bonds (more popularly referred to as "junk" bonds) will have less price volatility for a given change in yield than Treasury bonds because the former trade at a higher yield level than the latter.

SUMMARY

In this chapter we have discussed the price volatility properties of option-free bonds. Four properties of bond price volatility are demonstrated, and two characteristics that affect bond price volatility (coupon rate and maturity) are illustrated. The yield level affects price volatility.

EXHIBIT 11-8

The Effect of the Yield Level on Price Volatility

$$(Y_H' - Y_H) = (Y_H - Y_H'') = (Y_L' - Y_L) = (Y_L - Y_L'')$$
$$(P_H - P_H') < (P_L - P_L') \text{ and}$$
$$(P_H - P_H'') < (P_L - P_L'')$$

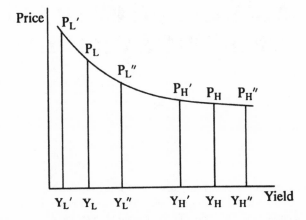

The lower the yield level, all other factors constant, the greater the price volatility for a given change in yield.

What market participants would like to have is a measure that can be used to quantify the price volatility of a bond. For example, suppose a portfolio manager expects that interest rates will fall and is considering purchasing one of the following two bonds: (1) bond A, 7%, 22-year bond selling to yield 8%, and (2) bond B, a zero-coupon, 15-year bond selling to yield 8.40%. With interest rates expected to decline, the portfolio manager will want to purchase the bond that offers the greater price volatility. Which has higher price volatility? On the one hand, bond B has a lower coupon than bond A, so it would seem that bond B has a greater price volatility. On the other hand, bond A has a longer maturity than bond B, so it would seem that bond A has more price volatility. Complicating this further is the fact that the two bonds are trading at different yield levels. In fact, none of the three factors (coupon rate, maturity, or yield) is equal for the two bonds. The purpose of the next two chapters is to discuss measures of bond price volatility appropriate for such a situation. One of the things we do know is that any measure of price volatility should take into consideration the three factors that affect price volatility: coupon rate, maturity, and yield level.

12

⑥ PRICE VOLATILITY MEASURES: PVBP AND YV OF A PRICE CHANGE

$\mathbf{P}$ortfolio managers, arbitrageurs, hedgers, and traders need to have a way to measure a bond's price volatility in order to implement strategies. The three measures commonly used are (1) price value of a basis point, (2) yield value of a price change, and (3) duration. The first two measures are the subject of this chapter; duration is discussed in the next chapter.

PRICE VALUE OF A BASIS POINT

The *price value of a basis point,* also referred to as the *dollar value of a basis point* or *DV01,* is the change in the price of the bond if the yield changes by one basis point. Note that this measure of price volatility indicates *dollar* price volatility as opposed to price volatility as a *percentage* of the initial price. The price value of a basis point is expressed as the absolute value of the change in price.

Property 2 of the price/yield relationship explained in the previous chapter states that for small changes in yield, price volatility is the same, regardless of the direction of the change in yield. Therefore, it does not make any difference if we increase or decrease the yield by one basis point to compute the price value of a basis point.

We will show how to calculate the price value of a basis point using the 12 bonds in Exhibit 11-1 of the previous chapter. For each bond, the initial price, the price after increasing the yield by one basis point (from 10.00% to 10.01%), and the price value of a basis point per $100 of par value (the difference between the two prices) are shown in the top panel of Exhibit 12-1. Similarly, if we decrease the yield by one basis point, from 10.00% to 9.99%, we would find approximately the same price value of a basis point for the 12 bonds, as shown in the bottom panel of Exhibit 12-1.

Exhibits 12-2A and 12-2B show graphically what happens to the price value of a basis point at different yields. Notice that the price value of a basis point is smaller, the higher the initial yield. The investment implication is that at higher yields, dollar price volatility is less.

Computation of the Price Value of a Basis Point

Bond Coupon (%)	Term (years)	Price ($) 10.00%	Price ($) 10.01%	Price Value of a Basis Point ($)*
.00%	5	$ 61.3913	$ 61.3621	$.0292
.00	15	23.1377	23.1047	.0330
.00	30	5.3536	5.3383	.0153
8.00	5	92.2783	92.2415	.0367
8.00	15	84.6275	84.5595	.0681
8.00	30	81.0707	80.9920	.0787
10.00	5	100.0000	99.9614	.0386
10.00	15	100.0000	99.9232	.0768
10.00	30	100.0000	99.9054	.0946
14.00	5	115.4435	115.4011	.0423
14.00	15	130.7449	130.6506	.0943
14.00	30	137.8586	137.7323	.1263

Bond Coupon (%)	Term (years)	Price ($) 10.00%	Price ($) 9.99%	Price Value of a Basis Point ($)
.00%	5	$ 61.3913	$ 61.4206	$.0292
.00	15	23.1377	23.1708	.0331
.00	30	5.3536	5.3689	.0153
8.00	5	92.2783	92.3150	.0367
8.00	15	84.6275	84.6957	.0681
8.00	30	81.0707	81.1496	.0788
10.00	5	100.0000	100.0386	.0386
10.00	15	100.0000	100.0769	.0769
10.00	30	100.0000	100.0947	.0947
14.00	5	115.4435	115.4858	.0424
14.00	15	130.7449	130.8393	.0944
14.00	30	137.8586	137.9851	.1265

*Absolute value per $100 of par value.

E X H I B I T 12–2

Graphical Illustration of the Price Value of a Basis Point

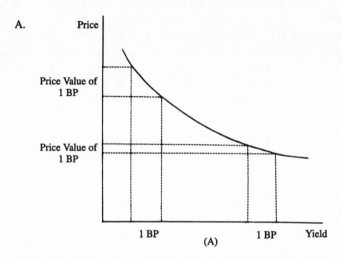

A.

(A)

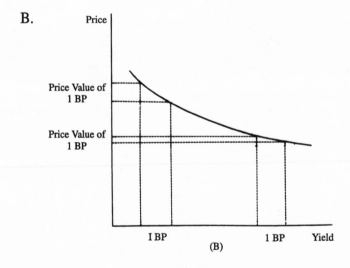

B.

(B)

Also notice that the larger the price value of a basis point, the greater the convexity. This can be seen by comparing the price value of a basis point in Exhibit 12-2A to that in Exhibit 12-2B, in which the curve is less convex.

The Price Value of More Than One Basis Point

In implementing a strategy, some investors will calculate the price value of a change of more than one basis point. The principle of calculating the price value of any number of basis points is the same. The price value of x basis points is found by computing the difference between the initial price and the price if the yield is changed by x basis points. For example, the price value per $100 of par value for several values of x for the 10% coupon, 15-year bond is found as follows if the yield is increased:

Change (x, in Basis Points)	Initial Price (10% yield; $)	Price at 10% + x yield ($)	Price Value of x Basis Points ($)
10	$100.00	$99.2357	$ .7643
50	100.00	96.2640	3.7360
100	100.00	92.7331	7.2669

For small changes in yield (such as 10 basis points), the price value of x basis points is roughly that found by multiplying the price value of one basis point by x. For example, the price value of 10 basis points computed by multiplying the price value of a basis point, namely, $.08, by 10 gives $.80, which is very close to the price value of 10 basis points computed above. In fact, the approximation is much better than indicated here because we computed the price value of a basis point to only two decimal places.

For a decrease in the yield, the price value of an x-basis-point change per $100 of par value is

Change (x, in basis points)	Initial Price (10% yield; $)	Price at 10% – x Yield ($)	Price Value of x Basis Points ($)
10	$100.00	$100.7730	$ .7730
50	100.00	103.9551	3.9551
100	100.00	108.1444	8.1444

Once again, note the approximate symmetry of the price change for small changes (10 basis points) in yield (Property 2 of the price/yield relationship). For larger changes in yield, however, there will be a difference between the price value of an x-basis-point movement, depending on whether the yield is increased or decreased. Many investors who use the price value of a large basis point movement in implementing a strategy will compute the average of the two price values. For example, the price value of 100 basis points would be approximated by averaging $7.2669 and $8.1444 to give $7.7057.

Application of Price Value of a Basis Point to Portfolio and Dealer Position

Suppose that a portfolio manager wants to know the price value of a basis point for a portfolio. Let's assume the following portfolio, comprised of three of our hypothetical bonds, all priced to yield 10%:

Bond	Par Amount Owned ($)	Price ($)
10%, 5-year	$4 million	$4,000,000
8%, 15-year	5 million	4,231,375
14%, 30-year	1 million	1,378,586

The price of a basis point per $100 of par value for each of these bonds, assuming an increase of 1 basis point, is:

Bond	Par Amount Owned ($)	Price Value for	
		$100 par ($)	Amount Owned ($)
10%, 5-year	$4 million	$.0386	$1,544
8%, 15-year	5 million	.0681	3,405
14%, 30-year	1 million	.1263	1,263

Thus, the portfolio's exposure to a one-basis-point movement is $6,212, that is, $1,544 + $3,405 + $1,263.

The same analysis can be used to determine the exposure of a bond dealer's inventory.

Price Change Versus Percentage Change

So far we have dealt with the dollar price change. If we want to know the percentage price change, we can find it by dividing the price value of a basis point by the initial price. That is,

$$\text{Percentage price change} = \frac{\text{Price value of a basis point}}{\text{Initial price}}.$$

Application to Hedging

To hedge a portfolio or bond position, a portfolio manager or trader wants to take an opposite position in a cash market security (or securities) or in a derivative instrument (option or futures contract) so that any loss in the position held is offset by a gain in the opposite position. To do so, the *dollar* price volatility of the position used to hedge must equal the *dollar* price volatility of the position to be hedged. That is, the objective in hedging is

Dollar price change in position to be hedged
= Dollar price change of hedging vehicle.

The hedger encounters two problems. First, for a given change in yield, the dollar price volatility of the bond to be hedged will not necessarily be equal to the dollar price volatility of the hedging vehicle. For example, if yields change by 50 basis points, the price of the bond to be hedged may change by X, while the price of the hedging vehicle may change by more or less than X. The second problem is that factors that result in a change in the yield of a given number of basis points for the bond to be hedged may not result in a change of the same number of basis points for the hedging vehicle. That is, if yields change by x basis points for the bond to be hedged, the yield for the hedging vehicle may change by more or less than x basis points.

Consequently, a portfolio manager or trader attempting to hedge a $10 million long position in some bond will not necessarily take a $10 million short position in the vehicle used for hedging because the relative dollar price volatility of the two positions will not necessarily be the same. The hedger would have to consider the relative dollar price volatility of the two positions in constructing the hedge. As a result, the objective in hedging can be restated as follows:

Dollar price change of bond to be hedged

= Dollar price change of hedging vehicle

$\times \dfrac{\text{Dollar price volatility of bond to be hedged}}{\text{Dollar price volatility of hedging vehicle}}$.

The last ratio is commonly referred to as the *hedge ratio*. The hedge ratio can be computed from the price value of a basis point by the following formula:

$\dfrac{\text{Price value of a basis point for bond to be hedged}}{\text{Price value of a basis point for hedging vehicle}}$

$\times \dfrac{\text{Change in yield for bond to be hedged}}{\text{Change in yield for hedging vehicle}}$.

The first ratio shows the price change for the bond to be hedged relative to the price change for the hedging vehicle, both based on a yield change of one basis point. The second ratio indicates the relative change in the yield of the two instruments. This ratio is commonly referred to as the *yield beta* and is estimated using the statistical technique of regression analysis, which is described in Chapter 23. Therefore, the hedge ratio can be rewritten as

$\dfrac{\text{Price value of a basis point for bond to be hedged}}{\text{Price value of a basis point for hedging vehicle}} \times \text{Yield beta}$.

To illustrate this relationship, we'll look at how to hedge a $10 million long position in a 15-year, 8% coupon bond selling to yield 10% with a 10% coupon bond with the same maturity and selling at the same yield. The following information is known:

Bond to be hedged = 15-year, 8% bond selling to yield 10%;
Hedging vehicle = 15-year, 10% bond selling to yield 10%;

For bond to be hedged,
Price value of a basis point per $100 of par = 0.0681;

For hedging vehicle,
Price value of a basis point per $100 of par = 0.0768.

For this illustration, we shall assume that the yield beta is 1. The hedge ratio is then

$$\frac{0.0681}{0.0768} \times 1 = .8867.$$

The hedge ratio of .8867 means that for every $1 of par value of the 15-year, 8% coupon bond to be hedged, the hedger should short $.8867 of $1 par of the hedging vehicle. Since this illustration involves a long position of $10 million of the 15-year, 8% coupon bond, a short position of $8.867 million of the 15-year, 10% bond should be taken.

To demonstrate that this hedge ratio will result in equal dollar price changes for the bond to be hedged and the hedging vehicle, suppose interest rates rise by 10 basis points. The price of the bond to be hedged will decline from $84.6275 per $100 of par to $83.9505, resulting in a loss for the $10 million position of $67,700. The short position, however, will gain. The price of the 15-year, 10% coupon bond will decline from $100 per $100 of par to $99.2357, resulting in a gain of $67,770 for the $8.867 million position. The gain is almost identical to the loss.

YIELD VALUE (YV) OF A PRICE CHANGE

Some investors use another measure of the dollar price volatility of a bond: the change in the yield for a specified price change. This is found by first calculating the bond's yield if the bond's price is increased by, say, $X. Then the difference between the initial yield and the new yield is the yield value of the $X price change.

The smaller the yield value of an $X price change, the greater the *dollar* price volatility. This is because it would take a larger $X price movement to change the yield a specified number of basis points. This is illustrated graphically in Exhibit 12-3.

EXHIBIT 12–3

Graphical Illustration of Yield Value of $X Price Change

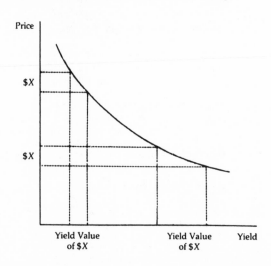

Yield Value of a 32nd for Treasury Securities

Treasury notes and bonds are quoted in 32nds of a percentage point of par. Consequently, investors in this market compute the yield value of a 32nd. The yield value of a 32nd for three 10% coupon bonds selling to yield 10% is computed below.

Decreasing the price by a 32nd:

Bond	Initial Price − One 32nd ($)	Yield at New Price	Initial Yield	Yield Value of a 32nd
10%, 5-year	$99.96875	.1000810	.10000	.0000810
10%, 15-year	99.96875	.1000407	.10000	.0000407
10%, 30-year	99.96875	.1000330	.10000	.0000330

Increasing the price by a 32nd:

Bond	Initial Price + One 32nd ($)	Yield at New Price	Initial Yield	Yield Value of a 32nd
10%, 5-year	$100.03125	.0999190	.10000	.0000810
10%, 15-year	100.03125	.0999593	.10000	.0000407
10%, 30-year	100.03125	.0999670	.10000	.0000330

Notice that the yield value of a 32nd for the 30-year bond is lower than for the 5-year bond. This agrees with our earlier statement that the lower the yield value of an X price change, the greater the dollar price volatility.

Yield Value of an 8th for Corporate and Municipal Securities

Corporate bonds and municipal bonds are traded in 8ths of a percentage point. Consequently, investors in these markets frequently compute the yield value of an 8th. The calculation of the yield value of an 8th for the three 10% coupon bonds selling to yield 10% is shown below.

Decreasing the price by an 8th:

Bond	Initial Price − One 8th ($)	Yield at New Price	Initial Yield	Yield Value of an 8th
10%, 5-year	$99.875	.10032	.10000	.00032
10%, 15-year	99.875	.10016	.10000	.00016
10%, 30-year	99.875	.10013	.10000	.00013

Increasing the price by an 8th:

Bond	Initial Price + One 8th ($)	Yield at New Price	Initial Yield	Yield Value of an 8th
10%, 5-year	$100.125	.09968	.10000	.00032
10%, 15-year	100.125	.09984	.10000	.00016
10%, 30-year	100.125	.09987	.10000	.00013

Application to Hedging

The hedge ratio can be rewritten as follows by using the yield value of a price change:

$$\frac{\text{Yield value of a price change for hedging vehicle}}{\text{Yield value of a price change for bond to be hedged}} \times \text{Yield beta.}$$

SUMMARY

There are three commonly used measures of price volatility: (1) price value of a basis point, (2) yield value of a price change, and (3) duration. Our focus in this chapter has been on the first two measures.

The price value of basis point (also called the dollar value of a basis point or DV01) is a measure of the dollar price change of a bond when the yield changes by one basis point. The yield value of a price change indicates how the yield will change if the price is changed by a certain amount. Those dealing with Treasury securities compute the yield value of a price change of one 32nd; for corporate and municipal securities, the yield of a price change of one 8th is computed.

These two measures can be used in hedging applications to calculate the appropriate hedge ratio. The principles can be extended to weighting trades so that a strategy employed will not be affected by yield changes.

13

⑥ PRICE VOLATILITY MEASURES: DURATION

In this chapter we discuss the third measure of bond price volatility: duration. We illustrate some applications of duration in portfolio strategies and discuss its limitations.

MACAULAY DURATION

In 1938, Frederick Macaulay constructed a measure that he could use as a proxy for the length of time a bond investment was outstanding.[1] He referred to this number as the *duration* of a bond and defined it as ·a weighted average term-to-maturity of the bond's cash flows. The weights in this weighted average are the present value of each cash flow as a percent of the present value of all the bond's cash flows (i.e., the weights are the present value of each cash flow as a percent of the bond's price). As we will see, Macaulay's measure is linked to the price volatility of a bond. First, let's look at how this measure, referred to as *Macaulay duration*, is computed.

Computing Macaulay Duration

Mathematically, Macaulay duration is computed as follows:

Macaulay duration (in periods)

$$= \frac{(1)\ PVCF_1 + (2)\ PVCF_2 + (3)\ PVCF_3 + \ldots + (n)\ PVCF_n}{PVTCF},$$

where

$PVCF_t$ = Present value of the cash flow in period t discounted at the prevailing period yield (in the case of a semiannual-pay bond, one-half the yield to maturity);

---

1. Frederick Macaulay, *Some Theoretical Problems Suggested by the Movements of Interest Rates, Bond Yields and Stock Prices in the United States Since 1865* (National Bureau of Economic Research, 1938).

t = Period when the cash flow is expected to be received ($t = 1, \ldots, n$);

n = Number of periods until maturity (specifically, number of years to maturity times k, rounded down to the nearest whole number);[2]

k = Number of periods, or payments, per year (i.e., $k = 2$ for semiannual-pay bonds, $k = 12$ for monthly-pay bonds);

$PVTCF$ = Total present value of the cash flow of the bond, where the present value is determined by using the prevailing yield to maturity.

For an *option-free bond* with semiannual payments, the cash flow for periods 1 to $n - 1$ is one-half the annual coupon interest. The cash flow in period n is the semiannual coupon interest plus the maturity value. Since the bond's price is equal to its cash flow discounted at the prevailing yield to maturity, $PVTCF$ is the current market price *plus* accrued interest.

The formula for Macaulay duration gives a value in terms of periods. Dividing by the number of payments per year converts Macaulay duration to years. That is,

$$\text{Macaulay duration (in years)} = \frac{\text{Macaulay duration (in periods)}}{k}.$$

Exhibits 13-1 and 13-2 show the calculation of Macaulay duration for two of our hypothetical bonds (the 10%, 5-year bond and the 14%, 5-year bond), assuming each bond is selling to yield 10%. The Macaulay duration in years for our 12 hypothetical bonds is given below:

Bond	Macaulay Duration (years)
0%, 5-year	5.00
0%, 15-year	15.00
0%, 30-year	30.00
8%, 5-year	4.18
8%, 15-year	8.45
8%, 30-year	10.20
10%, 5-year	4.05
10%, 15-year	8.07
10%, 30-year	9.94
14%, 5-year	3.85
14%, 15-year	7.58
14%, 30-year	9.63

Note in this summary that the Macaulay duration of a coupon bond is less than its maturity. It should be obvious from the formula that the Macaulay duration of a zero-coupon bond is equal to its maturity. The lower the coupon, generally the greater the duration of the bond.[3]

---

2 For example, if there are 5.2 years to maturity for a semiannual-pay bond (i.e., $k = 2$), then

$$n = 5.2 \times 2$$
$$= 10.4.$$

Rounding down to the nearest whole number gives a value of 10 for n.

EXHIBIT 13-1

Calculation of Macaulay Duration and Modified Duration for a 10%, 5-year Bond Selling to Yield 10%

Coupon rate = 10.00%;
Maturity (years) = 5;
Initial yield = 10.00%.

Period (t)	Cash Flow ($)*	Present Value of $1 at 5%	Present Value of Cash Flow (PVCF; ($))	t × PVCF ($)
1	$ 5.00	0.952380	$ 4.761905	$ 4.761905
2	5.00	0.907029	4.535147	9.070295
3	5.00	0.863837	4.319188	12.957563
4	5.00	0.822702	4.113512	16.454049
5	5.00	0.783526	3.917631	19.588154
6	5.00	0.746215	3.731077	22.386461
7	5.00	0.710681	3.553407	24.873846
8	5.00	0.676839	3.384197	27.073574
9	5.00	0.644608	3.223045	29.007401
10	105.00	0.613913	64.460892	644.608920
Total			$100.000000	$810.782168

*Cash flow per $100 of par value.

$$\text{Macaulay duration (in half years)} = \frac{810.782168}{100.000000} = 8.11.$$

$$\text{Macaulay duration (in years)} = \frac{8.11}{2} = 4.05.$$

$$\text{Modified duration (in years)} = \frac{4.05}{1.0500} = 3.86.$$

Notice the consistency between the properties of bond price volatility that we discussed earlier and the properties of duration. We showed that, all other factors constant, the greater the maturity, the greater the price volatility. A property of duration is that, all other factors constant, the greater the maturity, the greater the duration. We also showed that the lower the coupon rate, all other factors constant, the greater the bond price volatility. As we just noted, generally the lower the coupon rate, the greater the duration. It appears that duration is telling us something about bond price volatility.

---

3. This property does not necessarily hold for some long maturity deep discount coupon bonds, as explained below.

EXHIBIT 13–2

Calculation of Macaulay Duration and Modified Duration for a 14%, 5-year Bond Selling to Yield 10%

Coupon rate = 14.00%;
Maturity (years) = 5;
Initial yield = 10.00%.

Period (t)	Cash Flow ($)*	Present Value of $1 at 5%	Present Value of Cash Flow (PVCF; $)	t × PVCF ($)
1	$ 7.00	0.952380	$ 6.666667	$ 6.666667
2	7.00	0.907029	6.349206	12.698412
3	7.00	0.863837	6.046863	18.140589
4	7.00	0.822702	5.758917	23.035669
5	7.00	0.783526	5.484683	27.423415
6	7.00	0.746215	5.223508	31.341046
7	7.00	0.710681	4.974769	34.823385
8	7.00	0.676839	4.737876	37.903004
9	7.00	0.644608	4.512262	40.610361
10	107.00	0.613913	65.688718	656.887180
Total			$115.443470	$889.529728

*Cash flow per $100 of par value.

$$\text{Macaulay duration (in half years)} = \frac{889.529728}{115.443470} = 7.71.$$

$$\text{Macaulay duration (in years)} = \frac{7.71}{2} = 3.85.$$

$$\text{Modified duration (in years)} = \frac{3.85}{1.0500} = 3.67.$$

Short-Cut Formulas for Macaulay Duration

Mathematically, Macaulay duration for a semiannual-pay bond can be shown to be equivalent to:[4]

$$\text{Macaulay duration (in 6-month periods)}$$

$$= \left[\frac{1+y}{y}\right] H + \left[\frac{y-c}{y}\right] n\,(1-H),$$

---

4 The mathematical proof is given in Frank J. Fabozzi, *Bond Markets, Analysis and Strategies* (Englewood Cliffs, NJ: Prentice-Hall, 1993, 2nd ed), pp. 70–71.

where

  y = One-half the yield;
  H = Ratio of the present value of the annuity of the semiannual coupon payments to the price of the bond;
  c = One-half the annual coupon *rate*.

From Chapter 3, the present value of the semiannual coupon payments is:

$$100\,c\left[\frac{1-\left[\dfrac{1}{(1+y)^n}\right]}{y}\right].$$

Illustration 13-1   We can use the formula above to calculate Macaulay duration for the 14% coupon bond with 5 years to maturity, selling to yield 10%, by inserting the values:

  $y = .05\ (.10/2);$
  $c = .07\ (.14/2);$
  $n = 10\ (5 \times 2).$

The price of this bond is \$115.44 (see Exhibit 11-1 of Chapter 11). The present value of the coupon payments is

$$\$100\,(.07)\left[\frac{1-\left[\dfrac{1}{(1.05)^{10}}\right]}{.05}\right]$$

$$=\$7\left[\frac{1-.613913}{.05}\right]$$

$$=\$54.05.$$

Then,

$$H=\frac{\$54.05}{\$115.44}=.4682$$

and

Macaulay duration (in 6-month periods)

$$=\frac{1.05}{.05}\,(.4682)+\left[\frac{.05-.07}{.05}\right](10)\,(1-.4682)$$

$$=21(.4682)+(-.40)\,(10)\,(.5318)$$

$$=9.8322-2.1272$$

$$=7.705.$$

Dividing by 2 to give Macaulay duration in years, we have 3.85. Notice that this agrees with the Macaulay duration calculated for this bond in Exhibit 13-2.

  When a bond is selling at par, c is equal to y. The formula for Macaulay duration then reduces to

Macaulay duration for a bond selling at par (in 6-month periods)

$$= \left[\frac{1+y}{y}\right] H.$$

Illustration 13-2   In the formula for the Macaulay duration for a bond selling at par, the numbers needed to calculate Macaulay duration for the 10% coupon bond with 5 years to maturity selling to yield 10% are

$y = .05 \ (.10/2)$;
$c = .05 \ (.10/2)$;
$n = 10 \ (5 \times 2)$.

The present value of the coupon payments is

$$\$100 \ (.05) \left[\frac{1 - \left[\dfrac{1}{(1.05)^{10}}\right]}{.05}\right]$$

$$= \$5 \left[\frac{1 - .613913}{.05}\right]$$

$$= \$38.61.$$

Then,

$$H = \frac{\$38.61}{\$100} = .3861$$

and

Macaulay duration (in 6-month periods)

$$= \frac{1.05}{.05} \ (.3861)$$

$$= 21(.3861)$$

$$= 8.1081.$$

Dividing by 2 gives 4.05, the Macaulay duration in years. This result agrees with the calculation of Macaulay duration in Exhibit 13-1.

For a zero-coupon bond, the present value of the coupon payments is obviously zero, thus H is zero. The Macaulay duration for a zero-coupon bond in 6-month periods is

$$\left[\frac{1+y}{y}\right] H + \left[\frac{y-c}{y}\right] n \ (1-H)$$

$$= \left[\frac{1+y}{y}\right] 0 + \left[\frac{y-0}{y}\right] n \ (1-0)$$

$$= 0 + \left[\frac{y}{y}\right] n$$

$$= n.$$

Thus we see that the Macaulay duration of a zero-coupon bond in periods is just the number of 6-month periods. Dividing by 2 gives the term of the bond in years.

LINK BETWEEN DURATION AND BOND PRICE VOLATILITY

Now that we know how to compute Macaulay duration, how do we interpret it? Some investors continue to think of duration in the context in which it was developed by Macaulay—as a measure of the length of time a bond investment is outstanding. Forget it! The significance and interpretation of Macaulay duration lie in its link to bond price volatility.

The link between bond price volatility and Macaulay duration can be shown to be as follows:[5]

$$Approximate \text{ percentage change in price}$$

$$= - \left[\frac{1}{(1+y)} \right] \times \text{Macaulay duration} \times \text{Yield change},$$

where y = One-half the yield to maturity.

Generally, the first two terms are combined, and the resulting measure is called *modified duration;* that is,

$$\text{Modified duration} = \frac{\text{Macaulay duration}}{(1+y)}.$$

The relationship can then be expressed as

$$Approximate \text{ percentage change in price}$$

$$= - \text{Modified duration} \times \text{Yield change}.$$

Illustration 13-3   Consider the 8%, 15-year bond selling at 84.63 to yield 10%. The Macaulay duration for this bond is 8.45. Modified duration is 8.05:

$$\text{Modified duration} = \frac{8.45}{(1.05)} = 8.05.$$

If the yield increases instantaneously from 10.00% to 10.10%, a yield change of +0.0010, the *approximate* percentage change in price is

$$- 8.05 \times (+.0010) = -.00805 = -.81\%.$$

Exhibit 11-4 in Chapter 11 shows that the actual percentage change in price is –0.80%. Similarly, if the yield decreases instantaneously from 10.00% to 9.90% (a 10-basis-point decrease), the approximate percentage change in price would be +0.81%. Exhibit 11-4 shows that the actual percentage price change would be +0.80%. This example illustrates that for small changes in yield, modified duration provides a good approximation of percentage change in price.

---

5 Mathematically, this relationship is derived from the first term of a Taylor series of the price function.

Illustration 13-4   Instead of a small change in yield, let's assume that yields increase by 300 basis points, from 10% to 13% (a yield change of +.03). The approximate percentage change in price estimated using modified duration would be

$$- 8.05 \times (+.03) = - .2415 = 24.15\%.$$

How good is this approximation? As can be seen from Exhibit 11-4 in Chapter 11, the actual percentage change in price is only –20.41%. Moreover, if the yield decreases by 300 basis points, from 10% to 7%, the approximate percentage change in price based on duration would be +24.15%, compared to an actual percentage change in price of +29.03%. Thus, not only is the approximation off, but we can see that modified duration estimates a symmetric percentage change in price, which, as we pointed out in Chapter 11, is not a property of the price/yield relationship for bonds.

Exhibit 13-3 shows the estimated percentage change in price using modified duration for our 12 hypothetical bonds. The difference between the actual percentage price change, as reported in Exhibit 11-4, and the estimated percentage change in price using modified duration, as reported in Exhibit 13-3, is shown in Exhibit 13-4. The property that we just illustrated—that modified duration gives a good estimate of the percentage price change for small changes in yield but a poor estimate for large changes—can be seen in Exhibit 13-4. The percentage price change not explained by modified duration increases the greater the change in yield. For some bonds, however, the approximation is in error by less than others. For example, for the 14%, 30-year bond, the unexplained percentage price change for a 300-basis-point increase is 5.5%, while for the zero-coupon bond of the same maturity it is 28.41%.

The reason that modified duration provides a good approximation for small changes in yield but a poor approximation for large changes in yield lies in the convex shape of the price/yield relationship. This point is examined fully in the next chapter.

Modified Duration as a Measure of Percentage Price Change Per 100-Basis-Point Yield Change

For a 100-basis-point change in yield, the percentage change in the bond's price is

Modified duration $\times$ (.01).

For example, if the modified duration is 6, the approximate percentage change in the bond's price for a 100-basis-point change in yield is

$$6 \times (.01) = .06 \text{ or } 6\%.$$

Thus, a bond with a modified duration of 6 would change by approximately 6% for a 100-basis-point (1%) change in yield. Similarly, a bond with a modified duration of X would change by approximately $X\%$ for a 100-basis-point change in yield. For this reason, some investors refer to modified duration as the percentage price change of a bond per 100-basis-point change in yield. So, for example, a bond with a modified duration of 5.4 will change by approximately 5.4% for a 100-basis-point change in yield. For a 50-basis-point change in yield, the percentage price change would then be half of 5.4%, or 2.7%. For a 10-basis-point change in yield, the percentage price change would be one-tenth of 5.4%, or .54%.

EXHIBIT 13-3

Percentage Change in Price Estimated Using Modified Duration

			Yield Change (in basis points) from 10%					
			1	10	50	100	200	300
					New Yield Level			
Coupon (%)	Term (years)	Modified Duration (years)	10.01%	10.10%	10.50%	11.00%	12.00%	13.00%
.00%	5	4.76	-.05%	-.48%	-2.38%	-4.76%	-9.52%	-14.28%
.00	15	14.29	-.14	-1.43	-7.15	-14.29	-28.58	-42.87
.00	30	28.57	-.29	-2.86	-14.29	-28.57	-57.14	-85.71
8.00	5	3.98	-.04	-.40	-1.99	-3.98	-7.96	-11.94
8.00	15	8.05	-.08	-.81	-4.03	-8.05	-16.10	-24.15
8.00	30	9.72	-.10	-.97	-4.86	-9.72	-19.44	-29.16
10.00	5	3.86	-.04	-.39	-1.93	-3.86	-7.72	-11.58
10.00	15	7.69	-.08	-.77	-3.85	-7.69	-15.38	-23.07
10.00	30	9.46	-.09	-.95	-4.73	-9.46	-18.92	-28.38
14.00	5	3.67	-.04	-.37	-1.84	-3.67	-7.34	-11.01
14.00	15	7.22	-.07	-.72	-3.61	-7.22	-14.44	-21.66
14.00	30	9.17	-.09	-.92	-4.59	-9.17	-18.34	-27.51

EXHIBIT 13–3

Concluded

Coupon (%)	Term (years)	Modified Duration (years)	–1 9.99%	–10 9.90%	–50 9.50%	–100 9.00%	–200 8.00%	–300 7.00%
					Yield Change (in basis points) from 10%			
					New Yield Level			
.00%	5	4.76	.05%	.48%	2.38%	4.76%	9.52%	14.28%
.00	15	14.29	.14	1.43	7.15	14.29	28.58	42.87
.00	30	28.57	.29	2.86	14.29	28.57	57.14	85.71
8.00	5	3.98	.04	.40	1.99	3.98	7.96	11.94
8.00	15	8.05	.08	.81	4.03	8.05	16.10	24.15
8.00	30	9.72	.10	.97	4.86	9.72	19.44	29.16
10.00	5	3.86	.04	.39	1.93	3.86	7.72	11.58
10.00	15	7.69	.08	.77	3.85	7.69	15.38	23.07
10.00	30	9.46	.09	.95	4.73	9.46	18.92	28.38
14.00	5	3.67	.04	.37	1.84	3.67	7.34	11.01
14.00	15	7.22	.07	.72	3.61	7.22	14.44	21.66
14.00	30	9.17	.09	.92	4.59	9.17	18.34	27.51

EXHIBIT 13–4

Percentage Price Change Not Explained by Modified Duration

			Yield Change (in basis points) from 10%					
			1	10	50	100	200	300
					New Yield Level			
		Modified Duration (years)	10.01%	10.10%	10.50%	11.00%	12.00%	13.00%
Coupon (%)	Term (years)							
.00%	5	4.76	.00%	.00	.03%	.12%	.48%	1.06%
.00	15	14.29	.00	.01	.26	1.01	3.83	8.21
.00	30	28.57	.00	.04	.99	3.77	13.76	28.41
8.00	5	3.98	.00	.00	.02	.10	.38	.83
8.00	15	8.05	.00	.00	.12	.45	1.73	3.74
8.00	30	9.72	.00	.01	.20	.78	2.92	6.15
10.00	5	3.86	.00	.00	.02	.09	.36	.80
10.00	15	7.69	.00	.00	.11	.42	1.62	3.48
10.00	30	9.46	.00	.01	.19	.74	2.76	5.83
14.00	5	3.67	.00	.00	.02	.09	.34	.75
14.00	15	7.22	.00	.00	.10	.38	1.45	3.14
14.00	30	9.17	.00	.01	.18	.69	2.60	5.50

EXHIBIT 13—4

Concluded

Coupon (%)	Term (years)	Modified Duration (years)	Yield Change (in basis points) from 10%					
			−1	−10	−50	−100	−200	−300
			New Yield Level					
			9.99%	9.90%	9.50%	9.00%	8.00%	7.00%
.00%	5	4.76	.00%	.00%	.03%	.13%	.52%	1.20%
.00	15	14.29	.00	.01	.27	1.11	4.67	11.11
.00	30	28.57	.00	.04	1.09	4.59	20.43	51.39
8.00	5	3.98	.00	.00	.03	.10	.41	.93
8.00	15	8.05	.00	.00	.12	.49	2.06	4.88
8.00	30	9.72	.00	.01	.22	.90	3.91	9.57
10.00	5	3.86	.00	.00	.02	.10	.39	.89
10.00	15	7.69	.00	.00	.11	.45	1.91	4.52
10.00	30	9.46	.00	.01	.21	.86	3.70	9.04
14.00	5	3.67	.00	.00	.02	.09	.36	.83
14.00	15	7.22	.00	.00	.10	.41	1.72	4.06
14.00	30	9.17	.00	.01	.19	.79	3.43	8.36

Dollar Duration

The modified duration of a bond can be used to approximate the percentage change in price for a given change in yield. Similarly, the dollar price change can be approximated given the bond's modified duration, the bond's price, and a specified number of basis points. The dollar price change is referred to as *dollar duration.*

The dollar duration of a basis point change in yield can be calculated as follows:

Dollar duration of a basis point

$$= \frac{\text{Modified duration} \times \text{Price}}{10,000}$$

For example, consider an 8% coupon, 15-year bond selling to yield 10%. The price of this bond per $100 par value is $84.6275. The bond's modified duration is 8.05. Therefore,

Dollar duration of a basis point

$$= \frac{8.05 \times \$84.6275}{10,000} = \$.068125.$$

To find the dollar duration for more than one basis point, the dollar duration of a basis point is simply multiplied by the number of basis points. For example, for a 50-basis-point change in yield, the dollar duration would be $3.40625.

If the dollar duration for a par value different from $100 is sought, then the dollar duration per $100 par value must be scaled appropriately. For example, in our previous example if $1 million is the par value, then the market value of the bond is $8,462,750. The dollar duration of a basis point is $6,812.51.

It should be noted that there is no standard terminology used for dollar duration. More specifically, some market participants refer to "dollar duration" when they mean the "dollar duration of a basis point." In our example, the dollar duration would then be .0681, since this is the dollar duration of one basis point. The dollar duration of a basis point is equivalent to the price value of a basis point that we discussed in the previous chapter. Some market participants refer to the dollar duration in terms of the dollar duration of 100 basis points. In our example, the dollar duration would then be 6.81.

How good an estimate of the dollar price change is given by dollar duration? For small changes in yield, it will be good, as we saw in Illustration 13-3, where modified duration is used to estimate the percentage price change. For large changes in yield, the approximation is not as good. Recall from Illustration 13-4 that when the yield increases by 300 basis points, the estimated percentage decline in price is greater than the actual decline in price. This means that the estimated dollar price decline will be greater than the actual price decline, so that the estimated new price is less than the actual price at a higher yield. Also in Illustration 13-4, the estimated percentage price increase is less than the actual price increase when yield declines by 300 basis points. The actual price increase, therefore, is underestimated using modified duration, and the estimated price at a lower yield will be less than the actual price. Thus, whether the yield rises or falls by a large number of basis points, modified duration and dollar duration will underestimate what the new price will be. A graphical explanation for this fact is given in the next chapter.

PORTFOLIO DURATION

A portfolio's modified duration can be obtained by calculating the weighted average of the modified duration of the bonds in the portfolio. The weight is the proportion of the portfolio that a security comprises. Mathematically, a portfolio's modified duration can be calculated as follows:

$$w_1 D_1 + w_2 D_2 + w_3 D_3 + \cdots + w_K D_K,$$

where

w_i = Market value of bond i/market value of the portfolio;
D_i = Modified duration of bond i;
K = Number of bonds in the portfolio.

To illustrate this calculation, consider the three-bond portfolio used in the previous chapter to demonstrate how to calculate the price value of a basis point for a portfolio:

Bond	Par Amount Owned ($)	Market Value ($)
10%, 5-year	$4 million	$4,000,000
8%, 15-year	5 million	4,231,375
14%, 30-year	1 million	1,378,586

This illustration assumes that the next coupon payment for each bond is 6 months from now. The market value for the portfolio is $9,609,961. The market price per $100 par value of each bond, its yield to maturity, and its modified duration are as follows:

Bond	Price ($)	Yield to Maturity (%)	Modified Duration
10%, 5-year	$100.0000	10%	3.861
8%, 15-year	84.6275	10	8.047
14%, 30-year	137.8590	10	9.168

In this illustration, K is equal to 3, and

$w_1 = 4,000,000/9,609,961 = .416$ $D_1 = 3.861$
$w_2 = 4,231,375/9,609,961 = .440$ $D_2 = 8.047$
$w_3 = 1,378,586/9,609,961 = .144$ $D_3 = 9.168$

The portfolio's modified duration is:

$$.416 \,(3.861) + .440 \,(8.047) + .144 \,(9.168) = 6.47.$$

A portfolio modified duration of 6.47 means that for a 100-basis-point change in the yield for *all* three bonds, the market value of the portfolio will change by approximately 6.47%. But keep in mind that the yield on all three bonds must change by 100 basis points for the modified duration measure to be useful. This is a critical assumption and its importance can not be overemphasized. We shall return to this point in Chapter 15.

In the previous chapter, we calculated the price value of a basis point for this three-bond portfolio and found it to be $6,212. Since the dollar duration of a basis point change in yield will be the same as the price value of a basis point, let's see if this is true when we use our dollar duration of a basis point formula. The dollar duration of a basis point for the portfolio is

Portfolio dollar duration of a basis point

$$= \frac{\text{Portfolio modified duration} \times \text{Market value of portolio}}{10,000}.$$

Since the portfolio modified duration is 6.47 and the market value of the portfolio is $9,609,961, then

$$= \frac{6.47 \times \$9,609,961}{10,000}$$

$$= \$6,218.$$

This agrees with our calculation for the price value of a basis point (the difference of $6 is due to rounding).

Portfolio Duration for a Global Portfolio

Many global money managers calculate a duration for a portfolio consisting of bonds with cash flows denominated in several currencies. For example, a U.S. portfolio manager who has a portfolio of U.S. Treasury securities denominated in U.S. dollars, German government bonds denominated in deutschemarks, Japanese government bonds denominated in yen, and French government bonds denominated in francs might calculate a Macaulay duration and a modified duration for the portfolio. The question is what does a portfolio modified duration in such cases mean?

Since modified duration is a measure of the percentage price volatility of a bond to changes in yield, what yield is modified duration measuring price sensitivity to? U.S. yields, German yields, Japanese yields, or French yields? There is no answer to this question. Using the modified duration measure as discussed thus far in this chapter for a global portfolio is of questionable value.

APPROXIMATING DURATION

Since modified duration is a measure of the price sensitivity of a bond to interest rate changes, it can be approximated by simply changing yields by a small amount up and down, and then looking at how the price changes. More specifically, let

V_0 = Initial value or price of the security;
Δy = Change in the yield of a security;
V_- = Estimated value of the security if the yield is decreased by Δy;
V_+ = Estimated value of the security if the yield is increased by Δy.

Then for a small change decrease in yield, the percentage price change is

$$\frac{V_- - V_0}{V_0}.$$

The percentage price change per basis point change is found by dividing the percentage price change by the number of basis points ($\Delta y \times 100$). That is,

$$\frac{V_- - V_0}{V_0 (\Delta y) 100}.$$

Similarly, the percentage price change per basis point increase in yield is

$$\frac{V_0 - V_+}{V_+ (\Delta y) 100}.$$

As explained earlier, the percentage price change for an increase and decrease in interest rates will not be the same. Consequently, the average percentage price change per basis point change in yield can be calculated. This is done as follows:

$$\frac{1}{2}\left[\frac{V_- - V_0}{V_0(\Delta y)100} + \frac{V_0 - V_+}{V_0(\Delta y)100}\right],$$

or equivalently,

$$\frac{V_- - V_+}{2V_0(\Delta y)100}.$$

The approximate percentage price change for a 100 basis point change in yield is found by multiplying the previous formula by 100:

$$\text{Approximate duration} = \frac{V_- - V_+}{2V_0(\Delta y)}$$

To illustrate this formula for approximating modified duration, consider a 20-year, 7% coupon bond selling at \$74.26 to yield 10%. Suppose we evaluate the price changes for a 20-basis-point change up and down. Then,

$V_- = 75.64$;
$V_+ = 72.92$;
$V_0 = 74.26$;
$\Delta y = 0.002$.

Substituting into the formula:

$$\frac{75.64 - 72.92}{2(74.26)\,(0.002)} = 9.16.$$

The modified duration for this bond calculated using the formula presented earlier in this chapter is 9.18.

Effective Duration

The approximation formula above is important when we analyze bonds that are not option-free in later chapters; that is, when the bonds are putable or callable. Modified duration is not a good measure of the price sensitivity of such bonds to yield changes because it assumes that yield changes will not change the expected cash flows of a bond. For example, when a bond is callable, a decline in market yields may change the expected cash flows of the bond since it may increase the likelihood that the bond is called. In the case of mortgage-backed securities—the subject of Part VI of this book—a change in market yields will change prepayments of borrowers.

In such instances where the cash flow is interest-rate sensitive (interest-rate dependent), the price sensitivity of a bond to yield changes must take into consideration how yield changes affect the expected cash flows and, in turn, the price of a bond. A duration measure that does allow for changes in cash flows as yields change is called an *effective duration*. The formula we gave above for approximating the modified duration is the formula that is used to calculate the effective duration of a bond. We shall see how this formula is used for bonds with interest-rate sensitive cash flows in later chapters.

APPLICATIONS

Dollar Duration Weighting of Yield Spread Swap Strategies

A common active bond portfolio strategy is to position a portfolio to capitalize on expectations regarding the yield spread between sectors in the market. It is critical when assessing yield spread strategies to compare positions that have the same dollar duration. To understand why, consider two bonds, X and Y. Suppose that the price of bond X is $80 and has a modified duration of 5 while bond Y has a price of $90 and has a modified duration of 4. Since modified duration is the approximate percentage change per 100-basis-point change in yield, a 100 basis points change in yield for bond X would change its price by about 5%. Based on a price of $80, its price will change by about $4 per $80 of market value. Thus, its dollar duration for a 100 basis point change in yield is $4 per $80 of market value. Similarly, for bond Y, its dollar duration for a 100 basis-point-change in yield per $90 of market value can be determined. In this case it is $3.6. So, if bonds X and Y are being considered as alternative investments in some strategy other than one based on anticipating interest-rate movements, the amount of each bond in the strategy should be such that they will both have the same dollar duration.

To illustrate this, suppose that a portfolio manager owns $10 million of par value of bond X which has a market value of $8 million. The dollar duration of bond X per 100-basis-point change in yield for the $8 million market value is $400,000. Suppose further that this portfolio manager is considering exchanging bond X that it owns in its portfolio for bond Y. If the portfolio manager wants to have the same interest-rate exposure (i.e., dollar duration) for bond Y that she currently has for bond X, she will buy a market value amount of bond Y with the same dollar duration. If the portfolio manager purchased $10 million of *par value* of bond Y and therefore $9 million of *market value* of bond Y, the dollar price change per 100-basis-point change in yield would be only $360,000. If, instead, the portfolio manager purchased $10 million of *market value* of bond Y, the dollar duration per 100-basis-point change in yield would be

$400,000. Since bond Y is trading at $90, $11.11 million of par value of bond Y must be purchased to keep the dollar duration of the position for bond Y the same as for bond X.

Mathematically, this problem can be expressed as follows:

Let:

D_X = Dollar duration per 100-basis-point change in yield for bond X for the market value of bond X held;

MD_Y = Modified duration for bond Y;

MV_Y = Market value of bond Y needed to obtain the same dollar duration as bond X.

Then, the following equation sets the dollar duration for bond X equal to the dollar duration for bond Y:

$$\$D_X = (MD_Y/100) \, MV_Y.$$

Solving for MV_Y,

$$MV_Y = \$D_X \, / \, (MD_Y/100)$$

Dividing by the price per $1 of par value of bond Y gives the par value of bond Y that has an approximately equivalent dollar duration as bond X.

In our illustration, D_X is $400,000 and MD_Y is 4, so

$$MV_Y = \$400,000/(4/100) = \$10,000,000.$$

Since the market value of bond Y is $90 per $100 of par value, the price per $1 of par value is $0.9. Dividing $10 million by 0.9 indicates that the par value of bond Y that should be purchased is $11.11 million.

Failure to adjust a portfolio repositioning based on some expected change in yield spread so as to hold the dollar duration the same means that the outcome of the portfolio will be affected by not only the expected change in the yield spread but also a change in the yield level. Thus, a manager would be making a conscious yield spread bet and possibly an undesired bet on the level of interest rates.

Using Dollar Duration to Compute the Hedge Ratio

Modified duration is related to percentage price volatility. As explained in the previous chapter, in hedging we are interested in dollar price changes. Consequently, to compute the hedge ratio using duration, dollar duration should be used, not modified duration. The hedge ratio is computed from dollar duration as follows:

$$\frac{\text{Dollar duration for bond to be hedged}}{\text{Dollar duration for hedging vehicle}} \times \text{Yield beta.}$$

Recall that the dollar duration per basis point per $100 of par value is the same as the price value of a basis point. Therefore, dollar duration will produce the same hedge ratio as the price value of a basis point.

Role of Duration in Immunization Strategies

In Chapter 8, we explained that the return that is realized by investing in a coupon security will depend on the interest rate earned on the reinvestment of the coupon payments. When interest rates rise, interest on interest from the reinvestment of the coupon payments will be higher, but if the investment horizon is shorter than the maturity of the bond, a loss will be realized upon the sale of the bond. The reverse is true if interest rates fall: price appreciation will be realized when the bond is sold, but interest on interest from reinvesting the coupon payments will be lower. Because of these two risks, the investor cannot be assured of locking in the yield at the time of purchase.

Because interest rate risk and reinvestment risk offset each other, however, is it possible to select a bond or bond portfolio that will lock in the yield at the time of purchase regardless of interest rate changes in the future? That is, is it possible to *immunize* the bond or bond portfolio against interest rate changes? Fortunately, under certain circumstances, it is. This can be accomplished by constructing a portfolio so that its Macaulay duration is equal to the length of the investment horizon. Thus, a portfolio manager with an investment horizon of 5 years who wants to lock in a return over that time period should select a portfolio with a Macaulay duration of 5 years. This is demonstrated using an example.

Suppose a portfolio manager knows that a liability of $17,183,033 must be paid in 5.5 years. Also suppose that interest rates are currently 12.5% on a bond equivalent basis. The present value of the $17,183,033 liability 5.5 years from now assuming interest can be earned at a rate of 6.25% per 6-month period is $8,820,262. Thus, if the portfolio manager invested $8,820,262 at the current rate of 6.25% per 6-month period for the next 11 6-month periods, the accumulated value would be sufficient to satisfy the liability.

Suppose the portfolio manager buys $8,820,262 par value of a bond selling at par with a 12.5% yield to maturity that matures in 5.5 years. The Macaulay duration for this bond is 4.14 years, which is shorter than the length of the investment horizon. Will the portfolio manager be assured of realizing the target yield of 12.5% or, equivalently, a target accumulated value of $17,183,033? As we explained in Chapter 6, the portfolio manager will realize a 12.5% yield only if the coupon interest payments can be reinvested at 6.25% every 6 months. That is, the accumulated value will depend on the reinvestment rate.

To illustrate this, suppose that immediately after investing the $8,820,262 in the 12.5% coupon, 5.5-year maturity bond, yields in the market change and stay at the new level for the remainder of the 5.5 years. Exhibit 13-5 illustrates what happens at the end of 5.5 years. The first column shows the new yield. The second column shows the total coupon interest payments. The third column gives the interest on interest over the entire 5.5 years if the coupon interest payments are reinvested at the new yield shown in the first column. The price of the bond at the end of 5.5 years, shown in the fourth column, is the par value. The fifth column is the accumulated value from all three sources: coupon interest, interest on interest, and price of bond. The total return is shown in the last column.

When yields do not change, so that the coupon payments can be reinvested at 12.5% (6.25% every 6 months), the target accumulated value will be achieved by the portfolio manager. If market yields rise, an accumulated value (total return) higher than the target accumulated value (target yield) will be achieved, because the coupon interest payments can be reinvested at a rate higher than the initial yield to maturity. Contrast this circumstance with what happens when the yield declines. The accumulated value (total return) will be less than the target accumulated

EXHIBIT 13-5

Accumulated Value and Total Return:
5.5-Year, 12.5% Coupon Bond Selling to Yield 12.5%

Investment horizon (years) = 5.5;

Coupon rate = 12.5%;

Maturity (years) = 5.50;

Yield to maturity = 12.5%;

Price = 100.00000;

Par value purchased = $8,820,262;

Purchase price = $8,820,262;

Target accumulated value = $17,183,033.

			Over 5.5 Years		
New Yield (%)	Coupon ($)	Interest on Interest ($)	Price of Bond ($)	Accumulated Value ($)	Total Return (%)
16.0%	$6,063,930	$3,112,167	$8,820,262	$17,996,360	13.40%
15.5	6,063,930	2,990,716	8,820,262	17,874,908	13.26
14.5	6,063,930	2,753,177	8,820,262	17,637,369	13.00
14.0	6,063,930	2,637,037	8,820,262	17,521,230	12.88
13.5	6,063,930	2,522,618	8,820,262	17,406,810	12.75

EXHIBIT 13-5

Concluded

Over 5.5 Years

New Yield (%)	Coupon ($)	Interest on Interest ($)	Price of Bond ($)	Accumulated Value ($)	Total Return (%)
13.0%	$6,063,930	$2,409,894	$8,820,262	$17,294,086	12.62%
12.5	6,063,930	2,298,840	8,820,262	17,183,033	12.50
12.0	6,063,930	2,189,433	8,820,262	17,073,625	12.38
11.5	6,063,930	2,081,648	8,820,262	16,965,840	12.25
11.0	6,063,930	1,975,462	8,820,262	16,859,654	12.13
10.5	6,063,930	1,870,852	8,820,262	16,755,044	12.01
10.0	6,063,930	1,767,794	8,820,262	16,651,986	11.89
9.5	6,063,930	1,666,266	8,820,262	16,550,458	11.78
9.0	6,063,930	1,566,246	8,820,262	16,450,438	11.66
8.5	6,063,930	1,476,712	8,820,262	16,351,904	11.54
8.0	6,063,930	1,370,642	8,820,262	16,254,834	11.43
7.5	6,063,930	1,275,014	8,820,262	16,159,206	11.32
7.0	6,063,930	1,180,808	8,820,262	16,065,000	11.20
6.5	6,063,930	1,088,003	8,820,262	15,972,195	11.09
6.0	6,063,930	996,577	8,820,262	15,880,769	10.98
5.5	6,063,930	906,511	8,820,262	15,790,703	10.87
5.0	6,063,930	817,785	8,820,262	15,701,977	10.77

value (target yield). *Therefore, investing in a coupon bond with a yield to maturity equal to the target yield and a maturity equal to the investment horizon does not assure that the target accumulated value will be achieved.*

Suppose that instead of investing in a bond maturing in 5.5 years, the portfolio manager invests in a 15-year bond with a coupon rate of 12.5% and selling at par to yield 12.5%. The Macaulay duration for this bond is 7.12 years, which is longer than the 5.5-year investment horizon. The accumulated value and total return if the market yield changes immediately after the bond is purchased and remains at the new yield are presented in Exhibit 13-6. The fourth column in Exhibit 11-6 is the market price of a 12.5% coupon, 9.5-year bond (since 5.5 years have passed), assuming that the market yield is as shown in the first column. If the market yield increases, the portfolio will fail to achieve the target accumulated value; the opposite is true if the market yield decreases—the accumulated value (total return) will exceed the target accumulated value (target yield).

The reason for this result can be seen in Exhibit 13-7, which summarizes the change in interest on interest and the change in price resulting from a change in the market yield. For example, if the market yield rises instantaneously by 200 basis points, from 12.5% to 14.5%, interest on interest will be $454,336 greater; the market price of the bond, however, will decrease by $894,781. The net effect is that the accumulated value will be $440,445 less than the target accumulated value. The reverse is true if the market yield decreases: the change in the price of the bond will more than offset the decline in the interest on interest, resulting in an accumulated value that exceeds the target accumulated value. Exhibit 13-7 clearly demonstrates the trade-off between interest rate (or price) risk and reinvestment risk.

Consider an 8-year, 10.125% coupon bond selling at 88.20262 to yield 12.5%, which has a Macaulay duration of 5.5 years. Suppose $10,000,000 of par value of this bond is purchased for $8,820,262. For this bond, Exhibit 13-8 provides the same information as Exhibits 13-5 and 13-6. Looking at the last two columns, we see that the accumulated value and the total return are never less than the target accumulated value and the target yield. Thus, the target accumulated value is assured regardless of what happens to the market yield. Exhibit 13-9 shows why. When the market yield rises, the change in the interest on interest more than offsets the decline in price. On the other hand, when the market yield declines, the increase in price exceeds the decline in interest on interest.

Notice that the last bond, which assures that the target accumulated value will be achieved regardless of what happens to the market yield, has a Macaulay duration equal to the length of the investment horizon. This is the key. To immunize a portfolio's target accumulated value (target yield) against a change in the market yield, a portfolio manager must invest in a bond (or a bond portfolio) such that (1) the Macaulay duration is equal to the investment horizon,[6] and (2) the present value of the cash flow from the bond (or bond portfolio) equals the present value of the liability.

In this example, we assumed a one-time instantaneous change in the market yield. In practice, the market yield will fluctuate over the investment horizon. As a result, the Macaulay

---

6 This is equivalent to equating the modified duration of the portfolio to the modified duration of the investment horizon. This is because the Macaulay duration of the liability is the length of the investment horizon and dividing by one plus one-half the yield to maturity gives a modified duration that is the same as the portfolio.

EXHIBIT 13-6

Accumulated Value and Total Return:
15-Year, 12.5% Coupon Bond Selling to Yield 12.5%

Investment horizon (years) = 5.5;
Coupon rate = 12.5%;
Maturity (years) = 15;
Yield to maturity = 12.5%;
Price = $100.00000;
Par value purchased = $8,820,262;
Purchase price = $8,820,262;
Target accumulated value = $17,183,033.

Over 5.5 Years

New Yield (%)	Coupon ($)	Interest on Interest ($)	Price of Bond ($)	Accumulated Value ($)	Total Return (%)
16.0%	$6,063,930	$3,112,167	$7,337,902	$16,514,000	11.73%
15.5	6,063,930	2,990,716	7,526,488	16,581,134	11.81
14.5	6,063,930	2,753,177	7,925,481	16,742,587	12.00
14.0	6,063,930	2,637,037	8,136,542	16,837,510	12.11
13.5	6,063,930	2,522,618	8,355,777	16,942,325	12.23

EXHIBIT 13-6

Concluded

			Over 5.5 Years		
New Yield (%)	Coupon ($)	Interest on Interest ($)	Price of Bond ($)	Accumulated Value ($)	Total Return (%)
13.0%	$6,063,930	$2,409,894	$8,583,555	$17,057,379	12.36%
12.5	6,063,930	2,298,840	8,820,262	17,183,033	12.50
12.0	6,063,930	2,189,433	9,066,306	17,319,669	12.65
11.5	6,063,930	2,081,648	9,322,113	17,467,691	12.82
11.0	6,063,930	1,975,462	9,588,131	17,627,523	12.99
10.5	6,063,930	1,870,852	9,864,831	17,799,613	13.18
10.0	6,063,930	1,767,794	10,152,708	17,984,432	13.38
9.5	6,063,930	1,666,266	10,452,281	18,182,477	13.59
9.0	6,063,930	1,566,246	10,764,095	18,394,271	13.82
8.5	6,063,930	1,467,712	11,088,723	18,620,366	14.06
8.0	6,063,930	1,370,642	11,426,770	18,861,342	14.31
7.5	6,063,930	1,275,014	11,778,867	19,117,812	14.57
7.0	6,063,930	1,180,808	12,145,682	19,390,420	14.85
6.5	6,063,930	1,088,003	12,527,914	19,679,847	15.14
6.0	6,063,930	996,577	12,926,301	19,986,808	15.44
5.5	6,063,930	906,511	13,341,617	20,312,058	15.76
5.0	6,063,930	817,785	13,774,677	20,656,393	16.09

EXHIBIT 13-7

Change in Interest on Interest and Price Due to Interest Rate Change:
15-Year, 12.5% Coupon Bond Selling to Yield 12.5%

New Yield (%)	Change in Interest on Interest ($)	Change in Price ($)	Total Change in Accumulated Value ($)
16.0%	$813,327	−$1,482,360	−$669,033
15.5	691,875	−1,293,774	−601,898
14.5	454,336	−894,781	−440,445
14.0	338,197	−683,720	−345,523
13.5	223,778	−464,485	−240,707
13.0	111,054	−236,707	−125,654
12.5	0	0	0
12.0	−109,407	246,044	136,636
11.5	−217,192	501,851	284,659
11.0	−323,378	767,869	444,491
10.5	−427,989	1,044,569	616,581
10.0	−531,046	1,332,446	801,400
9.5	−632,574	1,632,019	999,445
9.0	−732,594	1,943,833	1,211,239
8.5	−831,128	2,268,461	1,437,333
8.0	−928,198	2,606,508	1,678,309
7.5	−1,023,826	2,958,605	1,934,779
7.0	−1,118,032	3,325,420	2,207,388
6.5	−1,210,838	3,707,652	2,496,814
6.0	−1,302,263	4,106,039	2,803,776
5.5	−1,392,329	4,521,355	3,129,026
5.0	−1,481,055	4,954,415	3,473,360

duration of the portfolio will change as the market yield changes. In addition, the Macaulay duration will change with the passage of time. In the face of changing market yields, a manager can still immunize a portfolio by rebalancing it so that the Macaulay duration of the portfolio is equal to the remainder of the investment horizon. For example, if the investment horizon is initially 5.5 years, the initial portfolio should have a Macaulay duration of 5.5 years. After 6 months, the remaining investment horizon is 5 years. The Macaulay duration then will probably be different from 5 years. Thus the portfolio must be rebalanced so that its Macaulay duration is equal to 5 years. Six months later, the portfolio must be rebalanced so that its Macaulay duration is equal to 4.5 years, etc.

Constructing a portfolio so that its Macaulay duration is equal to the investment horizon will assure that the target yield will be realized only if the yields on all bonds change by the

EXHIBIT 13–8

Accumulated Value and Total Return:
8-Year, 10.125% Coupon Bond Selling to Yield 12.5%

Investment horizon (years) = 5.5;
Coupon rate = 10.125%;
Maturity (years) = 8;
Yield to maturity = 12.5%;
Price = $88.20262;
Par value purchased = $10,000,000;
Purchase price = $8,820,262;
Target accumulated value = $17,183,033.

Over 5.5 Years

New Yield (%)	Coupon ($)	Interest on Interest ($)	Price of Bond ($)	Accumulated Value ($)	Total Return (%)
16.0%	$5,568,750	$2,858,028	$8,827,141	$17,253,919	12.58%
15.5	5,568,750	2,746,494	8,919,852	17,235,096	12.56
14.5	5,568,750	2,528,352	9,109,054	17,206,156	12.53
14.0	5,568,750	2,421,697	9,205,587	17,196,034	12.51
13.5	5,568,750	2,316,621	9,303,435	17,188,807	12.51

EXHIBIT 13-8

Concluded

Over 5.5 Years

New Yield (%)	Coupon ($)	Interest on Interest ($)	Price of Bond ($)	Accumulated Value ($)	Total Return (%)
13.0%	$5,568,750	$2,213,102	$9,402,621	$17,184,473	12.50%
12.5	5,568,750	2,111,117	9,503,166	17,183,033	12.50
12.0	5,568,750	2,010,644	9,605,091	17,184,485	12.50
11.5	5,568,750	1,911,661	9,708,420	17,188,831	12.51
11.0	5,568,750	1,814,146	9,813,175	17,196,071	12.51
10.5	5,568,750	1,718,078	9,919,380	17,206,208	12.53
10.0	5,568,750	1,623,436	10,027,059	17,219,245	12.54
9.5	5,568,750	1,530,199	10,136,236	17,235,185	12.56
9.0	5,568,750	1,438,347	10,246,936	17,254,033	12.58
8.5	5,568,750	1,347,859	10,359,184	17,275,793	12.60
8.0	5,568,750	1,258,715	10,473,006	17,300,472	12.63
7.5	5,568,750	1,170,897	10,588,428	17,328,075	12.66
7.0	5,568,750	1,084,383	10,705,477	17,358,610	12.70
6.5	5,568,750	999,156	10,824,180	17,392,086	12.73
6.0	5,568,750	915,197	10,944,565	17,428,511	12.77
5.5	5,568,750	832,486	11,066,660	17,467,895	12.82
5.0	5,568,750	751,005	11,190,494	17,510,248	12.86

EXHIBIT 13–9

Change in Interest on Interest and Price Due to Interest-Rate Change:
8-Year, 10.125% Coupon Bond Selling to Yield 12.5%

New Yield (%)	Change in Interest on Interest ($)	Change in Price ($)	Total Change in Accumulated Value ($)
16.0%	$746,911	–$676,024	$70,887
15.5	635,377	–583,314	52,063
14.5	417,235	–394,112	23,123
14.0	310,580	–297,579	13,001
13.5	205,504	–199,730	5,774
13.0	101,985	–100,544	1,441
12.5	0	0	0
12.0	–100,473	101,925	1,452
11.5	–199,456	205,254	5,798
11.0	–296,971	310,010	13,038
10.5	–393,039	416,215	23,176
10.0	–487,681	523,894	36,212
9.5	–580,918	633,071	52,153
9.0	–672,770	743,771	71,000
8.5	–763,258	856,019	92,760
8.0	–852,402	969,841	117,439
7.5	–940,221	1,085,263	145,042
7.0	–1,026,734	1,202,311	175,578
6.5	–1,111,961	1,321,014	209,053
6.0	–1,195,921	1,441,399	245,478
5.5	–1,278,632	1,563,494	284,862
5.0	–1,360,112	1,687,328	327,216

same amount. For example, if short-term yields fall but long-term yields rise, then the offsetting of interest rate risk and reinvestment risk by matching duration will not work. A decline in short-term yields will reduce reinvestment income, while a rise in long-term rates will result in a capital loss of bonds with a maturity greater than the investment horizon. This risk of failing to immunize can be reduced, however.[7]

---

7 See H. Gifford Fong and Oldrich Vasicek, "A Risk Minimizing Strategy for Multiple Liability Immunization," *Journal of Finance* (December 1984), pp. 1541–1546. For a less technical description, see H. Gifford Fong and Frank J. Fabozzi, *Fixed Income Portfolio Management* (Homewood, IL: Dow Jones–Irwin, 1985), pp. 133–136.

Duration of an Interest-Rate Swap

An interest-rate swap is an agreement whereby two parties (called counterparties) agree to exchange periodic interest payments. The dollar amount of the interest payments exchanged is based on some predetermined dollar principal, which is called the *notional principal amount*. The dollar amount each counterparty pays to the other is the agreed-upon periodic interest rate times the notional principal amount. The only dollars that are exchanged between the parties are the interest payments, not the notional principal amount. In the most common type of swap, one party agrees to pay the other party fixed interest payments at designated dates for the life of the contract. This party is referred to as the *fixed-rate payer*. The other party agrees to make interest-rate payments that float with some reference rate and is referred to as the *floating-rate payer*.

For example, suppose that for the next 5 years party X agrees to pay party Y 10% per year, while party Y agrees to pay party X 6-month LIBOR. Party X is a fixed-rate payer/floating-rate receiver, while party Y is a floating-rate payer/fixed-rate receiver. Assume that the notional principal amount is $50 million, and that payments are exchanged every 6 months for the next 5 years. This means that every 6 months, party X (the fixed-rate payer/floating-rate receiver) will pay party Y $2.5 million (10% times $50 million divided by 2). The amount that party Y (the floating-rate payer/fixed-rate receiver) will pay party X will be 6-month LIBOR times $50 million divided by 2. For example, if 6-month LIBOR is 7%, party Y will pay party X $1.75 million (7% times $50 million divided by 2). Note that we divide by two because one-half year's interest is being paid.

Interest rate benchmarks commonly used for the floating rate in an interest-rate swap are those on various money market instruments: Treasury bills, London interbank offered rate (LIBOR), commercial paper, bankers acceptance, certificates of deposit, federal funds rate, and prime rate.

One way to interpret an interest-rate swap position is as a package of cash flows from buying and selling cash market instruments. To understand why, consider the following. Suppose that an investor enters into the following transaction:

- Buys $50 million par of a 5-year floating-rate bond that pays 6-month LIBOR every 6 months;
- Finances the purchase of the 5-year floating-rate bond by borrowing $50 million for 5 years with the following terms: 10% annual interest rate paid every 6 months.

The cash flow of this transaction is presented in Exhibit 13-10. The second column of the exhibit sets out the cash flow from purchasing the 5-year floating-rate bond. There is a $50 million cash outlay and then cash inflows. The amount of the cash inflows is uncertain because they depend on future LIBOR. The third column shows the cash flow from borrowing $50 million on a fixed-rate basis. The last column shows the net cash flow from the entire transaction. As can be seen in the last column, there is no initial cash flow (no cash inflow or cash outlay). In all 10 6-month periods the net position results in a cash inflow of LIBOR and a cash outlay of $2.5 million. This net position, however, is identical to the position of a fixed-rate payer/floating-rate receiver.

It can be seen from the net cash flow in Exhibit 13-10 that a fixed-rate payer has a cash market position that is equivalent to a long position in a floating-rate bond and borrowing the

EXHIBIT 13-10

Cash Flow for the Purchase of a 5-Year Floating-Rate Bond Financed by Borrowing on a Fixed-Rate Basis

Transaction: Purchase for $50 million a 5-year floating-rate bond: floating rate = LIBOR, semiannual pay;

Borrow $50 million for 5 years: fixed rate = 10%, semiannual payments.

Cash Flow (in millions of dollars) from

6-Month Period	Floating-Rate Bond	Borrowing Cost	Net
0	−$ 50	+$50.0	$0
1	+(LIBOR$_1$/2) × 50	− 2.5	+(LIBOR$_1$/2) × 50 − 2.5
2	+(LIBOR$_2$/2) × 50	− 2.5	+(LIBOR$_2$/2) × 50 − 2.5
3	+(LIBOR$_3$/2) × 50	− 2.5	+(LIBOR$_3$/2) × 50 − 2.5
4	+(LIBOR$_4$/2) × 50	− 2.5	+(LIBOR$_4$/2) × 50 − 2.5
5	+(LIBOR$_5$/2) × 50	− 2.5	+(LIBOR$_5$/2) × 50 − 2.5
6	+(LIBOR$_6$/2) × 50	− 2.5	+(LIBOR$_6$/2) × 50 − 2.5
7	+(LIBOR$_7$/2) × 50	− 2.5	+(LIBOR$_7$/2) × 50 − 2.5
8	+(LIBOR$_8$/2) × 50	− 2.5	+(LIBOR$_8$/2) × 50 − 2.5
9	+(LIBOR$_9$/2) × 50	− 2.5	+(LIBOR$_9$/2) × 50 − 2.5
10	+(LIBOR$_{10}$/2) × 50 + 50	− 52.5	+(LIBOR$_{10}$/2) × 50 − 2.5

Note: The subscript for LIBOR indicates the 6-month LIBOR as per the terms of the floating-rate bond at time *t*.

funds to purchase the floating-rate bond on a fixed-rate basis. But the borrowing can be viewed as issuing a fixed-rate bond, or equivalently, being short a fixed-rate bond. Consequently, the position of a fixed-rate payer can be viewed as being long a floating-rate bond and short a fixed-rate bond.

What about the position of a floating-rate payer? It can be easily demonstrated that the position of a floating-rate payer is equivalent to purchasing a fixed-rate bond and financing that purchase at a floating rate, with the floating rate being the reference interest rate for the swap. That is, the position of a floating-rate payer is equivalent to a long position in a fixed-rate bond and a short position in a floating-rate bond.

As with any fixed-income contract, the dollar value of a swap will change as interest rates change. Duration is a measure of the sensitivity of a bond's price to a change in interest rates. From the perspective of the party who pays floating and receives fixed, the position can be viewed as follows:

Long a fixed-rate bond + Short a floating-rate bond.

This means that the dollar duration of an interest-rate swap from the perspective of a floating-rate payer is just the difference between the dollar duration of the two bond positions that make up the swap. That is,

Dollar duration of a swap
= Dollar duration of a fixed-rate bond − Dollar duration of a floating-rate bond.

Most of the interest rate sensitivity of a swap will result from the dollar duration of the fixed-rate bond since the dollar duration of the floating-rate bond will be small. It will always be less than the length of time to the next reset date. Therefore, the dollar duration of a floating-rate bond for which the coupon rate resets every 6 months will be less than 6 months. The dollar duration of a floating-rate bond is smaller, the closer the swap is to its reset date.

TOTAL RISK

Modified duration measures the percentage price change for a 100-basis-point change in rates. Dollar duration indicates the dollar price change. To assess the potential price risk of a portfolio, it is necessary to assess the volatility of yields themselves. For example, high-yield bonds (so-called junk bonds) trade at higher yield levels than same-maturity Treasury bonds. Given the properties of duration discussed in this chapter, this means that a Treasury bond would have a higher modified duration than a high-yield bond. Does this mean that high-yield bonds expose investors to less interest-rate risk? The answer is no. How much price volatility a portfolio will be exposed to depends on how volatile yields are. Since high-yield bonds have greater yield volatility (i.e., spreads to Treasuries change even when Treasury yields are unchanged), it would not be correct to say that there is less potential price volatility despite a lower duration.

Similarly, in Switzerland, 10-year government bonds trade at lower yields than U.S. 10-year government bonds. Thus, Swiss government bonds have a higher duration. However, the volatility of 10-year Swiss government bonds in Switzerland is less than that of 10-year U.S. government bonds. Consequently, there is greater potential price volatility for 10-year U.S. government bonds despite the lower duration.

The key to understanding the price volatility of a portfolio is to look not only at duration but yield volatility. We postpone our discussion of this topic to Chapter 21.

SUMMARY

In this chapter we have discussed a popular measure of price volatility called duration. Macaulay duration is related to price volatility and is commonly used as some measure of the weighted average life of a bond. Modified duration is the approximate percentage price change of a bond for a 100-basis-point change in interest rates. Dollar duration is a measure of the dollar price change of a bond to changes in interest rates; for a one-basis-point change in yield, dollar duration is equal to the price value of a basis point.

A portfolio's modified duration is found by computing the weighted average modified duration of all the bonds in the portfolio, where a particular bond's weight is the market value of the bond relative to the market value of the portfolio.

There are several problems with duration as a measure of the sensitivity of a bond or a portfolio to changes in yield:

1. Duration does a good job of estimating the sensitivity of a bond or portfolio to small changes in yield only. This is due to the convex shape of the price/yield relationship.

2. A portfolio's duration is a good measure of price sensitivity only if the yields of all bonds in the portfolio change by the same amount.

3. For a portfolio consisting of bonds denominated in multiple currencies, modified duration as conventionally calculated does not provide insight into the price sensitivity of the portfolio.

4. For bonds with interest-rate sensitive cash flows, modified duration is inappropriate since it assumes that cash flows will not change as yields change. A more appropriate measure in such instances is effective duration.

In the next chapter, we will take a look at the first problem. In Chapter 15, we will look at the second problem. Finally, when we look at bonds with embedded options, we will focus on the last problem.

There are several applications of duration: dollar duration weighting trades, determining the hedge ratio, immunizing a portfolio against interest rate changes, and determining the duration of an interest-rate swap.

CHAPTER

14

⑥ PRICE VOLATILITY
MEASURES: CONVEXITY

We're now ready to tie together the price/yield relationship and several of the properties about the bond price volatility that we discussed in previous chapters. Recall that the shape of the price/yield relationship is convex. It is the convex shape that gives rise to the properties.[1]

ESTIMATING PRICE WITH DURATION: A GRAPHICAL DEPICTION

In the previous chapter, we explained how duration (modified or dollar) can be used to estimate price change when yield changes. In Exhibit 14-1, a line is drawn tangent to the curve depicting the price/yield relationship at point y*.[2] The tangent line shows the rate of change of price with respect to a change in interest rates at that point (yield). Consequently, the tangent line is directly related to the dollar duration of the bond.[3]

How can the tangent line be used to approximate the new price if yield changes? If we draw a vertical line from any yield (on the horizontal axis), as we do in Exhibit 14-2, the distance between the horizontal axis and the tangent line represents the price as estimated using duration. Notice that the approximation will always underestimate the actual price at the new yield. This agrees with what we illustrated in the previous chapter: duration leads to an underestimate of the new price.

---

1 The formulas shown in this chapter are presented without proof. For a mathematical derivation of the formulas, see Frank
    J. Fabozzi, *Bond Markets, Analysis and Strategies* (Englewood Cliffs, NJ: Prentice-Hall, 1996, 3rd ed), Chapter 4.
2 In nontechnical terms, a tangent line is defined as a line that touches the price/yield relationship at the point y* and does
    not touch the price/yield relationship at any other point.
3 Technically, the slope of the tangent line is the change in price for a change in yield, sometimes referred to as *dP/dy*, a
    term adopted from calculus because the slope is the first derivative of the price function for a bond. The modified
    duration would be the slope of the tangent line if the price/yield relationship is drawn with the *natural logarithm* of
    the bond's price, rather than price, on the vertical axis. To simplify the discussion below, we shall refer to the slope
    of the tangent line as the dollar duration.

EXHIBIT 14-1

Tangent to Price/Yield Relationship

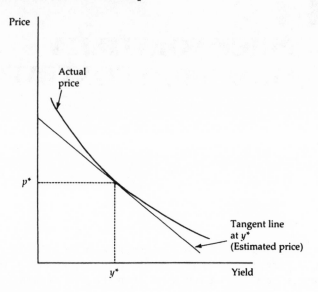

EXHIBIT 14-2

Comparison of Two Bonds with Different Convexities but the Same Duration

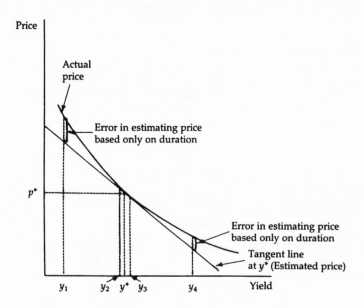

EXHIBIT 14-3

Comparison of Two Bonds with Different Convexities but the Same Duration

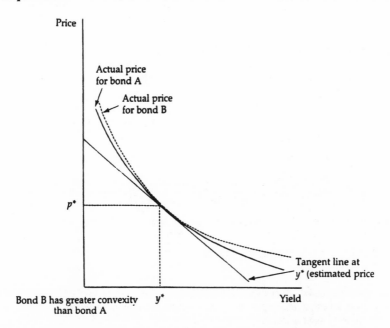

Bond B has greater convexity than bond A

For small changes in yield, the tangent line gives a satisfactory estimate of the actual price. However, the farther we move from the initial yield, y^*, the worse the approximation. It should be apparent that the accuracy of the approximation from using duration (the tangent line) depends on the convexity of the price/yield relationship for the bond. Exhibit 14-3 shows the convexity of two hypothetical bonds. Both have the same duration at y^*; but bond A has less convexity than bond B. As a result, the duration-based approximation of the price is better for bond A than bond B.

MEASURING CONVEXITY

Exhibit 14-3 indicates that how well we can approximate the new price will depend on the convexity of a bond. In this section, we give a formula for measuring the convexity of a bond at a given yield level. In the next section, we show how the price change due to convexity can be estimated.

The convexity of an option-free bond at a given yield level is measured as follows:[4]

Convexity (in periods)

$$= \frac{1(2)\, PVCF_1 + 2(3)\, PVCF_2 + 3(4)\, PVCF_3 + \cdots + n(n+1)\, PVCF_n}{(1+y)^2 \times PVTCF},$$

where

$PVCF_t$ = Present value of the cash flow in period t discounted at the prevailing period yield (in the case of a semiannual-pay bond, one-half the yield to maturity);

t = Period when the cash flow is expected to be received ($t = 1, \ldots, n$);

n = Number of periods until maturity;

y = One-half the yield to maturity;

$PVTCF$ = Total present value of the cash flow of the bond where the present value is determined by using the prevailing yield to maturity.

For a zero-coupon bond, the convexity in periods reduces to

$$\text{Convexity for a zero-coupon bond (in periods)} = \frac{n\,(n+1)}{(1+y)^2}.$$

To convert a bond's convexity from periods to years, the following formula is used:

$$\text{Convexity (in years)} = \frac{\text{Convexity (in periods)}}{k^2},$$

where

k = Number of payments per year (i.e., $k = 2$ for semiannual-pay bonds, $k = 12$ for monthly pay bonds).

For an option-free bond, the convexity measure will always be positive.

Exhibits 14-4 and 14-5 summarize the calculation of convexity for two of the hypothetical bonds (the 8%, 5-year bond and the 14%, 5-year bond) whose Macaulay durations are calculated in Exhibits 13-1 and 13-2 of Chapter 13, respectively, assuming each bond is selling to yield 10%. For the 5-year, zero-coupon bond, $n = 10$ (number of periods) and y is .05. Therefore

$$\text{Convexity} = \frac{10\,(10+1)}{(1.05)^2} = 24.94.$$

---

4 Sometimes this formula is used to approximate convexity (in periods):

$$\frac{(1)^2\, PVCF_1 + (2)^2\, PVCF_2 + (3)^2\, PVCF_3 + \cdots + (n)^2\, PVCF_n}{(1+y)^2 \times PVTCF}$$

EXHIBIT 14–4

Worksheet for Computation of Convexity for a 5-Year, 8% Coupon Bond Selling to Yield 10%

Coupon rate = 8%;
Term (years) = 5;
Initial yield = 10%;
Price = 92.27826.

Period (t)	Cash Flow	PVCF ($)	t(t + 1)	PVCF × t(t + 1) ($)
1	$ 4.00	$3.8095	2	$ 7.6190
2	4.00	3.6281	6	22.7687
3	4.00	3.4554	12	41.4642
4	4.00	3.2908	20	65.8162
5	4.00	3.1341	30	94.0231
6	4.00	2.9849	42	125.3642
7	4.00	2.8427	56	159.1926
8	4.00	2.7074	72	194.9297
9	4.00	2.5784	90	232.0592
10	104.00	63.8470	110	7,023.1676
			Total	$7,965.4046

$$\text{Convexity (in half years)} = \frac{7,965.4046}{(1.05)^2 \, 92.27826} = 78.2942.$$

$$\text{Convexity (in years)} = \frac{78.2942}{2^2} = 19.58.$$

EXHIBIT 14–5

Worksheet for Computation of Convexity for a 5-Year, 14% Coupon Bond Selling to Yield 10%

Coupon rate = 14%;

Term (years) = 5;

Initial yield = 10%;

Price = 115.4434.

Period (t)	Cash Flow ($)	PVCF ($)	t(t + 1)	PVCF × t(t + 1) ($)
1	$ 7.00	$6.6667	2	$ 13.333
2	7.00	6.3492	6	38.0952
3	7.00	6.0469	12	72.5624
4	7.00	5.7589	20	115.1783
5	7.00	5.4847	30	164.5405
6	7.00	5.2235	42	219.3873
7	7.00	4.9748	56	278.5871
8	7.00	4.7379	72	341.1270
9	7.00	4.5123	90	406.1036
10	107.00	65.6887	110	7,225.7590
			Total	$8,874.6738

$$\text{Convexity (in half years)} = \frac{8,874.6738}{(1.05)^2 \, 115.4434} = 69.7276.$$

$$\text{Convexity (in years)} = \frac{69.7276}{2^2} = 17.44.$$

The convexities in years for the 12 hypothetical bonds we examined in the previous chapters are

Coupon (%)	Maturity (years)	Convexity
.00%	5	24.94
.00	15	210.88
.00	30	829.94
8.00	5	19.58
8.00	15	94.36
8.00	30	167.56
10.00	5	18.74
10.00	15	87.62
10.00	30	158.70
14.00	5	17.44
14.00	15	78.90
14.00	30	148.28

What do these convexity numbers mean? How can they be used? We will answer these questions in the sections that follow.

PERCENTAGE PRICE CHANGE DUE TO CONVEXITY

Modified duration provides a first approximation to the percentage change in price. Convexity provides a second approximation, based on the following relationship:

Approximate percentage change in price due to convexity
$$= (.5) \times \text{Convexity} \times (\text{Yield change})^2.$$

Since the convexity measure is always positive for an option-free bond, the approximate percentage change in price due to convexity is positive for either an increase or a decrease in yield.

Illustration 14-1   Consider the 8%, 15-year bond selling to yield 10%. If the yield increases from 10% to 13% (a 300-basis-point or .03 yield change), then the percentage price change due to convexity is

$$(.5) \times 94.36 \times (.03)^2 \times 100 = .0425 = 4.25\%.$$

If the yield decreases by 300 basis points, from 10% to 7%, the percentage price change due to convexity is 4.25%.

Exhibit 14-6 shows the percentage price change due to convexity for various changes in yield for each of the 12 hypothetical bonds.

EXHIBIT 14–6

Percentage Price Change Due to Convexity

Coupon (%)	Term (years)	Convexity	Change (in basis points)					
			1	10	50	100	200	300
0%	5	24.94	.00%	.00%	.03%	.12%	.50%	1.12%
0	15	210.88	.00	.01	.26	1.05	4.22	9.49
0	30	829.94	.00	.04	1.04	4.15	16.60	37.35
8	5	19.58	.00	.00	.02	.10	.39	.88
8	15	94.36	.00	.00	.12	.47	1.89	4.25
8	30	167.56	.00	.01	.21	.84	3.35	7.54
10	5	18.74	.00	.00	.02	.09	.37	.84
10	15	87.62	.00	.00	.11	.44	1.75	3.94
10	30	158.70	.00	.01	.20	.79	3.17	7.14
14	5	17.44	.00	.00	.02	.09	.35	.78
14	15	78.90	.00	.00	.10	.39	1.58	3.55
14	30	148.28	.00	.01	.19	.74	2.97	6.67

PERCENTAGE PRICE CHANGE DUE TO DURATION AND CONVEXITY

The approximate percentage change in price resulting from both duration and convexity is found by simply adding the two estimates.

Illustration 14-2   For the 8%, 15-year bond selling to yield 10%, if yields change from 10% to 13%, we have

Price Change Based on	Approx. % Price Change
Duration	−24.15%
Convexity	+ 4.25
Total	−19.90%

The actual percentage change in price would be –20.41%.
   For a decrease of 300 basis points, from 10% to 7%:

Price Change Based on	Approx. % Price Change
Duration	+24.15%
Convexity	+ 4.25
Total	28.40%

The actual percentage price change would be +29.03%.
   Consequently, for large yield movements, a better approximation for bond price volatility is obtained by combining duration and convexity.
   Exhibit 14-7 shows the percentage price changes due to both duration and convexity for our 12 hypothetical bonds. The percentage price change not explained by duration and convexity is shown in Exhibit 14-8. As can be seen from this exhibit, most of the change in price is explained by using duration and convexity.

Dollar Convexity

In the previous chapter, we explained that dollar duration can be obtained by multiplying modified duration by the initial price. Dollar convexity can be obtained by multiplying convexity by the initial price:

Dollar convexity = Convexity × Initial price.

To determine the dollar price change, the following formula is used:

Dollar price change due to convexity
   $= (.5) \times$ Dollar convexity $\times$ (Yield change)^2.

EXHIBIT 14-7

Estimated Percentage Price Change Using Duration and Convexity

Coupon (%)	Term (years)	Yield Change (in basis points) from 10%					
		1	10	50	100	200	300
		New Yield Level					
		10.01%	10.10%	10.50%	11.00%	12.00%	13.00%
0%	5	-.05%	-.47%	-2.35%	-4.64%	-9.02%	-13.16%
0	15	-.14	-1.42	-6.88	-13.24	-24.36	-33.38
0	30	-.29	-2.82	-13.25	-24.42	-40.54	-48.36
8	5	-.04	-.40	-1.97	-3.88	-7.57	-11.06
8	15	-.08	-.80	-3.91	-7.58	-14.21	-19.90
8	30	-.10	-.96	-4.65	-8.88	-16.09	-21.62
10	5	-.04	-.39	-1.91	-3.77	-7.35	-10.74
10	15	-.08	-.76	-3.74	-7.25	-13.63	-19.13
10	30	-.09	-.94	-4.53	-8.67	-15.75	-21.24
14	5	-.04	-.37	-1.81	-3.58	-6.99	-10.23
14	15	-.07	-.72	-3.51	-6.83	-12.86	-18.11
14	30	-.09	-.91	-4.40	-8.43	-15.37	-20.84

EXHIBIT 14–7

Concluded

Coupon (%)	Term (years)	Yield Change (in basis points) from 10%					
		−1	−10	−50	−100	−200	−300
		New Yield Level					
		9.99%	9.90%	9.50%	9.00%	8.00%	7.00%
0%	5	.05%	.48%	2.41%	4.88%	10.02%	15.40%
0	15	.14	1.44	7.41	15.34	32.80	52.36
0	30	.29	2.90	15.32	32.72	73.74	123.06
8	5	.04	.40	2.01	4.08	8.35	12.82
8	15	.08	.81	4.14	8.52	17.99	28.40
8	30	.10	.98	5.07	10.56	22.79	36.70
10	5	.04	.39	1.95	3.95	8.09	12.42
10	15	.08	.77	3.95	8.13	17.13	27.01
10	30	.09	.95	4.93	10.25	22.09	35.52
14	5	.04	.37	1.86	3.76	7.69	11.79
14	15	.07	.73	3.71	7.61	16.02	25.21
14	30	.09	.92	4.77	9.91	21.31	34.18

EXHIBIT 14-8

Estimated Percentage Price Change Not Explained by Using Both Duration and Convexity

		Yield Change (in basis points) from 10%					
		1	10	50	100	200	300
		New Yield Level					
Coupon (%)	Term (years)	10.01%	10.10%	10.50%	11.00%	12.00%	13.00%
0%	5	.00%	.00%	.00%	.00%	−.02%	−.07%
0	15	.00	.00	.00	−.05	−.39	−1.28
0	30	.00	.00	−.05	−.38	−2.83	−8.94
8	5	.00	.00	.00	.00	−.02	−.05
8	15	.00	.00	.00	−.02	−.15	−.51
8	30	.00	.00	−.01	−.06	−.43	−1.39
10	5	.00	.00	.00	.00	−.01	−.05
10	15	.00	.00	.00	−.01	−.14	−.46
10	30	.00	.00	−.01	−.06	−.42	−1.31
14	5	.00	.00	.00	.00	−.01	−.04
14	15	.00	.00	.00	−.02	−.13	−.41
14	30	.00	.00	−.01	−.05	−.36	−1.17

EXHIBIT 14–8
Concluded

		Yield Change (in basis points) from 10%					
		−1	−10	−50	−100	−200	−300
		New Yield Level					
Coupon (%)	Term (years)	9.99%	9.90%	9.50%	9.00%	8.00%	7.00%
0%	5	.00%	.00%	.00%	.00%	.02%	.07%
0	15	.00	.00	.00	.05	.46	1.62
0	30	.00	.00	.05	.44	3.83	14.05
8	5	.00	.00	.00	.00	.02	.05
8	15	.00	.00	.00	.02	.18	.64
8	30	.00	.00	.01	.06	.56	2.03
10	5	.00	.00	.00	.00	.02	.05
10	15	.00	.00	.00	.02	.16	.58
10	30	.00	.00	.01	.07	.53	1.90
14	5	.00	.00	.00	.00	.01	.04
14	15	.00	.00	.00	.02	.14	.51
14	30	.00	.00	.01	.05	.46	1.69

Illustration 14-3   For the 8%, 15-year bond selling to yield 10%, the dollar convexity per $100 of par value is

$$94.36 \times \$84.63 = \$7,985.69.$$

The dollar price change due to convexity per $100 of par value for a 100-basis-point change is

$$(.5) \times \$7,985.69 \times (.01)^2 = \$.399.$$

Thus, for a 100-basis-point change, the price of the bond will change by approximately $.40 per $100 par value due to convexity.

For a 200-basis-point change, the dollar price change per $100 of par value due to convexity is

$$(.5) \times \$7,985.69 \times (.02)^2 = \$1.597.$$

For a 200-basis-point change, the dollar price change due to convexity is approximately $1.60 per $100 of par value—quadruple the $.40 for a 100-basis-point change. Consequently, unlike dollar duration in which the dollar price change due to duration is proportionate to the change in yield—doubling the yield change from 100 basis points to 200 basis points, for example, doubles the dollar price change due to duration—the dollar price change due to convexity changes more than proportionately.

CONVEXITY AS A MEASURE OF THE CHANGE IN DOLLAR DURATION

The tangent line in Exhibit 14-1 is a measure of the dollar duration of the price/yield relationship at point y^*. The steeper the tangent lines, the greater is the dollar duration; the flatter the lines, the lower is the dollar duration.

Exhibit 14-9 graphically depicts what happens to the dollar duration as the yield changes. Notice that for an option-free bond, as the yield declines below y^*, the dollar duration increases; as the yield increases above y^*, the dollar duration decreases. This is true for all option-free bonds: *the dollar duration increases as the yield decreases and decreases as the yield increases.* Exhibit 14-10 shows the dollar durations for our 12 hypothetical bonds for various yields and confirms our graphical illustration.

Why is this property of an option-free bond attractive? As the yield declines, an investor who is long a bond would want its price to increase as much as possible—hence, an investor wants dollar duration to increase. The opposite is true if the yield increases. An investor wants the dollar duration to decline when the yield increases. For this reason, investors commonly refer to the shape of the price/yield relationship for an option-free bond as having "positive" convexity, "positive" indicating that it is a good attribute of a bond. It is because of positive convexity that we observed the property in Chapter 9 that the increase in price will be greater than the decrease in price for a given change in yield. In Chapter 17, we'll discuss bonds that have "negative" convexity, which means that dollar duration does not change in the desired direction.

Exhibit 14-11 is the same as Exhibit 14-3, which shows the price/yield relationship of two bonds, A and B, with different convexities. Bond B has greater convexity than bond A, while both have the same duration. Bond B is preferred over bond A because it provides a higher bond

EXHIBIT 14-9

Dollar Duration at Different Yields

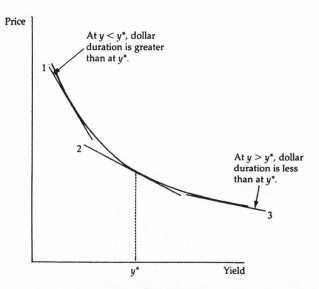

price regardless of how yield changes—greater price appreciation if yield declines, and smaller price loss if yield increases. Notice that the steepness of bond B is greater than that of bond A at yields below y^*. This means that the dollar duration of bond B is greater than bond A if the yield decreases. Thus, the investor realizes greater price appreciation from bond B than from bond A. Look at what happens if the yield increases above y^*. The tangent line is flatter for bond B than for bond A, indicating a lower dollar duration for bond B than for bond A. The investor in bond B realizes a smaller price decline than the investor in bond A.

Exhibit 14-12 shows for each of our 12 hypothetical bonds the percentage change in dollar duration per 100 basis points per $100 par value, assuming an initial yield of 10%. This exhibit is constructed from the dollar durations in Exhibit 14-10. Also shown is the convexity for each bond at a 10% yield. Notice that the change in dollar duration is greater the higher the convexity. *Convexity measures the rate of change of dollar duration for a bond.*

SUMMARY OF PROPERTIES OF CONVEXITY

The convexity properties of all option-free bonds are summarized below.

Property 1   As the yield increases (decreases) the dollar duration of a bond decreases (increases). We demonstrated this in the previous section.

Property 2   For a given yield and maturity, the lower the coupon, the greater the convexity of a bond. This can be seen from the computed convexity of our 12 hypothetical bonds. An

EXHIBIT 14-10

Dollar Duration Per 100 Basis Points Per $100 Par Value

Coupon (%)	Term (years)	Yield Level						
		4%	6%	8%	10%	12%	14%	16%
0%	5	$4.02	$3.61	$3.25	$2.92	$2.63	$2.38	$2.14
0	15	8.12	6.00	4.45	3.31	2.46	1.84	1.38
0	30	8.96	4.94	2.74	1.53	.86	.48	.27
8	5	5.14	4.65	4.21	3.82	3.47	3.16	2.87
8	15	14.72	11.45	8.98	7.10	5.67	4.57	3.71
8	30	26.48	17.34	11.75	8.24	5.98	4.48	3.46
10	5	5.42	4.91	4.45	4.04	3.68	3.35	3.06
10	15	16.37	12.81	10.11	8.05	6.47	5.25	4.30
10	30	30.86	20.44	14.00	9.92	7.26	5.48	4.26
14	5	5.97	5.43	4.93	4.49	4.10	3.74	3.42
14	15	19.67	15.53	12.38	9.95	8.07	6.61	5.46
14	30	39.61	26.64	18.50	13.27	9.82	7.48	5.85

EXHIBIT 14-11

Dollar Duration for Different Convexities

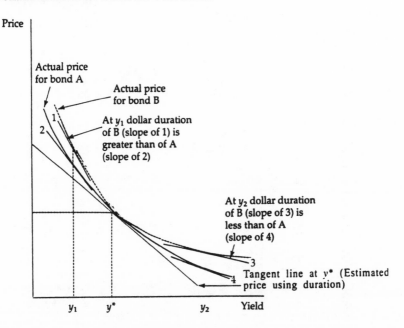

Bond B has greater convexity
than bond A

implication of this property is that for two bonds with the same maturity, a zero-coupon bond has greater convexity than a coupon bond.

Property 3 For a given yield and modified duration, the lower the coupon, the smaller the convexity. The investment implication of this property is that zero-coupon bonds have the lowest convexity for a given modified duration.

To see this, consider three bonds:

Coupon (%)	Maturity (years)	Yield to Maturity (%)	Modified Duration (years)	Convexity
11.625%	10.00	10%	6.05	50.48
5.500	8.00	10	6.02	44.87
0	6.33	10	6.03	39.24

EXHIBIT 14-12

Percentage Change in Dollar Duration Per 100 Basis Points Per $100 Par Value (Initial Yield is 10%)

Assumption: Initial yield = 10%;
Convexity computed at 10% yield.

Coupon (%)	Term (years)	Convexity	Yield Level					
			4%	6%	8%	12%	14%	16%
0	5	24.94	37.6%	23.6%	11.1%	-9.9%	-18.7%	-26.6%
0	15	210.88	145.6	81.5	34.5	-25.5	-44.3	-58.2
0	30	829.94	486.1	223.2	79.3	-43.9	-68.4	-82.1
8	5	19.58	34.5	21.7	10.2	-9.2	-17.4	-24.8
8	15	94.36	107.2	61.2	26.4	-20.2	-35.7	-47.7
8	30	167.56	221.4	110.5	42.6	-27.4	-45.6	-58.0
10	5	18.74	33.9	21.3	10.1	-9.0	-17.1	-24.4
10	15	87.62	103.3	59.1	25.6	-19.6	-34.8	-46.6
10	30	158.70	211.2	106.1	41.2	-26.8	-44.7	-57.1
14	5	17.44	33.0	20.8	9.8	-8.8	-16.7	-23.9
14	15	78.90	97.6	56.1	24.4	-18.9	-33.6	-45.1
14	30	148.28	198.5	100.7	39.4	-26.0	-43.6	-55.9

Notice that all three bonds are selling to yield 10% and have a modified duration of approximately 6 years.[5] The convexity of the bonds decreases as the coupon rate decreases.

Property 4   The convexity of a bond increases at an increasing rate as duration increases. This is depicted in Exhibit 14-13. Doubling duration, for example, will more than double convexity.

VALUE OF CONVEXITY

Look again at Exhibit 14-3, where bonds A and B have the same duration but different convexities. We stated that bond B would be preferred to bond A because both have the same price (same yield) and the same duration, but bond B has greater convexity than bond A. Thus, it offers better price performance if yield changes.

Generally, the market will take the greater convexity of bond B compared to bond A into account in pricing the two bonds. That is, the market prices convexity. Consequently, while there may be times when a situation such as depicted in Exhibit 14-3 may exist, generally the market will require investors to "pay up" (accept a lower yield) for the greater convexity offered by bond B.

EXHIBIT 14–13

Property 4:
Relationship between Duration and Convexity

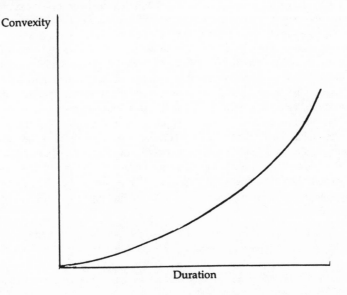

---

5 A 6-year, zero-coupon bond has a Macaulay duration equal to its maturity. It has a modified duration that is less than 6 years.

How much should the market want investors to pay for convexity? Look again at Exhibit 14-3. Notice that if investors expect that yields will change by very little—that is, they expect low interest rate volatility—the advantage of owning bond B over bond A is insignificant because the two bonds will offer approximately the same price performance for small changes in yield. Thus, investors should not be willing to pay much for convexity. In fact, if the market is pricing convexity high, which means that bond A will be offering a higher yield than bond B, then investors with expectations of low interest rate volatility would probably be willing to "sell convexity"—sell bond B if they own it, and buy bond A. In contrast, if investors expect substantial interest rate volatility, bond B would probably sell at a much lower yield than bond A.

Illustration 14-4   To see how two portfolios with the same dollar duration but with different convexities can perform differently, consider the three bonds shown in Exhibit 14-14 and the following two portfolios.[6] One portfolio consists of only bond C, the 10-year bond and shall be referred to as the "bullet portfolio." A second portfolio consists of 50.2% of bond A and 49.8% of bond B; this portfolio shall be referred to as the "barbell portfolio." The dollar duration per 100-basis-point change in yield of the bullet portfolio is 6.43409. Recall from Chapter 13 that dollar duration is a measure of the dollar price sensitivity of a bond or a portfolio. As shown in Exhibit 14-14, the dollar duration per 100-basis-point change in yield of the barbell—which is just the weighted average of the dollar duration of the two bonds—is the same as the bullet portfolio. In fact, the barbell portfolio was designed to produce this result. The dollar convexity of the two portfolios, shown in Exhibit 14-14, is not equal. The dollar convexity of the bullet portfolio is less than that of the barbell portfolio.

The "yield" for the two portfolios is not the same. The yield (yield to maturity) for the bullet is simply the yield to maturity of bond C, 9.25%. The traditional yield calculation for the barbell portfolio, which is found by taking a weighted average of the yield to maturity of the two bonds included in the portfolio, is 8.998%. This would suggest that the "yield" of the bullet portfolio is 25.2 basis points greater than the barbell portfolio. Alternatively, a cash flow yield can be approximated for the barbell portfolio by calculating the dollar-duration market-weighted yield of the portfolio. As shown in Exhibit 14-14, the cash flow yield of the barbell portfolio is 9.187%, suggesting that the "yield" of the bullet portfolio is 6.3 basis points greater than the barbell portfolio. Thus, both portfolios have the same dollar duration but, using either yield measure, the yield of the bullet portfolio is greater than the yield of the barbell portfolio. However, the dollar convexity of the barbell portfolio is greater than that of the bullet portfolio. The difference in the two yields is sometimes referred to as the "cost of convexity."

Exhibit 14-15 shows the difference in the total return over a 6-month investment horizon for the two portfolios, assuming that the yields for all three bonds change by the same number of basis points shown in the first column.[7] The total return reported in the second column of Exhibit 14-15 is

Bullet portfolio's total return – Barbell portfolio's total return.

---

6 This illustration is adapted from Ravi E. Dattatreya and Frank J. Fabozzi, *Active Total Return Management of Fixed Income Portfolios* (Chicago: Probus Publishing, 1989).

7 Note that no assumption is needed for the reinvestment rate since the three bonds shown in Exhibit 14-14 are assumed to be trading right after a coupon payment has been made and therefore there is no accrued interest.

EXHIBIT 14–14

Barbell-Bullet Analysis

Three Bonds Used in Analysis

Bond	Coupon (%)	Maturity (years)	Price Plus Accrued	Yield (%)	Dollar Duration*	Dollar Convexity*
A	8.50%	5	100	8.50%	4.00544	19.8164
B	9.50	20	100	9.50	8.88151	124.1702
C	9.25	10	100	9.25	6.43409	55.4506

Bullet portfolio = Bond C;

Barbell portfolio = Bonds A and B;

Composition of barbell portfolio = 50.2% of bond A; 49.8% of bond B.

Dollar duration of barbell
$$= .502 \times 4.00544 + .498 \times 8.88151 = 6.434.$$

Average yield of barbell
$$= .502 \times 8.50 + .498 \times 9.5 = 8.998.$$

Cash flow yield of barbell[†]
$$= \frac{(8.5 \times .502 \times 4.00544) + (9.5 \times .498 \times 8.88151)}{6.434} = 9.187.$$

Yield pickup = Yield on bullet − Cash flow yield of barbell
$$= 9.25 - 9.187 = .063, \text{ or } 6.3 \text{ basis points.}$$

Analysis based on duration, convexity, and average yield:

Dollar convexity of barbell
$$= .502 \times 19.8164 + .498 \times 124.1702 = 71.7846.$$

Yield pickup = Yield on bullet = Average yield of barbell
$$= 9.25 - 8.998 = .252, \text{ or } 25.2 \text{ basis points}$$

Convexity giveup = Convexity of barbell − Convexity of bullet
$$= 71.7846 - 55.4506 = 16.334.$$

*Per 100-basis-point change in yield.
[†]The calculation shown is actually a dollar-duration weighted yield, a very close approximation to cash flow yield.

EXHIBIT 14–15

Relative Performance of Bullet Portfolio and Barbell Portfolio over a 6-Month Investment Horizon

Yield Change	Difference in Total Return	Yield Change	Difference in Total Return
−5.000	−7.19	.250	.24
−4.750	−6.28	.500	.21
−4.500	−5.44	.750	.16
−4.250	−4.68	1.000	.09
−4.000	−4.00	1.250	.01
−3.750	−3.38	1.500	−.08
−3.500	−2.82	1.750	−.19
−3.250	−2.32	2.000	−.31
−3.000	−1.88	2.250	−.44
−2.750	−1.49	2.500	−.58
−2.500	−1.15	2.750	−.73
−2.250	−.85	3.000	−.88
−2.000	−.59	3.250	−1.05
−1.750	−.38	3.500	−1.21
−1.500	−.20	3.750	−1.39
−1.250	−.05	4.000	−1.57
−1.000	.06	4.250	−1.75
−.750	.15	4.500	−1.93
−.500	.21	4.750	−2.12
−.250	.24	5.000	−2.31
.000	.25		

*Note: Performance is based on the difference in total return over the 6-month investment horizon. Specifically

Bullet portfolio's total return − Barbell portfolio's total return.

Therefore a negative value means that the barbell portfolio outperformed the bullet portfolio.

Thus, a positive sign in the second column means that the bullet portfolio outperformed the barbell portfolio, while a negative sign means that the barbell portfolio outperformed the bullet portfolio.

Which portfolio is the better investment alternative if the yields of all three bonds change by the same amount *and* the investment horizon is 6 months? The answer depends on the amount by which yields change. Notice in the second column that if yields change by less than 100 basis points, the bullet portfolio will outperform the barbell portfolio. The reverse is true if yields change by more than 100 basis points.

The key point here is that looking at measures such as yield (yield to maturity or some type of portfolio yield measure), duration, or convexity tells us little about performance over some investment horizon because performance depends on the magnitude of the change in yields. Moreover, as we shall see in Chapter 15, the relative performance will also depend on the relative change in yields of each bond.

APPROXIMATING CONVEXITY: EFFECTIVE CONVEXITY

The convexity measure of any bond can be approximated using the following formula:

$$\text{Convexity} = \frac{V_+ + V_- - 2V_0}{V_0(\Delta y)^2},$$

where

V_0 = Initial value or price of the security;

Δy = Change in the yield of a security;

V_- = Estimated value of the security if the yield is decreased by Δy;

V_+ = Estimated value of the security if the yield is increased by Δy.

These are the same values used for approximating duration.

For example, consider the 20-year, 7% coupon bond selling at 74.26 to yield 10% that we used in the previous chapter to illustrate how to approximate modified duration. Suppose we evaluate the price changes for a 20-basis-point change up and down. Then,

V_+ = 72.92;

V_- = 75.64;

V_0 = 74.26;

Δy = 0.002.

Substituting these values in the formula:

$$\frac{72.92 + 75.64 - 2\,(74.26)}{(74.26)(0.002)^2} = 134.66$$

The convexity is equal to 132.08. The approximated convexity (134.66) has proven itself to be a good approximation of convexity (132.08).

Effective Convexity

Just as in the case of modified duration, the convexity measure discussed in this chapter does not take into consideration how the cash flows may change if yield changes. In later chapters, we can use the formula above to calculate the convexity of a bond when there are interest-rate sensitive cash flows. When the formula above is used in this way, the resulting convexity is called an *effective convexity* because it allows the cash flow to change as yields change.

SUMMARY

In this chapter, we have presented a graphical explanation of how duration is used to approximate the change in price when yield changes. We showed why duration will underestimate the new price and why the error in estimating price becomes greater for large yield changes. The explanation lies in the convex shape of the price/yield relationship for an option-free bond. We then introduced a convexity measure for an option-free bond to provide a formula that links the convexity measure to price change.

The convexity of a bond will determine its price performance when yield changes. For two bonds with the same duration and the same yield to maturity, the bond with the greater convexity will be the more attractive. Typically, convexity does not come without a cost, however. The cost is the yield give-up necessary to improve convexity. Just how much investors should be willing to pay for better convexity depends on their expectations about the volatility of future interest rates. The greater the expected volatility, the more investors should be willing to pay for convexity. Trades that hold duration constant and improve convexity may enhance return over some specified holding period if the movement in yield is sufficient to offset the cost of obtaining the better convexity.

15

---

⑥ DURATION AND THE YIELD CURVE

$\mathbf{A}$s we explained in Chapter 7, the yield curve describes the relationship between maturity and yield on U.S. Treasury securities. The shape of the yield curve changes over time. Because a portfolio consists of bonds of different maturities, changes in the shape of the yield curve will have different effects on each bond's price.

Our objective in this chapter is threefold. First, we illustrate how the duration measure discussed in Chapter 13 when applied to a portfolio of bonds does not capture the effect of changes in the shape of the yield curve. Second, we review the types of yield curve shifts that have been observed in the Treasury market. Finally, we provide one duration measure that indicates the exposure of a portfolio to yield curve shifts.

DURATION AND NONPARALLEL YIELD CURVE SHIFTS

Two portfolios that have the same duration may perform quite differently if the yield curve does not shift in a parallel fashion. To illustrate this point, consider the three bonds in Illustration 14-4 of Chapter 14 and summarized in Exhibit 14-14.[1] Two portfolios were created from these three bonds: a bullet portfolio consisting of bond C and a barbell portfolio consisting of roughly equal amounts of bonds A and B. As explained in Chapter 14, both portfolios have the same dollar duration. However, the dollar convexity of the two portfolios is not equal. The dollar convexity of the bullet portfolio is less than that of the barbell portfolio. Also, the "yield" for the two portfolios is not the same. The yield for the bullet is simply the yield to maturity of bond C, 9.25%. For the barbell portfolio, the traditional yield calculation is found by taking a weighted average of the yield to maturity of the two bonds included in the portfolio, which is 8.998%.

---

1   This illustration is adapted from Ravi E. Dattatreya and Frank J. Fabozzi, *Active Total Return Management of Fixed Income Portfolios* (Chicago: Probus Publishing, 1995).

Thus, the "yield" of the bullet portfolio is 25.2 basis points higher than that of the barbell portfolio.

Exhibit 15-1, column 2, shows the difference in the total return over a 6-month investment horizon for the two portfolios, assuming that the yield curve shifts in a "parallel" fashion.[2] By parallel we mean that the yields for the short-term bond (A), the intermediate-term bond (C), and the long-term bond (B) change by the same number of basis points, as shown in the first column of the exhibit. The total return reported in the second column of Exhibit 15-1 is

Bullet portfolio's total return – Barbell portfolio's total return.

EXHIBIT 15–1

Relative Performance of Bullet Portfolio and Barbell Portfolio Over a 6-Month Investment Horizon*

Yield Change (%)	Parallel Shift (%)	Nonparallel Shift (%)**	Nonparallel Shift (%)***
–5.000%	–7.19%	–10.69%	–3.89%
–4.750	–6.28	–9.61	–3.12
–4.500	–5.44	–8.62	–2.44
–4.250	–4.68	–7.71	–1.82
–4.000	–4.00	–6.88	–1.27
–3.750	–3.38	–6.13	–0.78
–3.500	–2.82	–5.44	–0.35
–3.250	–2.32	–4.82	0.03
–3.000	–1.88	–4.26	0.36
–2.750	–1.49	–3.75	0.65
–2.500	–1.15	–3.30	0.89
–2.250	–0.85	–2.90	1.09
–2.000	–0.59	–2.55	1.25
–1.750	–0.38	–2.24	1.37
–1.500	–0.20	–1.97	1.47
–1.250	–0.05	–1.74	1.53
–1.000	0.06	–1.54	1.57
–0.750	0.15	–1.38	1.58
–0.500	0.21	–1.24	1.57
–0.250	0.24	–1.14	1.53

Continued

2 Note that no assumption is needed for the reinvestment rate since the three bonds are assumed to be trading right after a coupon payment has been made and therefore there is no accrued interest.

EXHIBIT 15-1

Concluded

Yield Change (%)	Parallel Shift (%)	Nonparallel Shift (%)**	Nonparallel Shift (%)***
0.000	0.25	−1.06	1.48
0.250	0.24	−1.01	1.41
0.500	0.21	−0.98	1.32
0.750	0.16	−0.97	1.21
1.000	0.09	−0.98	1.09
1.250	0.01	−1.00	0.96
1.500	−0.08	−1.05	0.81
1.750	−0.19	−1.10	0.66
2.000	−0.31	−1.18	0.49
2.250	−0.44	−1.26	0.32
2.500	−0.58	−1.36	0.14
2.750	−0.73	−1.46	−0.05
3.000	−0.88	−1.58	−0.24
3.250	−1.05	−1.70	−0.44
3.500	−1.21	−1.84	−0.64
3.750	−1.39	−1.98	−0.85
4.000	−1.57	−2.12	−1.06
4.250	−1.75	−2.27	−1.27
4.500	−1.93	−2.43	−1.48
4.750	−2.12	−2.58	−1.70
5.000	−2.31	−2.75	−1.92

*Performance is based on the difference in total return over a 6-month investment horizon. Specifically

Bullet portfolio's total return − Barbell portfolio's total return.

Therefore a negative value means that the barbell portfolio outperformed the bullet portfolio.

**Change in yield for bond C. Nonparallel shift as follows (flattening of yield curve):

Yield change bond A = Yield change bond C + 25 basis points;
Yield change bond B = Yield change bond C − 25 basis points.

***Change in yield for bond C. Nonparallel shift as follows (steepening of yield curve):

Yield change bond A = Yield change bond C − 25 basis points;
Yield change bond B = Yield change bond C + 25 basis points.

Thus a positive value in the second column means that the bullet portfolio outperforms the barbell portfolio, while a negative sign means that the barbell portfolio outperforms the bullet portfolio. As explained in Illustration 14-4, the better investment alternative depends on the amount by which yields change. If the yields change by less than 100 basis points, the bullet portfolio will outperform the barbell portfolio. The reverse is true if yields change by more than 100 basis points.

Now let's look at what happens if the yield curve does not shift in a parallel fashion. The third and fourth columns of Exhibit 15-1 show the relative performance of the two portfolios for a nonparallel shift of the yield curve. Specifically, the third column assumes that if the yield on bond C (the intermediate-term bond) changes by the amount shown in the first column, the yield on bond A (the short-term bond) will change by the same amount plus 25 basis points, while the yield on bond B (the long-term bond) will change by the same amount shown in the first column less 25 basis points. In this case, the nonparallel shift assumed is a flattening of the yield curve. For this yield curve shift, the barbell will always outperform the bullet.

In the fourth column, the nonparallel shift assumes that for a change in bond C's yield, the yield on bond A will change by the same amount less 25 basis points, while that on bond B will change by the same amount plus 25 points. That is, this nonparallel shift means that the yield curve will steepen. In this case, the bullet portfolio would outperform the barbell portfolio so long as the yield on bond C does not rise by more than 250 basis points or fall by more than 325 basis points.

The key point here is that measures such as yield (yield to maturity or some type of portfolio yield measure), duration, or convexity tell us little about performance over some investment horizon, because performance depends on the magnitude of the change in yields and how the yield curve shifts.

TYPES OF YIELD CURVE SHIFTS

Frank Jones provides empirical evidence of the importance of changes in the yield curve in determining returns of Treasury securities for various maturity sectors from 1979 to 1990.[3] Historically, three basic yield curve shift patterns have been observed, each shown in Exhibit 15-2:

- A parallel shift;
- A twist in the slope of the yield curve (i.e., a flattening or steepening of the yield curve);
- A change in the humpedness of the yield curve (referred to as a *butterfly shift*).

Jones finds that parallel shifts and twists in the yield curve are responsible for 91.6% of Treasury returns, while 3.4% of changes are attributable to butterfly shifts, and the balance, 5%, to unexplained factor shifts.[4] The three types of yield curve shifts are not independent, but

---

3   Frank J. Jones, "Yield Curve Strategies," *Journal of Fixed Income* (September 1991), pp. 33–41.

4   These findings are consistent with those reported in Robert Litterman and José Scheinkman, "Common Factors Affecting Bond Returns," *Journal of Fixed Income* (June 1991), pp. 54–61.

EXHIBIT 15-2

Types of Yield Curve Shifts

(a) Parallel shifts

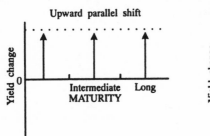
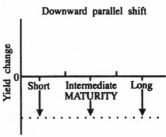

(b) Twists

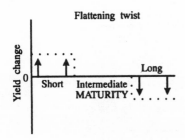
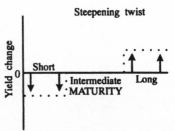

(c) Butterfly shifts

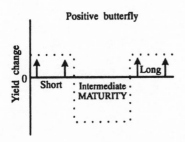
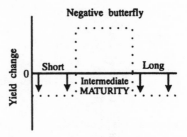

correlated. For example, an upward parallel shift in the yield curve and a flattening of the yield curve have a correlation of .41. Jones's statistical analysis suggests that an upward shift of the yield curve by 10 basis points is consistent with a 2.5 basis point flattening of the yield curve. Moreover, he finds that an upward shift and flattening of the yield curve is correlated with a positive butterfly (less humpedness), while a downward shift and steepening of the yield curve is correlated with a negative butterfly (more humpedness). These two types of shifts in the yield curve are depicted in Exhibit 15-3.

EXHIBIT 15-3

Combination of Yield Curve Shifts

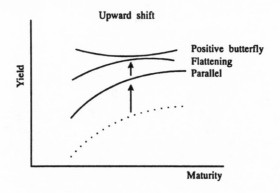

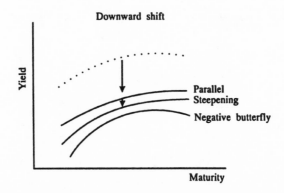

YIELD CURVE SHIFTS AND THE VALUE OF CONVEXITY

In Chapter 14 it was stated that there is a trade-off between convexity and yield. This statement is not correct once nonparallel shifts in the yield curve are considered. This should not be surprising since as argued in earlier chapters, the yield measure is not a good indicator of the potential return. To illustrate this, consider the three hypothetical bonds shown in Exhibit 15-4.[5] A barbell portfolio with the same dollar duration as the bullet portfolio was constructed. At the bottom of the exhibit are the yield, dollar duration, and dollar convexity. Notice that the average yield and the dollar convexity are greater for the barbell portfolio than for the bullet portfolio.

Thus, it would seem that the barbell portfolio in our illustration would perform better than the bullet portfolio over a 6-month investment horizon. This is, in fact, the case for a parallel shift in the yield, as can be seen in Exhibit 15-5. However, this is not the case for a nonparallel yield curve shift. Exhibit 15-6 shows that if the yield curve steepens as assumed in the exhibit, the bullet outperforms the barbell over the 6-month investment horizon.

EXHIBIT 15-4

Three Hypothetical Bonds to Illustrate the Lack of Trade-Off Between Yield and Convexity

Bond	Coupon Rate (%)	Price ($)	Yield to maturity (%)	Maturity (years)
X	7.900%	$100	7.900%	2
Y	8.800	100	8.800	7
Z	8.200	100	8.200	4

Bullet portfolio = Bond Z;

Barbell portfolio = Bonds X and Y;

Composition of barbell portfolio = 53.86% of bond X; 46.14% of bond Y.

Summary of parameters:

Portfolio	Yield (%)	Dollar Duration	Dollar Convexity
Bullet	8.20%	3.35253	6.90699
Barbell	8.32	3.35253	8.89010

5   This illustration is taken from Chapter 11 of Frank J. Fabozzi, *Bond Portfolio Management* (New Hope, PA: Frank J. Fabozzi Associates, 1996).

EXHIBIT 15-5

Performance of Bullet and Barbell Portfolios Over a 6-Month Horizon Assuming a Parallel Yield Curve Shift

Yield Change (in basis points)	Price Plus Coupon ($)			Total Return (%)		
	X	Y	Z	Bullet	Barbell	Difference*
-300	$108.2382	$120.4549	$113.5879	27.18%	27.75%	-0.57%
-250	107.5063	117.5671	111.9321	23.86	24.30	-0.43
-200	106.7813	114.7679	110.3069	20.61	20.93	-0.32
-150	106.0633	112.0545	108.7117	17.42	17.66	-0.23
-100	105.3522	109.4239	107.1459	14.29	14.46	-0.17
-50	104.6477	106.8733	105.6089	11.22	11.35	-0.13
-25	104.2980	105.6272	104.8510	9.70	9.82	-0.12
0	103.9500	104.4000	104.1000	8.20	8.32	-0.12
25	103.6036	103.1915	103.3559	6.71	6.83	-0.12
50	103.2589	102.0013	102.6187	5.24	5.36	-0.12
100	102.5742	99.6748	101.1644	2.33	2.47	-0.14
150	101.8960	97.4180	99.7365	-0.53	-0.34	-0.19
200	101.2242	95.2286	98.3345	-3.33	-3.08	-0.25
250	100.5587	93.1044	96.9579	-6.08	-5.76	-0.32
300	99.8993	91.0431	95.6061	-8.79	-8.37	-0.41

* A positive sign indicates that the bullet portfolio outperformed the barbell portfolio; a negative sign indicates that the barbell portfolio outperformed the bullet portfolio.

EXHIBIT 15–6

Performance of Bullet and Barbell Portfolios Over a 6-Month Horizon Assuming a Steepening of the Yield Curve

Yield Change for Z (in basis points)	Price Plus Coupon ($)			Total Return (%)		
	X	Y	Z	Bullet	Barbell	Difference*
–0.0300	$108.6807	$118.7114	$113.5879	27.18%	26.62%	0.56%
–0.0250	107.9446	115.8771	111.9321	23.86	23.21	0.65
–0.0200	107.2155	113.1298	110.3069	20.61	19.89	0.72
–0.0150	106.4933	110.4664	108.7117	17.42	16.65	0.77
–0.0100	105.7780	107.8842	107.1459	14.29	13.50	0.79
–0.0050	105.0696	105.3802	105.6089	11.22	10.43	0.79
–0.0025	104.7179	104.1568	104.8510	9.70	8.92	0.78
0.0000	104.3678	102.9520	104.1000	8.20	7.43	0.77
0.0025	104.0195	101.7655	103.3559	6.71	5.96	0.75
0.0050	103.6728	100.5969	102.6187	5.24	4.51	0.73
0.0100	102.9842	98.3125	101.1644	2.33	1.66	0.67
0.0150	102.3022	96.0964	99.7365	–0.53	–1.12	0.60
0.0200	101.6265	93.9464	98.3345	–3.33	–3.83	0.50
0.0250	100.9572	91.8602	96.9579	–6.08	–6.48	0.40
0.0300	100.2942	89.8356	95.6061	–8.79	–9.06	0.28

Assumptions:

Change in yield of bond Z (column 1) results in a change in the yield of bond X minus 30 basis points;

Change in yield of bond Z (column 1) results in a change in the yield of bond Y plus 30 basis points.

* A positive sign indicates that the bullet portfolio outperformed the barbell portfolio; a negative sign indicates that the barbell portfolio outperformed the bullet portfolio.

YIELD CURVE RESHAPING DURATIONS

While the total return framework clearly demonstrates the performance potential of a bond portfolio, money managers still seek measures of the interest rate sensitivity of their portfolio, i.e., duration and convexity. The weakness of the traditional modified duration, as we have just illustrated, is that it assumes that the yield curve shifts in a parallel fashion.

The sensitivity of a portfolio to changes in the shape of the yield curve can be approximated. There have been several approaches suggested in the literature to accomplish this.[6] The methodology described here is the one proposed by Klaffky, Ma, and Nozari.[7] They refer to the sensitivity of a portfolio to changes in the shape of the yield curve as *reshaping durations*.

To explain reshaping durations, we can use the illustration developed by Klaffky, Ma, and Nozari. Exhibit 15-7 shows two Treasury portfolios, portfolio A and portfolio B, constructed from three on-the-run Treasury securities: the 2-year, 10-year, and 30-year. The analysis is based on the yield curve as of the close of May 29, 1992. The yield for each issue on that date was 5.18% for the 2-year issue, 7.33% for the 10-year issue, and 7.84% for the 30-year issue. Also shown in the exhibit is the modified duration for each Treasury issue.[8] The modified duration for both portfolios is 7. Consequently, for a 50-basis-point change for all three maturities of the yield curve, each portfolio should change by approximately 3.5%.

EXHIBIT 15-7

Two Portfolios with Similar Durations but Different Yield Curve Exposures

On-the-run Treasury Issue	Modified Duration	Market Weight (%)	
		Portfolio A	Portfolio B
5.125% of 5/31/94	1.9	20%	39%
7.50% of 5/12/02	7.1	60	20
8.0% of 11/15/21	11.1	20	41
Portfolio modified duration		7	7

Source: Adapted from Thomas E. Klaffky, Y.Y. Ma, and Ardavan Nozari, "Managing Yield Curve Exposure: Introducing Reshaping Durations," *Journal of Fixed Income* (December 1992).

---

6 For a description of these measures, see Frank J. Fabozzi, *Measuring and Controlling Interest Rate Risk* (New Hope, PA: Frank J. Fabozzi, 1996), Chapter 4.

7 Thomas E. Klaffky, Y.Y. Ma, and Ardavan Nozari, "Managing Yield Curve Exposure: Introducing Reshaping Durations," *Journal of Fixed Income* (December 1992).

8 Klaffky, Ma, and Nozari present a generalized approach in which Treasury and non-Treasury securities are included in the portfolio. The latter includes bonds with embedded options (i.e., callable and putable bonds). The valuation of these bonds is discussed in Part V of this book. As will be explained, for bonds with embedded options, a more appropriate measure of price sensitivity is effective duration, a measure we introduced in Chapter 13. Thus, in their article, Klaffky, Ma, and Nozari refer to the effective duration rather than modified duration. For a noncallable Treasury issue, the two are almost identical, so the modified duration is used in our explanation of their methodology.

Let's look at the actual percentage price change for the two portfolios under three different yield curve scenarios. In the first scenario, suppose that the yield curve shifts in a parallel fashion so that the yield for all Treasury issues declines by 50 basis points. Under this scenario, the actual percentage price increase is 3.52% for portfolio A and 3.56% for portfolio B. Thus, the two portfolios would have similar performance. Note that the percentage price change is what would be projected using modified duration (3.5%).

In the next two scenarios, assume a reshaping of the yield curve. In the second scenario, suppose that the 2-year yield declines by 50 basis points, while the 10-year and 30-year yields do not change (i.e., the yield curve steepens). In contrast to the first scenario, portfolio A's price change will be .19%, while portfolio B's will be .36%. Thus, portfolio A will outperform portfolio B by .17%. In the third scenario, assume that the 2-year and 10-year yields do not change, but the 30-year yield declines by 50 basis points (i.e., the yield curve flattens). In this scenario, portfolio B will outperform portfolio A by 1.25%, 2.42% versus 1.17%.

What we seek is a duration measure that takes into account how the reshaping of the yield curve affects price changes. In the measures discussed below, we focus on three points on the yield curve—2-year, 10-year, and 30-year—and the spread between the 10-year and 2-year issue and between the 30-year and 10-year issue. The former spread is referred to as the *short-end of the yield curve*, and the latter spread as the *long-end of the yield curve*. Klaffky, Ma, and Nozari refer to the sensitivity of a portfolio to changes in the short end of the yield curve as *short-end duration* (SEDUR), and to changes in the long end of the yield curve as *long-end duration* (LEDUR). These concepts, however, are applicable to other points on the yield curve.

Calculating Reshaping Duration

To calculate the SEDUR of each bond in the portfolio, the percentage change in the bond's price is calculated for (1) a steepening of the yield curve at the short end by 50 basis points, and (2) a flattening of the yield curve at the short end of the yield curve by 50 basis points. Then the bond's SEDUR is computed as follows:

$$\text{SEDUR} = \frac{P_s - P_f}{P_0} \times 100,$$

where

P_s = Bond's price if the short end of the yield curve steepens by 50 basis points;
P_f = Bond's price if the short end of the yield curve flattens by 50 basis points;
P_0 = Bond's current market price.

To calculate the LEDUR, we use the same procedure for each bond in the portfolio: calculate the price for (1) a flattening of the yield curve at the long end by 50 basis points, and (2) a steepening of the yield curve at the long end of the yield curve by 50 basis points. Then the bond's LEDUR is computed in the following manner:

$$\text{SEDUR} = \frac{P_f - P_s}{P_0} \times 100.$$

The SEDUR and the LEDUR calculations are equivalent to the formula for approximating duration given in Chapter 13 when a 50 basis point change is used in the formula. Since in our illustration we are using Treasury issues, the modified duration for each bond is the appropriate measure. For example, the SEDUR for the 2-year Treasury in Exhibit 15-7 is 1.9, and its LEDUR is zero. The SEDUR for the 30-year bond is zero, and its LEDUR is 11.1. The analysis proceeds from the shifting of the yield curve holding the 10-year yield constant, so the SEDUR and the LEDUR for the 10-year issue are zero.

The portfolio SEDUR and LEDUR are the weighted average of the corresponding durations for each bond in the portfolio. For example, the SEDUR for the two portfolios is calculated as follows:

Portfolio A: .2 (1.9) + .4 (0) +   .2 (0) = 3.8;
Portfolio B: .39 (1.9) + .2 (0) + .41 (0) = 7.4.

A SEDUR of 3.8 means that if the short end of the yield curve shifts by 50 basis points, the portfolio value will change by approximately 1.9%. A similar shift for portfolio B will result in a 3.7% change in the portfolio's value.

The LEDUR for the two portfolios is calculated in the following manner:

Portfolio A: .2 (0) + .4 (0) +   .2 (11.1) = 2.2;
Portfolio B: .39 (0) + .2 (0) + .41 (11.1) = 4.6.

So far, we have looked at only bonds with maturities at the three points on the yield curve that are used to define the short end and long end. The methodology can be generalized to other maturities as follows.

1. The shift in yields begins with the 10-year Treasury.

2. At the short end, the steepening or flattening of the yield curve for any maturity other than 2 years is proportionate to the 10-year to 2-year spread. For example, suppose that the 10-to-2-year spread is 200 basis points and that the 10-to-7-year spread is 120 basis points. Assume that the yield spread widens by 50 basis points, a 25% increase in the spread. The yield spread for the 10-to-7-year spread is then assumed to widen by 20 basis points (50 basis points – .25 × 120). The SEDUR for the 7-year is then calculated assuming a 20-basis-point change in the spread, not 50 basis points.

3. At the long end, the steepening or widening for any bond with a maturity of greater than 10 years is assumed to be proportionate to the change in the 30- to-10-year spread.

SUMMARY

In this chapter the limitation of duration when the yield curve does not shift in a parallel fashion is illustrated. Three types of yield curve shifts have been observed: parallel shifts, a twist in the slope of the yield curve, and a change in the humpedness of the yield curve. The convexity/yield trade-off does not hold when the yield curve can shift in a nonparallel fashion. To measure the exposure of a portfolio to yield curve shifts, yield curve reshaping durations can be calculated.

⑥ ANALYZING BONDS WITH EMBEDDED OPTIONS

CHAPTER

16

⑥ CALL OPTIONS: INVESTMENT AND PRICE CHARACTERISTICS

In previous chapters, we described the investment characteristics of option-free bonds. Most of the bonds that we encounter in the market, however, are not option-free. To establish a basis for understanding the price/yield relationship and price volatility characteristics of bonds with embedded options, we review the investment and price characteristics of options in this chapter. Our focus is on *call* options because most corporate bonds and municipal bonds and all mortgage pass-through securities have embedded call options.

WHAT IS AN OPTION?

An option is an agreement granting the buyer of the option the right to purchase from or sell to the writer of the option a designated instrument at a specified price within a specified period of time. The writer, also referred to as the seller, grants this right to the buyer in exchange for a sum of money called the *option price* or *option premium*. The price at which the instrument may be bought or sold is called the *exercise price* or *strike price*. The date after which an option is void is called the *expiration date* or *maturity date*. An option is called an *American option* if the buyer may exercise the option at any time up to and including the expiration date. An option is called a *European option* if the buyer may exercise the option on only the expiration date.

When an option grants the buyer the right to purchase the designated instrument from the writer, it is called a *call option*. When the option buyer has the right to sell the designated instrument to the writer (seller), the option is called a *put option*. The buyer of an option is said to be *long the option;* the writer (seller) is said to be *short the option*.

The most popular exchange-traded interest-rate options are options in which the designated instrument is an interest-rate futures contract. In this chapter we focus on options on cash market bonds because we will be applying the principles and concepts in this chapter to bonds with embedded options in which the cash market bond is the underlying instrument.

PAYOFFS FROM BUYING AND SELLING OPTIONS

The maximum amount that an option buyer can lose is the option price. The maximum profit that the option writer (seller) can realize is the option price. The option buyer has substantial upside return potential while the option writer has substantial downside risk.

We describe the profit/loss or payoff profile for four basic option positions: (1) long call (buying a call option), (2) short call (selling or writing a call option), (3) long put (buying a put option), and (4) short put (selling or writing a put option). The discussion assumes that a position in only one option is taken. That is, no position is taken in another option or bond. *The profit/loss profiles presented assume that each option position is held to the expiration date and not exercised early.* Also, to simplify the illustrations we assume there are no transaction costs in implementing the position.

Long Call Position (Buying a Call Option)

An investor who purchases a call option is said to be in a *long call position*. This is the most straightforward option for allowing the investor to participate in an anticipated decrease in interest rates (increase in the price of bonds).

To illustrate this strategy, assume that there is a call option on a particular 10% coupon bond with a par value of $100 and 15 years and 2 months to maturity. The call option expires in 2 months, the strike price is $100, and the option price is $5.

Suppose that the current price of the bond is $100 (i.e., the bond is selling at par), which means that the yield on this bond is 10%. The payoff from this position will depend on the price of the bond at the expiration date. The price, in turn, will depend on the yield on 15-year bonds with 10% coupons, because in 2 months the bond will have only 15 years to maturity.

If the price of the bond at the expiration date is less than or equal to $100 (which means that the market yield is greater than or equal to 10%), then the investor would not exercise the option. The option buyer will lose the entire option price of $5. Notice, however, that this is the maximum loss that the option buyer will realize, no matter how far the price of the bond declines.

If the price of the bond is higher than $100 (that is, the market yield at expiration is less than 10%), the option buyer will exercise the option. To exercise, the option buyer purchases the bond for $100 (the strike price) and then can sell it in the market for a higher price. The option buyer will realize a loss at expiration if the price of the bond is more than $100 but less than $105 (which corresponds to a market yield at expiration of 10% and approximately 9.35%, respectively). The option buyer will break even if the price of the bond at expiration is $105. This is the break-even price because it costs the option buyer $5 to acquire the call option and $100 to exercise the option to purchase the bond. A profit will be realized if the price of the bond at expiration is more than $105 (that is, the market yield declines to at least 9.35%).

Exhibit 16-1 shows the profit/loss profile. While the break-even point and the loss will depend on the option price, the shape of the curve shown in the exhibit will hold for all buyers of call options. The shape indicates that the maximum loss is the option price and that there is substantial upside potential.

EXHIBIT 16–1

Profit/Loss for a Long Call Position

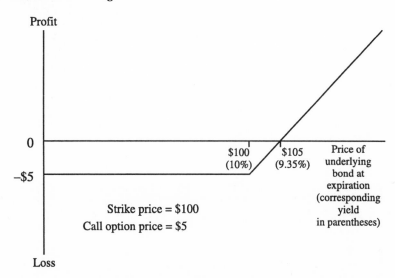

Short Call Position (Selling or Writing a Call Option)

An investor who sells or writes a call option is said to be in a *short call position*. Investors who believe that interest rates will rise or change very little can, if their expectations are realized, generate income by writing (selling) a call option.

To illustrate this option position we can use the call option used to illustrate the long call position. The profit/loss profile of the short call position is the mirror image of the payoff of the long call strategy. That is, the profit (loss) of the short call position for any given price of the bond at the expiration date is the same as the loss (profit) of the long call position. Consequently, the maximum profit that the short call position can produce is the option price; the maximum loss is limited only by how much the price of the bond can increase (i.e., how far the market yield can fall) by the expiration date, less the option price. This can be seen in Exhibit 16-2, which shows the profit/loss profile for this short call position.

Long Put Position (Buying a Put Option)

The most straightforward option position an investor can take to benefit from an expected increase in interest rates is to buy a put option. This investment position is called a *long put position*.

To illustrate the payoff profile for this position, we'll assume a hypothetical put option for a 10% coupon bond with a par value of $100, 15 years and 2 months to maturity, and a strike price of $100, selling for $5.50. The current price of the bond is $100 (yield of 10%). The payoff for this strategy at the expiration date depends on the market yield at the time.

EXHIBIT 16–2

Profit/Loss for a Short Call Position

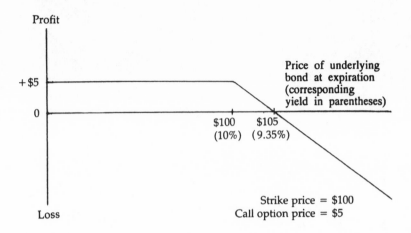

If the price of the bond is equal to or more than $100 because the market yield has fallen below 10%, the buyer of the put option will not exercise it, thereby incurring a loss of $5.50 (the option price). The investor will exercise the option when the price of the bond at expiration is less than $100 (the market yield at expiration is above 10%). If the market yield is higher than approximately 10.75%, the price of the bond will be lower than $94.50, resulting in a profit from the position. For market yields between 10% and about 10.75%, the investor will realize a loss but the loss is less than $5.50. The break-even market yield is approximately 10.75%, since this will result in a bond price of $94.50.

Exhibit 16-3 shows the profit/loss profile for this position. As with all long option positions, the loss is limited to the option price. The profit potential, however, is substantial; the theoretical maximum profit is generated if the bond price falls to zero.

Short Put Position (Selling or Writing a Put Option)

The *short put position* involves the selling (writing) of a put option. This position is taken if the investor expects interest rates to fall or stay flat so that the price of the bond will increase or stay the same. The profit/loss profile for a short put position is the mirror image of the long put option. The maximum profit from this strategy is the option price. The maximum loss is limited only by how low the price of the bond can fall by the expiration date less the option price received for writing the option. Exhibit 16-4 graphically depicts the profit/loss profile.

Considering the Time Value of Money

Our illustrations of the four basic option positions have neglected the time value of money. Specifically, the buyer of an option must pay the seller the option price at the time the option is purchased. Thus, the buyer must finance the purchase of the option or, if the funds do not

EXHIBIT 16–3

Profit/Loss for a Long Put Position

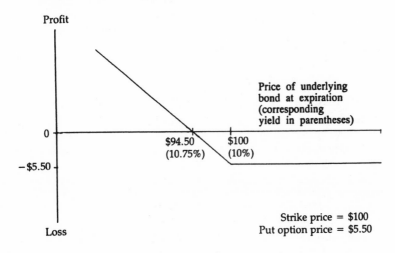

EXHIBIT 16–4

Profit/Loss for a Short Put Position

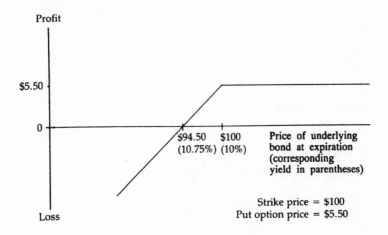

have to be borrowed, the buyer loses the interest that could be earned by investing the option price. In contrast, assuming that the seller does not have to use the option price as margin for the short position, the seller has the opportunity to invest the option price.

The time value of money changes the profit profile of the option positions. The break-even price for the buyer and the seller of an option will not be the same as in our illustrations. For example, the break-even price for the underlying instrument at the expiration date is higher for the buyer of a call option; for the seller, it is lower.

THE INTRINSIC VALUE AND TIME VALUE OF AN OPTION

The cost to the buyer of an option is primarily a reflection of the option's *intrinsic* value and any additional amount over its intrinsic value. The premium over intrinsic value is often referred to as *time value*. This expression, "time value," should not be confused with our earlier use of the term to describe the valuation of cash flows.

Intrinsic Value of an Option

The intrinsic value of an option is the economic value of the option if it is exercised immediately. Since the buyer of an option need not exercise the option and, in fact, will not do so if no economic value will result from exercising, the intrinsic value cannot be less than zero.

The intrinsic value of a call option on a bond is the difference between the current bond price and the strike price. For example, if the *strike price* for a call option is $100 and the *current bond price* is $107, the intrinsic value is $7. That is, if the option buyer exercised the option and simultaneously sold the bond, the option buyer would realize $107 from the sale of the bond, which would be covered by acquiring the bond from the option writer for $100, thereby netting $7.

When a call option has intrinsic value, it is said to be "in the money." Our call option with a strike price of $100 is in the money when the price of the underlying bond is greater than $100. When the strike price of a call option exceeds the current bond price, the call option is said to be "out of the money" and has no intrinsic value. A call option for which the strike price is equal to the current bond price is said to be "at the money."

These relationships are summarized below for a call option:

If the current bond price is higher than the strike price, then the

1. Intrinsic value is the difference between the current bond price and strike price;
2. Option is said to be "in the money."

If the current bond price equals the strike price, then the

1. Intrinsic value is zero;
2. Option is said to be "at the money."

If the current bond price is lower than the strike price, then the

1. Intrinsic value is zero;
2. Option is said to be "out of the money."

For a put option, the intrinsic value is equal to the amount by which the current bond price is below the strike price. For example, if the strike price of a put option is $100, and the current bond price is $88, the intrinsic value is $12. That is, if the buyer of the put option exercises it and simultaneously buys the bond, he or she will net $12. The bond will be sold to the writer for $100 and purchased in the market for $88.

When the put option has intrinsic value, the option is said to be "in the money." For our put option with a strike price of $100, the option will be in the money when the bond price is less than $100. A put option is "out of the money" when the current bond price exceeds the strike price. A put option is "at the money" when the strike price is equal to the current bond price.

These relationships are summarized below for a put option:

If the current bond price is lower than the strike price, then the

1. Intrinsic value is the difference between the strike price and current bond price;
2. Option is said to be "in the money."

If the current bond price equals the strike price, then the

1. Intrinsic value is zero;
2. Option is said to be "at the money."

If the current bond price is higher than the strike price, then the

1. Intrinsic value is zero;
2. Option is said to be "out of the money."

Time Value of an Option

The time value of an option is the amount by which the option price exceeds the intrinsic value. That is,

Time value of an option = Option price – Intrinsic value.

For example, if the price of a call option with a strike price of $100 is $18 when the current bond price is $107, then for this option:

Intrinsic value = $107 – $100 = $7;
Time value of option = $18 – $7 = $11.

If the current bond price is $88 instead of $107, then the time value of this option is $18 since the option has no intrinsic value. Notice that for an at-the-money or out-of-the-money option, the time value of the option is equal to the option price because the intrinsic value is zero.

At the expiration date, the time value of the option will be zero. The option price at the expiration date will be equal to its intrinsic value.

Why would an option buyer be willing to pay a premium over the intrinsic value for an option? The reason is that the option buyer believes that at some time prior to expiration, changes in the market yield will increase the value of the rights conveyed by the option.

THE OPTION PRICE

In the next chapter we shall see that the price of a bond with an embedded option is determined by the price of the underlying bond and the value of the option. While we can easily determine the value of an option at the expiration date and the intrinsic value of an option at any time prior to the expiration date, the fair value or price of the option at any time prior to the expiration date must be estimated. In this section, we will discuss the factors that influence the fair or "theoretical" value of an option.[1]

Factors that Influence the Option Price

Six factors influence the option price:

1. Current price of the underlying bond;
2. Strike price;
3. Time to expiration;
4. Short-term risk-free interest rate over the life of the option;
5. Coupon rate;
6. Expected interest-rate volatility over the life of the option.

The effect of each of these factors depends on whether (1) the option is a call or a put and (2) the option is an American option (an option that may be exercised up to and including the expiration date) or a European option (an option that may be exercised only at the expiration date).[2]

Current Price of the Underlying Bond
For a call option, as the current price of the underlying bond increases (decreases), the option price increases (decreases). For a put option, as the current price of the bond decreases (increases), the option price increases (decreases).

Strike Price
All other factors constant, the higher the strike price is, the lower is the price of a call option. For a put option, the opposite is true: the higher the strike price, the higher the price of a put option.

Time to Expiration
For American options, all other factors constant, the longer the time to expiration, the higher is the option price. No general statement can be made for European options.

Short-Term Risk-Free Interest Rate over the Life of the Option
Holding all other factors constant, the price of a call option on a bond will increase as the

---

1 For a more detailed discussion of the impact of these factors on the price of an option, see Mark Pitts and Frank J. Fabozzi, *Interest Rate Futures and Options* (Chicago: Probus Publishing, 1989).
2 The option price also will depend on whether the underlying instrument is a cash market bond or an interest-rate futures contract. Our focus in this chapter is on options on cash market bonds.

short-term risk-free interest rate rises. For a put option, the opposite is true: an increase in the short-term risk-free interest rate will reduce the price of a put option.

Coupon Rate

Coupons for options on bonds tend to reduce the price of a call option because the coupons make it more attractive to hold the bond than the option. Thus, call options on coupon-bearing bonds will tend to be priced lower than other similar call options on noncoupon-bearing bonds. For put options, coupons tend to increase their price.

Expected Interest-Rate Volatility over the Life of the Option

As the expected interest-rate volatility over the life of the option increases, the price of an option increases. The reason is that the more the expected volatility, as measured by the standard deviation or variance of interest rates,[3] the greater the probability that the price of the underlying bond will move in the direction that will benefit the option buyer.

Option Pricing Model

Several models have been developed to estimate the theoretical or fair price of an option. These models are based on an arbitrage or riskless hedge valuation model. Our purpose here is not to describe option pricing models, but instead, to mention some of the models that are commercially available from software vendors. Most of the dealer firms have developed their own option pricing models, which typically are not available to clients.

The most popular option pricing model for American call options on common stocks is the Black–Scholes option pricing model.[4] The key insight of the Black-Scholes option pricing model is that a synthetic option can be created by taking an appropriate position in the underlying common stock and borrowing or lending funds at the riskless interest rate.[5]

There are several problems in applying the Black–Scholes option pricing model to price interest rate options. To illustrate these problems, consider a 3-month European call option on a 3-year zero-coupon bond.[6] The maturity value of the underlying bond is $100, and the strike price is $120. Suppose further that the current price of the bond is $75.13, the 3-year risk-free rate is 10% annually, and expected price volatility is 4%. What would be the fair value for this option? Do you really need an option pricing model to determine the value of this option?

Think about it. This zero-coupon bond will never have a price above $100 because that is the maturity value. As the strike price is $120, the option will never be exercised; its value is therefore zero. If you can get anyone to buy such an option, any price you obtain will be free money. Yet an option buyer armed with the Black–Scholes option pricing model will input the variables we assume above and come up with a value for this option of $5.60! Why is the Black–Scholes model off by so much? The answer lies in the underlying assumptions.

---

3   These statistical measures are explained in Chapter 21.
4   Fischer Black and Myron Scholes, "The Pricing of Corporate Liabilities," *Journal of Political Economy* (May–June 1973), pp. 637–659.
5   The appropriate position in the underlying common stock depends on how the price of the option will change when the price of the stock changes. This relationship between the change in price of the option and the change in price of the underlying common stock is called the *delta* of the option and is discussed later in this chapter.
6   Lawrence Dyer and David Jacob, "Guide to Fixed Income Option Pricing Models," in Frank J. Fabozzi (ed.), *The Handbook of Fixed Income Options* (Chicago: Probus Publishing, 1989).

There are three assumptions underlying the Black–Scholes model that limit its use in pricing options on interest rate instruments. First, the probability distribution for the prices assumed by the Black–Scholes option pricing model is a lognormal distribution, which permits some probability—no matter how small—that the price can take on any positive value. In the case of the zero-coupon bond, that means the price can take on a value above $100. In the case of a coupon bond, we know that the price cannot exceed the sum of the coupon payments plus the maturity value. For example, for a 5-year 10% coupon bond with a maturity value of $100, the price cannot be more than $150 (5 coupon payments of $10 plus the maturity value of $100). The only way a bond's price can exceed the maximum value is if negative interest rates are permitted. This is not likely to occur, so any probability distribution for prices assumed by an option pricing model that permits bond prices to be more than the maximum bond value can generate nonsensical option prices. The Black–Scholes model does allow bond prices to exceed the maximum bond value (or, equivalently, allows negative interest rates). This is one of the reasons we obtained the nonsensical option price for the 3-month European call option on the 3-year zero-coupon bond.

The second assumption of the Black–Scholes option pricing model is that the short-term interest rate is constant over the life of the option. Yet the price of an interest rate option does change as interest rates change. A change in the short-term interest rate changes the rates along the yield curve. Therefore, to assume that the short-term rate will be constant is inappropriate for interest rate options.

The third assumption is that the variance of prices is constant over the life of the option. Recall from Chapter 5 that as a bond moves closer to maturity, its price volatility declines. Therefore, the assumption that price variance is constant over the life of the option is inappropriate.

A binomial option pricing model based on the price distribution of the underlying bond suffers from the same problems as the Black–Scholes model. A way around the problem of negative interest rates is to use a model based on the distribution of yields rather than prices.

While the binomial option pricing model based on yields is superior to models based on prices, it still has a theoretical drawback. All option pricing models to be valid theoretically must satisfy the put-call parity relationship (explained later in the chapter). The problem with the binomial model based on yields is that it does not satisfy this relationship. It violates the relationship in that it fails to take into consideration the yield curve, thereby allowing arbitrage opportunities.

The most elaborate models that take the yield curve into consideration and as a result do not permit arbitrage opportunities are called *arbitrage-free option pricing models* or *yield curve option pricing models*. These models can incorporate different volatility assumptions along the yield curve. The binomial model discussed in the next chapter to value a bond with an embedded option is based on an arbitrage-free option pricing model.

Implied Interest-Rate Volatility

Option pricing models provide a theoretical option price based on the six factors that we discussed earlier. Of the six factors, the only one that is not known and must be estimated is the expected interest-rate volatility over the life of the option. A popular methodology for assessing

EXHIBIT 16–5

The Process of Obtaining Implied Interest-Rate Volatility

A. To obtain theoretical option price

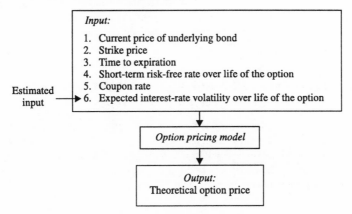

B. To obtain implied interest-rate volatility

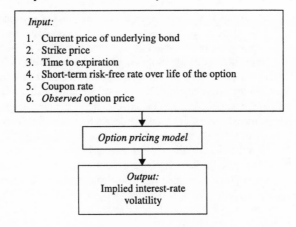

whether an option is fairly priced is to assume that the option is priced correctly and to estimate the interest-rate volatility that is implied by an option pricing model. Exhibit 16-5 describes the process for computing implied interest-rate volatility.

For example, suppose that a money manager—using some option pricing model, the current price of the option, and the five factors that determine the price of an option—computes an implied interest-rate volatility of 12%. If the money manager expects that the interest-rate volatility over the life of the option will be greater than the implied interest-rate volatility of 12%, the option is undervalued. If the money manager's expected interest-rate volatility over the life of the option is less than the implied interest-rate volatility, the option is overvalued.

While we have focused on the option price, the key to understanding the options market is that trading and investment strategies in this market involve buying and selling interest-rate volatility. Looking at the implied interest-rate volatility and comparing it to the trader's or money manager's expectations of future interest-rate volatility is just another way of evaluating options.

SENSITIVITY OF THE THEORETICAL CALL OPTION PRICE TO CHANGES IN FACTORS

When any one of the six factors that affect the price of an option changes, the option price will change. Since the price of a bond with an embedded option will be affected by how the price of the embedded option changes, we will look at the sensitivity of the option price to three of the factors—the price of the underlying bond, time to expiration, and expected interest-rate volatility. We focus our attention on call options.[7]

The Call Option Price and the Price of the Underlying Bond

Exhibit 16-6 shows the theoretical price of a call option based on the price of the underlying bond. The horizontal axis is the price of the underlying bond at any time. The vertical axis is the option price. The shape of the curve representing the theoretical price of a call option, given the price of the underlying bond, would be the same regardless of the actual option pricing model used. Specifically, the relationship between the price of the underlying bond and the theoretical call option price is convex. Thus, option prices also exhibit convexity.

The line from the origin to the strike price on the horizontal axis in Exhibit 16-6 is the intrinsic value of the call option when the price of the underlying bond is less than the strike price, since the intrinsic value is zero. The 45-degree line extending from the horizontal axis is the intrinsic value of the call option once the price of the underlying bond exceeds the strike price. The reason is that the intrinsic value of the call option will increase by the same amount as the increase in the price of the underlying bond. For example, if the exercise price is $100, and the price of the underlying bond increases from $100 to $101, the intrinsic value will increase by $1. If the price of the bond increases from $101 to $110, the intrinsic value of the option will increase from $1 to $10. Thus, the slope of the line representing the intrinsic value after the strike price is reached is 1.

Since the theoretical call option price is shown by the convex line, the difference between the theoretical call option price and the intrinsic value at any given price for the underlying bond is the time value of the option.

---

7   For a detailed discussion of the role of these measures in option strategies, see Mark Pitts and Frank J. Fabozzi, *Interest Rate Futures and Options;* and Richard M. Bookstaber, *Option Pricing and Investment Strategies* (Chicago: Probus Publishing, 1987), Chapter 4.

EXHIBIT 16–6

Theoretical Call Price and the Price of the Underlying Bond

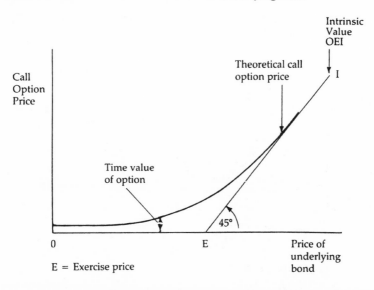

E = Exercise price

Exhibit 16-7 shows the theoretical call option price, but with a tangent line drawn at the price of p^*. Recall from Chapter 14 that the tangent line was used to estimate the new price of a bond at a new yield level. Here we have an analogous situation. The tangent line in Exhibit 16-7 can be used to estimate what the new option price will be (and therefore what the change in the option price will be) if the price of the underlying bond changes. Once again, because of the convexity of the relationship between the option price and the price of the underlying bond, the tangent line closely approximates the new option price for a small change in the price of the underlying bond. For large changes, however, the tangent line does not provide as good an approximation of the new option price.

The slope of the tangent line shows how the theoretical call option price will change for small changes in the price of the underlying bond. The slope of the tangent line is commonly referred to as the *delta* of the option.[8] Specifically,

$$\text{Delta} = \frac{\text{Change in price of call option}}{\text{Change in price of underlying bond}}.$$

For example, a delta of .5 means that a $1 change in the price of the underlying bond will change the price of the call option by $.50.

---

8   Delta is also referred to as the *hedge ratio*.

EXHIBIT 16–7

Delta of a Call Option

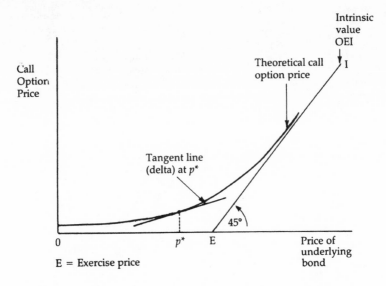

E = Exercise price

Exhibit 16-8 shows the curve of the theoretical call option price with three tangent lines drawn. The steeper the slope of the tangent line, the greater the delta. When an option is deep out of the money (that is, the price of the underlying bond is substantially below the strike price), the tangent line is nearly flat (see Line 1 in Exhibit 16-8). This means that the delta is close to 0. To understand why, consider a call option with a strike price of $100 and 2 months to expiration. If the price of the underlying bond is $20, the option price would not increase by much if the price of the underlying bond increased by $1, from $20 to $21.

For a call option that is deep in the money, the delta will be close to 1. That is, the call option price will increase almost dollar for dollar with an increase in the price of the underlying bond. In terms of Exhibit 16-8, the slope of the tangent line approaches the slope of the intrinsic value line after the strike price. As we stated earlier, the slope of that line is 1.

Thus, the delta for a call option varies from 0 (for call options deep out of the money) to 1 (for call options deep in the money). The delta for a call option at the money is approximately .5.

Related to the delta is the *lambda* of an option, which measures the percentage change in the price of the option for a 1% change in the price of the underlying bond. That is,

$$\text{Lambda} = \frac{\text{Percentage change in the price of the call option}}{\text{Percentage change in the price of the underlying bond}}.$$

EXHIBIT 16-8

Delta of a Call Option at Three Prices for the Underlying Bond

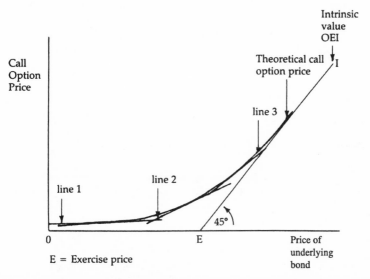

For example, a lambda of 1.5 indicates that if the price of the call option changes by 1%, the call option's price will change by 1.5%. The lambda of a call option will be greater than 1 because of the leverage offered by an option. As the price of the underlying bond increases, the option's lambda decreases.

In the previous chapter, we measured the convexity of an option-free bond. We also can measure the convexity of a call option. Recall from the previous chapter that the convexity of a bond measures the rate of change in dollar duration. For call options, convexity measures the rate of change in delta. The measure of convexity for options is commonly referred to as *gamma*, defined as follows:

$$\text{Gamma} = \frac{\text{Change in delta}}{\text{Change in price of underlying bond}}.$$

The Call Option Price and Time to Expiration

All other factors constant, the longer the time to expiration, the higher the option price. Since each day the option moves closer to the expiration date, the time to expiration decreases. The *theta* of an option measures the change in the option price as the time to expiration decreases.

That is,

$$\text{Theta} = \frac{\text{Change in price of option}}{\text{Decrease in time to expiration}}.$$

Assuming that the price of the underlying bond does not change so that the intrinsic value of the option does not change, theta measures how quickly the time value of the option changes as the option moves toward expiration.

The Call Option Price and Expected Interest-Rate Volatility

All other factors constant, a change in the expected interest-rate volatility will change the option price. The *kappa* (or *vega*) of an option measures the dollar price change in the price of the option for a 1% change in the expected interest-rate volatility. That is,

$$\frac{\text{Kappa}}{(\text{Vega})} = \frac{\text{Change in option price}}{1\% \text{ change in expected interest–rate volatility}}.$$

DURATION OF AN OPTION

The modified duration of a bond is an indicator of its price sensitivity to changes in interest rates. We can similarly define a modified duration for an option as follows:

Modified duration for an option

$$= \left(\begin{array}{c}\text{Modified duration of the} \\ \text{underlying instrument}\end{array}\right) \times \text{Delta} \times \left(\frac{\text{Price of underlying instrument}}{\text{Price of option}}\right).$$

Therefore, the modified duration for an option depends on three factors: (1) the modified duration of the underlying instrument, (2) the delta of the option, and (3) the ratio of the price of the underlying instrument to the price of the option. This last factor can be thought of as a measure of the "leverage" in the option.

Put–Call Parity Relationship

There is a relationship between the price of a call option and the price of a put option on the same underlying bond, with the same strike price and the same expiration date. This relationship is commonly referred to as the *put–call parity relationship*. For coupon bearing bonds it is

Put price = Call price + Present value of strike price
+ Present value of coupon – Price of underlying bond

This relationship is one form of the put–call parity relationship for European options. It is approximately true for American options. The relationship is based on arbitrage arguments.

SUMMARY

In this chapter we have explained the investment and price characteristics of options, focusing on call options because they are the most common type of option embedded in bonds. The key concepts to be understood are as follows. First, the maximum profit that an option writer (seller) can realize is the option price; the option writer, however, is exposed to substantial downside risk. For an option buyer, the maximum loss is the option price. The option buyer retains all the upside potential (reduced by the option price).

Second, there are six factors that influence an option's price: current price of the underlying bond, strike price, time to expiration, short-term risk-free interest rate over the life of the option, coupon rate, and expected interest-rate volatility over the life of the option. Option pricing models attempt to estimate the theoretical price of an option.

Third, buying and selling of options involves buying and selling expected interest-rate volatility. Recall that we said the same thing in Chapter 14 when we explained that the value of convexity depends on expected interest-rate volatility over some investment horizon. Rather than looking at the value of an option in terms of price, it is common for investors to compute the implied interest-rate volatility of an option and compare it to expected interest-rate volatility.

Fourth, there are measures used to assess the sensitivity of the option price to a change in factors such as the price of the underlying bond (delta and lambda), time (theta), and expected interest-rate volatility (kappa or vega). A graph of the relationship between the theoretical call price and the price of the underlying bond is convex. Gamma measures the convexity (that is, how the delta changes). A duration for an option can be calculated.

Finally, the put–call parity relationship defines the relationships among the prices of a put option, a call option, and the underlying bond.

17

⑥ VALUATION AND PRICE VOLATILITY OF BONDS WITH EMBEDDED OPTIONS

Now that we understand the fundamental characteristics of options, in this chapter we turn to the analysis of bonds with embedded options. By an embedded option we mean that either the issuer or the bondholder has the right to alter the bond's cash flow. Bonds with embedded options include callable bonds, putable bonds, range notes, floaters with restrictions on the coupon rate (i.e., cap and/or floor), and mortgage-backed securities. In each case, the cash flow depends on the future level of interest rates. Bonds with embedded options also include convertible bonds in which the bondholder can convert the bond into common stock and foreign currency bonds in which either the issuer or bondholder has the option to select the currency in which a coupon and/or the principal are paid.

The analysis of a bond with an embedded option involves determining the fair value of the bond (i.e., its theoretical value) and its price volatility. Our focus will be on the most popular type of bond with an embedded option, callable bonds. The principles are applicable to other bonds whose cash flows are sensitive to interest rates.

The valuation model that will be described in this chapter is the *binomial model*. This model is based on a consistent framework for valuing both option-free bonds and bonds with embedded options. The valuation principles that we have discussed so far in this book are used here. Specifically, we saw in Chapter 7 two important things. First, it is inappropriate to use a single rate to discount all the cash flows of a bond. Second, the correct rate to use to discount each cash flow is the spot rate. This is equivalent to discounting at a series of forward rates. What we have to add to the valuation process is how interest-rate volatility affects the value of a bond through its effects on the embedded options.

An alternative valuation model used by some dealers and vendors is the Monte Carlo model. Since this model is more commonly used for the valuation of mortgage-backed securities, we postpone discussion of this model until Chapter 20 when the analysis of these securities is explained.

EXHIBIT 17–1

Price/Yield Relationship for an Option-Free Bond and a Callable Bond

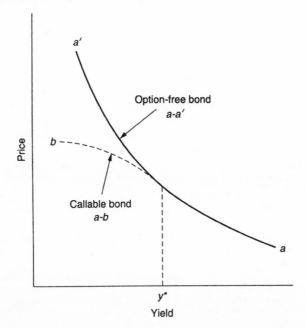

The price volatility of a bond with an embedded option can then be assessed given the valuation model. More specifically, we will see how to determine the effective duration and convexity using the binomial model.

PRICE/YIELD RELATIONSHIP FOR A CALLABLE BOND

As explained in Chapter 4, the price/yield relationship for an option-free (i.e., noncallable/non-putable) bond is convex. Exhibit 17-1 shows the price/yield relationship for both an option-free bond and the same bond if it is callable. The convex curve a-a' is the price/yield relationship for the noncallable (option-free) bond. The unusual shaped curve denoted by a-b is the price/yield relationship for the callable bond.

The reason for the shape of the price/yield relationship for the callable bond is as follows. When the prevailing market yield for comparable bonds is higher than the coupon interest on the bond, it is unlikely that the issuer will call the bond. For example, if the coupon rate on a bond is 8% and the prevailing yield on comparable bonds is 16%, it is highly improbable that the issuer will call an 8% coupon bond so that it can issue a 16% coupon bond. Since the bond is unlikely to be called, the callable bond will have the same price/yield relationship as an option-free bond. However, even when the coupon rate is just below the market yield, investors may not pay the same price for the callable bond had it been noncallable because there is still the chance the market yield may drop further, making it beneficial for the issuer to call the bond.

As yields in the market decline, the likelihood that yields will decline further so that the issuer will benefit from calling the bond increases. The exact yield level at which investors begin to view the issue likely to be called may not be known, but we do know that there is some level. In Exhibit 17-1, at yield levels below y^*, the price/yield relationship for the callable bond departs from the price/yield relationship for the option-free bond. For example, suppose the market yield were such that an option-free bond was selling for $109. Suppose instead the bond is callable with a call price of $104. Investors would not be willing to pay $109 for this callable bond. If they did and the bond were called, investors would receive $104 (the call price) for a bond they purchased for $109. Notice that for a range of yields below y*, there is price compression; that is, there is limited price appreciation as yields decline. The portion of the callable bond price/yield relationship below y^* is said to be *negatively convex*.

Negative convexity means that the price appreciation will be less than the price depreciation for a large change in yield of a given number of basis points. For a bond that is option-free and exhibits positive convexity, the price appreciation will be greater than the price depreciation for a large change in yield. The price changes resulting from bonds exhibiting positive convexity and negative convexity can be expressed as follows:

	Absolute Value of Percentage Price Change for	
Change in Interest Rates	Positive Convexity	Negative Convexity
−100 basis points	X%	less than Y%
+100 basis points	less than X%	Y%

THE COMPONENTS OF A BOND WITH AN EMBEDDED OPTION

To develop an analytical framework for valuing a bond with an embedded option, it is necessary to decompose a bond into its component parts. A callable bond, for example, is a bond in which the bondholder has sold the issuer an option (more specifically, a call option) that allows the issuer to repurchase the contractual cash flows of the bond from the time the bond is first callable until the maturity date.

Consider the following two bonds: (1) a callable bond with an 8% coupon, 20 years to maturity, and callable in 5 years at $104 and (2) a 9% coupon, 10-year bond callable immediately at par. For the first bond, the bondholder owns a 5-year option-free bond and has sold a call option granting the issuer the right to call away from the bondholder 15 years of cash flows 5 years from now for a price of $104. The investor who owns the second bond has a 10-year option-free bond and has sold a call option granting the issuer the right to immediately call the entire 10-year contractual cash flows, or any cash flows remaining at the time the issue is called, for $100.

Effectively, the owner of a callable bond is entering into two separate transactions. First, he buys an option-free bond from the issuer for which he pays some price. Then, he sells the issuer a call option for which he receives the option price. Therefore, we can summarize the position of a callable bondholder as follows:

> Long a callable bond
> = Long an option-free bond + Sold a call option.

In terms of price, the price of a callable bond is therefore equal to the price of the two components parts. That is,

> Callable bond price
> = Option-free bond price – Call option price.

The reason the call option price is subtracted from the price of the option-free bond is that when the bondholder sells a call option, he receives the option price. Graphically this can be seen in Exhibit 17-1. The difference between the price of the option-free bond and the callable bond at any given yield is the price of the embedded call option.

Actually, the position is more complicated than we just described. The issuer may be entitled to call the bond at the first call date and any time thereafter, or at the first call date and any subsequent coupon anniversary. Thus the investor has effectively sold an American-type call option to the issuer but the call price may vary with the date the call option is exercised. This is because the call schedule for a bond typically has a different call price depending on the call date. Moreover, the underlying bond for the call option is the remaining coupon payments that would have been made by the issuer had the bond not been called. For exposition purposes, it is easier to understand the principles associated with the investment characteristics of callable bonds by describing the investor's position as long an option-free bond and short a call option.

The same logic applies to putable bonds. In the case of a putable bond, the bondholder has the right to sell the bond to the issuer at a designated price and time. A putable bond can be broken into two separate transactions. First, the investor buys an option-free bond. Second, the investor buys an option from the issuer that allows the investor to sell the bond to the issuer. This type of option is called a *put* option. Therefore, the position of a putable bondholder can be described as

> Long a putable bond
> = Long an option-free bond + Own a put option.

The price of a putable bond is then

> Price of a putable bond
> = Option-free bond price + Put option price.

TRADITIONAL VALUATION METHODOLOGY

When a bond is callable, the practice has been to calculate a yield to call as well as a yield to maturity. The former yield calculation assumes that the issuer will call the bond at the first call date. As explained in Chapter 6, the procedure for calculating the yield to call is the same as for any yield calculation: determine the interest rate that will make the present value of the expected cash flows equal to the price. In the case of yield to call, the expected cash flows are the coupon payments to the first call date and the call price.

According to the traditional approach, conservative investors should compute the yield to call and yield to maturity for a callable bond selling at a premium, selecting the lower of the two as a measure of potential return. The smaller of the two yield measures should be used to evaluate the relative value of a callable bond. More recently, the traditional approach has been extended to compute not just the yield to the first call date, but the yield to all possible call dates. Since most bonds can be called at any time after the first call date, the approach has been to compute the yield to every coupon anniversary date following the first call date. Then, all the yields to calls calculated and the yield to maturity are compared. The lowest of these yields is called the *yield to worst*, which is the yield that the traditional approach has investors believing should be used in relative value analysis.

The limitations of the yield to call as a measure of the potential return of a security are given in Chapter 4. The yield to call does consider all three sources of potential return from owning a bond. However, as in the case of the yield to maturity, it assumes that all cash flows can be reinvested at the computed yield—in this case the yield to call—until the assumed call date. Moreover, the yield to call assumes that (1) the investor will hold the bond to the assumed call date, and (2) the issuer will call the bond on that date.

Oftentimes, these underlying assumptions about the yield to call are unrealistic since they do not take into account how an investor will reinvest the proceeds if the issue is called. For example, consider two bonds, M and N. Suppose that the yield to maturity for bond M, a 5-year option-free bond, is 10% while the yield to call for bond N is 10.5% assuming the bond will be called in 3 years. Which bond is better for an investor with a 5-year investment horizon? It is not possible to tell from the yields cited. If the investor intends to hold the bond for 5 years and the issuer calls the bond after 3 years, the total dollars that will be available at the end of 5 years will depend on the interest rate that can be earned from investing funds from the call date to the end of the investment horizon.

BINOMIAL MODEL FOR VALUING BONDS WITH EMBEDDED OPTIONS[1]

The discussion in the previous section provides a useful way to conceptualize a bond with an embedded option. Specifically, the value of a callable bond equals the value of a comparable option-free bond less the value of the call option. This insight led to the first generation of valuation models for callable bonds. These early models attempted to directly estimate the value of the embedded call option, but without explicitly incorporating the shape of the yield curve.

Instead of relying on an external option pricing model, the binomial model discussed here is based on an internally consistent framework appropriate to bonds with and without embedded options. The difference between the values of a bond with an embedded option and an otherwise identical bond without that option is the value of the option.

---

1 This section is adapted from Andrew Kalotay, George O. Williams, and Frank J. Fabozzi, "A Model for the Valuation of Bonds and Embedded Options," *Financial Analysts Journal* (May–June 1993), pp. 35–46.

As we saw in Chapter 7, instead of discounting all cash flows at the same rate, one should discount each cash flow at its own spot rate. This is equivalent to discounting at a sequence of forward rates. Both the spot rates and the implied forward rates can be calculated by the bootstrapping methodology described in Chapter 7. What was not considered was how expected interest-rate volatility affects spot rates and forward rates and, in turn, how interest-rate volatility affects the value of a bond through its effects on the embedded options.

Valuation of Option-Free Bonds

We begin with a review of the valuation technique for bonds without any embedded options. The price of an option-free bond is the present value of the cash flows discounted at the spot rates. To illustrate this, we start with the on-the-run yield curve for the particular issuer whose bonds we want to value. The starting point is the Treasury's on-the-run yield curve. To obtain a particular issuer's on-the-run yield curve, an appropriate credit spread is added to each on-the-run Treasury issue. The credit spread need not be constant for all maturities. For example, the credit spreads may increase with maturity.

In our illustration, we use the following hypothetical on-the-run issue for an issuer:

Maturity (years)	Yield to Maturity (%)	Market Price ($)
1	3.50%	$100
2	4.00	100
3	4.50	100

Each bond is trading at par value ($100) so the coupon rate is equal to the yield to maturity. We will simplify the illustration by assuming annual-pay bonds.

Determined by using the bootstrapping methodology, the spot rates are given below:

Year	Spot Rate (%)
1	3.500%
2	4.010
3	4.531

The corresponding 1-year forward rates are

Current 1-year forward rate = 3.500%;

1-year forward rate 1-year from now = 4.523%;

1-year forward rate 2-years from now = 5.580%.

Now consider an option-free bond with 3 years remaining to maturity and a coupon rate of 5.25%. The value of this bond can be calculated in one of two ways, both producing the same value. First, the coupon payments can be discounted at the zero-coupon rates as shown below:

$$\frac{\$5.25}{(1.035)} + \frac{\$5.25}{(1.0401)^2} + \frac{\$100 + \$5.25}{(1.04531)^3} = \$102.075.$$

The second way is to discount by the 1-year forward rates as shown below:

EXHIBIT 17-2

3-Year Binomial Interest-Rate Tree

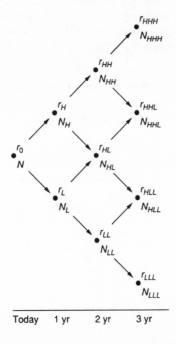

$$\frac{\$5.25}{(1.035)} + \frac{\$5.25}{(1.035)(1.04523)} + \frac{\$100 + \$5.25}{(1.035)(1.04523)(1.0558)} = \$102.075.$$

Binomial Interest Rate Tree

Once we allow for embedded options, consideration must be given to interest-rate volatility. This can be done by introducing a *binomial interest rate tree*. This tree is nothing more than a graphical depiction of the 1-period forward rates over time based on some assumption about interest-rate volatility. How this tree is constructed is illustrated below.

Exhibit 17-2 shows an example of a binomial interest rate tree. In this tree, each node (bold circle) represents a time period that is equal to 1 year from the node to its left. Each node is labeled with an N, representing node, and a subscript that indicates the path that 1-year forward rates took to get to that node. L represents the lower of the two 1-year forward rates and H represents the higher of the two 1-year forward rates. For example, node N_{HH} means to get to that node the following path for 1-year forward rates occurred: the 1-year forward rate realized is the higher of the two forward rates in the first year and then the higher of the 1-year forward rates in the second year.[2]

Look first at the point denoted by just N in Exhibit 17-2. This is the root of the tree and is nothing more than the current 1-year rate, or equivalently the current 1-year forward rate, which we denote by r_0. What we have assumed in creating this tree is that the 1-year forward rate can take on two possible values the next period and the two forward rates have the same probability of occurring. One forward rate will be higher than the other. It is assumed that the 1-year forward rate can evolve over time based on a random process called a lognormal random walk with a certain volatility.

We use the following notation to describe the tree in the first year. Let

σ = Assumed volatility of the 1-year forward rate;

$r_{1,L}$ = Lower 1-year forward rate 1 year from now;

$r_{1,H}$ = Higher 1-year forward rate 1 year from now.

The relationship between $r_{1,L}$ and $r_{1,H}$ is as follows:

$$r_{1,H} = r_{1,L}(e^{2\sigma})$$

where e is the base of the natural logarithm 2.71828.

For example, suppose that $r_{1,L}$ is 4.074% and σ is 10% per year. Then

$$r_{1,H} = 4.074\% \ (e^{2 \times .10}) = 4.976\%.$$

In the second year, there are three possible values for the 1-year forward rate, which we will denote as follows:

$r_{2,LL}$ = 1-year forward rate in the second year assuming the lower forward rate in the first year and the lower forward rate in the second year;

$r_{2,HH}$ = 1-year forward rate in the second year assuming the higher forward rate in the first year and the higher forward rate in the second year;

$r_{2,HL}$ = 1-year forward rate in the second year assuming the higher forward rate in the first year and the lower forward rate in the second year *or,* equivalently, the lower forward rate in the first year and the higher forward rate in the second year.

The relationship between $r_{2,LL}$ and the other two forward rates is as follows:

$$r_{2,HH} = r_{2,LL}(e^{4\sigma})$$

and

$$r_{2,HL} = r_{2,LL}(e^{2\sigma}).$$

So, for example, if $r_{2,LL}$ is 4.53%, and assuming once again that σ is 10%, then

$$r_{2,HH} = 4.53\% \ (e^{4 \times .10}) = 6.757\%$$

and

---

2 Note that N_{HL} is equivalent to N_{LH} in the second year. Also, in the third year, N_{HHL} is equivalent to N_{HLH} and N_{LHH} and N_{HLL} is equivalent to N_{LLH}. We have simply selected one label for a node rather than clutter up the figure with unnecessary information.

EXHIBIT 17–3

3-Year Binomial Interest-Rate Tree with 1-Year Forward Rates

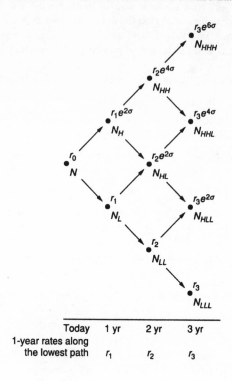

Today	1 yr	2 yr	3 yr
1-year rates along the lowest path	r_1	r_2	r_3

$$r_{2,HL} = 4.53\% \ (e^{2 \times .10}) = 5.532\%.$$

Exhibit 17-2 shows the notation for the binomial interest-rate tree in the third year. We can simplify the notation by letting r_t be the 1-year forward rate t years from now for the lower forward rate since all the other forward rates t years from now depend on that rate. Exhibit 17-3 shows the interest-rate tree using this simplified notation.

Before we go on to show how to use this binomial interest-rate tree to value bonds, let's focus on two issues here. First, what does the volatility parameter σ in the expression $e^{2\sigma}$ represent? Second, how do we find the value of the bond at each node?

Volatility and the Standard Deviation

It can be shown that the standard deviation of the 1-year forward rate is equal to $r_0\sigma$.[3] As will be explained in Chapter 21, the standard deviation is a statistical measure of volatility. In that chapter it will be shown how the standard deviation of interest rates can be estimated. For now

EXHIBIT 17–4

Calculating a Value at a Node

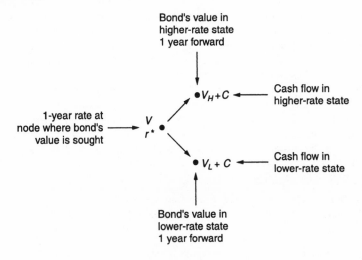

it is important to see that the process that we assumed generates the binomial interest-rate tree (or equivalently the forward rates) implies that volatility is measured relative to the current level of rates. For example, if σ is 10% and the 1-year rate (r_0) is 4%, then the standard deviation of the 1-year forward rate is 4% × 10% = .4% or 40 basis points. However, if the current 1-year rate is 12%, the standard deviation of the 1-year forward rate would be 12% × 10% or 120 basis points.

Determining the Value at a Node

To find the value of the bond at a node, we first calculate the bond's value at the two nodes to the right of the node we are interested in. For example, in Exhibit 17-3, suppose we want to determine the bond's value at node N_H. The bond's value at node N_{HH} and N_{HL} must be determined. Don't be concerned now with how we get these two values because as we will see the process involves starting from the last year in the tree and working backwards to get the final solution we want, so these two values will be known.

Effectively what we are saying is that if we are at some node, then the value at that node will depend on the future cash flows. In turn, the future cash flows depend on (1) the bond's

---

3 This can be seen by noting that $e^{2\sigma} \approx 1 + 2\sigma$. Then the standard deviation of 1-period forward rates is

$$\frac{re^{2\sigma} - r}{2} \approx \frac{r + 2\sigma r - r}{2} = \sigma r.$$

value 1 year from now and (2) the coupon payment 1 year from now. The latter is known. The former depends on whether the 1-year forward rate is the higher or lower rate. The bond's value if the rate is higher or lower is reported at the two nodes to the right of the node that is the focus of our attention. So, the cash flow at a node will be either (1) the bond's value if the forward rate is the higher rate plus the coupon payment, or (2) the bond's value if the forward rate is the lower rate plus the coupon payment. For example, suppose that we are interested in the bond's value at N_H. The cash flow will be either the bond's value at N_{HH} plus the coupon payment or the bond's value at N_{HL} plus the coupon payment.

To get the bond's value at a node we follow the fundamental rule for valuation: the value is the present value of the expected cash flows. The appropriate discount rate to use is the 1-year forward rate at the node. Now there are two present values in this case: the present value if the 1-year forward rate is the higher rate and one if it is the lower rate. Since it is assumed that the probabilities of both outcomes are equal, an average of the two present values is computed. This is illustrated in Exhibit 17-4 for any node assuming that the 1-year forward rate is r_* at the node where the valuation is sought and letting

V_H = Bond's value for the higher 1-year forward rate;
V_L = Bond's value for the lower 1-year forward rate;
C = Coupon payment.

Using our notation, the cash flow at a node is either

$$V_H + C \text{ for the higher 1-year forward rate}$$

or

$$V_L + C \text{ for the lower 1-year forward rate.}$$

The present value of these two cash flows using the 1-year forward rate at the node, r_*, is

$$\frac{V_H + C}{(1 + r_*)} = \text{Present value for the higher 1-year forward rate;}$$

$$\frac{V_L + C}{(1 + r_*)} = \text{Present value for the lower 1-year forward rate.}$$

Then, the value of the bond at the node is found as follows:

$$\text{Value at a node} = \frac{1}{2}\left[\frac{V_H + C}{(1 + r_*)} + \frac{V_L + C}{(1 + r_*)}\right].$$

Constructing the Binomial Interest-Rate Tree

To see how to construct the binomial interest-rate tree, let's use the assumed on-the-run yields we used earlier. We will assume that volatility, σ, is 10% and construct a 2-year tree using the 2-year bond with a coupon rate of 4%.

Exhibit 17-5 shows a more detailed binomial interest-rate tree with the cash flow shown at each node. We'll see how all the values reported in the figure are obtained. The root rate for the tree, r_0, is simply the current 1-year rate, 3.5%.

EXHIBIT 17-5

**Find the 1-Year Forward Rates for Year 1 by Using the 2-Year, 4%
On-the-Run Issue: First Trial**

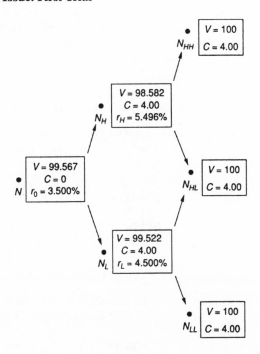

In the first year there are two possible 1-year forward rates, the higher forward rate and the lower forward rate. What we want to find are the two forward rates that will be consistent with the volatility assumption, the process that is assumed to generate the forward rates, and the observed market value of the bond. There is no simple formula for this. It must be found by an iterative process (i.e., trial and error). The steps are described and illustrated below.

Step 1 Select a value for r_1. Recall that r_1 is the lower 1-year forward rate. In this first trial, we *arbitrarily* selected a value of 4.5%.

Step 2 Determine the corresponding value for the higher 1-year forward rate. As explained earlier, this rate is related to the lower 1-year forward rate as follows: $r_1e^{2\sigma}$. Since r_1 is 4.5%, the higher 1-year forward rate is 5.496% (= 4.5% $e^{2\times.10}$). This value is reported in Exhibit 17-5 at node N_H.

Step 3 Compute the bond value's 1 year from now. This value is determined as follows:

3a. Determine the bond's value 2 years from now. In our example, this is simple. Since we are using a 2-year bond, the bond's value is its maturity value ($100) plus its final coupon payment ($4). Thus, it is $104.

3b. Calculate the present value of the bond's value found in 3a for the higher forward rate in the second year. The appropriate discount rate is the higher 1-year forward rate, 5.496% in our example. The present value is $98.582 (= $104/1.05496) This is the value of V_H that we referred to earlier.

3c. Calculate the present value of the bond's value assumed in (3a) for the lower forward rate. The discount rate assumed for the lower 1-year forward rate is 4.5%. The present value is $99.522 (= $104/1.045) and is the value of V_L.

3d. Add the coupon to both V_H and V_L to get the cash flow at N_H and N_L, respectively. In our example we have $102.582 for the higher forward rate and $103.522 for the lower forward rate.

3e. Calculate the present value of the two values using the 1-year forward rate r_*. At this point in the valuation, r_* is the root rate, 3.50%. Therefore,

$$\frac{V_H + C}{1 + r_*} = \frac{\$102.582}{1.035} = \$99.113$$

and

$$\frac{V_L + C}{1 + r_*} = \frac{\$103.522}{1.035} = \$100.021.$$

Step 4   Calculate the average present value of the two cash flows in Step 3. This is the value we referred to earlier as

$$\text{Value at a node} = \frac{1}{2}\left[\frac{V_H + C}{(1 + r_*)} + \frac{V_L + C}{(1 + r_*)}\right].$$

In our example, we have

$$\text{Value at a node} = \frac{1}{2}[\$99.113 + \$100.021] = \$99.567.$$

Step 5   Compare the value in Step 4 to the bond's market value. If the two values are the same, then the r_1 used in this trial is the one we seek. This is the 1-year forward rate that would then be used in the binomial interest-rate tree for the lower forward rate and the corresponding higher forward rate. If, instead, the value found in Step 4 is not equal to the market value of the bond, this means that the value r_1 in this trial is not the 1-year forward rate that is consistent with (1) the volatility assumption of 10%, (2) the process assumed to generate the 1-year forward rate, and (3) the observed market value of the bond. In this case, the five steps are repeated with a different value for r_1.

EXHIBIT 17-6

The 1-Year Forward Rates for Year 1 by Using the 2-Year, 4% On-the-Run Issue

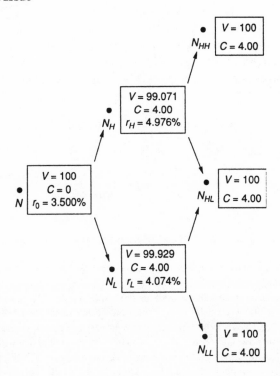

When r_1 is 4.5%, a value of $99.567 results in Step 4, which is less than the observed market price of $100. Therefore, 4.5% is too large and the five steps must be repeated, trying a lower rate for r_1.

Let's jump right to the correct rate for r_1 in this example and rework Steps 1 through 5. This occurs when r_1 is 4.074%. The corresponding binomial interest-rate tree is shown in Exhibit 17-6.

Step 1   In this trial we select a value of 4.074% for r_1, the lower 1-year forward rate.

Step 2   The corresponding value for the higher 1-year forward rate is 4.976% (= 4.074% $e^{2 \times .10}$).

Step 3   The bond's value 1 year from now is determined as follows:

3a. The bond's value 2 years from now is $104, just as in the first trial.

3b. The present value of the bond's value found in (3a) for the higher 1-year forward rate, V_H, is $99.071 (= $104/1.04976).

3c. The present value of the bond's value found in (3a) for the lower 1-year forward rate, V_L, is $99.929 (= $104/1.04074).

3d. Adding the coupon to V_H and V_L, we get $103.071 as the cash flow for the higher forward rate and $103.929 as the cash flow for the lower forward rate.

3e. The present value of the two cash flows using the 1-year forward rate at the node to the left, 3.5%, gives

$$\frac{V_H + C}{(1 + r_*)} = \frac{\$103.071}{1.035} = \$99.586$$

and

$$\frac{V_L + C}{1 + r_*} = \frac{\$103.929}{1.035} = \$100.414.$$

Step 4   The average present value is $100, which is the value at the node.

Step 5   Since the average present value is equal to the observed market price of $100, r_1 or $r_{1,L}$ is 4.074% and $r_{1,H}$ is 4.976%.

We're not done. Suppose that we want to "grow" this tree for one more year—that is, we want to determine r_2. Now we will use the 3-year on-the-run issue, the 4.5% coupon bond, to get r_2. The same five steps are used in an iterative process to find the 1-year forward rates in the tree 2 years from now. Our objective is now to find the value of r_2 that will produce a bond value of $100 (since the 3-year on-the-run issue has a market price of $100) and is consistent with (1) a volatility assumption of 10%, (2) a current 1-year forward rate of 3.5%, and (3) the two forward rates 1 year from now of 4.074% (the lower forward rate) and 4.976% (the higher forward rate).

We explain how this is done using Exhibit 17-7. Let's look at how we get the information in the exhibit. The maturity value and coupon payment 3 years from now are shown in the boxes at the four nodes. Since the 3-year on-the-run issue has a maturity value of $100 and a coupon payment of $4.5, these values are the same in the box shown at each node. For the three nodes 2 years from now the coupon payment of $4.5 is shown. Unknown at these three nodes are (1) the three forward rates 2 years from now and (2) the value of the bond 2 years from now. For the two nodes 1 year from now, the coupon payment is known, as are the 1-year forward rates 1 year from now. These are the forward rates found earlier. The value of the bond, which depends on the bond values at the nodes to the right, are unknown at these two nodes.

Exhibit 17-8 is the same as Exhibit 17-7 complete with the values previously unknown. As can be seen from Exhibit 17-8, the value of r_2, or equivalently $r_{2,LL}$, which will produce the desired result is 4.53%. We showed earlier that the corresponding forward rates $r_{2,HL}$ and $r_{2,HH}$ would be 5.532% and 6.757%, respectively. To verify that these are the 1-year forward rates 2

EXHIBIT 17–7

Information for Deriving the 1-Year Forward Rates for Year 2 by Using the 3-Year, 4.5% On-the-Run Issue

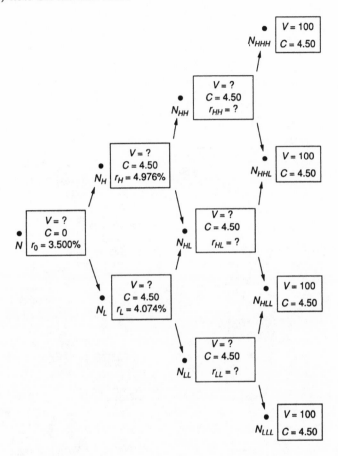

years from now, work backwards from the four nodes at the right of the tree in Exhibit 17-8. For example, the value in the box at N_{HH} is found by taking the value of \$104.5 at the two nodes to its right and discounting at 6.757%. The value is \$98.886. (Since it is the same value for both nodes to the right, it is also the average value.) Similarly, the value in the box at N_{HL} is found by discounting \$104.50 by 5.532% and at N_{LL} by discounting at 4.53%. The same procedure used in Exhibits 17-5 and 17-6 is used to get the values at the other nodes.

EXHIBIT 17–8

The 1-Year Forward Rates for Year 2 by Using the 3-Year, 4.5% On-the-Run Issue

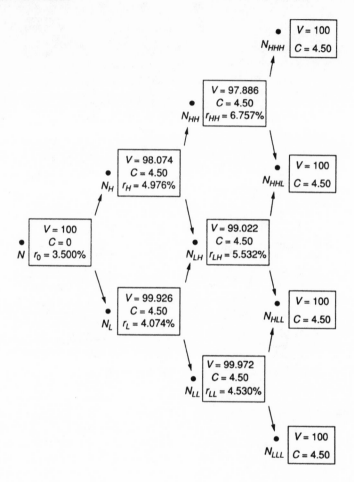

Valuing an Option-Free Bond

Exhibit 17-9 shows the 1-year forward rates or binomial interest-rate tree that can then be used to value any 1-year, 2-year, or 3-year bond for this issuer. To illustrate how to use the binomial interest-rate tree, consider a 5.25% option-free bond of this issuer with 3 years remaining to maturity. Also assume that the issuer's on-the-run yield curve is the one given earlier and hence

EXHIBIT 17–9

Binomial Interest-Rate Tree for Valuing Up to a 3-Year Bond for Issuer

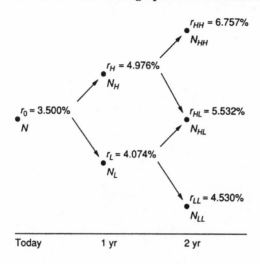

Today	1 yr	2 yr

the appropriate binomial interest-rate tree is the one in Exhibit 17-9. Exhibit 17-10 shows the various values in the discounting process and produces a bond value of $102.075.

It is important to note that this value is identical to the bond value found earlier when we discounted at either the spot rates or the 1-year forward rates. We should expect to find this result since our bond is option-free. This clearly demonstrates that the valuation model is consistent with the standard valuation model for an option-free bond.

Valuing a Callable Bond

Now we will demonstrate how the binomial interest-rate tree can be applied to value a callable bond. The valuation process proceeds in the same fashion as in the case of an option-free bond, but with one exception: when the call option may be exercised by the issuer, the bond value at a node must be changed to reflect the lesser of its value if it is not called (i.e., the value obtained by applying the recursive valuation formula described above) and the call price.

For example, consider a 5.25% bond with 3 years remaining to maturity that is callable in 1 year at $100. To simplify the illustration, let's assume the issuer will call the bond if its price exceeds $100. Exhibit 17-11 shows the values at each node of the binomial interest-rate tree. The discounting process is identical to that shown in Exhibit 17-10 except that at two nodes N_L and N_{LL} the values from the recursive valuation formula ($101.002 at N_L and $100.689 at N_{LL}) exceed the call price ($100) and therefore have been struck out and replaced with $100. Each time a value derived from the recursive valuation formula has been replaced, the process for

EXHIBIT 17–10

Valuing an Option-Free Bond of Issuer with 3 Years to Maturity and a Coupon Rate of 5.25%

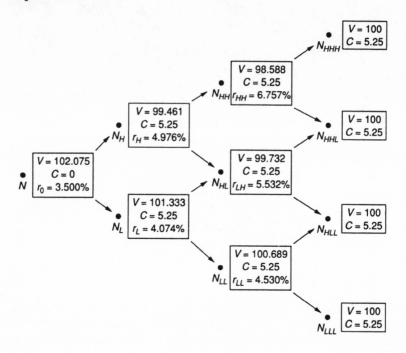

finding the values at that node is reworked starting with the period to the right. The value for this callable bond is $101.432.

The question that we have not addressed in our illustration, but which is nonetheless important, is under which circumstances the issuer will call the bond. A detailed explanation of the call rule is beyond the scope of this chapter. Basically, it involves determining when it is economic for the issuer on an after-tax basis to call the issue.

Since the value of a callable bond is equal to the value of an option-free bond minus the value of the call option, this means that

> Value of the call option
>
> = Value of the option-free bond – Value of the callable bond.

But we have just seen how the value of an option-free bond and the value of a callable bond can be determined. The difference between the two values is therefore the value of the call option.

EXHIBIT 17–11

Valuing a Callable Bond with 3 Years to Maturity, a Coupon Rate of 5.25%, and Callable in 1 Year at $100*

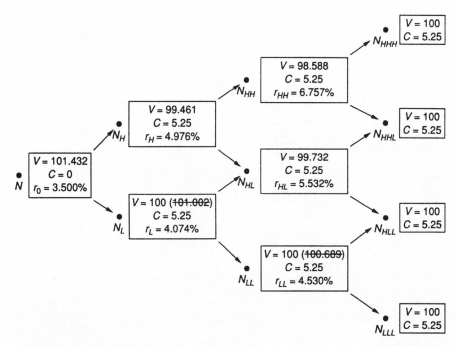

*Bond assumed to be called if value exceeds $100.

In our illustration, since the value of the option-free bond is $102.075 and the value of the callable bond is $101.432, the value of the call option is $0.643.

Extension to Other Embedded Options

The bond valuation framework presented here can be used to analyze other embedded options such as put options, caps and floors on floating-rate notes, step-up notes, range notes, and the optional accelerated redemption granted to an issuer in fulfilling its sinking fund requirement.[4] For example, let's consider a putable bond. Suppose that a 5.25% bond with 3 years remaining

---

4 The valuation of floating-rate notes with embedded options, floating-rate notes with caps and/or floors, range notes, and step-up notes using the binomial model are presented in Richard S. Wilson and Frank J. Fabozzi, *Corporate Bonds: Structures and Analysis* (New Hope, PA: Frank J. Fabozzi Associates, 1996). For an explanation of the valuation of

EXHIBIT 17–12

Valuing a Putable Bond with 3 Years to Maturity, a Coupon Rate of 5.25%, and Putable in 1 Year at $100*

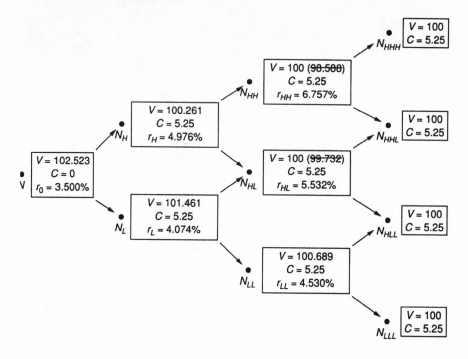

to maturity is putable in 1 year at par ($100). Also assume that the appropriate binomial interest-rate tree for this issuer is the one in Exhibit 17-9. Exhibit 17-12 shows the binomial interest-rate tree with the bond values altered at two nodes (N_{HH} and N_{HL}) because the bond values at these two nodes falls below $100, the assumed value at which the bond can be put. The value of this putable bond is $102.523.

Since the value of an option-free bond can be expressed as the value of a putable bond minus the value of a put option on that bond, this means that

> Value of the put option
> = Value of the option-free bond – Value of the putable bond.

---

sinking fund options, see Andrew J. Kalotay and George O. Williams, "The Valuation and Management of Bonds with Sinking Fund Provisions," *Financial Analysts Journal* (March–April 1992), pp. 59–67.

In our example, since the value of the putable bond is $102.523 and the value of the corresponding option-free bond is $102.075, the value of the put option is –$0.448. The negative sign indicates the issuer has sold the option or, equivalently, the investor has purchased the option.

The framework can also be used to value a bond with multiple or interrelated embedded options. The bond values at each node are altered based on whether one of the options is exercised.

Interest-Rate Volatility and the Theoretical Value

In our illustration, interest-rate volatility was assumed to be 10%. The volatility assumption has an important impact on the theoretical value. More specifically, the higher the expected volatility, the higher the value of an option. The same is true for an option embedded in a bond. Correspondingly, this affects the value of the bond with an embedded option.

For example, for a callable bond, a higher interest-rate volatility assumption means that the value of the call option increases and, since the value of the option-free bond is not affected, the value of the callable bond must be lower. For a putable bond, higher interest-rate volatility means that its value will be higher.

OPTION-ADJUSTED SPREAD

The valuation model gives the theoretical value of a bond. For example, if the observed price of the 3-year, 5.25% callable bond is $101 and the theoretical value is $101.432, this means that this bond is cheap by $.432 according to the valuation model. Bond market participants, however, prefer to think not in terms of a bond's price being cheap or expensive in dollar terms but rather in terms of a yield spread—a cheap bond trades at a higher yield spread and an expensive bond at a lower yield spread.

The market convention is to think of a yield spread as the difference between the yield to maturity on a particular bond and the yield on a comparable maturity Treasury. However, this is inappropriate because, as we have explained, there is not one rate at which all cash flows should be discounted but a set of spot rates or, equivalently, forward rates. Given that this is the correct procedure for discounting, market participants determine the spread over the issuer's spot rate curve or forward rates. In terms of our binomial interest-rate tree, it is the constant spread that when added to all the forward rates on the tree will make the theoretical value equal to the market price. The constant spread that satisfies this condition is called the *option-adjusted spread* (OAS). The spread is referred to as an "option-adjusted" spread since the spread takes into consideration the option embedded in the issue.

Returning to our illustration, if the observed market price is $101, the OAS would be the constant spread added to every forward rate in Exhibit 17-9 that will make the theoretical value equal to $101. In this case, that spread is 23.2 basis points, as can be verified in Exhibit 17-13.

As with the value of a bond with an embedded option, the OAS will depend on the volatility assumption. For a given bond price, the higher the interest-rate volatility assumed, the lower the OAS for a callable bond and the higher the OAS for a putable bond.

EXHIBIT 17–13

Demonstration of the Option-Adjusted Spread

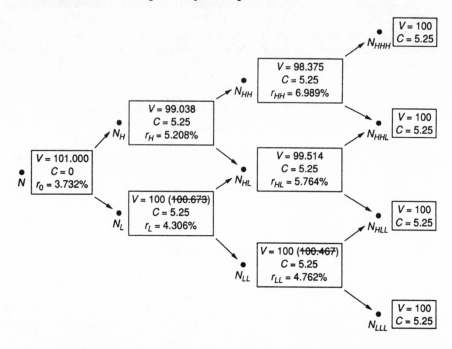

The interpretation of the OAS depends on the benchmark on-the-run issue used in the model. For example, some dealers use the Treasury on-the-run to generate the binomial tree. In this case, the OAS captures the credit spread, a liquidity premium, and any richness or cheapness of the bond being valued after adjusted for the embedded option. In contrast, some dealers use the issuer's on-the-run issue to construct the binomial tree and, as result, the spread has already accounted for the credit risk. Thus, the OAS reflects a liquidity premium and the richness or cheapness of the issue after considering the embedded option.

It is critical to understand that OAS is not a valuation model. Rather, it is a product of a valuation model. If the valuation model is poor, the OAS will be meaningless.

PRICE VOLATILITY OF BONDS WITH EMBEDDED OPTIONS

In Chapter 11 the price volatility characteristics of option-free bonds were explained. In Chapter 13, duration was introduced as a measure of interest-rate risk. More specifically, the concept of modified duration was explained. Modified duration is a measure of the sensitivity of a bond's price to interest-rate changes, *assuming that the expected cash flow does not change with interest rates*. Consequently, modified duration may not be an appropriate measure for bonds with embedded options because the expected cash flows change as interest rates change. For example, when interest rates fall, the binomial tree changes resulting in a change in the expected cash flow for a bond with an embedded option.

While modified duration may be inappropriate as a measure of a bond's price sensitivity to interest-rate changes, there is a duration measure that is more appropriate for bonds with embedded options. Since duration measures price responsiveness to changes in interest rates, the duration for a bond with an embedded option can be estimated by letting interest rates change by a small number of basis points above and below the prevailing yield, and seeing how the prices change. As explained and illustrated in Chapter 13, the duration for *any* bond can be *approximated* as follows:

$$\text{Approximate duration} = \frac{V_- - V_+}{2V_0\,(\Delta y)},$$

V_0 = Initial value or price of the security;
V_- = Estimated value of the security if the yield is decreased by Δy;
V_+ = Estimated value of the security if the yield is increased by Δy;
Δy = Change in the yield of a security.

Effective Duration

Application of this formula to an option-free bond gives the modified duration because the cash flows do not change when yields change. When the approximate duration formula is applied to a bond with an embedded option, the new prices at the higher and lower yield levels should reflect the change in the cash flow. Duration calculated in this way is called *effective duration* or *option-adjusted duration*.

Exhibit 17-14 summarizes the distinction between modified duration and effective duration.

The difference between modified duration and effective duration for fixed-income securities with an embedded option can be quite dramatic. For example, a callable bond could have a modified duration of 4 but an effective duration of only 2. For certain mortgage-backed securities, the modified duration could be 7 and the effective duration 40! Thus, using modified duration as a measure of the price sensitivity of a security to a parallel shift in the yield curve would be misleading. The more appropriate measure for any security with an embedded option is effective duration.

Calculating the Effective Duration by Using the Binomial Model

The procedure for calculating the values to be substituted into the duration formula by using the binomial model is described below. First, V_+ is determined as follows:

Step 1   Calculate the option-adjusted spread (OAS) for the issue.

Step 2   Shift the on-the-run yield curve up by a small number of basis points.

EXHIBIT 17–14

Modified Duration versus Effective Duration

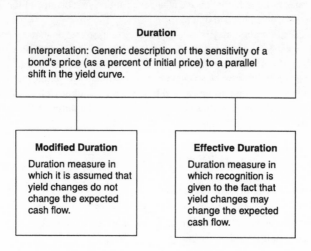

Step 3   Construct a binomial interest-rate tree based on the new yield curve in Step 2.

Step 4   Add the OAS to each of the forward rates in the binomial interest-rate tree to obtain an "adjusted tree."

Step 5   Use the adjusted tree found in Step 4 to determine the value of the security, which is V_+.

To determine the value of V_-, the same 5 steps are followed except that in Step 2, the on-the-run yield curve is shifted down by a small number of basis points.

Let's return to the example of the callable 5.25% 3-year bond. Given the yield curve and volatility assumptions we have been using, V_0 is $101.432. Following the five steps above for a shift of the yield curve by 10 basis points down and up gives values for V_- and V_+ of $101.628 and $101.234, respectively. The effective duration is then

$$\text{Effective duration} = \frac{\$101.628 - \$101.234}{2(101.432)(0.001)} = 1.94.$$

Effective Convexity

In the same manner, the standard convexity measure explained in Chapter 14 may be inappropriate for a bond with embedded options because it does not consider the effect of a change in interest rates on the bond's cash flow. The convexity of any bond can be approximated using the following formula:

$$\text{Convexity} = \frac{V_+ + V_- - 2V_0}{V_0(\Delta y)^2}.$$

The values in the formula are the same values used in the duration formula.

When the prices used in this formula assume that the cash flows do not change when yields change, the resulting convexity is a good approximation of the standard convexity for an option-free bond. When the prices used in the formula are derived by changing the cash flows when yields change, the resulting convexity is called *effective convexity* or *option-adjusted convexity*. In our illustration, the effective convexity is

$$\text{Effective convexity} = \frac{\$101.628 + \$101.234 - 2(101.432)}{(101.432)(0.001)^2} = 6.77.$$

SUMMARY

In this chapter a valuation framework that can be used to value any bond is explained. It involves generating a binomial interest-rate tree based on (1) an issuer's on-the-run yield curve, (2) an assumed interest-rate generation process, and (3) an assumed interest-rate volatility. The binomial interest-rate tree provides the appropriate volatility-dependent 1-period forward rates that should be used to discount the expected cash flows of a bond. The value of the embedded option is the difference between the value of an option-free bond and the value of the bond with the embedded option.

The option-adjusted spread is the constant spread that when added to the forward rates in the binomial interest-rate tree will produce a valuation for the bond equal to the market price of the bond. It is simply a way of recasting the difference between the theoretical value and the observed market price in terms of a yield spread.

Modified duration and standard convexity used to measure the interest-rate sensitivity of an option-free bond may be inappropriate for a bond with an embedded option because these measures assume that cash flows do not change as interest rates change. The duration and convexity can be approximated for any bond whether it is option-free or has an embedded option. The approximation involves determining how the price of the bond changes if interest rates go up or down by a small number of basis points. If when interest rates are changed it is assumed that the cash flows do not change, then the resulting measures are modified duration and standard convexity. However, when the cash flows are allowed to change when interest rates change, the resulting measures are called effective duration and effective convexity.

PART

VI

⑥ ANALYZING MORTGAGE-BACKED SECURITIES

18

⑥ CASH FLOW CHARACTERISTICS OF MORTGAGES

A mortgage is a pledge of real estate to secure the payment of the loan originated for the purchase of that real property. The mortgage gives the lender (*mortgagee*) the right to foreclose on the loan and seize the property in order to ensure that the loan is paid off if the borrower (*mortgagor*) fails to make the contracted payments.

A mortgage loan specifies the interest rate of the loan, the frequency of payment, and the number of years to maturity. In this chapter we show how to compute the cash flow of mortgages. While there are many types of mortgages, we focus in this chapter on level-payment fixed-rate mortgages. A level-payment fixed-rate mortgage has the following features: (1) the term of the loan is fixed, (2) the interest rate is fixed, and (3) the amount of the monthly mortgage payment is fixed for the entire term of the loan (i.e., the mortgage is "level-pay").

A characteristic that mortgages share with callable bonds is that their cash flow is not known with certainty. For callable bonds, this happens because the bondholder has effectively granted the issuer the option to call the issue. For mortgages, the lender has effectively granted the homeowner the right to repay *all* or *any part* of the mortgage balance at any time.

Mortgages are the underlying collateral for mortgage-backed securities.[1] In the next chapter we describe the cash flow characteristics of mortgage-backed securities, along with the effect of prepayments.

---

1 Other types of mortgages can serve as the underlying collateral for mortgage-backed securities. These include adjustable-rate mortgages and balloon mortgages. For a discussion of the characteristics of these mortgages, see Frank J. Fabozzi and Franco Modigliani, *Mortgage and Mortgage-Backed Securities* (Boston: Harvard Business School Press, 1992).

DETERMINING THE MONTHLY MORTGAGE PAYMENT

In Chapter 3 we explained calculation of the present value of an ordinary annuity. To compute the monthly mortgage payment for a level-payment fixed-rate mortgage requires application of the formula for the present value of an ordinary annuity formula, which is

$$PV = A\left[\dfrac{1 - \left[\dfrac{1}{(1+i)^n}\right]}{i}\right],$$

where

PV = Present value of an annuity ($);
A = Amount of the annuity ($);
i = Periodic interest rate;
n = Number of periods.

We can redefine these terms to yield a formula for a level-payment fixed-rate mortgage as follows:

$$MB_0 = MP\left[\dfrac{1 - \left[\dfrac{1}{(1+i)^n}\right]}{i}\right],$$

where

MB_0 = Original mortgage balance ($);
MP = Monthly mortgage payment ($);
i = Simple monthly interest rate (annual interest rate/12);
n = Number of months.

Solving for the monthly mortgage payment (MP) gives

$$MP = \dfrac{MB_0}{\left[\dfrac{1 - \left[\dfrac{1}{(1+i)^n}\right]}{i}\right]}.$$

This can be expressed in a simplified form as follows:

$$MP = MB_0\left[\dfrac{i(1+i)^n}{[(1+i)^n - 1]}\right].$$

Illustration 18-1   Suppose a homeowner enters into a mortgage for $100,000 for 360 months (30 years) at a mortgage rate of 9.5%. The monthly mortgage payment is determined as follows:

MB_0 = $100,000;
i = .0079167 (= .095/12);
n = 360.

The monthly mortgage payment is then

$$MP = \$100,000 \left[\frac{.0079167\ (1.0079167)^{360}}{[(1.0079167)^{360} - 1]} \right]$$

$$= \$100,000\ \frac{[.0079167\ (17.095)]}{[17.095 - 1]}$$

$$= \$840.85.$$

CASH FLOW OF A LEVEL-PAYMENT FIXED-RATE MORTGAGE

Each monthly mortgage payment for a level-payment fixed-rate mortgage due on the first of each month consists of

1. Interest of one-twelfth of the fixed annual interest rate times the amount of the outstanding mortgage balance at the beginning of the previous month (interest "in arrears");

2. Repayment of a portion of the outstanding mortgage balance (principal).

The difference between the monthly mortgage payment and the portion of the payment that represents interest equals the amount that is applied to reduce the outstanding mortgage balance. The monthly mortgage payment is designed so that after the last scheduled monthly payment of the loan is made, the amount of the outstanding mortgage balance is zero (i.e., the mortgage is fully repaid).

Illustration 18-2   Consider the mortgage in Illustration 18-1. Exhibit 18-1 shows how each monthly mortgage payment is divided between interest and repayment of principal. At the beginning of month 1, the mortgage balance is $100,000, the amount of the original loan. The mortgage payment for month 1 includes interest for the month on the $100,000 borrowed. Since the interest rate is 9.5%, the monthly interest rate is .0079167 (.095 divided by 12). Interest for month 1 is therefore $791.67 ($100,000 times .0079167). The portion of the monthly mortgage payment that represents repayment of principal is the difference between the monthly mortgage payment of $840.85 and the interest of $791.67. Thus, the scheduled principal repayment is $49.18, and the mortgage balance is reduced by this amount.[2]

The mortgage balance at the end of month 1 (beginning of month 2) is then $99,950.81 ($100,00 minus $49.19). The interest for the second month is $791.28, the monthly interest rate (.0079167) times the mortgage balance at the end of month 1 ($99,950.81). The difference between the $840.85 monthly mortgage payment and the $791.28 interest is $49.57, representing the amount of the mortgage balance paid off with that monthly mortgage payment.

The last line of Exhibit 18-1 shows the last monthly mortgage payment is sufficient to pay off the remaining mortgage balance. When a loan repayment schedule is structured so that the payments made by the borrower will completely pay off the interest and principal, the loan is said to be *self-amortizing*. Exhibit 18-1 is thus referred to as an amortization schedule.

---

2 Because Exhibit 18-1 is computer-generated, rounding resulted in the values of $49.19 and $49.18 shown in the exhibit.

EXHIBIT 18–1

Amortization Schedule for a Level-Payment Fixed-Rate Mortgage

Mortgage loan = $100,000;

Mortgage rate = 9.5%;

Monthly payment = $840.85;

Term of loan = 30 years (360 months).

Month	Beginning Mortgage Balance ($)	Monthly Mortgage Payment ($)	Interest for Month ($)	Principal Repayment ($)	Ending Mortgage Balance ($)
1	$100,000.00	$840.85	$791.67	$49.19	$99,950.81
2	99,950.81	840.85	791.28	49.58	99,901.24
3	99,901.24	840.85	790.88	49.97	99,851.27
4	99,851.27	840.85	790.49	50.37	99,800.90
5	99,800.90	840.85	790.09	50.76	99,750.14
6	99,750.14	840.85	789.69	51.10	99,698.97
7	99,698.97	840.85	789.28	51.57	99,647.40
8	99,647.40	840.85	788.88	51.90	99,595.42
9	99,595.42	840.85	788.46	52.39	99,543.03
10	99,543.03	840.85	788.05	52.81	99,490.23
11	99,490.23	840.85	787.63	53.22	99,437.00
12	99,437.00	840.85	787.21	53.64	99,383.36
13	99,383.36	840.85	786.78	54.07	99,329.29
14	99,329.29	840.85	786.36	54.50	99,274.79
15	99,274.79	840.85	785.93	54.93	99,219.86

Continued

EXHIBIT 18-1

Continued

Month	Beginning Mortgage Balance ($)	Monthly Mortgage Payment ($)	Interest for Month ($)	Principal Repayment ($)	Ending Mortgage Balance ($)
16	$99,219.86	$840.85	$785.49	$55.36	$99,164.50
17	99,164.50	840.85	785.05	55.80	99,108.70
18	99,108.70	840.85	784.61	56.24	99,052.45
19	99,052.45	840.85	784.17	56.69	98,995.77
20	98,995.77	840.85	783.72	57.14	98,938.63
21	98,938.63	840.85	783.26	57.59	98,881.04
22	98,881.04	840.85	782.81	58.05	98,822.99
23	98,822.99	840.85	782.35	58.51	98,764.49
24	98,764.49	840.85	781.89	58.97	98,705.52
25	98,705.52	840.85	781.42	59.44	98,646.08
26	98,646.08	840.85	780.95	59.91	98,586.18
27	98,586.18	840.85	780.47	60.38	98,525.80
28	98,525.80	840.85	780.00	60.86	98,464.94
29	98,464.94	840.85	779.51	61.34	98,403.60
30	98,403.60	840.85	779.03	61.83	98,341.77
31	98,341.77	840.85	778.54	62.32	98,279.46
32	98,279.46	840.85	778.05	62.81	98,216.65
33	98,216.65	840.85	777.55	63.31	98,153.34
34	98,153.34	840.85	777.05	63.81	98,089.53
35	98,089.53	840.85	776.54	64.31	98,025.22

Continued

307

EXHIBIT 18–1

Continued

Month	Beginning Mortgage Balance ($)	Monthly Mortgage Payment ($)	Interest for Month ($)	Principal Repayment ($)	Ending Mortgage Balance ($)
36	$98,025.22	$840.85	$776.03	$ 64.82	$97,960.40
:	:	:	:	:	:
:	:	:	:	:	:
:	:	:	:	:	:
98	92,862.54	840.85	735.16	105.69	92,756.85
99	92,756.85	840.85	734.33	106.53	92,650.32
100	92,650.32	840.85	733.48	107.37	92,542.95
101	92,542.95	840.85	732.63	108.22	92,434.72
102	92,434.72	840.85	731.77	109.08	92,325.64
103	92,325.64	840.85	730.91	109.94	92,215.70
104	92,215.70	840.85	730.04	110.81	92,104.89
105	92,104.89	840.85	729.16	111.69	91,993.20
106	91,993.20	840.85	728.28	112.57	91,880.62
107	91,880.62	840.85	727.39	113.47	91,767.16
108	91,767.16	840.85	726.49	114.36	91,652.79
109	91,652.79	840.85	725.58	115.27	91,537.52
110	91,537.52	840.85	724.67	116.18	91,421.34
111	91,421.34	840.85	723.75	117.10	91,304.24
112	91,304.24	840.85	722.83	118.03	91,186.21
113	91,186.21	840.85	721.89	118.96	91,067.25

Continued

EXHIBIT 18-1

Continued

Month	Beginning Mortgage Balance ($)	Monthly Mortgage Payment ($)	Interest for Month ($)	Principal Repayment ($)	Ending Mortgage Balance ($)
114	$91,067.25	$840.85	$720.95	$119.91	$90,947.34
115	90,947.34	840.85	720.00	120.85	90,826.49
...	......	......	......	......	......
...	......	......	......	......	......
...	......	......	......	......	......
201	76,135.92	840.85	602.74	238.11	75,897.80
202	75,897.80	840.85	600.86	240.00	75,657.81
203	75,657.81	840.85	598.96	241.90	75,415.91
204	75,415.91	840.85	597.04	243.81	75,172.10
205	75,172.10	840.85	595.11	245.74	74,926.36
206	74,926.36	840.85	593.17	247.69	74,678.67
207	74,678.67	840.85	591.21	249.65	74,429.02
208	74,429.02	840.85	589.23	251.62	74,177.40
209	74,177.40	840.85	587.24	253.62	73,923.78
210	73,923.78	840.85	585.23	255.62	73,668.16
211	73,668.16	840.85	583.21	257.65	73,410.51
212	73,410.51	840.85	581.17	259.69	73,150.82
213	73,150.82	840.85	579.11	261.74	72,889.08
214	72,889.08	840.85	577.04	263.82	72,625.26
215	72,625.26	840.85	574.95	265.90	72,359.36

Continued

EXHIBIT 18-1

Continued

Month	Beginning Mortgage Balance ($)	Monthly Mortgage Payment ($)	Interest for Month ($)	Principal Repayment ($)	Ending Mortgage Balance ($)
216	$72,359.36	$840.85	$572.84	$268.01	$72,091.35
217	72,091.35	840.85	570.72	270.13	71,821.22
218	71,821.22	840.85	568.58	272.27	71,548.95
219	71,548.95	840.85	566.43	274.43	71,274.52
220	71,274.52	840.85	564.26	276.60	70,997.93
⋮	⋮	⋮	⋮	⋮	⋮
⋮	⋮	⋮	⋮	⋮	⋮
⋮	⋮	⋮	⋮	⋮	⋮
342	14,778.59	840.85	117.00	723.86	14,054.73
343	14,054.73	840.85	111.27	729.59	13,325.15
344	13,325.15	840.85	105.49	735.36	12,589.78
345	12,589.78	840.85	99.67	741.19	11,848.60
346	11,848.60	840.85	93.80	747.05	11,101.55
347	11,101.55	840.85	87.89	752.97	10,348.58
348	10,348.58	840.85	81.93	758.93	9,589.65
349	9,589.65	840.85	75.92	764.94	8,824.71
350	8,824.71	840.85	69.86	770.99	8,053.72
351	8,053.72	840.85	63.76	777.10	7,276.63
352	7,276.63	840.85	57.61	783.25	6,493.38
353	6,493.38	840.85	51.41	789.45	5,703.93

Continued

EXHIBIT 18-1

Concluded

Month	Beginning Mortgage Balance ($)	Monthly Mortgage Payment ($)	Interest for Month ($)	Principal Repayment ($)	Ending Mortgage Balance ($)
354	$5,703.93	$840.85	$45.16	$795.70	$4,908.23
355	4,908.23	840.85	38.86	802.00	4,106.24
356	4,106.24	840.85	32.51	808.35	3,297.89
357	3,297.89	840.85	26.11	814.75	2,483.14
358	2,483.14	840.85	19.66	821.20	1,661.95
359	1,661.95	840.85	13.16	827.70	834.25
360	834.25	840.85	6.60	834.25	0.00

311

As Exhibit 18-1 clearly shows, *the portion of the monthly mortgage payment applied to interest declines each month, and the portion that goes to reducing the mortgage balance increases.* The reason for this is that as the mortgage balance is reduced with each monthly mortgage payment, the interest on the mortgage balance declines. Since the monthly mortgage payment is fixed, a larger part of the monthly payment is applied to reduce the principal each month.

It is not necessary to construct an amortization schedule such as Exhibit 18-1 in order to determine the remaining mortgage balance for any month. The following formula can be used:

$$MB_t = MB_0 \left[\frac{[(1+i)^n - (1+i)^t]}{[(1+i)^n - 1]} \right],$$

where

MB_t = Mortgage balance after t months ($);
MB_0 = The original mortgage balance ($);
  i = Simple monthly interest rate (annual interest rate/12);
  n = Original number of months of mortgage.

Illustration 18-3   For the mortgage in Illustration 18-1, the mortgage balance after the 210th month is

$t = 210$;
$MB_0 = \$100,000$;
  $i = .0079167$;
  $n = 360$.

$$MB_{210} = \$100,000 \left[\frac{[(1.0079167)^{360} - (1.0079167)^{210}]}{[(1.0079167)^{360} - 1]} \right]$$

$$= \$100,000 \left[\frac{(17.095 - 5.2381)}{(17.095 - 1)} \right]$$

$$= \$73,668.$$

This agrees with the ending mortgage balance for month 210 shown in Exhibit 18-1.

Another formula can be used to determine the amount of the scheduled principal repayment in month t:

$$P_t = MB_0 \left[\frac{[i(1+i)^{t-1}]}{[(1+i)^n - 1]} \right],$$

where

P_t = Scheduled principal repayment for month t.

Illustration 18-4   The scheduled principal repayment for the 210th month for the mortgage in Illustration 18-1 is

$$\$100,000 \left[\frac{[.0079167 \ (1.0079167)^{210-1}]}{[(1.0079167)^{360} - 1]} \right]$$

$$= \$100,000 \left[\frac{[.0079167 \ (5.19696)]}{[17.095 - 1]} \right]$$

$$= \$255.62.$$

Once again, this agrees with Exhibit 18-1.

To compute the interest paid for month t, a final formula can be used:

$$I_t = MB_0 \left[\frac{i[(1 + i)^n - (1 + i)^{t-1}]}{[(1 + i)^n - 1]} \right],$$

where

I_t = Interest for month t.

Illustration 18-5   For the 210th month, the interest for the mortgage in Illustration 18-1 is

$$I_{210} = \$100,000 \left[\frac{.0079167 \ [(1.0079167)^{360} - (1.0079167)^{210-1}]}{[(1.0079167)^{360} - 1]} \right]$$

$$= \$100,000 \left[\frac{.0079167 \ (17.095 - 5.19696)}{(17.095 - 1)} \right]$$

$$= \$585.23.$$

This result can be confirmed by examination of Exhibit 18-1.

CASH FLOW AND SERVICING FEE

An investor who owns a mortgage receives the monthly mortgage payment as the *scheduled* cash flow. A mortgage, however, requires monitoring to ensure that the borrower complies with the terms of the mortgage. In addition, the investor must periodically supply certain information to the borrower. These activities are referred to as *servicing* the mortgage. More specifically, servicing of the mortgage involves collecting monthly payments from mortgagors, sending payment notices to mortgagors, reminding mortgagors when payments are overdue, maintaining records of mortgage balances, furnishing tax information to mortgagors, administering an escrow account for real estate taxes and insurance purposes, and, if necessary, initiating foreclosure proceedings. Part of the mortgage rate includes the cost of servicing the mortgage. The servicing fee is a fixed percentage of the outstanding mortgage balance.

An investor who acquires a mortgage may either service the mortgage or sell the right to service the mortgage. In the former case, the investor's cash flow is the entire cash flow from the mortgage. In the latter case it is the cash flow net of the servicing fee.

The monthly cash flow from the mortgage can therefore be decomposed into three parts:

1. The amount to service the mortgage;
2. The interest payment net of the servicing fee;
3. The scheduled principal repayment.

EXHIBIT 18-2

Cash Flow for a Mortgage with Servicing Fee

Mortgage loan = $100,000;

Mortgage rate = 9.5%;

Servicing fee = 0.5%;

Monthly payment = $840.85;

Term of loan = 30 years (360 months).

Month	Beginning Mortgage Balance ($)	Monthly Mortgage Payment ($)	Net Interest for Month ($)	Servicing Fee ($)	Principal Repayment ($)	Ending Mortgage Balance ($)
1	$100,000.00	$840.85	$750.00	$41.67	$49.19	$99,950.81
2	99,950.81	840.85	749.63	41.65	49.58	99,901.24
3	99,901.24	840.85	749.26	41.63	49.97	99,851.27
4	99,851.27	840.85	748.88	41.60	50.37	99,800.90
5	99,800.90	840.85	748.51	41.58	50.76	99,750.14
6	99,750.14	840.85	748.13	41.56	51.17	99,698.97
7	99,698.97	840.85	747.74	41.54	51.57	99,647.40
8	99,647.40	840.85	747.36	41.52	51.98	99,595.42
9	99,595.42	840.85	746.97	41.50	52.39	99,543.03
10	99,543.03	840.85	746.57	41.48	52.81	99,490.23
11	99,490.23	840.85	746.18	41.45	53.22	99,437.00
12	99,437.00	840.85	745.78	41.43	53.64	99,383.36
13	99,383.36	840.85	745.38	41.41	54.07	99,329.29

Continued

EXHIBIT 18-2

Continued

Month	Beginning Mortgage Balance ($)	Monthly Mortgage Payment ($)	Net Interest for Month ($)	Servicing Fee ($)	Principal Repayment ($)	Ending Mortgage Balance ($)
14	$99,329.29	$840.85	$744.97	$41.39	$54.50	$99,274.79
15	99,274.79	840.85	744.56	41.36	54.93	99,219.86
16	99,219.86	840.85	744.15	41.34	55.36	99,164.50
17	99,164.50	840.85	743.73	41.32	55.80	99,108.70
18	99,108.70	840.85	743.32	41.30	56.24	99,052.45
19	99,052.45	840.85	742.89	41.27	56.69	98,995.77
20	98,995.77	840.85	742.47	41.25	57.14	98,938.63
21	98,938.63	840.85	742.04	41.22	57.59	98,881.04
22	98,881.04	840.85	741.61	41.20	58.05	98,822.99
23	98,822.99	840.85	741.17	41.18	58.51	98,764.49
24	98,764.49	840.85	740.73	41.15	58.97	98,705.52
25	98,705.52	840.85	740.29	41.13	59.44	98,646.08
26	98,646.08	840.85	739.85	41.10	59.91	98,586.18
27	98,586.18	840.85	739.40	41.08	60.38	98,525.80
28	98,525.80	840.85	738.94	41.05	60.86	98,464.94
29	98,464.94	840.85	738.49	41.03	61.34	98,403.60
30	98,403.60	840.85	738.03	41.00	61.83	98,341.77
31	98,341.77	840.85	737.56	40.98	62.32	98,279.46
32	98,279.46	840.85	737.10	40.95	62.81	98,216.65
33	98,216.65	840.85	736.62	40.92	63.31	98,153.34

Continued

315

EXHIBIT 18-2

Continued

Month	Beginning Mortgage Balance ($)	Monthly Mortgage Payment ($)	Net Interest for Month ($)	Servicing Fee ($)	Principal Repayment ($)	Ending Mortgage Balance ($)
34	$98,153.34	$840.85	$736.15	$40.90	$63.81	$98,089.53
35	98,089.53	840.85	735.67	40.87	64.31	98,025.22
36	98,025.22	840.85	735.19	40.84	64.82	97,960.40
:	::::::	::::::	::::::	::::::	::::::	::::::
:	::::::	::::::	::::::	::::::	::::::	::::::
:	::::::	::::::	::::::	::::::	::::::	::::::
98	92,862.54	840.85	696.47	38.69	105.69	92,756.85
99	92,756.85	840.85	695.68	38.65	106.53	92,650.32
100	92,650.32	840.85	694.88	38.60	107.37	92,542.95
101	92,542.95	840.85	694.07	38.56	108.22	92,434.72
102	92,434.72	840.85	693.26	38.51	109.08	92,325.64
103	92,325.64	840.85	692.44	38.47	109.94	92,215.70
104	92,215.70	840.85	691.62	38.42	110.81	92,104.89
105	92,104.89	840.85	690.79	38.38	111.69	91,993.20
106	91,993.20	840.85	689.95	38.33	112.57	91,880.62
107	91,880.62	840.85	689.10	38.28	113.47	91,767.16
108	91,767.16	840.85	688.25	38.24	114.36	91,652.79
109	91,652.79	840.85	687.40	38.19	115.27	91,537.52
110	91,537.52	840.85	686.53	38.14	116.18	91,421.34
111	91,421.34	840.85	685.66	38.09	117.10	91,304.24

Continued

EXHIBIT 18–2

Continued

Month	Beginning Mortgage Balance ($)	Monthly Mortgage Payment ($)	Net Interest for Month ($)	Servicing Fee ($)	Principal Repayment ($)	Ending Mortgage Balance ($)
112	$91,304.24	$840.85	$684.78	$38.04	$118.03	$91,186.21
113	91,186.21	840.85	683.90	37.99	118.96	91,067.25
114	91,067.25	840.85	683.00	37.94	119.91	90,947.34
115	90,947.34	840.85	682.11	37.89	120.85	90,826.49
:	:	:	:	:	:	:
:	:	:	:	:	:	:
:	:	:	:	:	:	:
201	76,135.92	840.85	571.02	31.72	238.11	75,897.80
202	75,897.80	840.85	569.23	31.62	240.00	75,657.81
203	75,657.81	840.85	567.43	31.52	241.90	75,415.91
204	75,415.91	840.85	565.62	31.42	243.81	75,172.10
205	75,172.10	840.85	563.79	31.32	245.74	74,926.36
206	74,926.36	840.85	561.95	31.22	247.69	74,678.67
207	74,678.67	840.85	560.09	31.12	249.65	74,429.02
208	74,429.02	840.85	558.22	31.01	251.62	74,177.40
209	74,177.40	840.85	556.33	30.91	253.62	73,923.78
210	73,923.78	840.85	554.43	30.80	255.62	73,668.16
211	73,668.16	840.85	552.51	30.70	257.65	73,410.51
212	73,410.51	840.85	550.58	30.59	259.69	73,150.82
213	73,150.82	840.85	548.63	30.48	261.74	72,889.08
214	72,889,08	840.85	546.67	30.37	263.82	72,625.26

Continued

EXHIBIT 18–2

Continued

Month	Beginning Mortgage Balance ($)	Monthly Mortgage Payment ($)	Net Interest for Month ($)	Servicing Fee ($)	Principal Repayment ($)	Ending Mortgage Balance ($)
215	$72,625.26	$840.85	$544.69	$30.26	$265.90	$72,359.36
216	72,359.36	840.85	542.70	30.15	268.01	72,091.35
217	72,091,35	840.85	540.69	30.04	270.13	71,821.22
218	71,821.22	840.85	538.66	29.93	272.27	71,548.95
219	71,548.95	840.85	536.62	29.81	274.43	71,274.52
220	71,274.52	840.85	534.56	29.70	276.60	70,997.93
:	:	:	:	:	:	:
:	:	:	:	:	:	:
:	:	:	:	:	:	:
342	14,778.59	840.85	110.84	6.16	723.86	14,054.73
343	14,054.73	840.85	105.41	5.86	729.59	13,325.15
344	13,325.15	840.85	99.94	5.55	735.36	12,589.78
345	12,589.78	840.85	94.42	5.25	741.19	11,848.60
346	11,848.60	840.85	88.86	4.94	747.05	11,101.55
347	11,101.55	840.85	83.26	4.63	752.97	10,348.58
348	10,348.58	840.85	77.61	4.31	758.93	9,589.65
349	9,589.65	840.85	71.92	4.00	764.94	8,824.71
350	8,824.71	840.85	66.19	3.68	770.99	8,053.72
351	8,053.72	840.85	60.40	3.36	777.10	7,276.63
352	7,276.63	840.85	54.57	3.03	783.25	6,493.38
353	6,493.38	840.85	48.70	2.71	789.45	5,703.93

Continued

EXHIBIT 18–2

Concluded

Month	Beginning Mortgage Balance ($)	Monthly Mortgage Payment ($)	Net Interest for Month ($)	Servicing Fee ($)	Principal Repayment ($)	Ending Mortgage Balance ($)
354	$5,703.93	$840.85	$42.78	$2.38	$795.70	$4,908.23
355	4,908.23	840.85	36.81	2.05	802.00	4,106.24
356	4,106.24	840.85	30.80	1.71	808.35	3,297.89
357	3,297.89	840.85	24.73	1.37	814.75	2,483.14
358	2,483.14	840.85	18.62	1.03	821.20	1,661.95
359	1,661.95	840.85	12.46	0.69	827.70	834.25
360	834.25	840.85	6.60	0.38	834.25	0

Illustration 18-6   Consider once again the 30-year mortgage loan for $100,000 with a mortgage rate of 9.5%. Suppose the servicing fee is .5% per year. Exhibit 18-2 shows the cash flow for the mortgage assuming this servicing fee. The monthly mortgage payment is unchanged from Exhibit 18-1, and so is the amount of the principal repayment. The difference is that the interest is reduced by the amount of the servicing fee. The servicing fee, just like the interest, declines each month because the mortgage balance declines.

SUMMARY

In this chapter we have shown how to determine the cash flow of a level-payment fixed-rate mortgage. The cash flow of a mortgage consists of the monthly interest plus the scheduled principal repayment. Each month, the mortgage balance declines, resulting in a lower monthly dollar interest than in the previous month, with more of the fixed monthly mortgage payment applied to reduction of the mortgage balance. The cash flow can be partitioned further by dividing the interest into (1) a servicing fee and (2) interest net of the servicing fee. Exhibit 18-3 summarizes the formulas presented in the chapter.

EXHIBIT 18-3

Summary of Formulas for Cash Flow of Level-Payment Fixed-Rate Mortgages (Assuming No Prepayments)

1. The monthly mortgage payment:

$$MP = MB_0 \left[\frac{[i(1+i)^n]}{[(1+i)^n - 1]} \right],$$

where

MP = Monthly mortgage payment (\$);
MB_0 = Original mortgage balance (\$);
i = Simple monthly interest rate (annual interest rate/12);
n = Number of months.

2. The remaining mortgage balance at the end of month t:

$$MB_t = MB_0 \left[\frac{[(1+i)^n - (1+i)^t]}{[(1+i)^n - 1]} \right],$$

where

MB_t = Mortgage balance after t months (\$);
n = Original number of months of mortgage.

3. The scheduled principal repayments in month t:

$$P_t = MB_0 \left[\frac{[(i(+i)^{t-1}]}{[(1+i)^n - 1]} \right],$$

where

P_t = Scheduled principal repayment for month t.

4. The interest for month t:

$$I_t = MB_0 \left[\frac{i[(1+i)^n - (1+i)^{t-1}]}{[(1+i)^n - 1]} \right],$$

where
I_t = Interest for month t.

CHAPTER

19

⑥ CASH FLOW CHARACTERISTICS OF MORTGAGE-BACKED SECURITIES

A mortgage-backed security (MBS) is created by pooling mortgage loans and using this pool of mortgage loans as collateral for the security. There are three types of mortgage-backed securities: a mortgage pass-through security, a collateralized mortgage obligation, and a stripped MBS. The cash flow of any MBS depends on the cash flow of the underlying mortgage pool. Since the cash flow of an individual mortgage loan is uncertain because of the potential of prepayments, the same is true for MBSs.

In this chapter we focus on the various conventions for projecting the cash flow of an MBS. We show how to project the cash flow for a mortgage pass-through security as well as for the other products, collateralized mortgage obligations, and a stripped MBS. We then look at the convention for constructing cash flow for nonagency mortgage-backed securities where defaults must be considered, and another mortgage-related product—asset-backed securities backed by a pool of home equity loans.

THE PREPAYMENT OPTION AND THE CASH FLOW

In our illustration of the cash flow from a level-payment fixed-rate mortgage in the previous chapter, we assumed that the homeowner would not pay any portion of the mortgage balance off prior to the scheduled due date. But homeowners do pay off some or all of their mortgage balance prior to the maturity date. Payments made in excess of the scheduled principal repayments are called *prepayments*.

Prepayments occur for one of several reasons. First, homeowners pay off the entire mortgage when they sell their home. The sale of a home may be due to (1) a change of employment that necessitates moving, (2) the purchase of a more expensive home ("trading up"), or (3) a divorce settlement requiring sale of the marital residence. Second, borrowers have an incentive to prepay a mortgage loan as mortgage rates in the market fall below the specified rate on their mortgage loan. Third, in the case of homeowners who cannot meet their mortgage obligations, the property may be repossessed and sold, with the proceeds from the sale used to pay off the mortgage loan. Finally, if property is destroyed by fire or another insured catastrophe occurs, the insurance proceeds are used to pay off the mortgage.

The effect of the right to prepay is that the cash flow from a mortgage is not known with certainty. This is true for all mortgage loans, not just level-payment fixed-rate mortgages.

OVERVIEW OF MORTGAGE-BACKED SECURITIES

We illustrate the creation of mortgage-backed securities using Exhibits 19-1 through 19-4. Exhibit 19-1 shows 10 mortgage loans (each loan depicted as a home) and the cash flows from these loans. For the sake of simplicity, we assume that the amount of each loan is $100,000 so that the aggregate value of all 10 loans is $1 million. The cash flows are monthly and consist of three components:

1. Interest;
2. Scheduled principal repayment;
3. Payments in excess of the regularly scheduled principal repayment.

How (1) and (2) are determined is explained in Chapter 18. The third component, payments in excess of the scheduled principal payment, is what we said is a prepayment. It is the amount and timing of this component of the cash flow from a mortgage that makes the entire cash flow (and therefore analysis of mortgages and mortgage-backed securities) complicated. This is referred to as *prepayment risk*. Creation of mortgage-backed securities does not alter the total amount of prepayment risk. The distribution of that risk among investors, however, can be altered.

An investor who owns any one of the mortgage loans shown in Exhibit 19-1 faces prepayment risk. For an individual loan, it may be difficult to predict prepayments, but if an individual investor purchased all 10 loans, there could be a way to predict prepayments better. In fact, if there were 500 mortgage loans in Exhibit 19-1 rather than 10, we could use historical prepayment experience to improve predictions about prepayments. But an investor would have to invest $1 million to buy 10 loans and $50 million to buy 500 loans assuming each loan is for $100,000.

Mortgage Pass-Through Securities

Suppose, instead, that some entity purchases all 10 loans in Exhibit 19-1 and pools them. The 10 loans can be used as collateral for the issuance of a security whose cash flow would reflect the cash flow from the 10 loans, as depicted in Exhibit 19-2. Suppose there are 40 units of this security issued. Thus, each unit is initially worth $25,000 ($1 million divided by 40). Each unit would be entitled to 2.5% (1/40) of the cash flow. The security created is called a *mortgage pass-through security* or, simply, a *pass-through*. The majority of pass-throughs are guaranteed by a government-related entity, the Government National Mortgage Association (GNMA, nicknamed "Ginnie Mae"), and two government-sponsored enterprises, the Federal National Mortgage Association (FNMA, nicknamed "Fannie Mae") and the Federal Home Loan Mortgage Corporation (FHLMC, nicknamed "Freddie Mac"). Pass-throughs are also issued by private entities; these securities are referred to as *non-agency pass-throughs* or *private label pass-throughs*.

EXHIBIT 19-1

10 Mortgage Loans

Monthly cash flow

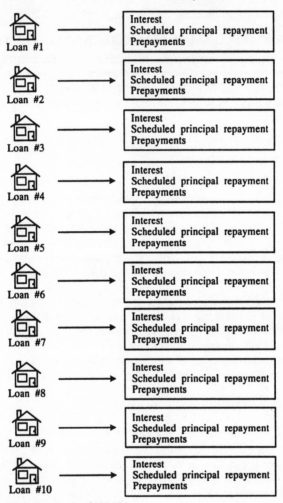

Each loan is for $100,000
Total loans: $1 million

E X H I B I T   19-2

Creation of a Pass-Through Security

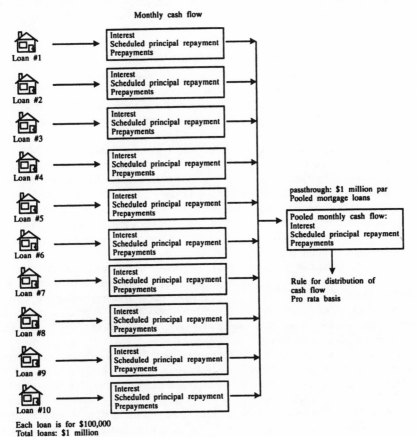

Monthly cash flow

Each loan is for $100,000
Total loans: $1 million

Let's see what has been accomplished by creating the pass-through. The total amount of prepayment risk has not changed. Instead, with an investment of less than $1 million, the investor is now exposed to the total prepayment risk of all 10 loans rather than facing the risk of an individual mortgage loan.

So far, this financial "engineering" has not resulted in creation of a totally new instrument, as an individual investor could have achieved the same outcome by purchasing all 10 loans. The pass-through does reduce the $1 million requirement and increases the liquidity of the security. Moreover, by selling a pass-through the investor can dispose of all 10 loans rather than having to dispose of each loan one by one. Thus, a pass-through can be viewed as a more transactionally efficient vehicle for investing in mortgages than the purchase of individual mortgages would be.

Mortgage loans that are included in a pool to create a pass-through are said to be *securitized.* The process of creating a pass-through is referred to as the securitization of mortgage loans.

Collateralized Mortgage Obligations

An investor in a pass-through is still exposed to the total prepayment risk associated with the pool of mortgage loans underlying the security. A way to change this is instead of distributing the monthly cash flow on a pro rata basis, as in the case of a pass-through, to distribute the principal (both scheduled and prepayments) on some prioritized basis. How this may be done is illustrated in Exhibit 19-3.

Exhibit 19-3 shows the cash flow of our original 10 mortgage loans and the pass-through. Also shown are three classes of bonds of different par values, with a set of rules indicating how the principal from the pass-through is to be distributed to each. The sum of the par value of the three classes is equal to $1 million. While it is not shown in the exhibit, for each of the three classes there are units representing a proportionate interest in the class. Each unit then receives a proportionate share of what is received by the class. For example, suppose that for class A, which has a par value of $400,000, there are 50 units issued. Class A holders then receive proportionate shares of 2% of the distribution of principal.

The rule for the distribution of principal shown in Exhibit 19-3 is that class A will receive all principal (both scheduled and prepayments) until that class receives its entire par value of $400,000. Then, class B receives all principal payments until it receives its par value of $350,000. Finally, after class B is completely paid off, class C receives principal payments. The rule for the distribution of interest in Exhibit 19-3 indicates that each of the three classes will receive interest based on the amount of par value outstanding.

The mortgage-backed security that has been created is called a *collateralized mortgage obligation* (CMO). The collateral for a loan may be either one or more pass-throughs or a pool of mortgage loans that have not been securitized. The ultimate source for the CMO's cash flow is the pool of mortgage loans.

Let's evaluate what has been accomplished. Once again, the total prepayment risk for the CMO remains the same as the total prepayment risk for the 10 mortgage loans. Creation of three classes, however, means that the prepayment risk is distributed differently among the three classes of the CMO. Class A absorbs prepayments first, next class B, and last of all class C. The result is that class A effectively holds a shorter-term security than the other two classes; class C has the longest maturity. Institutional investors will be attracted to the different classes given the varying nature of their liability structure and the effective maturity of the CMO class. Moreover, the cash flow distribution rules mitigate the uncertainty about the maturity of each class of the CMO.

Thus, redirection of the cash flow from the underlying mortgage pool creates classes of bonds that may be more attractive to institutional investors to satisfy asset/liability objectives than a pass-through.

The CMO we depict in Exhibit 19-3 has a simple set of rules for prioritizing the distribution of principal. Today, much more complicated CMO structures exist, such as *planned amortization class (PAC) bonds, targeted amortization class (TAC) bonds,* and *very accurately deter-*

EXHIBIT 19-3

Creation of a Collateralized Mortgage Obligation

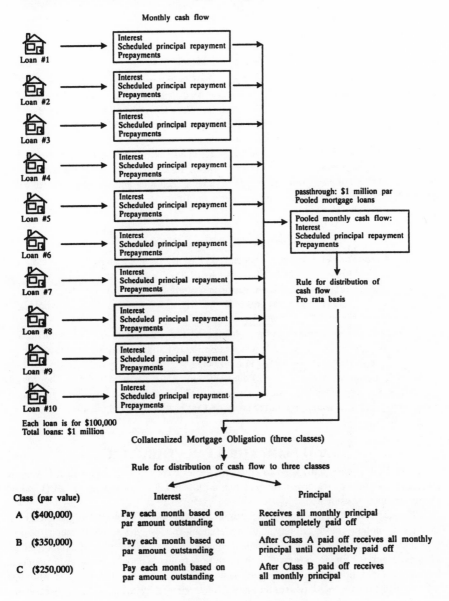

Class (par value)	Interest	Principal
A ($400,000)	Pay each month based on par amount outstanding	Receives all monthly principal until completely paid off
B ($350,000)	Pay each month based on par amount outstanding	After Class A paid off receives all monthly principal until completely paid off
C ($250,000)	Pay each month based on par amount outstanding	After Class B paid off receives all monthly principal

mined maturity (VADM) bonds. These CMO structures are intended to expose certain CMO classes to less prepayment risk. Note, however, that this can occur only if the reduction in prepayment risk for some classes is absorbed by other classes in the CMO structure, which are referred to as *support bonds* or *companion bonds.*

Stripped MBS

The CMO in Exhibit 19-3 specified a set of rules for prioritizing the distribution of the principal payments among the various classes. A stripped MBS calls for dividing all the principal and all the interest between two bond classes. One class is entitled to receive all the principal; the other class, all the interest. The former class is called the *principal-only* or *PO* class and the latter the *interest-only* or *IO* class. This is depicted in Exhibit 19-4.

It may be less clear why stripped mortgage-backed securities are created. Suffice it to say that the risk/return characteristics of stripped MBSs make them attractive for purposes of hedging a portfolio of pass-throughs, creating synthetic securities, and hedging a portfolio of a mortgage-related product such as mortgage servicing rights.

Mortgage Servicing Rights

There is yet another asset whose value depends on the cash flow of a mortgage pool. Consider that the cash flow to investors in Exhibits 19-1 to 19-4 omits an important component: a fee paid to service a mortgage loan. If an investor in a mortgage-backed security were forced to maintain a staff to service the underlying pool of mortgage loans, these securities would have much less appeal to institutional investors.

Fortunately, the servicing of mortgage loans can be separated from the investment in those loans. This is depicted in Exhibit 19-5, which is similar to Exhibit 19-2 but now shows that the cash flow is separated into two parts: (1) a servicing fee (which is a fixed percentage of the outstanding mortgage balance), and (2) the cash flow minus the servicing fee. The right to service the mortgage loans is an asset whose cash flow is uncertain because of the uncertainty about prepayments, as well as the future costs associated with servicing the mortgages.

CASH FLOW FOR A PASS-THROUGH

A pass-through is commonly used as collateral for a CMO and a stripped MBS. Given the estimated cash flow of the pass-through, the cash flow of CMO bond classes and PO and IO classes can then be estimated.

The cash flow of a pass-through depends on the cash flow of the underlying mortgages. It consists of monthly mortgage payments representing interest, the scheduled repayment of principal, and any prepayments. Payments are made to security holders each month. Neither the amount nor the timing, however, of the cash flow from the pool of mortgages is identical to that of the cash flow passed through to investors. The monthly cash flow for a pass-through is less than the monthly cash flow of the underlying mortgages by an amount equal to servicing and other fees. The other fees are those charged by the issuer or guarantor of the pass-through

EXHIBIT 19–4

Creation of a Stripped Mortgage-Backed Security

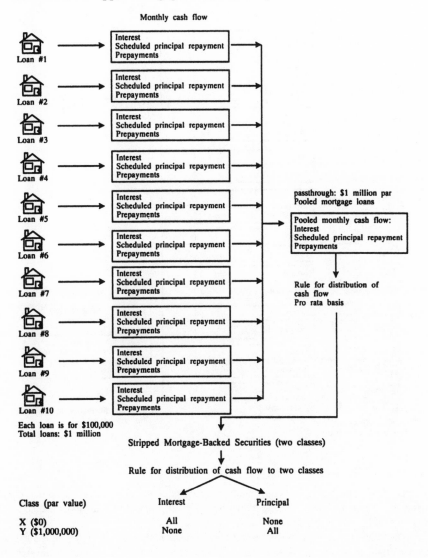

Monthly cash flow

Each loan is for $100,000
Total loans: $1 million

passthrough: $1 million par
Pooled mortgage loans

Pooled monthly cash flow:
Interest
Scheduled principal repayment
Prepayments

Rule for distribution of cash flow
Pro rata basis

Stripped Mortgage-Backed Securities (two classes)

Rule for distribution of cash flow to two classes

Class (par value)	Interest	Principal
X ($0)	All	None
Y ($1,000,000)	None	All

EXHIBIT 19–5

Cash Flow When Servicing Is Considered

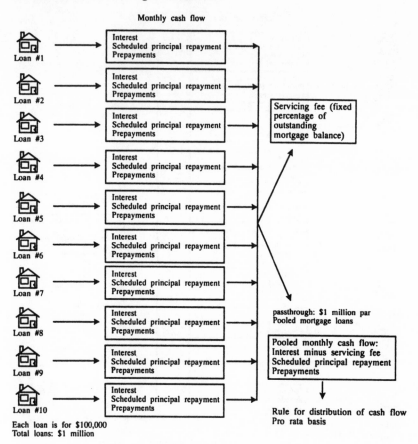

Monthly cash flow

Loan #1 — Interest / Scheduled principal repayment / Prepayments

Loan #2 — Interest / Scheduled principal repayment / Prepayments

Loan #3 — Interest / Scheduled principal repayment / Prepayments

Loan #4 — Interest / Scheduled principal repayment / Prepayments

Loan #5 — Interest / Scheduled principal repayment / Prepayments

Loan #6 — Interest / Scheduled principal repayment / Prepayments

Loan #7 — Interest / Scheduled principal repayment / Prepayments

Loan #8 — Interest / Scheduled principal repayment / Prepayments

Loan #9 — Interest / Scheduled principal repayment / Prepayments

Loan #10 — Interest / Scheduled principal repayment / Prepayments

Servicing fee (fixed percentage of outstanding mortgage balance)

passthrough: $1 million par
Pooled mortgage loans

Pooled monthly cash flow:
Interest minus servicing fee
Scheduled principal repayment
Prepayments

Rule for distribution of cash flow
Pro rata basis

Each loan is for $100,000
Total loans: $1 million

for guaranteeing the issue.[1] The coupon rate on a pass-through, called the *pass-through rate*, is less than the contract rate on the underlying pool of mortgage loans by an amount equal to the servicing and guaranteeing fees.

The timing of the cash flow is also different. The monthly mortgage payment is due from each mortgagor on the first day of each month. There is a delay in passing through the corresponding monthly cash flow to the security holders, which varies by the type of pass-through. Because of prepayments, the cash flow of a pass-through is not known with certainty.

---

1   Actually, the servicer pays the guarantee fee to the issuer or guarantor.

Prepayment Benchmark Conventions

Estimating the cash flow from a pass-through requires forecasting prepayments. Current practice is to use the Public Securities Association (PSA) prepayment benchmark. This benchmark is based on a series of conditional prepayment rates.[2]

Conditional Prepayment Rate

One way to project prepayments and cash flow is to assume that some fraction of the remaining principal in the pool is prepaid *each* month for the remaining term of the mortgages. The prepayment rate assumed for a pool, called the *conditional prepayment rate (CPR)*, is based on the characteristics of the pool (including its historical prepayment experience) and the current and expected economic environment.

The CPR is an annual prepayment rate. To estimate monthly prepayments, the CPR must be converted into a monthly prepayment rate, commonly referred to as the *single monthly mortality rate* (SMM). The following formula can be used to determine the SMM for a given CPR:

$$SMM = 1 - (1 - CPR)^{1/12}.$$

Illustration 19-1   Suppose that the CPR used to project prepayments is 6%. The corresponding SMM is

$$SMM = 1 - (1 - .06)^{1/12}$$
$$= 1 - (.94)^{.083333} = .005143.$$

An SMM of $w\%$ means that approximately $w\%$ of the remaining mortgage balance at the beginning of the month after subtracting the scheduled principal payment will prepay that month. That is,

Prepayment for month = SMM
× (Beginning mortgage balance − Scheduled principal for month).

Illustration 19-2   Suppose that an investor owns a pass-through whose remaining mortgage balance at the beginning of some month is $50,525. Assuming that the SMM is .5143% and the scheduled principal payment is $67, the estimated prepayment for the month is

---

2   In the early stages of the development of the pass-through market, cash flows were calculated assuming no prepayments for 12 years. In the twelfth year, all the mortgages in the pool would be assumed to prepay. This naive approach was replaced by the "FHA prepayment experience" for 30-year mortgages derived from an FHA probability table on mortgage survivals. On the basis of FHA experience, the cash flow is projected for a mortgage pool, assuming that the prepayment rate is the same as the FHA experience ("100% FHA") or some multiple of FHA experience (faster than FHA experience or slower than FHA experience).

   Despite its popularity at one time, prepayment projections based on FHA experience were not necessarily indicative of the prepayment rate for a particular pool. This is so because FHA experience represents an estimate of prepayments on all FHA-insured mortgages originated *over various interest-rate periods*. Prepayment rates, of course, are tied to interest-rate cycles, so an average prepayment rate over various cycles is not of much value for estimating prepayments. In addition, new FHA tables are published periodically, leading to confusion as to which FHA table prepayments should be based on. Consequently, as estimated prepayments using FHA experience may be misleading, the resulting cash flow is not meaningful for valuing pass-throughs.

$$.005143 \times (\$50,525 - \$67) = \$260.$$

PSA Standard Prepayment Benchmark

The Public Securities Association (PSA) standard prepayment benchmark[3] is expressed as a monthly series of annual CPRs. The benchmark PSA model assumes that prepayment rates will be low for newly originated mortgages, and then will speed up as the mortgages become seasoned.

More specifically, the PSA standard prepayment benchmark assumes the following prepayment rates for 30-year mortgages:

1. A CPR of .2% for the first month, increased by .2% per month for the next 30 months, when it reaches 6% per year;

2. A 6% CPR for the remaining years.

This benchmark is referred to as "100% PSA" and can be expressed as follows:

$$\text{If } t \leq 30, \text{ then } CPR = \frac{6\% \ t}{30};$$
$$\text{if } t > 30, \text{ then } CPR = 6\%;$$

where t is the number of months since the mortgage originated. Exhibit 19-6 illustrates this benchmark.

Slower or faster speeds than the benchmark are then referred to as some percentage of PSA. For example, 50% PSA means one-half the CPR of the PSA prepayment rate; 150% PSA means one-and-a-half the CPR of the PSA prepayment rate. This is illustrated in Exhibit 19-7. The CPR is converted to an SMM using the formula presented earlier.

EXHIBIT 19-6

100% PSA

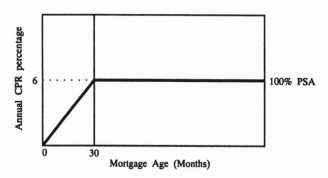

---

3 This benchmark is commonly referred to as a prepayment model, suggesting that it can be used to estimate prepayments. In fact, this is an inappropriate characterization.

EXHIBIT 19–7

Multiples of PSA

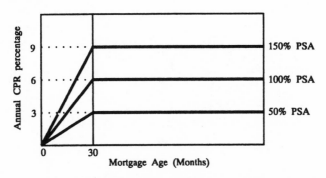

Illustration 19-3 The SMM for month 5, month 20, and months 31 through 360, assuming 100% PSA, are calculated as follows:

For month 5:

$$CPR = \frac{6\% \ (5)}{30} = 1\% = .01;$$
$$SMM = 1 - (1 - .01)^{1/12}$$
$$= 1 - (.99)^{.083333} = .000837.$$

For month 20:

$$CPR = \frac{6\% \ (20)}{30} = 4\% = .04;$$
$$SMM = 1 - (1 - .04)^{1/12}$$
$$= 1 - (.96)^{.083333} = .003396 .$$

For months 31–360:

$$CPR = 6\%;$$
$$SMM = 1 - (1 - .06)^{1/12}$$
$$= 1 - (.94)^{.08333} = .005143.$$

Illustration 19-4 The SMM for month 5, month 20, and months 31 through 360, assuming 150% PSA, are computed as follows:

For month 5:

$$CPR = \frac{6\% \ (5)}{30} = 1\% = .01;$$

$$150\% \ PSA = 1.5(.01) = .015;$$
$$SMM = 1 - (1-.015)^{1/12}$$
$$= 1 - (.985)^{.083333} = .001259.$$

For month 20:

$$CPR = \frac{6\% \ (20)}{30} = 4\% = .04;$$
$$150\% \ PSA = 1.5 \ (.04) = .06;$$
$$SMM = 1 - (1 - .06)^{1/12}$$
$$= 1 - (.94)^{.083333} = .005143.$$

For months 31–360:

$$CPR = 6\% = .06;$$
$$150\% \ PSA = 1.5 \ (.06) = .09;$$
$$SMM = 1 - (1 - .09)^{1/12}$$
$$= 1 - (.91)^{.083333} = .007828.$$

Notice that the SMM assuming 150% PSA is not just 1.5 times the SMM assuming 100% PSA. It is the CPR that is a multiple of the CPR assuming 100% PSA.

Illustration 19.5   The SMM for month 5, month 20, and months 31 through 360, assuming 50% PSA, are as follows:

For month 5:

$$CPR = \frac{6\% \ (5)}{30} = 1\% = .01;$$
$$50\% \ PSA = .5 \ (.01) = .005;$$
$$SMM = 1 - (1 - .005)^{1/12}$$
$$= 1 - (.995)^{.083333} = .000418.$$

For month 20:

$$CPR = \frac{6\% \ (20)}{30} = 4\% = .04;$$
$$50\% \ PSA = .5(.04) = .02;$$
$$SMM = 1 - (1 - .02)^{1/12}$$
$$= 1 - (.98)^{.083333} = .001682.$$

For months 31–360:

$$CPR = 6\% = .06;$$
$$50\% \ PSA = .5 \ (.06) = .03;$$

$$SMM = 1 - (1 - .03)^{1/12}$$
$$= 1 - (.97)^{.083333} = .002535.$$

Once again, notice that the SMM assuming 50% PSA is not just half the SMM assuming 100% PSA. It is the CPR that is a multiple of the CPR assuming 100% PSA.

CONSTRUCTING THE PROJECTED CASH FLOW

We can construct a cash flow schedule for a mortgage pass-through security on the basis of some assumed prepayment rate (or rates), using several formulas. First, the formula to obtain the projected monthly mortgage payment for any month is

$$\overline{MP}_t = \overline{MB}_{t-1} \left[\frac{i(1+i)^{n-t+1}}{(1+i)^{n-t+1} - 1} \right],$$

where

$\overline{MP}_t$ = Projected monthly mortgage payment for month t;

$\overline{MB}_{t-1}$ = Projected mortgage balance at the end of month t given prepayments have occurred in the past (which is the projected mortgage balance at the beginning of month t);

i = Simple monthly interest rate (annual interest rate/12);

n = Original number of months of mortgage.

Second, to compute the portion of the projected monthly mortgage payment that is interest, the formula is

$$\overline{I}_t = \overline{MB}_{t-1} \, i,$$

where

$\overline{I}_t$ = Projected monthly interest for month t.

This formula states that the projected monthly interest is found by multiplying the mortgage balance at the end of the previous month by the monthly interest rate. The projected monthly interest rate can be divided into two parts: (1) the projected net monthly interest rate after the servicing fee and (2) the servicing fee. The formulas are as follows:

$$\overline{NI}_t = \overline{MB}_{t-1} \, (i - s),$$
$$\overline{S}_t = \overline{MB}_{t-1} \, s,$$

where

$\overline{NI}_t$ = Projected interest net of servicing fee for month t;

s = Servicing fee rate;

$\overline{S}_t$ = Projected servicing fee for month t.

The projected monthly scheduled principal payment is found by subtracting from the projected monthly mortgage payment the projected monthly interest. In terms of our notation,

$$\overline{SP_t} = \overline{MP_t} - \overline{I_t},$$

where

$\overline{SP_t}$ = Projected monthly scheduled principal payment for month t.

As explained earlier, the projected monthly principal prepayment is found by multiplying the SMM by the difference between the outstanding balance at the beginning of the month (the ending balance in the previous month) and the projected scheduled principal payment for the month. That is,

$$\overline{PR_t} = \text{SMM}_t \, (\overline{MB_{t-1}} - \overline{SP_t}),$$

where

$\overline{PR_t}$ = Projected monthly principal prepayment for month t;
SMM_t = Assumed single monthly mortality rate for month t.

The cash flow to the investor is then the sum of (1) the projected monthly interest net of the servicing fee, (2) the projected monthly scheduled principal payment, and (3) the projected monthly principal prepayment. That is,

$$\overline{CF_t} = \overline{NI_t} + \overline{SP_t} + \overline{PR_t},$$

where

$\overline{CF_t}$ = Projected cash flow for month t.

Alternatively, this can be expressed as

$$\overline{CF_t} = \overline{I_t} + \overline{SP_t} + \overline{PR_t} - \overline{S_t}.$$

The next three illustrations demonstrate application of these formulas.

Illustration 19-6   Suppose that an investor owns a pass-through with an original mortgage balance of $100 million, mortgage rate of 9.5%, a .5% servicing fee, and 360 months to maturity. The pass-through rate is therefore 9%. Suppose that the PSA prepayment benchmark is used to project prepayments for the pass-through. In particular, assume that the investor believes that the mortgages will prepay at 100% PSA.

Using our notation:

MB_0 = $100,000,000;
n = 360;
i = .0079167 (.095/12);
s = .0004167 (.005/12).

Exhibit 19-8 shows the cash flow for the pass-through for selected months. The SMMs shown in the third column agree with those computed earlier.

EXHIBIT 19-8

Projected Cash Flow Assuming 100% PSA

Original balance = $100 million – dollar values shown per $100,000 loan;

Mortgage rate = 9.5%;

Servicing fee = 0.5%;

Term = 360 months.

(1) t	(2) $\overline{MB}_{t-1}$ ($)	(3) SMM_t	(4) $\overline{b}_{t-1}$	(5) $\overline{MP}_t$ ($)	(6) $\overline{SP}_t$ ($)	(7) $\overline{I}_t$ ($)	(8) $\overline{PR}_t$ ($)	(9) $\overline{S}_t$ ($)	(10) $\overline{CF}_t$ ($)	(11) $\overline{MB}_t$ ($)
1	$100,000	0.000166	1.00000	$841	$49	$792	$ 17	$42	$ 816	$99,934
2	99,934	0.000333	0.99983	841	50	791	33	42	832	99,851
3	99,851	0.000501	0.99950	840	50	790	50	42	849	99,751
4	99,751	0.000669	0.99900	840	50	790	67	42	865	99,634
5	99,634	0.000837	0.99833	839	51	789	83	42	881	99,500
6	99,500	0.001005	0.99749	839	51	788	100	41	897	99,349
7	99,349	0.001174	0.99649	838	51	787	117	41	913	99,181
8	99,181	0.001343	0.99532	837	52	785	133	41	929	98,996
9	98,996	0.001512	0.99398	836	52	784	150	41	994	98,795
10	98,795	0.001682	0.99248	835	52	782	166	41	959	98,576
11	98,576	0.001852	0.99081	833	53	780	182	41	975	98,341
12	98,341	0.002022	0.98898	832	53	779	199	41	989	98,089
13	98,089	0.002192	0.98698	830	53	777	215	41	1,004	97,821
14	97,821	0.002363	0.98481	828	54	774	231	41	1,018	97,536
15	97,536	0.002535	0.98248	826	54	772	247	41	1,033	97,235

Continued

EXHIBIT 19–8

Continued

(1) t	(2) $\overline{MB}_{t-1}$ ($)	(3) SMM_t	(4) $\bar{b}_{t-1}$	(5) $\overline{MP}_t$ ($)	(6) $\overline{SP}_t$ ($)	(7) $\bar{I}_t$ ($)	(8) $\overline{PR}_t$ ($)	(9) $\bar{S}_t$ ($)	(10) $\overline{CF}_t$ ($)	(11) $\overline{MB}_t$ ($)
16	$97,235	0.002706	0.97999	$824	$54	$770	$263	$41	$1,047	$96,917
17	96,917	0.002878	0.97734	822	55	767	279	40	1,060	96,584
18	96,584	0.003050	0.97453	819	55	765	294	40	1,074	96,235
19	96,235	0.003223	0.97155	817	55	762	310	40	1,087	95,870
20	95,870	0.003396	0.96842	814	55	759	325	40	1,100	95,489
21	95,489	0.003569	0.96513	812	56	756	341	40	1,113	95,093
⋮										
31	90,860	0.005143	0.92392	777	58	719	467	38	1,206	90,336
32	90,336	0.005143	0.91917	773	58	715	464	38	1,200	89,814
33	89,814	0.005143	0.91444	769	58	711	462	37	1,193	89,294
34	89,294	0.005143	0.90974	765	58	707	459	37	1,187	88,777
35	88,777	0.005143	0.90506	761	58	703	456	37	1,180	88,263
36	88,263	0.005143	0.90041	757	58	699	454	37	1,174	87,751
⋮										
98	60,735	0.005143	0.65403	550	69	481	312	25	837	60,354
99	60,354	0.005143	0.65067	547	69	478	310	25	832	59,975
100	59,975	0.005143	0.64732	544	70	475	308	25	827	59,597
⋮										
209	27,372	0.005143	0.36901	310	94	217	140	11	439	27,138
210	27,138	0.005143	0.36711	309	94	215	139	11	436	26,905

Continued

EXHIBIT 19-8

Concluded

(1) t	(2) $\overline{MB}_{t-1}$ ($)	(3) SMM_t	(4) $\overline{b}_{t-1}$	(5) $\overline{MP}_t$ ($)	(6) $\overline{SP}_t$ ($)	(7) $\overline{I}_t$ ($)	(8) $\overline{PR}_t$ ($)	(9) $\overline{S}_t$ ($)	(10) $\overline{CF}_t$ ($)	(11) $\overline{MB}_t$ ($)
211	$26,905	0.005143	0.36522	$307	$ 94	$213	$138	$11	$434	$26,673
. . .	. . .	. . .	. . .	. . .	. . .	. . .	. . .	. . .	. . .	. . .
357	567	0.005143	0.17203	145	140	4	1	0	147	425
358	425	0.005143	0.17115	144	141	3	1	0	145	283
359	283	0.005143	0.17027	143	141	2	1	0	144	141
360	141	0.005143	0.16939	142	141	1	0	0	142	0

Key:

$\overline{MB}_{t-1}$ = Projected mortgage balance at the end of month $t-1$;

SMM_t = Single monthly mortality rate;

$\overline{b}_{t-1}$ = $(1 - SMM_{t-1})(1 - SMM_{t-2}) \ldots (1 - SMM_1)$;

$\overline{MP}_t$ = Projected monthly mortgage payment for month t;

$\overline{SP}_t$ = Projected monthly scheduled principal payment for month t;

$\overline{I}_t$ = Projected monthly interest for month t;

$\overline{PR}_t$ = Projected monthly principal prepayment for month t;

$\overline{S}_t$ = Projected servicing fee for month t;

$\overline{CF}_t$ = Projected cash flow for month t.

Let's look at the components of the cash flow for the first month. The initial monthly mortgage payment for this pass-through, shown in column (5), is $841,000. The monthly interest is the monthly interest rate of .0079167 (.095 divided by 12) multiplied by the original mortgage balance, $100 million. The regularly scheduled principal is the difference between the monthly mortgage payment for the month, $841,000 in the first month, and the monthly interest of $792,000. The difference, $49,000, is shown in column (6).

The prepayment for the month is found by multiplying the SMM for the month by the difference between the mortgage balance at the beginning of the month and the regularly scheduled principal repayment. In the first month, since the SMM is .000166, and the difference between the beginning mortgage balance of $100 million and the projected scheduled principal payment of $49,000 is $99,510,000, the projected prepayment for the month is $17,000, shown in column (8).

The amount of the monthly servicing fee is found by multiplying the mortgage balance at the beginning of the month by the servicing fee. For the first month, in our illustration it is .0004166 (.005 divided by 12) multiplied by $100 million. The product is $42,000, which is shown in column (9).

The monthly cash flow is then the projected monthly mortgage payment ($841,000) plus the projected monthly prepayment ($17,000) minus the amount of the servicing fee ($42,000). Alternatively, the monthly cash flow is the monthly interest net of servicing ($792,000 minus $42,000) plus the projected principal repayment, which consists of the projected monthly regularly scheduled principal repayment ($49,000) and the monthly projected prepayment ($17,000). The projected monthly cash flow of $816,000 is shown in column (10).

Finally, the last column shows the end-of-month mortgage balance, found by subtracting the projected principal repayment from the mortgage balance at the beginning of the month. In the first month, the ending mortgage balance is $100,000,000 minus $66,000 ($49,000 + $17,000), or $99,934,000. This amount is then the beginning mortgage balance for month 2. From this amount, the cash flow can be calculated for the second month.

Notice that the monthly mortgage payment declines over time. This is because mortgages in the pool are assumed to be prepaying.

Illustration 19-7 Now suppose that instead of 100% PSA, 150% PSA is assumed. Exhibit 19-9 shows the cash flow for the mortgage pass-through security for selected months. The SMMs shown in column (3) are the same as those computed in Illustration 19-6.

Illustration 19-8 Suppose the prepayment rate is assumed to be 50% PSA. For selected months, Exhibit 19-10 shows the cash flow.

In the formulas we develop above, the process begins with determination of the mortgage balance at the beginning of the month, given prepayments that have occurred in the past. While this balance can be determined by using the procedure shown in Exhibits 19-8 to 19-10, there are formulas that can be used to compute the projected cash flow without knowing the mortgage balance at the beginning of the month. First, it is necessary to introduce the following concept.[4]

---

[4] See the appendix to Lakhbir S. Hayre and Cyrus Mohebbi, "Mortgage Pass-Through Securities," in Frank J. Fabozzi (ed.), *Advances and Innovations in the Bond and Mortgage Markets* (Chicago: Probus Publishing, 1989), pp. 259–304.

EXHIBIT 19-9

Projected Cash Flow Assuming 150% PSA*

Original balance = $100 million – dollar values per $100,000 loan;

Mortgage rate = 9.5%;

Servicing fee = 0.5%;

Term = 360 months;

(1) t	(2) $\overline{MB}_{t-1}$ ($)	(3) SMM_t	(4) $\bar{b}_{t-1}$	(5) $\overline{MP}_t$ ($)	(6) $\overline{SP}_t$ ($)	(7) $\bar{I}_t$ ($)	(8) $\overline{PR}_t$ ($)	(9) $\bar{S}_t$ ($)	(10) $\overline{CF}_t$ ($)	(11) $\overline{MB}_t$ ($)
1	$100,000	0.000250	1.00000	$841	$49	$792	$ 25	$42	$ 824	$99,926
2	99,926	0.000501	0.99975	841	50	791	50	42	849	99,826
3	99,826	0.000753	0.99925	840	50	790	75	42	874	99,701
4	99,701	0.001005	0.99850	840	50	789	100	42	898	99,551
5	99,551	0.001258	0.99749	839	51	788	125	41	923	99,375
6	99,375	0.001512	0.99624	838	51	787	150	41	947	99,174
7	99,174	0.001767	0.99473	836	51	785	175	41	970	98,947
8	98,947	0.002022	0.99297	835	52	783	200	41	994	98,695
9	98,695	0.002278	0.99096	833	52	781	225	41	1,017	98,419
10	98,419	0.002535	0.98871	831	52	799	249	41	1,040	98,117
11	98,117	0.002792	0.98620	829	52	777	274	41	1,062	97,791
12	97,791	0.003050	0.98345	827	53	774	298	41	1,084	97,440
13	97,440	0.003309	0.98045	824	53	771	322	41	1,106	97,065

Continued

*See the key in Exhibit 19-8.

EXHIBIT 19-9

Continued

(1) t	(2) $\overline{MB}_{t-1}$ ($)	(3) SMM_t	(4) $\overline{b}_{t-1}$	(5) $\overline{MP}_t$ ($)	(6) $\overline{SP}_t$ ($)	(7) $\overline{I}_t$ ($)	(8) $\overline{PR}_t$ ($)	(9) $\overline{S}_t$ ($)	(10) $\overline{CF}_t$ ($)	(11) $\overline{MB}_t$ ($)
14	$97,065	0.003569	0.97720	$822	$53	$768	$346	$40	$1,127	$96,665
15	96,665	0.003829	0.97371	819	53	765	370	40	1,148	96,242
16	96,242	0.004090	0.96998	816	54	762	393	40	1,169	95,794
17	95,794	0.004352	0.96602	812	54	758	417	40	1,189	95,324
18	95,324	0.004615	0.96181	809	54	755	440	40	1,209	94,830
19	94,830	0.004878	0.95737	805	54	751	462	40	1,228	94,313
20	94,313	0.005143	0.95270	801	54	747	485	39	1,247	93,774
21	93,774	0.005407	0.94780	797	55	742	507	39	1,266	93,2l3
.										
.										
31	87,224	0.007828	0.88695	746	55	691	682	36	1,392	86,487
32	86,487	0.007828	0.88001	740	55	685	677	36	1,381	85,755
33	85,755	0.007828	0.87312	734	55	679	671	36	1,369	85,028
34	85,028	0.007828	0.86628	728	55	673	665	35	1,358	84,308
35	84,308	0.007828	0.85950	723	55	667	660	35	1,347	83,593
36	83,593	0.007828	0.85277	717	55	662	654	35	1,335	82,884
.										
.										
98	48,647	0.007828	0.52386	400	55	385	380	20	801	48,211
99	48,211	0.007828	0.51976	437	55	382	377	20	794	47,779
100	47,779	0.007828	0.51569	434	55	378	374	20	787	47,350

Continued

EXHIBIT 19-9

Concluded

(1) t	(2) $\overline{MB}_{t-1}$ ($)	(3) SMM_t	(4) $\bar{b}_{t-1}$	(5) $\overline{MP}_t$ ($)	(6) $\overline{SP}_t$ ($)	(7) $\bar{I}_t$ ($)	(8) $\overline{PR}_t$ ($)	(9) $\bar{S}_t$ ($)	(10) $\overline{CF}_t$ ($)	(11) $\overline{MB}_t$ ($)
209	$16,241	0.007828	0.21895	$184	$56	$129	$127	$7	$304	$16,059
210	16,059	0.007828	0.21724	183	56	127	125	7	301	15,878
211	15,878	0.007828	0.21554	181	56	126	124	7	299	15,699
. . .										
357	226	0.007828	0.06842	58	56	1	1	0	58	169
358	169	0.007828	0.06789	57	56	1	1	0	58	112
359	112	0.007828	0.06735	57	56	1	0	0	57	56
360	56	0.007828	0.06683	56	56	0	0	0	56	0

EXHIBIT 19-10

Projected Cash Flow Assuming 50% PSA*

Original balance = $100 million – dollar values for $100,000 loan;

Mortgage rate = 9.5%;

Servicing fee = 0.5%;

Term = 360 months.

(1) t	(2) $\overline{MB}_{t-1}$ ($)	(3) SMM_t	(4) $\overline{b}_{t-1}$	(5) $\overline{MP}_t$ ($)	(6) $\overline{SP}_t$ ($)	(7) $\overline{I}_t$ ($)	(8) $\overline{PR}_t$ ($)	(9) $\overline{S}_t$ ($)	(10) $\overline{CF}_t$ ($)	(11) $\overline{MB}_t$ ($)
1	$100,000	0.000083	1.00000	$841	$49	$792	$ 8	$42	$808	$99,942
2	99,942	0.000166	0.99992	841	50	791	17	42	816	99,876
3	99,876	0.000250	0.99975	841	50	791	25	42	824	99,801
4	99,801	0.000333	0.99950	840	50	790	33	42	832	99,718
5	99,718	0.000417	0.99917	840	51	789	42	42	840	99,625
6	99,625	0.000501	0.99875	840	51	789	50	42	848	99,524
7	99,524	0.000585	0.99825	839	51	788	58	41	856	99,415
8	99,415	0.000669	0.99766	839	52	787	66	41	864	99,296
9	99,296	0.000753	0.99700	838	52	786	75	41	872	99,169
10	99,169	0.000837	0.99625	838	53	785	83	41	879	99,034
11	99,034	0.000921	0.99541	837	53	784	91	41	887	98,890
12	98,890	0.001005	0.99449	836	53	783	99	41	894	98,737
13	98,737	0.001089	0.99349	835	54	782	108	41	902	98,576

Continued

*See the key in Exhibit 19-8.

EXHIBIT 19-10

Continued

(1) t	(2) $\overline{MB}_{t-1}$ ($)	(3) SMM_t	(4) $\overline{b}_{t-1}$	(5) $\overline{MP}_t$ ($)	(6) $\overline{SP}_t$ ($)	(7) $\overline{I}_t$ ($)	(8) $\overline{PR}_t$ ($)	(9) $\overline{S}_t$ ($)	(10) $\overline{CF}_t$ ($)	(11) $\overline{MB}_t$ ($)
14	$98,576	0.001174	0.99241	$834	$54	$780	$116	$41	$ 909	$98,406
15	98,406	0.001258	0.99125	833	54	779	124	41	916	98,227
16	98,227	0.001343	0.99000	832	55	778	132	41	923	98,041
17	98,041	0.001427	0.98867	831	55	776	140	41	930	97,846
18	97,846	0.001512	0.98726	830	56	775	148	41	937	97,642
19	97,642	0.001597	0.98576	829	56	773	156	41	944	97,431
20	97,431	0.001682	0.98419	828	56	771	164	41	951	97,211
21	97,211	0.001767	0.98253	826	57	770	172	41	957	96,982
.	.	.	.	.	.	.	.	.	.	.
31	94,566	0.002535	0.96161	809	60	749	240	39	1,009	94,267
32	94,267	0.002535	0.95917	807	60	746	239	39	1,006	93,968
33	93,968	0.002535	0.95674	804	61	744	238	39	1,003	93,669
34	93,669	0.002535	0.95431	802	61	742	237	39	1,001	93,371
35	93,371	0.002535	0.95189	800	61	739	237	39	998	93,073
36	93,073	0.002535	0.94948	798	62	737	236	39	995	92,776
.	.	.	.	.	.	.	.	.	.	.
98	75,332	0.002535	0.81122	682	86	596	191	31	841	75,056
99	75,056	0.002535	0.80917	680	86	594	190	31	839	74,779
100	74,779	0.002535	0.80711	679	87	592	189	31	837	74,503

Continued

EXHIBIT 19–10

Concluded

(1) t	(2) $\overline{MB}_{t-1}$ ($)	(3) SMM_t	(4) $\overline{b}_{t-1}$	(5) $\overline{MP}_t$ ($)	(6) $\overline{SP}_t$ ($)	(7) $\overline{I}_t$ ($)	(8) $\overline{PR}_t$ ($)	(9) $\overline{S}_t$ ($)	(10) $\overline{CF}_t$ ($)	(11) $\overline{MB}_t$ ($)
209	$45,399	0.002535	0.61204	$515	$155	$359	$115	$19	$610	$45,129
210	45,129	0.002535	0.61049	513	156	357	114	19	609	44,859
211	44,859	0.002535	0.60894	512	157	355	113	19	607	44,589
. . .										
357	1,386	0.002535	0.42037	353	342	11	3	1	356	1,041
358	1,041	0.002535	0.41930	353	344	8	2	0	354	695
359	695	0.002535	0.41824	352	346	6	1	0	352	348
360	348	0.002535	0.41718	351	348	3	0	0	351	0

Let

$$\overline{b}_t = (1 - SMM_t)(1 - SMM_{t-1}) \cdots (1 - SMM_2)(1 - SMM_1),$$

where

$\overline{b}_t$ = Projected mortgage balance in month t per \$1 of the original mortgage, given prepayments through month t.

Then, the projected monthly mortgage payment in month t is

$$\overline{MP}_t = \overline{b}_{t-1}MP,$$

where

MP = Monthly mortgage payment on the original principal, assuming no prepayments.

The projected scheduled principal payment is found as follows:

$$\overline{SP}_t = \overline{b}_{t-1}P_t,$$

where

P_t = Scheduled principal payment on the original balance, assuming no prepayments.

Once MP and P_t are computed, the other values necessary to compute the projected cash flow can be easily determined.

(The formulas for obtaining MP and P_t were given in the previous chapter.)

Illustration 19-9   Consider the pass-through we have been using in all previous illustrations. Assuming a prepayment speed of 100% PSA, the projected monthly mortgage payment for month 8 is

$$\overline{MP}_8 = \overline{b}_7 MP.$$

The monthly mortgage payment assuming no principal prepayments is \$840,850. The SMM for each month is shown in column (3) of Exhibit 19-8. Then

$$\overline{b}_8 = (1 - .000166)(1 - .000333)(1 - .000501)(1 - .000669)$$
$$\times (1 - .000837)(1 - .001005)(1 - .001174) = .99532.$$

So,

$$\overline{MP}_8 = (.99532)\,\$840,850 = \$836,915.$$

The projected scheduled principal payment is

$$\overline{SP}_8 = \overline{b}_7 P_8.$$

The scheduled principal payment in month 8 assuming no prepayments is \$52,000. The projected scheduled principal payment is then

$$\overline{SP}_8 = (.99532)\,\$52,000 = \$51,757.$$

Notice that both of the values computed here agree with the values for month 8 shown in Exhibit 19-8 ($837,000 for $\overline{MP_8}$ and $52,000 for $\overline{SP_8}$).

WAC, WAM, WALA, and CAGE

In our illustrations we assumed that all the mortgage loans in the pool have the same mortgage rate (9.5%), the same servicing fee (0.5%), and the same number of months remaining to maturity (360). In practice, within a pool the mortgage loans can have different mortgage rates, servicing fees, and remaining months to maturity.

To construct the cash flow for a pass-through, the parameters used for the mortgage rate and the remaining months to maturity are the *weighted average coupon rate* (WAC) and the *weighted average maturity* (WAM), respectively. The WAC is the weighted average of all the mortgage rates in the pool, where the weight used for each mortgage loan is the amount of the balance outstanding. The WAM is the weighted average of the number of months to maturity of all the mortgage loans in the pool, where the weight for each mortgage loan is the amount of the balance outstanding.

Once a mortgage is seasoned, additonal information is needed about the underlying mortgage pool for a pass-through. Remaining average maturity changes. The WAM after the issuance date is sometimes referred to as the *weighted average remaining maturity* (WARM) or *weighted average remaining time* (WART).

For Freddie Mac pass-throughs, the remaining number of months are reported. This measure is called the *weighted average loan age* (WALA). Due to partial prepayments, called *curtailments*, the WALA is not simply the original term of the mortgages less the WARM. A measure similar to WALA to measure the remaining number of months for the underlying mortgages is reported by Fannie Mae. This measure is called the *calculated loan age* (CAGE).

Beware of Prepayment Conventions

The PSA prepayment benchmark is simply a market convention, originally introduced to provide a standard measure for pricing mortgage-backed securities backed by 30-year fixed-rate, fully amortizing mortgages. It is a product of a study by the PSA that evaluated the mortality rates of residential loans insured by the FHA. Data that the PSA committee examined seemed to suggest that mortgages became "seasoned" (i.e., prepayment rates tended to level off) after 29 months at which time the CPR tended to hover at approximately 6%. How did the PSA come up with the CPRs used for months 1 through 29? It was not based on recent empirical evidence of FHA mortgages. Instead, a linear increase from month 1 to month 30 was arbitrarily selected, so that at month 1 the CPR assumption is .2% and at month 30 the CPR assumption is 6%.

In adopting this convention, the seasonal nature of prepayment activity was assumed away as were the differences in underlying borrower characteristics. FHA/VA borrowers, conventional borrowers, and jumbo borrowers all evidence different prepayment behavior not to mention the fact that FHA/VA loans are assumable while conventional loans carry due-on-sale provisions. Moreover, the same benchmark or seasoning process is used in quoting pass-throughs regardless of the collateral—30- and 15-year loans, balloon loans, fixed- and adjustable-rate loans.

Astute money managers recognize that the CPR is a convenient convention, useful for quoting yield and/or price, but that it also has many limitations in determining the value of a pass-through. The message is that analysts must take care in using any measure that is based on the PSA prepayment benchmark. It is simply a market convention.

Vector Analysis

One approach market participants take to overcome the limitations of the PSA benchmark is to assume that the PSA speed can change over time. This technique is referred to as *vector analysis*. A "vector" is simply a set of numbers. In the case of prepayments, it is a vector of prepayment speeds.

In Illustrations 19-6 to 19-8, this would be done by replacing the SMMs in the relevant exhibits with the appropriate values based on the vector of PSA prepayment speeds. Specifically, consider Illustration 19-6, where it is assumed that the prepayment speed is 100% PSA for the entire life of the pass-through. Suppose instead that the following vector of prepayment speeds is assumed:

Months   1–43 = 100% PSA;

Months   44–204 = 150% PSA;

Months 205–360 = 50% PSA.

To construct the cash flow given this vector of prepayment speeds, the SMMs would be as follows. For months 1–43, the SMM would be the same as in Exhibit 19-8. The SMM for months 44–204 would be the SMM given in Exhibit 19-9 for the same months. Finally, for months 205–360, the SMM would be the same as for the corresponding months in Exhibit 19-10.

PREPAYMENT MODELS

A prepayment model attempts to predict the prepayment activity of a mortgage pool and begins by modeling the statistical relationships among the factors that are expected to affect prepayments. Such factors are (1) the prevailing mortgage rate, (2) characteristics of the underlying mortgage pool, (3) seasonal factors, and (4) general economic activity.[5]

The current mortgage rate affects prepayments in three ways. First, the spread between the prevailing mortgage rate and the contract rate affects the incentive to refinance. Second, the path of mortgage rates since the loan was originated affects prepayments through a phenomenon referred to as *refinancing burnout*. Both the spread and path of mortgage rates affect prepayments that are the product of refinancing. The third way in which the prevailing mortgage rate affects prepayments is through its effect on the affordability of housing and housing turnover.

The following characteristics of the underlying mortgage loans affect prepayments: (1) the contract rate; (2) whether the loans are FHA/VA-guaranteed or conventional; (3) the amount of seasoning; (4) the type of loan, for example, a 30-year level-payment mortgage, 5-year balloon mortgage, etc.; and (5) the geographical location of the underlying properties.

---

5   For a further discussion of these factors, see Frank J. Fabozzi, Chuck Ramsey, and Frank R. Ramirez, *Collateralized Mortgage Obligations: Structures and Analysis* (Buckingham, PA: Frank J. Fabozzi Associates, 1994), Chapter 3.

There is a well-documented seasonal pattern in prepayments. This pattern is related to activity in the primary housing market, with home buying increasing in the spring and gradually reaching a peak in the late summer. Home buying declines in the fall and winter. Mirroring this activity are the prepayments that result from the turnover of housing as home buyers sell their existing homes and purchase new ones. Prepayments are low in the winter months and begin to rise in the spring, reaching a peak in the summer months. However, probably because of delays in passing through prepayments, the peak may not be observed until early fall. Economic theory would suggest that general economic activity affects prepayment behavior through its effect on housing turnover. The link is as follows: a growing economy results in a rise in personal income and in opportunities for worker migration; this increases family mobility and, as a result, increases housing turnover.

The factors are then combined into one model. For example, in the Goldman, Sachs prepayment model the effects interact proportionally through the following multiplicative function, which is used to project prepayments:

Monthly prepayment rate

= (Refinancing incentive) × (Seasoning multiplier) × (Month multiplier)

× (Burnout multiplier),

where the various multipliers are adjustments for the effects we discussed above.

The product of a prepayment forecast is not one prepayment rate but a set of prepayment rates for each month of the remaining term of a mortgage pool. The set of monthly prepayment rates, however, is not reported by Wall Street firms or vendors. Instead, a single prepayment rate is reported. One way to convert a set of monthly prepayment rates into a single prepayment rate is to calculate a simple average of the prepayment rates. The obvious drawback to this approach is that it does not take into consideration the outstanding balance each month. An alternative approach is to use some type of weighted average, selecting the weights to reflect the amount of the monthly cash flow corresponding to a monthly prepayment rate. This is done by first computing the cash flow yield (discussed in Chapter 20) for a pass-through given its market price and the set of monthly prepayment rates. Then a single prepayment rate (CPR or PSA multiple) that gives the same cash flow yield is found.

HOME EQUITY LOAN ASSET-BACKED SECURITIES

Asset-backed securities are securities backed by pools of loans. Mortgage-backed securities are a form of asset-backed security in which the mortgage loans are first liens against the property. There are asset-backed securities backed by home equity loans, referred to as HELS (home equity loan securities).

As with a mortgage-backed security, the cash flow of HELS depends on prepayments. The prepayment modeling used for HELS builds on the prepayment experience and modeling for mortgage-backed securities. There is also a prepayment convention that has been adopted by some market participants developed by Prudential Securities.[6]

---

6 "HEP—A New Curve for Home Equity Prepayments," *Spread Talk: The Mortgage- and Asset-Backed Securities Strategist* (New York: Prudential Securities, October 10, 1994), pp. 7–8.

The Prudential benchmark is based on historical prepayment rates of home equity loan transactions issued from 1991 to 1993. The benchmark curve developed, called the Home Equity Prepayment Curve or HEP^{sm}, is a series of CPRs. The benchmark curve ramps up for 10 months and then seasons. Thus, seasoning begins at 10 months for HELS compared to 30 months for the PSA benchmark for mortgage-backed securities. The increase from month 1 to month 10 is linear, as with the PSA benchmark. The HEP^{sm} benchmark is expressed in terms of the terminal CPR. Thus, a 20% HEP^{sm} means that in month 1 the CPR is 2% (20% divided by 10) and increases by 2% each month until month 10 when the CPR reaches 20%. A 10% HEP^{sm} means that in month 1 the CPR is 1% (10% divided by 10) and increases by 1% each month until month 10 when the CPR reaches 10%.

The same factors that affect prepayments on mortgage-backed securities appear to affect those on HELS, except that refinancing is not as significant. In addition, there is a factor that does not affect prepayments on agency mortgage-backed securities that does affect HELS. This factor is defaults.[7]

PSA STANDARD DEFAULT ASSUMPTION BENCHMARK

Mortgage-backed securities issued by Ginnie Mae, Fannie Mae, and Freddie Mac are guaranteed by these entities. Consequently, defaults are ignored. Investors in nonagency mortgage-backed securities must be concerned with defaults.

With the increase in the issuance of nonagency mortgage-backed securities, a standardized benchmark for default rates has been introduced by the Public Securities Association. The PSA standard default assumption (SDA) benchmark gives the annual default rate for a mortgage pool as a function of the seasoning of the mortgages. The PSA SDA benchmark, or 100 SDA, specifies the following:

1. The default rate in month 1 is 0.02% and increases by 0.02% up to month 30, so that in month 30 the default rate is 0.60%;

2. From month 30 to month 60, the default rate remains at 0.60%;

3. From month 61 to month 120, the default rate declines from 0.60% to 0.03%;

4. From month 120 on, the default rate remains constant at 0.03%.

This pattern is illustrated in Exhibit 19-11.

As with the PSA prepayment benchmark, multiples of the benchmark are found by multiplying the default rate by the assumed multiple. For example, 200 SDA means the following pattern:

1. The default rate in month 1 is 0.04% and increases by 0.04% up to month 30, so that in month 30 the default rate is 1.20%;

2. From month 30 to month 60, the default rate remains at 1.20%;

3. From month 61 to month 120, the default rate declines from 1.20% to 0.06%;

---

7   For a further discussion of prepayments on HELS, see Charles Huang, *An Inside Look at Home-Equity Prepayments* (New York: Prudential Securities, January 1995).

EXHIBIT 19-11

PSA Standard Default Assumption Benchmark (100 SDA)

Mortgage Age (in months)

4. From month 120 on, the default rate remains constant at 0.06%.

A 0 SDA means that no defaults are assumed.

CASH FLOW FOR A CMO, A STRIPPED MBS, AND MORTGAGE SERVICING RIGHTS

Given the cash flow for a pass-through, we can determine the cash flow for any derivative of a pass-through such as a CMO bond class and a stripped MBS.

Illustration 19-10   Consider a stripped MBS whose collateral is the pass-through in Illustrations 19-6 through 19-8. Then for a principal-only security with this collateral, the cash flow assuming 100% PSA can be determined from Exhibit 19-8. The cash flow is only the principal. Since the principal is equal to the sum of the regularly scheduled principal repayment and prepayments, the cash flow for this PO security is the sum of columns (6) and (8) in the exhibit. The cash flow for the corresponding interest-only security assuming the same prepayment speed of 100% PSA is the net interest. In Exhibit 19-8, this is the difference between the gross interest reported in column (7) and the servicing fee in column (9).

Illustration 19-11   Suppose that the same pass-through is used as collateral for a CMO with two bond classes, A and B. Suppose further that the coupon rate for both bond classes is 9.0% (the same as the pass-through in our illustration) and the par value for class A is $54,333,000 and for class B is $45,667,000. The rules for distributing the cash flow to the two bond classes are as follows.

For the principal:

Pay all principal to class A until it is fully paid off, then
pay class B all the principal.

For the interest:

Pay interest to both classes based on the balance outstanding
at the beginning of the month.

According to these disbursement rules, and assuming a prepayment speed of 150% PSA, the cash flow for each bond class can be determined from Exhibit 19-9. At the end of month 104 (not shown in the exhibit), the remaining mortgage balance is $45,667,000. This means that $54,333,000 of principal has been repaid. Since this is the amount of the par value assumed for class A, the principal payments to this bond class will be paid off by month 104. The principal payments for class A are therefore those shown in months 1 through 104 in Exhibit 19-9. The principal payment in each month is the sum of columns (6) and (8).

The interest payment is determined by first calculating the balance for class A at the beginning of the month and then multiplying by the pass-through rate, .75% (9%/12). For example, at the beginning of month 1, the balance for class A is $54,333,000. The principal payment to class A in month 1 is $74,000 ($49,000 + $25,000). The monthly interest for class A is then $407,498 ($54,333,000 × .75%). The balance at the beginning of month 2 is then $54,259,000 ($54,333,000 − $74,000). In month 2, the interest for class A is then $406,943 ($54,259,000 × .75). The cash flow for class A is then the principal payments and monthly interest for months 1 through 104.

For class B, the principal payments are as shown in Exhibit 19-9 for months 105 through 360. For months 1 through 104, the monthly interest is simply the difference between the interest to class A and the net interest shown in the exhibit. For months 105 through 360, the interest is the net interest in the exhibit.

Illustration 19-12   For the same pass-through as in the two previous illustrations, the cash flow for a servicer who purchased the right to service all the mortgages in the pool would depend on the prepayment speed assumed. Assuming a prepayment speed of 150% PSA, the cash flow that would be expected is shown in column (9) of Exhibit 19-9.

SUMMARY

In this chapter we showed how to construct the projected cash flow for any mortgage-backed security (pass-through, CMO, and stripped MBS), as well as a mortgage-related product such as a portfolio of servicing rights. The cash flow depends on the cash flow of the underlying pool of mortgage loans, which in turn depends on prepayments. The market convention to determine prepayment speed is the PSA benchmark, which is simply a series of conditional prepayment rates. Once prepayments are determined for a pass-through, the cash flow for any other MBS can be determined according to the rules for allocating principal and interest payments.

Exhibit 19-12 summarizes the formulas presented in this chapter.

EXHIBIT 19-12

Summary of Formulas

1. To convert from CPR to SMM:

$$SMM = 1 - (1 - CPR)^{1/12}.$$

2. Benchmark PSA prepayment model:

$$\text{If } t < 30, \text{ then CPR} = \frac{6\% \, t}{30},$$
$$\text{if } t > 30, \text{ then CPR} = 6\%.$$

where t is the number of months since the mortgage originated.

3. Constructing the Cash Flow:

Let

$\overline{MP_t}$ = Projected monthly mortgage payment for month t;

$\overline{MB_{t-1}}$ = Projected mortgage balance at the end of month $t - 1$, given prepayments that have occurred in the past (which is the projected mortgage balance at the beginning of month t);

i = Simple monthly interest rate (annual interest rate/12);

n = Original number of months of mortgage;

$\overline{I_t}$ = Projected monthly interest for month t;

$\overline{NI_t}$ = Projected interest, net of servicing fee, for month t;

s = Servicing Fee rate;

$\overline{S_t}$ = Projected servicing fee for month t;

$\overline{SP_t}$ = Projected monthly scheduled principal prepayment for month t;

$\overline{PR_t}$ = Projected monthly principal prepayment for month t;

$\overline{CF_t}$ = Projected cash flow for month t.

$$\overline{MP_t} = \overline{MB_{t-1}} \left[\frac{i(1 + i)^{n-t+1}}{(1 + i)^{n-t+1}} \right],$$

then

$$\overline{I_t} = \overline{MB_{t-1}} i \, ;$$
$$\overline{NI_t} = \overline{MB_{t-1}} \, (i - s) \, ;$$
$$\overline{S_t} = \overline{MB_{t-1}} s \, ;$$
$$\overline{SP_t} = \overline{MB_t} - \overline{I_t} \, ;$$
$$\overline{PR} = SMM_t \, (MB_{t-1} - \overline{SP_t}) \, ;$$
$$\overline{CF_t} = \overline{NI_t} + \overline{SP_t} + \overline{PR_t} \, ;$$
$$\text{or } \overline{CF_t} = \overline{I_t} + \overline{SP_t} + \overline{PR_t} - \overline{S_t} \, .$$

Continued

EXHIBIT 19–12

Concluded

Alternatively, let

$\overline{b}_t$ = Projected mortgage balance in month t per \$1 of the original mortgage, given prepayments through month t;

SMM_t = Assumed single monthly mortality rate for month t;

MP = Monthly mortgage payment on the original principal, assuming no prepayments;

P_t = Scheduled princcipal payment on the original balance, assuming no prepayments.

Then,

$$\overline{b}_t = (1 - \text{SMM}_t)(1 - \text{SMM}_{t-1}) \cdots (1 - \text{SMM}_2)(1 - \text{SMM}_1);$$

$$\overline{MP}_t = \overline{b}_{t-1}\, MP;$$

$$\overline{SP}_t = \overline{b}_{t-1}\, P_t.$$

20

⑥ ANALYSIS OF MORTGAGE-BACKED SECURITIES

With our understanding of the characteristics of mortgages and mortgage-backed securities, we can now look at the various methodologies for analyzing mortgage-backed securities. Specifically, we will look at two valuation models: the static cash flow model and the Monte Carlo simulation model. We will also discuss how to estimate the effective duration of a mortgage-backed security for each valuation model. In the last section we explain how to calculate the total return for a mortgage-backed security.

STATIC CASH FLOW MODEL

The static cash flow model involves estimating the cash flow based on a single prepayment assumption. No consideration is given to how changes in interest rates in the future will affect the cash flows (i.e., prepayments).

Cash Flow Yield

Recall from Chapter 4 that the yield is the interest rate that will make the present value of the expected cash flows equal to the price (plus accrued interest). A yield computed in this manner is called a *cash flow yield.*

The cash flow for an MBS is typically monthly. Thus, the cash flow yield as just described must be annualized. The convention is to compare the yield on an MBS with that of Treasury coupon securities by calculating the bond equivalent yield of the MBS. Recall that the bond equivalent yield for a Treasury coupon security is found by doubling the semiannual yield. It is not correct to do this for an MBS. The reason is that since an MBS pays monthly, the investor has the opportunity to generate greater interest by reinvesting the cash flows.

The market practice is to calculate a yield so as to make it comparable to the yield to maturity on a bond equivalent yield basis. The formula for annualizing the monthly cash flow yield on an MBS is

$$\text{Bond equivalent yield} = 2\ [(1 + i_M)^6 - 1],$$

where i_M is the interest rate that will equate the present value of the projected monthly cash flow to the price of the MBS. The bond equivalent semiannual yield for a monthly-pay MBS is

$$(1 + i_M)^6 - 1.$$

Illustration 20-1   Suppose that a pass-through with a mortgage rate of 9.5%, a servicing fee of 0.5%, 360 months remaining to maturity (new pass-through), and an original mortgage balance of $100,000 can be purchased for $94,521. To compute the cash flow yield, a prepayment assumption must be made. Assuming that the prepayment rate is 100% PSA, the cash flows would be as shown in Exhibit 19-8 of Chapter 19.

Assuming that the first monthly cash flow will occur 30 days from now, the interest rate that will make the present value of the cash flows, assuming 100% PSA, equal to the price of $94,521 is .8333% (.008333). The bond equivalent yield is then 10.21%, as shown below:

$i_M = .008333;$

$$\text{Bond equivalent yield} = 2[(1.008333)^6 - 1] = .1021 = 10.21\%.$$

Illustration 20-2   Suppose that the pass-through in the previous illustration can be purchased for $105,985. Assuming a prepayment rate of 200% PSA, the interest rate that will make the present value of the cash flows equal to $105,985 is .006667 (.6667%). The bond equivalent yield is found as follows:

$i_M = .006667;$

$$\text{Bond equivalent yield} = 2[(1.006667)^6 - 1] = .0813 = 8.13\%.$$

Drawbacks of the Cash Flow Yield Measure

As we note several times throughout this book, the yield to maturity has two shortcomings as a measure of a bond's potential return: (1) the coupon payments must be reinvested at a rate equal to the yield to maturity, and (2) the bond must be held to maturity. These shortcomings are equally applicable to the cash flow yield measure: (1) the projected cash flows are assumed to be reinvested at the cash flow yield, and (2) the mortgage-backed security is assumed to be held until the final payout based on some prepayment assumption.

The importance of reinvestment risk, the risk that the cash flows must be reinvested at a rate below the cash flow yield, is particularly important for most mortgage-backed securities because payments are monthly or quarterly. In addition, the cash flow yield is dependent on realization of the projected cash flows according to some prepayment rate. If the prepayment experience is different from the prepayment rate assumed, the cash flow yield will not be realized.

Spread to Treasuries

It should be clear that at the time of purchase it is not possible to determine an exact yield for a mortgage-backed security; the yield depends on the actual prepayment experience of the mortgages in the pool. Nevertheless, the convention in all fixed-income markets is to measure the yield on a non-Treasury security to that of a "comparable" Treasury security.

In comparing the yield of a mortgage-backed security to a comparable Treasury, it is inappropriate to use the stated maturity of the MBS because of the potential for prepayments. Instead, market participants have used two measures: Macaulay duration and average life.

Macaulay Duration

Calculating Macaulay duration requires a projection of the cash flows, which, in turn, requires a prepayment rate assumption. We can then use the projected cash flows, the price of the MBS, and the periodic interest rate (computed from the yield on a bond equivalent basis) to compute Macaulay duration, as illustrated in Chapter 13. Macaulay duration is converted into years by dividing the periodic Macaulay duration by 12 in the case of a monthly-pay MBS.

Illustration 20-3   For the pass-through in Illustration 20-1, selling for $94,521 and yielding 10.21% (assuming 100% PSA), Macaulay duration is 6.17, as shown below.

The numerator of the Macaulay duration is the present value of the projected cash flows using a monthly interest rate of 0.8333% times the time period (the month). For our pass-through, the numerator is $6,998,347. Macaulay duration is then found by dividing by the price of the pass-through.

Thus,

$$\text{Macaulay duration (in months)} = \frac{\$6,998,347}{\$94,521} = 74.04.$$

To convert the Macaulay duration in months to Macaulay duration in years:

$$\text{Macaulay duration (in years)} = \frac{74.04}{12} = 6.17.$$

Average Life

A second measure commonly used to compare Treasury securities and MBSs is the average life (or weighted average life) which is the average time to receipt of principal payments (projected scheduled principal and projected principal prepayments), weighted by the amount of principal expected divided by the total principal to be repaid.

Mathematically, the average life is expressed as follows:

$$\text{Average life} = \frac{1}{12} \sum_{t=1}^{n} \frac{t\,(\text{Principal received at time } t)}{\text{Total principal received}},$$

where n is the number of months remaining. (The *tail* is defined as the principal payments that extend from the average life to the last principal payment.)

Illustration 20-4   For the pass-through in the previous illustration, assuming the same prepayment rate (100% PSA), the principal payments are shown in columns (6) and (8) of Exhibit 19-8 of Chapter 19. Adding the principal payments in these two columns and applying the formula above, the average life is 12.18 years.

Price

Given the required yield for an MBS, the price is simply the present value of the projected cash flows. Care must be taken, however, in determining the monthly interest rate that should be used to compute the present value of each cash flow.

To convert a bond equivalent yield to a monthly interest rate, we can use the following formula:

$$i_M = [1 + (.5) \text{ Bond equivalent yield}]^{1/6} - 1.$$

Illustration 20-5 Once again, consider the pass-through in Illustration 20-1. Suppose that the investor (1) requires an 8.13% yield on a bond equivalent basis and (2) assumes a prepayment rate of 150% PSA. The corresponding monthly interest rate for a bond equivalent yield of 8.13% is .6667% (.006667), as shown below:

$$i_M = [1 + (.5) .0813]^{1/6} - 1$$
$$= [1.04065]^{.16667} - 1$$
$$= .006667.$$

The projected cash flows, based on 150% PSA, would be the same as Exhibit 19-9 in Chapter 19. Discounting the projected cash flow at .6667% gives a price of $106,710.

Illustration 20-6 Suppose that instead of 8.13%, the investor wants a yield of 12.30%. Also assume that the investor believes that a 25% PSA rate is appropriate to project the cash flow. The monthly interest rate is determined as follows:

$$i_M = [1 + (.5) .1230]^{1/6} - 1$$
$$= [1.0615]^{.16667} - 1$$
$$= .01.$$

Discounting the cash flows projected on the basis of 25% PSA would give a price of $79,976.

The cash flows of IO and PO securities depend on the cash flows of the underlying pass-through, which, in turn, depends on the cash flows of the underlying pool of mortgages. Thus, to determine the price of an IO or PO, a prepayment rate must be assumed. The price of an IO is the present value of the projected interest payments net of the servicing fee. The price of a PO is the present value of the projected principal payments (projected scheduled principal payments and projected principal prepayments).

Illustration 20-7 For the 9.5% pass-through with a .5% servicing fee and 360 months to maturity, the projected interest payments net of the servicing fee and the projected principal payments assuming 100% PSA are shown in Exhibit 19-8 of Chapter 19 for selected months. Assuming a required yield of 10.21%, then

Price of pass-through	$94,521
Price of IO	55,548
Price of PO	38,973

Illustration 20-8   Assuming that the required yield is 12.30% rather than 10.21%, and the prepayment rate is 25% PSA rather than 100% PSA, then

Price of pass-through	$79,976
Price of IO	61,010
Price of PO	18,966

Notice what has happened to the price of the IO security in Illustration 20-7 compared to Illustration 20-8. As interest rates increased from 10.21% to 12.30%, the price of the IO increased. This is to be expected, as the holder of an IO security benefits when prepayments slow; that is, the longer the mortgages are outstanding because of fewer prepayments, the longer the IO receives interest. The PO portion decreases as interest rates increase.

Illustration 20-9   Assuming that the required yield is 8.14% rather than 10.21% and the prepayment rate is 200% PSA rather than 100% PSA, then

Price of pass-through	$105,985
Price of IO	47,875
Price of PO	58,110

The price of the IO in Illustration 20-9 has decreased as a result of both a lower required yield and a higher prepayment rate compared to Illustration 20-7. The opposite is true for the PO.

From the last two illustrations we can see that IOs move in the same direction as interest rates, while POs move inversely with interest rates.

Effective Duration and Convexity

Modified duration is a measure of the sensitivity of a bond's price to interest rate changes, assuming that the expected cash flows do not change with interest rates. Consequently, modified duration (as well as Macaulay duration) is not an appropriate measure for mortgage-backed securities, because mortgage prepayments mean that the projected cash flows change as interest rates change. When interest rates decline (rise), prepayments are expected to rise (fall). As a result, when interest rates decline (increase), duration may decline (increase) rather than increase (decline). This property, as we explained in Chapter 17, is referred to as negative convexity.

To see this effect, consider the modified duration for the 9.5% pass-through (assuming 100% PSA) selling to yield 10.21%. If the required yield decreases to 8.14% instantaneously, and the prepayment rate is assumed not to change, modified duration will increase from 6.17 to 6.80. Suppose, however, that when the yield declines to 8.14%, the assumed prepayment rate changes to 150% PSA. The modified duration would decline to 5.91 rather than increase.

Negative convexity has the same impact on the price performance of a mortgage-backed security as it does for a callable bond (discussed in Chapter 17). When interest rates decline, a bond with an embedded call option such as a mortgage-backed security will not perform as well as an option-free bond.

For example, if the required yield decreases instantaneously from 10.21% to 8.14%, the price will increase from $94,521 to $107,596. If the prepayment rate increases to 150% PSA, however, the price will rise to only $106,710.

Effective Duration

The proper measure to use is the effective duration. This measure allows for the cash flow to change when interest rates changes. The formula to approximate duration is

$$\text{Approximate duration} = \frac{V_- - V_+}{2\,V_0(\Delta y)},$$

where

V_0 = Initial value or price of the security;

V_- = Estimated value of the security if the yield is decreased by Δy;

V_+ = Estimated value of the security if the yield is increased by Δy;

Δy = Change in the yield of a security.

The approximate duration is the effective duration when the two values V_- and V_+ are obtained from a valuation model that allows for the cash flow to change due to prepayments when interest rates change. The values are obtained from a valuation model. The two models that we are discussing in this chapter are the static cash flow model and the Monte Carlo simulation model. Here we focus on the values obtained from the former model.

When computing effective duration using the static cash flow model, the price at the higher and lower interest rates will depend on the prepayment rate assumed. A higher prepayment rate is typically assumed at the lower interest rate than at a higher interest rate. Thus, calculation of effective duration requires a prepayment model to determine how prepayments are expected to change as interest rates change.

Illustration 20-10   To illustrate the calculation of effective duration using the static cash flow model, consider the pass-through in Exhibit 19-8 of Chapter 19. The price assuming 100% PSA and a yield of 10.21% is $94,521, or 94.521 per $100 of par value. Let's look at what would happen to the price if the yield changes by 50 basis points. Suppose that if the yield decreases by 50 basis points to 9.71%, the prepayment rate is assumed to be unchanged at 100% PSA. However, if the yield increases by 50 basis points to 10.71%, the prepayment rate is assumed to decrease to 75% PSA. The price at 9.71% and 10.71% would be $97,520 (97.520 per $100 of par value) and $90,992 (90.992 per $100 of par value), respectively. Therefore,

$V_0 = 94.521$;
$V_- = 97.520$;
$V_+ = 90.992$;
$\Delta y = 0.005$.

Then

$$\text{Effective duration} = \frac{97.520 - 90.992}{2(94.521)(0.005)} = 6.91.$$

Effective Convexity

The formula to approximate convexity is

$$\text{Approximate convexity} = \frac{V_+ + V_- - 2V_0}{V_0(\Delta y)^2}.$$

Once again, if the values used in the formula are those allowing for the cash flow to change, then the resulting convexity is the effective convexity.

Illustration 20-11   For the pass-through we used in our previous illustration:

$$\text{Effective convexity} = \frac{90.992 + 97.520 - 2(94.521)}{(94.521)(0.005)^2}$$

$$= \frac{-0.530}{94.521(0.005)^2} = -224.29.$$

Notice that the effective convexity of this pass-through is negative.

Drawback of the Static Cash Flow Methodology

For the static cash flow yield model, the yield spread for a mortgage-backed security is the difference between the cash flow yield and the yield to maturity of a comparable Treasury. The latter is obtained from the yield curve. The drawback of this procedure is that neither the cash flow yield for either the mortgage-backed security or Treasury security is calculated properly because it fails to take into consideration (1) the term structure of interest rates for Treasuries (i.e., the theoretical spot rate curve) and (2) expected interest-rate volatility that will alter the expected cash flow for the pass-through due to changes in prepayments. The next valuation model discussed overcomes these drawbacks.

MONTE CARLO SIMULATION MODEL[1]

Conceptually, the valuation of pass-throughs using the Monte Carlo method is simple. In practice, however, it is very complex. The simulation involves generating a set of cash flows based on simulated future mortgage refinancing rates, which in turn imply simulated prepayment rates.

Valuation modeling for CMOs is similar to valuation modeling for pass-throughs, although the difficulties are amplified because the issuer has sliced and diced both the prepayment and interest-rate risk into smaller pieces called *tranches*. The sensitivity of the pass-throughs comprising the collateral to these two risks is not transmitted equally to every tranche. Some of the tranches wind up more sensitive to prepayments and interest-rate risk than the collateral, while some of them are much less sensitive.

Using Simulation to Generate Interest-Rate Paths and Cash Flows

The typical model that Wall Street firms and commercial vendors use to generate random interest-rate paths takes as input today's term structure of interest rates and a volatility assumption. The term structure of interest rates is the theoretical spot rate (or zero coupon) curve

---

1 Portions of the material in this section and the one to follow are adapted from Frank J. Fabozzi and Scott F. Richard, "Valuation of CMOs," Frank J. Fabozzi (ed.), *CMO Portfolio Management* (Summit, NJ: Frank J. Fabozzi Associates, 1994), Chapter 6.

implied by today's Treasury securities. The volatility assumption determines the dispersion of future interest rates in the simulation. The simulations should be normalized so that the average simulated price of a zero-coupon Treasury bond equals today's actual price.

Each model has its own model of the evolution of future interest rates and its own volatility assumptions. Typically, there are no significant differences in the interest-rate models of dealer firms and vendors, although their volatility assumptions can be significantly different.

The random paths of interest rates should be generated from an arbitrage-free model of the future term structure of interest rates. By arbitrage-free it is meant that the model replicates today's term structure of interest rates, an input of the model, and that for all future dates there is no possible arbitrage within the model. We will explain how this is done later.

The simulation works by generating many scenarios of future interest-rate paths. In each month of the scenario, a monthly interest rate and a mortgage refinancing rate are generated. The monthly interest rates are used to discount the projected cash flows in the scenario. The mortgage refinancing rate is needed to determine the cash flow because it represents the opportunity cost the mortgagor is facing at that time.

If the refinancing rates are high relative to the mortgagor's original coupon rate (i.e., the rate on the mortgagor's loan), the mortgagor will have less incentive to refinance, or even a positive disincentive (i.e., the homeowner will avoid moving in order to avoid refinancing). If the refinancing rate is low relative to the mortgagor's original coupon rate, the mortgagor has an incentive to refinance.

Prepayments are projected by feeding the refinancing rate and loan characteristics, such as age, into a prepayment model. Given the projected prepayments, the cash flow along an interest-rate path can be determined.

To make this more concrete, consider a newly issued mortgage pass-through security with a maturity of 360 months. Exhibit 20-1 shows N simulated interest-rate path scenarios. Each scenario consists of a path of 360 simulated 1-month future interest rates. Just how many paths should be generated is explained later. Exhibit 20-2 shows the paths of simulated mortgage refinancing rates corresponding to the scenarios shown in Exhibit 20-1. Assuming these mortgage refinancing rates, the cash flow for each scenario path is shown in Exhibit 20-3.

Calculating the Present Value for a Scenario Interest-Rate Path

Given the cash flow on an interest-rate path, its present value can be calculated. The discount rate for determining the present value is the simulated spot rate for each month on the interest-rate path plus an appropriate spread. The spot rate on a path can be determined from the simulated future monthly rates. The relationship that holds between the simulated spot rate for month T on path n and the simulated future 1-month rates is

$$z_T(n) = \left\{ [1 + f_1(n)] \, [1 + f_2(n)] \cdots [1 + f_T(n)] \right\}^{1/T} - 1,$$

where

$z_T(n)$ = Simulated spot rate for month T on path n;

$f_j(n)$ = Simulated future 1-month rate for month j on path n.

Consequently, the interest-rate path for the simulated future 1-month rates can be converted to the interest-rate path for the simulated monthly spot rates as shown in Exhibit 20-4.

EXHIBIT 20–1

Simulated Paths of 1-Month Future Interest Rates

	Interest-Rate Path Number					
Month	1	2	3	$\cdots$	n	$\cdots$	N
1	$f_1(1)$	$f_1(2)$	$f_1(3)$	$\cdots$	$f_1(n)$	$\cdots$	$f_1(N)$
2	$f_2(1)$	$f_2(2)$	$f_2(3)$	$\cdots$	$f_2(n)$	$\cdots$	$f_2(N)$
3	$f_3(1)$	$f_3(2)$	$f_3(3)$	$\cdots$	$f_3(n)$	$\cdots$	$f_3(N)$
t	$f_t(1)$	$f_t(2)$	$f_t(3)$	$\cdots$	$f_t(n)$	$\cdots$	$f_t(N)$
358	$f_{358}(1)$	$f_{358}(2)$	$f_{358}(3)$	$\cdots$	$f_{358}(n)$	$\cdots$	$f_{358}(N)$
359	$f_{359}(1)$	$f_{359}(2)$	$f_{359}(3)$	$\cdots$	$f_{359}(n)$	$\cdots$	$f_{359}(N)$
360	$f_{360}(1)$	$f_{360}(2)$	$f_{360}(3)$	$\cdots$	$f_{360}(n)$	$\cdots$	$f_{360}(N)$

Key:

$f_t(n)$ = 1-month future interest rate for month t on path n;

N = Total number of interest-rate paths.

EXHIBIT 20–2

Simulated Paths of Mortgage Refinancing Rates

	Interest-Rate Path Number					
Month	1	2	3	$\cdots$	n	$\cdots$	N
1	$r_1(1)$	$r_1(2)$	$r_1(3)$	$\cdots$	$r_1(n)$	$\cdots$	$r_1(N)$
2	$r_2(1)$	$r_2(2)$	$r_2(3)$	$\cdots$	$r_2(n)$	$\cdots$	$r_2(N)$
3	$r_3(1)$	$r_3(2)$	$r_3(3)$	$\cdots$	$r_3(n)$	$\cdots$	$r_3(N)$
t	$r_t(1)$	$r_t(2)$	$r_t(3)$	$\cdots$	$r_t(n)$	$\cdots$	$r_t(N)$
358	$r_{358}(1)$	$r_{358}(2)$	$r_{358}(3)$	$\cdots$	$r_{358}(n)$	$\cdots$	$r_{358}(N)$
359	$r_{359}(1)$	$r_{359}(2)$	$r_{359}(3)$	$\cdots$	$r_{359}(n)$	$\cdots$	$r_{359}(N)$
360	$r_{360}(1)$	$r_{360}(2)$	$r_{360}(3)$	$\cdots$	$r_{360}(n)$	$\cdots$	$r_{360}(N)$

Key:

$r_t(n)$ = Mortgage refinancing rate for month t on path n;

N = Total number of interest-rate paths.

EXHIBIT 20-3

Simulated Cash Flow on Each of the Interest-Rate Paths

	Interest-Rate Path Number						
Month	1	2	3	$\cdots$	n	$\cdots$	N
1	$C_1(1)$	$C_1(2)$	$C_1(3)$	$\cdots$	$C_1(n)$	$\cdots$	$C_1(N)$
2	$C_2(1)$	$C_2(2)$	$C_2(3)$	$\cdots$	$C_2(n)$	$\cdots$	$C_2(N)$
3	$C_3(1)$	$C_3(2)$	$C_3(3)$	$\cdots$	$C_3(n)$	$\cdots$	$C_3(N)$
t	$C_t(1)$	$C_t(2)$	$C_t(3)$	$\cdots$	$C_t(n)$	$\cdots$	$C_t(N)$
358	$C_{358}(1)$	$C_{358}(2)$	$C_{358}(3)$	$\cdots$	$C_{358}(n)$	$\cdots$	$C_{358}(N)$
359	$C_{359}(1)$	$C_{359}(2)$	$C_{359}(3)$	$\cdots$	$C_{359}(n)$	$\cdots$	$C_{359}(N)$
360	$C_{360}(1)$	$C_{360}(2)$	$C_{360}(3)$	$\cdots$	$C_{360}(n)$	$\cdots$	$C_{360}(N)$

Key:

$C_t(n)$ = Cash flow for month t on path n;

N = Total number of interest-rate paths.

EXHIBIT 20-4

Simulated Paths of Monthly Spot Rates

	Interest-Rate Path Number						
Month	1	2	3	$\cdots$	n	$\cdots$	N
1	$z_1(1)$	$z_1(2)$	$z_1(3)$	$\cdots$	$z_1(n)$	$\cdots$	$z_1(N)$
2	$z_2(1)$	$z_2(2)$	$z_2(3)$	$\cdots$	$z_2(n)$	$\cdots$	$z_2(N)$
3	$z_3(1)$	$z_3(2)$	$z_3(3)$	$\cdots$	$z_3(n)$	$\cdots$	$z_3(N)$
t	$z_t(1)$	$z_t(2)$	$z_t(3)$	$\cdots$	$z_t(n)$	$\cdots$	$z_t(N)$
358	$z_{358}(1)$	$z_{358}(2)$	$z_{358}(3)$	$\cdots$	$z_{358}(n)$	$\cdots$	$z_{358}(N)$
359	$z_{359}(1)$	$z_{359}(2)$	$z_{359}(3)$	$\cdots$	$z_{359}(n)$	$\cdots$	$z_{359}(N)$
360	$z_{360}(1)$	$z_{360}(2)$	$z_{360}(3)$	$\cdots$	$z_{360}(n)$	$\cdots$	$z_{360}(N)$

Key:

$z_t(n)$ = Spot rate for month t on path n;

N = Total number of interest-rate paths.

Therefore the present value of the cash flow for month T on interest-rate path n discounted at the simulated spot rate for month T plus some spread is

$$PV\left[C_T(n)\right] = \frac{C_T(n)}{\left[1 + z_T(n) + K\right]^{1/T}},$$

where

$PV[C_T(n)]$ = Present value of cash flow for month T on path n;

$\quad C_T(n)$ = Cash flow for month T on path n;

$\quad z_T(n)$ = Spot rate for month T on path n;

$\quad\quad K$ = Spread.

The present value for path n is the sum of the present value of the cash flow for each month on path n. That is,

$$PV[\text{Path}(n)] = PV[C_1(n)] + PV[C_2(n)] + \cdots + PV[C_{360}(n)],$$

where $PV[\text{Path}(n)]$ is the present value of interest-rate path n.

Determining the Theoretical Value

The present value of a given interest-rate path can be thought of as the theoretical value of a pass-through if that path was actually realized. The theoretical value of the pass-through can be determined by calculating the average of the theoretical value of all the interest-rate paths. That is,

$$\text{Theoretical value} = \frac{PV[\text{Path}(1)] + PV\text{Path}(2)] + \cdots + PV[\text{Path}(N)]}{N}.$$

where N is the number of interest-rate paths.

This procedure for valuing a pass-through is also followed for a CMO tranche. The cash flow for each month on each interest-rate path is found according to the principal repayment and interest distribution rules of the deal. In order to do this, a CMO structuring model is needed. In any analysis of CMOs, one of the major stumbling blocks is getting a good CMO structuring model.

Distribution of Path Present Values

The Monte Carlo simulation method is a commonly used management science tool in business. It is employed when the outcome of a business decision depends on the outcome of several random variables. The product of the simulation is the average value and the probability distribution of the possible outcomes.

Unfortunately, the use of Monte Carlo simulation to value fixed-income securities has been limited to just the reporting of the average value, which is referred to as the theoretical value of the security. This means that all of the information about the distribution of the path present values is ignored. Yet, this information is quite valuable.

For example, consider a well-protected PAC bond. The distribution of the present value for the paths should be concentrated around the theoretical value. That is, the standard deviation should be small. In contrast, for a support tranche, the distribution of the present value for the paths could be wide, or equivalently, the standard deviation could be large.

Therefore, before using the theoretical value for a mortgage-backed security generated from the Monte Carlo method, a portfolio manager should ask for information about the distribution of the path's present values.

Option-Adjusted Spread

As explained in Chapter 17, the option-adjusted spread (OAS) is a measure of the yield spread that can be used to convert dollar differences between value and price. It represents a spread over the issuer's spot rate curve or benchmark.

In the Monte Carlo model, the OAS is the spread K that when added to all the spot rates on all interest-rate paths will make the average present value of the paths equal to the observed market price (plus accrued interest). Mathematically, OAS is the spread that will satisfy the following condition:

$$\text{Market price} = \frac{PV[\text{Path}(1)] + PV[\text{Path}(2)] + \cdots + PV[\text{Path}(N)]}{N},$$

where N is the number of interest-rate paths.

Zero-Volatility Spread

The proper way to evaluate mortgage-backed securities of the same duration but with different coupon rates is to compare them with a portfolio of zero-coupon Treasury securities that have the same cash flow stream as projected for the mortgage-backed security. Assuming the mortgage-backed security's cash flows are riskless, its value is equal to the portfolio value of all of the zero-coupon Treasuries, with cash flows valued at the spot rates. A mortgage-backed security's value will be less than the portfolio of zero-coupon Treasury securities because investors demand a spread for the risk associated with holding a mortgage-backed security rather than a riskless package (in the sense of default risk and certainty of the cash flows) of Treasury securities.

The *zero-volatility spread* (also called the *static spread*) to Treasuries is determined as follows. It is the spread that will make the present value of the projected cash flows from the mortgage-backed security when discounted at the spot rate plus a spread equal to its market price. A trial-and-error procedure is required to determine this spread.

Option Cost

Using the decomposition principle for a callable bond discussed in Chapter 17, we can obtain the implied cost of the option embedded in a mortgage-backed security by calculating the difference between the option-adjusted spread at the assumed volatility of interest rates and the zero-volatility spread. That is,

Option cost = Zero-volatility spread – Option-adjusted spread.

The option cost measures the prepayment (or option) risk embedded in the security.

Some Technical Issues

In the binomial method for valuing bonds discussed in Chapter 17, the interest-rate tree is constructed so that it is arbitrage-free. That is, if any on-the-run issue is valued, the value produced by the model is equal to the market price. This means that the tree is calibrated to the market. In contrast, in our discussion of the Monte Carlo method, there is no mechanism that we have described above that will assure that the valuation model will produce a value for an on-the-run Treasury security (the benchmark in the case of agency mortgage-backed securities) equal to the market price. In practice, this is accomplished by adding a *drift term* to the short-term return generating process (Exhibit 20-1) so that the value produced by the Monte Carlo method for all on-the-run Treasury securities is their market price.[2] A technical explanation of this process is beyond the scope of this chapter.[3]

There is also another adjustment made to the interest-rate paths. Restrictions on interest-rate movements must be built into the model to prevent interest rates from reaching levels that are believed to be unreasonable (e.g., an interest rate of zero or an interest rate of 30%). This is done by incorporating *mean reversion* into the model. By this it is meant that at some point, the interest rate is forced toward some estimated average (mean) value.

The specification of the relationship between short-term rates and refinancing rates is necessary. Empirical evidence on the relationship is also necessary. More specifically, the correlation between the short-term and long-term rates must be estimated.

The number of interest-rate paths determines how "good" the estimate is, not relative to the truth but relative to the valuation model used. The more paths, the more the theoretical value tends to settle down. It is a statistical sampling problem. Most Monte Carlo models employ some form of *variance reduction* to cut down on the number of sample paths necessary to get a good statistical sample. Variance reduction techniques allow us to obtain value estimates within a tick. By this we mean 'that if the model is used to generate more scenarios, value estimates from the model will not change by more than a tick. So, for example, if 1,024 paths are used to obtain the estimate value for a security, there is little more information to be had from the model by generating more than that number of paths. (For some very sensitive CMO tranches, more paths may be needed to estimate value within one tick.)

Effective Duration and Convexity

With the Monte Carlo simulation model, effective duration and convexity can be computed by increasing and decreasing short-term Treasury rates by a small amount. When these interest rates are changed, the option-adjusted spread is kept constant. This will produce two average

2 This is equivalent to saying that the OAS produced by the model is zero.
3 For an explanation of how this is done, see Lakhbir S. Hayre and Kenneth Lauterbach, "Stochastic Valuation of Debt Securities," in Frank J. Fabozzi (ed.), *Managing Institutional Assets* (New York: Harper & Row, 1990), pp. 321–361.

total present values: one when short-term interest rates increase, and one when short-term interest rates decrease. These average total present values can be viewed as the theoretical values under small interest rate changes. These values are then substituted into the formula for effective duration and convexity.

When effective duration is calculated using the Monte Carlo simulation model to produce the two prices for a higher and lower yield, the result is commonly referred to as an *OAS-duration*. Thus, effective duration means in general that the duration is calculated after allowing for the cash flows to change as yields change. The OAS-duration is a special case where price sensitivity is determined within the Monte Carlo simulation framework.

MARKET-BASED APPROACHES TO DURATION ESTIMATION FOR AN MBS

For mortgage-backed securities, two market-based approaches have been used to estimate duration: empirical duration and coupon curve duration.

Empirical Duration

Empirical duration, sometimes referred to as *implied duration*, is the sensitivity of a mortgage-backed security as estimated empirically from historical prices.[4] Regression analysis, a statistical technique described in Chapter 23, is used to estimate the relationship. More specifically, the relationship estimated is the percentage change in the price of the security of interest to the change in the general level of Treasury yields. In Chapter 23, we explain empirical duration in more detail.

Coupon Curve Duration

The *coupon curve duration* is a second approach that uses market prices to estimate the duration of an MBS. It is an easier approach to duration estimation than empirical duration. The approach, first suggested by Douglas Breeden,[5] starts with the coupon curve of prices for similar MBSs. By rolling up and down the coupon curve of prices, the duration can be obtained. Because of the way it is estimated, this approach to duration estimation was referred to by Breeden as the "roll-up, roll-down approach." The prices obtained from rolling up and rolling down the coupon curve of prices are substituted into the approximation formula for duration.

To illustrate this approach, let's use the coupon curve of prices for Ginnie Maes in June 1994. A portion of the coupon curve of prices for that month was as follows:

Coupon ($)	Price
7%	$ 92.06
8	98.38
9	103.34

---

4 The first attempt to calculate empirical duration was by Scott M. Pinkus and Marie A. Chandola, "The Relative Price Volatility of Mortgage Securities," *Journal of Portfolio Management* (Summer 1986), pp. 9–22.

5 Douglas Breeden, "Risk, Return, and Hedging of Fixed-Rate Mortgages," *Journal of Fixed Income* (September 1991), pp. 85–107.

Suppose that the coupon curve duration for the 8s is sought. If the yield declines by 100 basis points, the assumption is that the price of the 8s will increase to the price of the 9s. Thus, the price will increase from $98.38 to $103.34. Similarly, if the yield increases by 100 basis points, the assumption is that the price of the 8s will decline to the price of the 7s ($92.06). Using the approximate duration formula, the corresponding values are

V_0 = $98.38;
V_- = $103.34;
V_+ = $92.06;
y = 0.01.

The estimated duration based on the coupon curve is then

$$\text{Duration} = \frac{\$103.34 - \$92.06}{2(\$98.38)(0.01)} = 5.73 \ .$$

TOTAL RETURN

The total return framework can be used to assess the relative attractiveness of an MBS over some investment horizon. The total receipts resulting from investing in an MBS consist of the following:

1. The projected cash flows of the MBS from
   a. the projected interest payments (net of servicing fee),
   b. the projected principal repayment (scheduled plus prepayments);
2. The interest earned on the reinvestment of the projected interest payments and the projected principal repayments;
3. The projected price of the MBS at the end of the investment horizon.

To obtain (1), a prepayment rate over the investment horizon must be assumed. To calculate (2), a reinvestment rate must be assumed. Finally, to calculate (3) the investor must make two assumptions. First, the investor must project what the bond equivalent yield will be for the MBS at the end of the investment horizon. Second, the investor must project what prepayment rate the market will assume at the end of the investment horizon. Obviously, the first and second assumptions are not independent. The projected prepayment rate will depend on the projected yield in the market.

As we have stressed throughout this book, an investor should not use one set of projections to determine the total return. Instead, an investor should assess the performance of a security over a range of likely assumptions.

The monthly total return is then found by using the formula:

$$\left[\frac{\text{Total future amount}}{\text{Price of the MBS}} \right]^{1/\text{Number of months}} - 1.$$

The monthly total return can be annualized on the basis of the bond equivalent yield given earlier or by computing the effective annual yield as follows:

$$(1 + \text{Monthly total return})^{12} - 1.$$

Illustration 20-12   Suppose a portfolio manager is considering investing in a pass-through with a 9.5% mortgage rate, .5% servicing fee, 360 months remaining to maturity, and an original mortgage balance of $100,000. The price of this security is $94,521. The cash flow yield, assuming 100% PSA, is 10.21% (see Illustration 20-1). The portfolio manager has a 6-month investment horizon and believes the following:

1. For the next six months the prepayment rate will be 100% PSA;
2. The projected cash flows can be reinvested at .5% per month;
3. The pass-through will sell to yield 7.62% at the end of the investment horizon;
4. The projected PSA prepayment rate at the end of the investment horizon will be 185% PSA.

On the basis of the first assumption, the projected cash flows (projected interest net of servicing fee, projected scheduled principal, and projected principal prepayment) for the first 6 months are

End of Month	Projected Cash Flow ($)
1	$816
2	832
3	849
4	865
5	881
6	897

The projected cash flow is obtained from Exhibit 19-8 of Chapter 19.

The projected cash flow, plus interest from reinvesting the cash flow at .5% per month, is

End of Month	Projected Cash Flow ($)	Projected Cash Flows Plus Reinvestment Income ($)
1	$816	$837
2	832	849
3	849	862
4	865	874
5	881	885
6	897	897
	Total	$5,204

At the end of the investment horizon, our original pass-through would have a remaining mortgage balance of $99,379 (see Exhibit 19-8 of Chapter 19) and remaining maturity of 354 months. Assuming a required yield of 7.62% and a prepayment rate of 185% PSA, the projected price of this pass-through would be $106,210.

The total future amount is then

Projected cash flows plus reinvestment income $5,204
Projected price   106,210
Total $111,414

The monthly total return is

$$\left[\frac{\$111,414}{\$94,521}\right]^{\frac{1}{6}} - 1 = .02778.$$

On a bond equivalent basis, the total return is

$$2[(1.02778)^6 - 1] = .3574 = 35.74\%.$$

On an effective annual yield basis, the total return is

$$(1.02778)^{12} - 1 = .3893 = 38.93\%.$$

Illustration 20-13   Suppose that a portfolio manager wants to assess the performance of the pass-through in the previous illustration over a 6-month investment horizon on the basis of the following assumptions.

1. For the next 6 months the prepayment rate will be 100% PSA;
2. The projected cash flow can be reinvested at .75% per month;
3. The pass-through will sell to yield 12.30% at the end of the investment horizon;
4. The projected PSA prepayment rate at the end of the investment horizon will be 50% PSA.

On the basis of the first assumption, the projected cash flows for the first 6 months are the same as in the previous illustration. The projected cash flows plus interest from reinvesting the cash flow at 0.75% per month are computed below:

End of Month	Projected Cash Flow ($)	Projected Cash Flow Plus Reinvestment Income ($)
1	$816	$847
2	832	857
3	849	868
4	865	878
5	881	888
6	897	897
	Total	$5,235

At the end of the investment horizon, our original pass-through would have a remaining balance of $99,174 and remaining maturity of 354 months. Assuming a required yield of 12.30% and a prepayment rate of 50% PSA, the projected price of this pass-through would be $78,757.
The total future amount is then

Projected cash flows plus reinvestment income	$ 5,235
Projected price	78,757
Total	$83,992

The monthly total return is

$$\left[\frac{\$83,992}{\$94,521}\right]^{\frac{1}{6}} - 1 = -.019491.$$

On a bond equivalent basis, the total return is

$$2[(0.98051)^6 - 1] = -.2228 = -22.28\%.$$

On an effective annual yield basis, the total return is

$$(0.98051)^{12} - 1 = -.2104 = -21.04\%.$$

SUMMARY

In this chapter, two models for valuing mortgage-backed securities are explained: static cash flow model and the Monte Carlo simulation model. The drawbacks of the former model are that it fails to recognize the term structure of interest rates and does not recognize how changes in future rates can affect prepayments and therefore cash flow.

The Monte Carlo simulation model overcomes both of these drawbacks. However, it is not a perfect model since prepayment models are only statistical models and interest-rate volatility is not known with certainty. An option-adjusted spread and option cost can be calculated using the Monte Carlo simulation model.

Effective duration and convexity can be calculated using both models. Two market-based approaches to estimating duration for mortgage-backed securities are empirical duration and coupon curve duration.

VII

⑥ STATISTICAL AND OPTIMIZATION TECHNIQUES

21

⑥ PROBABILITY THEORY

In most instances of fixed-income analysis or fixed-income portfolio management, a decision's outcome depends on variables that are not known with certainty at the time the decision is made. Stochastic or probabilistic analysis is often used in these circumstances to aid in making such decisions. This involves estimating probabilities of the various outcomes that may result from a decision. In this chapter, we establish the fundamentals of probability theory and show some applications. One particularly important application is estimation of interest-rate volatility from historical data.

OBJECTIVE VERSUS SUBJECTIVE PROBABILITIES

Probabilities can be determined through objective or subjective analysis. The *objective approach* to probability theory basically asserts that probabilities relate to long-run frequencies of occurrence. That is, the objective probability of an outcome or event can be defined as the relative frequency with which an event would occur, given a large number of observations. An objectivist would assign a probability of 1/6 (one in six), for example, to the outcome or event that a value of "1" would appear if a fair die is rolled and a probability of 4/52 to the outcome or event that an ace of any suit would be drawn from a fair deck of 52 cards.

The *subjective approach* basically maintains that probabilities measure the decision maker's degree of belief in the likelihood of a given outcome. It is a broad and flexible approach, allowing assignment of probabilities to outcomes for which no objective data may exist, or in circumstances where there may be a combination of objective data and subjective belief.

BASIC CONCEPTS IN PROBABILITY THEORY

Some basic concepts in probability theory hold true whether the objective or the subjective approach is taken.

Simple and Compound Events

Suppose an experiment is performed that involves tossing a fair die. There are then six possible outcomes: 1,2,3,4,5, or 6. Each of these outcomes is referred to as a *simple event*. The characteristic of a simple event is that it cannot be decomposed into other events. A *compound event* is one that can be decomposed into simple events. For example, an outcome that an even number will occur when a fair die is tossed is a compound event, because it can be decomposed into three simple events: getting a 2, 4, or 6.

Illustration 21-1   Suppose that a portfolio manager is considering buying a 20.5-year bond with a coupon rate of 10% and selling at par to yield 10%. The next coupon payment is exactly 6 months from now. Suppose also that the portfolio manager has a 6-month investment horizon. The portfolio's total return will depend only on the yield for 20-year bonds 6 months from now. We refer to this yield as the *horizon yield*. The portfolio manager believes that only the following nine possible horizon yields for 20-year bonds 6 months from now will result:

Possible Horizon Yields
12.0%
11.5
11.0
10.5
10.0
9.5
9.0
8.5
8.0

Each of these horizon yields is a simple event. The event that the horizon yield will be less than the yield today (10%) is a compound event. It can be decomposed into four simple events: 8.0%, 8.5%, 9.0%, and 9.5%.

Mutually Exclusive Events

If two events or outcomes have nothing in common, they are referred to as *mutually exclusive events*. That is, if an experiment can result in only one of the two events occurring, then the events are mutually exclusive. For example, in the tossing of a die, the probability of a 1 and a 2 occurring is zero. Both cannot appear simultaneously. Hence the events defining an outcome of 1 and an outcome of 2 are mutually exclusive.

Conditional Probabilities

Conditional probabilities are probabilities obtained after the initial conditions have changed. For example, the probability of picking an ace with one draw of a card from the deck of 52 cards is 4/52. Suppose that the card drawn is not an ace. If you then pick another card without replacing the original card in the deck, the probability of drawing an ace is now 4/51. This probability is a conditional probability because it is conditional on the withdrawal and nonreplacement of a card that is not an ace. In probability notation, the probability of some event E_i conditional on the occurrence of some other event E_j is denoted by $P(E_i\backslash E_j)$.[1]

As another example of a conditional probability, suppose that an investor is trying to estimate the probability that an issuer will default on a 5-year debt instrument. Today, the investor assigns a probability that the issuer will default 2 years from now. A conditional probability would be the probability that the issuer does not default 2 years from now, given that the issuer does not default in the first year.

Joint Probabilities

Joint probabilities refer to the probability that more than one event will occur simultaneously. For example, suppose a single card selection experiment defines one outcome as selecting an ace and a second outcome as selecting a card that is a heart. The joint event of the two events defined above would be selecting the ace of hearts. The probability of this joint event is 1/52. In probability notation, the joint probability of two events E_i and E_j is denoted by $P(E_i \,\&\, E_j)$.

BASIC RULES OF PROBABILITY THEORY

From the concepts of probability theory described above, we can state four basic rules of probability theory.

Rule 1
Given an experiment with n possible simple events or outcomes denoted by $E_1, E_2, \ldots , E_n$, a nonnegative number is assigned to each outcome. This is denoted mathematically by

$$P(E_i) \geq 0.$$

Rule 2
The sum of the probabilities of all possible simple events is one; that is,

$$P(E_1) + P(E_2) + \cdots + P(E_n) = 1.$$

Rule 3
For two mutually exclusive events, E_i and E_j, the probability of either occurring is the sum of the two probabilities. That is,

$$P(E_i \text{ or } E_j) = P(E_i) + P(E_j).$$

Rule 4
Two events are *statistically independent* if the occurrence of one does not affect the probability of the other. When two events E_i and E_k are statistically independent, then

---

1   In the notation of probability theory, a backslash (\) means "given." for example, $P(E_i\backslash E_k)$ means the probability of event i occurring *given* that event k occurs.

$$P(E_i \backslash E_k) = P(E_i) \text{ or } P(E_k \backslash E_i) = P(E_k).$$

Alternatively, two events are statistically independent if the following holds:

$$P(E_i \& E_k) = P(E_i)\, P(E_k).$$

That is, if two events are statistically independent, the joint probability can be obtained by multiplying the probabilities of the two events.

To illustrate statistical independence, suppose a fair coin is tossed twice. Define the first event as a head appearing on the first toss, and the second event as a head appearing on the second toss. If a head in fact does turn up on the first toss, how does this affect the probability of obtaining a head on the second toss? It does not, as a probability of 1/2 is still correct for a head occurring on the second toss. Hence, the two events are statistically independent.

RANDOM VARIABLE AND PROBABILITY DISTRIBUTION

A *random variable* is a variable for which a probability can be assigned to each possible result (value) that the variable can take. A *probability distribution* or *probability function* is a function that describes all the values that the random variable can take and the probability associated with each. For example, suppose that two dice are rolled. There are 36 possible outcomes. The pairs of values in each parenthesis represent the value appearing on the first and second die.

(1,1)	(2,1)	(3,1)	(4,1)	(5,1)	(6,1)
(1,2)	(2,2)	(3,2)	(4,2)	(5,2)	(6,2)
(1,3)	(2,3)	(3,3)	(4,3)	(5,3)	(6,3)
(1,4)	(2,4)	(3,4)	(4,4)	(5,4)	(6,4)
(1,5)	(2,5)	(3,5)	(4,5)	(5,5)	(6,5)
(1,6)	(2,6)	(3,6)	(4,6)	(5,6)	(6,6)

If X represents the sum of the two values appearing on the two dice, then X can take on integer values from 2 to 12. The probability distribution for X is shown in Exhibit 21-1. For example, the outcomes that result in a value of 5 for the random variable X are (1,4), (2,3), (3,2), and (4,1). Thus 4 of the 36 possible outcomes will sum to 5. The probability of this is therefore 4/36 or 1/9.

A *cumulative probability distribution* is a function that shows the probability that the random variable will attain a value less than or equal to each value that the random variable can take on. For the dice rolling experiment, for example, the probability that X will realize a value less than or equal to 5 is equal to the sum of the probabilities associated with X realizing a value of 2, 3, 4, and 5, which is 10/36 or 5/18. The cumulative probability distribution is also shown in Exhibit 21-1.

A subscript is used to denote specific values of the random variable. For example, in the dice-rolling experiment, there are 11 possible values that can occur for the random variable X, as follows:

i	1	2	3	4	5	6	7	8	9	10	11
X	2	3	4	5	6	7	8	9	10	11	12

EXHIBIT 21-1

Probability Distribution and Cumulative Probability Distribution for the Sum of the Values Appearing when Two Dice Are Tossed

Sum of Values (X)	No. of Outcomes That Will Result in X	Probability Distribution	Cumulative Probability
2	1	$\dfrac{1}{36}$	$\dfrac{1}{36}$
3	2	$\dfrac{2}{36} = \dfrac{1}{18}$	$\dfrac{3}{36} = \dfrac{1}{12}$
4	3	$\dfrac{3}{36} = \dfrac{1}{12}$	$\dfrac{6}{36} = \dfrac{1}{6}$
5	4	$\dfrac{4}{36} = \dfrac{1}{9}$	$\dfrac{10}{36} = \dfrac{5}{18}$
6	5	$\dfrac{5}{36}$	$\dfrac{15}{36} = \dfrac{5}{12}$
7	6	$\dfrac{6}{36} = \dfrac{1}{6}$	$\dfrac{21}{36} = \dfrac{7}{12}$
8	5	$\dfrac{5}{36}$	$\dfrac{26}{36} = \dfrac{13}{18}$
9	4	$\dfrac{4}{36} = \dfrac{1}{9}$	$\dfrac{30}{36} = \dfrac{5}{6}$
10	3	$\dfrac{3}{36} = \dfrac{1}{12}$	$\dfrac{33}{36} = \dfrac{11}{12}$
11	2	$\dfrac{2}{36} = \dfrac{1}{18}$	$\dfrac{35}{36}$
12	1	$\dfrac{1}{36}$	$\dfrac{36}{36} = 1$

These possible values can be denoted as X_i where i refers to the ith value for the random variable X. Thus, X_4 is the fourth value for the random variable X, which is the value 5, expressed as follows:

$$X_4 = 5.$$

The probability that X will be equal to 5 can be expressed as follows:

$$P(X = 5) = P(X_4).$$

In the examples in this chapter, we denote the probability of a specific value for the random variable X by stating the specific value [i.e., $P(X = \text{specific value})$] or by using the subscript notation [i.e., $P(X_i)$].

EXHIBIT 21-2

Probability Distribution for the 6-Month Total Return for a 20.5-Year, 10% Coupon Bond Selling Initially at Par

i	Horizon Yield (%)	Probability	Cumulative Probability	Price at Horizon ($)	Total Return (%)
1	12.0%	.05	.05	$ 84.85	−10.15%
2	11.5	.08	.13	88.35	−6.65
3	11.0	.10	.23	91.98	−3.02
4	10.5	.16	.39	95.85	0.85
5	10.0	.22	.61	100.00	5.00
6	9.5	.16	.77	104.44	9.44
7	9.0	.10	.87	109.20	14.20
8	8.5	.08	.95	114.31	19.31
9	8.0	.05	1.00	119.79	24.79

*Note: Since the initial price is $100 and the 6-month coupon is $5 per $100 of par value, the 6-month total return is found as follows:

$$(100 - \text{Price at Horizon} + 5)/100.$$

Illustration 21-2   To illustrate these basic rules, we continue the bond return problem in Illustration 21-1. Exhibit 21-2 shows the nine possible horizon yields and the assumed probability that each horizon yield will occur. Notice that the sum of the probabilities is one. The random variable in this illustration is the horizon yield, which can take on nine possible outcomes, but the total return can also be considered the random variable. A total return corresponds to each horizon yield, with the probability distribution for the total return the same as the probability distribution for the horizon yield.

The probability that the total return will be 14.2% is 10%. That is, $P(X = 14.2\%)$ or $P(X_7)$ is 10%. The probability that the total return will be less than 14.2% is the cumulative probability shown in the fourth column of Exhibit 21-2. The probability is 77%.

STATISTICAL MEASURES OF A PROBABILITY DISTRIBUTION

Various measures are used to summarize the probability distribution of a random variable. The two most often used measures are the expected value and the variance (or standard deviation).

Expected Value

The *expected value* of a probability distribution is the weighted average of the distribution. The weights in this case are the probabilities associated with the random variable X. The expected value of a random variable is denoted by $E(X)$ and is computed using the following expression:

$$E(X) = P_1 X_1 + P_2 X_2 + \cdots + P_n X_n,$$

where P_i is the probability associated with the outcome X_i.

Illustration 21-3 The expected value for the 6-month total return for the probability distribution in Exhibit 21-2 is found as follows:

$$E(X) = .05\,(-10.15) + .08\,(-6.65) + .10\,(-3.02)$$
$$+ .16\,(0.85) + .22\,(5.00) + .16\,(9.44) + .10\,(14.20)$$
$$+ .08\,(19.31) + .05\,(24.79) = 5.61\%.$$

The expected value for the 6-month total return is 5.61%.

Variance

A portfolio manager is interested not only in the expected value of a probability distribution but also in the dispersion of the random variable around the expected value. A measure of dispersion of the probability distribution is the *variance* of the distribution. The variance of a random variable X, denoted by var(X), is computed as

$$\text{var}(X) = [X_1 - E(X)]^2 P_1 + [X_2 - E(X)]^2 P_2 + \ldots + [X_n - E(X)]^2 P_n .$$

Notice that the variance is simply a weighted average of the deviations of each possible outcome from the expected value, where the weight is the probability of an outcome occurring. The greater the variance is, the wider is the distribution of the possible outcomes for the random variable. The reason that the deviations from the expected value are squared is so that outcomes above and below the expected value will not cancel each other out.

The problem with using the variance as a measure of dispersion is that it is expressed in terms of squared units of the random variable. Consequently, we use the square root of the variance, called the *standard deviation*, as a better measure of the degree of dispersion. Mathematically this can be expressed as follows:

$$\text{std}(X) = \sqrt{\text{var}(X)},$$

where std(X) denotes the standard deviation of the random variable X.

Illustration 21-4 The variance for the 6-month total return whose probability distribution is given in Exhibit 21-2 is calculated as follows:

$$\text{var}(X) = (-10.15 - 5.61)^2 \,.05 + (-6.65 - 5.61)^2 \,.08 + (-3.02 - 5.61)^2 \,.10$$
$$+ (0.85 - 5.61)^2 \,.16 + (5.00 - 5.61)^2 \,.22 + (9.44 - 5.61)^2 \,.16$$
$$+ (14.20 - 5.61)^2 \,.10 + (19.31 - 5.61)^2 \,.08 + (24.79 - 5.61)^2 \,.05$$
$$= 78.73\%.$$

The standard deviation is 8.87%, which is the square root of the variance, 78.73%.

DISCRETE VERSUS CONTINUOUS PROBABILITY DISTRIBUTION

A probability distribution can be classified according to the values that a random variable can realize. When the value of the random variable can only take on specific values, then the probability distribution is referred to as a *discrete probability distribution*. For example, in our illustration, we assumed only nine specific values for the random variable. Hence, to this point we have been working with a discrete probability distribution. If, instead, the random variable can take on any possible value within the range of outcomes, then the probability distribution is said to be a *continuous probability distribution*.

When a random variable is either the price or the return on a traded financial asset, the distribution can be assumed to be a continuous probability distribution. This means that it is possible to obtain, for example, a price of $95.43231 or $109.34872 and any value in between. In practice, we know that financial assets are not quoted in such a way. Nevertheless, there is no loss in describing the distribution as continuous. However, what is important in using a continuous distribution is that in moving from one price to the next, there is no major jump. For example, if the price declines from $95.14 to $70.50, it is assumed that there are trades that are executed at prices at small increments below $95.14 before getting to $70.50. In contrast, if the price can just "jump" from $95.14 to $70.50, then the distribution is referred to as a *jump process*.

NORMAL PROBABILITY DISTRIBUTION

In many applications involving probability distributions, it is assumed that the underlying probability distribution is a *normal distribution*. An example of a normal distribution is shown in Exhibit 21-3.

The area under the normal distribution (or normal curve) between any two points on a horizontal axis represents the probability of obtaining a value between those two values. For example, the probability of realizing a value for the random variable X that is between X_1 and X_2 in Exhibit 21-3 is shown by the shaded area. Mathematically, the probability of realizing a value for X between these two values can be written as follows:

$$P(X_1 < X < X_2).$$

The entire area under the normal curve is equal to 1. This follows from the second rule of probability theory, which states that the sum of the probabilities of all possible simple events is 1.

Properties of the Normal Distribution

The normal distribution has the following properties:

1. The point in the middle of the normal curve is the expected value for the distribution.
2. The distribution is symmetric around the expected value. That is, half of the distribution is to the left of the expected value and the other half is to the right. Thus, the probability of obtaining a value less than the expected value is 50%. The probability of obtaining a value greater than the expected value is also 50%. Mathematically, this is expressed as follows:

$$P[X < E(X)] = .5 \text{ and } P[X > E(X)] = .5.$$

EXHIBIT 21-3

Normal Distribution (or Normal Curve)

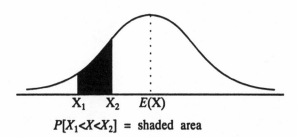

$$X_1 \quad X_2 \quad E(X)$$

$$P[X_1 < X < X_2] = \text{shaded area}$$

3. The probability that the actual outcome will be within a range of one standard deviation above the expected value and one standard deviation below the expected value is 68.26%, rounded to 68.3%.
4. The probability that the actual outcome will be within a range of two standard deviations above the expected value and two standard deviations below the expected value is 95.46%, rounded to 95.5%.
5. The probability that the actual outcome will be within a range of three standard deviations above the expected value and three standard deviations below the expected value is 99.74%, rounded to 99.7%.

Illustration 21-5   Suppose that the 1-year total return for a portfolio has an expected value of 7% and a standard deviation of 4%, and that the probability distribution is a normal distribution. The probability is 68.3% that the 1-year total return will be between 3% (the expected value of 7% minus one standard deviation of 4%) and 11% (the expected value of 7% plus one standard deviation of 4%). The probability is 95.5% that the 1-year total return will be between –1% (the expected value minus two standard deviations) and 15% (the expected value plus two standard deviations).

Illustration 21-6   Suppose that the standard deviation for the 1-year total return in the previous illustration is 2% rather than 4%. Then the probability is 68.3% that the 1-year total return will be between 5% and 9%; the probability is 95.5% that the 1-year total return will be between 3% and 11%.

   Notice that the smaller the standard deviation, the narrower the range of the possible outcome for a given probability.

Using Normal Distribution Tables

Tables are available that give the probability of obtaining a value between any two values of a normal probability distribution. All that must be known in order to determine the probability is the expected value and the standard deviation. However, the normal distribution table is constructed for a normal distribution that has an expected value of 0 and a standard deviation of 1. In order to use the table, therefore, it is necessary to convert the normal distribution under consideration into a distribution that has an expected value of 0 and standard deviation of 1. This is done by standardizing the values of the distribution under consideration.

The procedure is as follows. Suppose that a normal distribution for some random variable X has an expected value $E(X)$ and a standard deviation denoted by std(X). To standardize any particular value, say X_1, the following is computed:

$$z_1 = \frac{X_1 - E(X)}{\text{std}(X)},$$

where z_1 is the *standardized value* for X_1. The standardized value is also called the *normal deviate*.

Exhibit 21-4 is an abridged normal distribution table that shows the area under the normal curve, which, as stated before, represents probability. This particular table shows the probability of obtaining a value greater than some specified value in standardized form in the right-hand tail of the distribution. This is the shaded area shown in the normal curve at the top of Exhibit 21-4.

We demonstrate how to use the table in the next 11 illustrations. In Illustrations 21-7 to 21-13 it is assumed that a life insurance company has estimated that the value of one of its long-term Treasury bond portfolios is normally distributed with an expected value of $10 million and a standard deviation of $2 million.

Illustration 21-7   Suppose that the portfolio manager wants to know the probability of realizing a portfolio value greater than $14 million. The standardized value corresponding to $14 million in this case is 2, as shown below:

$$\frac{\$14 \text{ million} - \$10 \text{ million}}{\$2 \text{ million}} = 2.$$

The probability of obtaining a value greater than $14 million is the same as a standardized value greater than 2. (See Exhibit 21-5.) From Exhibit 21-4, the probability of obtaining a value greater than 2 is .0228 or 2.28%, expressed as follows:

$$P(X > \$14 \text{ million}) = P(z > 2) = .0228.$$

Illustration 21-8   Suppose the probability of obtaining a value greater than $11 million is wanted. The standardized value is .5, as shown below:

$$\frac{\$11 \text{ million} - \$10 \text{ million}}{\$2 \text{ million}} = .5.$$

From Exhibit 21-4, the probability of obtaining a value greater than .5 is .3085 or 30.85%, expressed as follows:

$$P(X > \$11 \text{ million}) = P(z > .5) = .3085.$$

Illustration 21-9   Suppose that the probability of obtaining a value less than $14 million is wanted. This is simple, because the entire area under the normal curve is equal to 1. If the

EXHIBIT 21-4

Normal Distribution Table for Standardized Value (or Normal Deviate) z

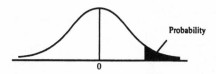

z	.00	.01	.02	.03	.04	.05	.06	.07	.08	.09
0.0	.5000	.4960	.4920	.4880	.4840	.4801	.4761	.4721	.4681	.4641
0.1	.4602	.4562	.4522	.4483	.4443	.4404	.4364	.4325	.4286	.4247
0.2	.4207	.4168	.4129	.4090	.4052	.4013	.3974	.3936	.3897	.3859
0.3	.3821	.3783	.3745	.3707	.3669	.3632	.3594	.3557	.3520	.3483
0.4	.3446	.3409	.3372	.3336	.3300	.3264	.3228	.3192	.3156	.3121
0.5	.3085	.3050	.3015	.2981	.2946	.2912	.2877	.2843	.2810	.2776
0.6	.2743	.2709	.2676	.2643	.2611	.2578	.2546	.2514	.2483	.2451
0.7	.2420	.2389	.2358	.2327	.2296	.2266	.2236	.2206	.2177	.2148
0.8	.2110	.2090	.2061	.2033	.2005	.1977	.1949	.1922	.1894	.1867
0.9	.1841	.1814	.1788	.1762	.1736	.1711	.1685	.1660	.1635	.1611
1.0	.1587	.1562	.1539	.1515	.1492	.1469	.1449	.1423	.1401	.1379
1.1	.1357	.1335	.1314	.1292	.1271	.1251	.1230	.1210	.1190	.1170
1.2	.1151	.1131	.1112	.1093	.1075	.1056	.1038	.1020	.1003	.0985
1.3	.0968	.0951	.0934	.0918	.0901	.0885	.0869	.0853	.0838	.0823
1.4	.0808	.0793	.0778	.0764	.0749	.0735	.0721	.0708	.0694	.0681
1.5	.0668	.0655	.0643	.0630	.0618	.0606	.0594	.0582	.0571	.0559
1.6	.0548	.0537	.0526	.0516	.0505	.0495	.0485	.0475	.0465	.0455
1.7	.0446	.0436	.0427	.0418	.0409	.0401	.0392	.0384	.0375	.0367
1.8	.0359	.0351	.0344	.0336	.0329	.0322	.0314	.0307	.0301	.0294
1.9	.0287	.0281	.0274	.0268	.0262	.0256	.0250	.0244	.0239	.0233
2.0	.0228	.0222	.0217	.0212	.0207	.0202	.0197	.0192	,0188	,0183
2.1	.0179	.0174	.0170	.0166	.0162	.0158	.0154	.0150	.0146	.0143
2.2	.0139	.0136	.0132	.0129	.0125	.0122	.0119	.0116	.0113	.0110
2.3	.0107	.0104	.0102	.0099	.0096	.0094	.0091	.0089	.0087	.0084
2.4	.0082	.0080	.0078	.0075	.0073	.0071	.0069	.0068	.0066	.0064
2.5	.0062	.0060	.0059	.0057	.0055	.0054	.0052	.0051	.0049	.0048
2.6	.0047	.0045	.0044	.0043	.0041	.0040	.0039	.0038	,0037	.0036
2.7	.0035	.0034	.0033	.0032	.0031	,0030	.0029	.0028	,0027	.0026
2.8	.0026	.0025	.0024	.0023	.0023	.0022	.0021	.0021	.0020	.0019
2.9	.0019	.0018	.0018	.0017	.0016	.0016	.0015	.0015	.0014	.0014
3.0	.0013	.0013	.0013	.0012	.0012	.0011	.0011	.0011	.0010	.0010

EXHIBIT 21-5

Relationship Between Normal Distribution of X and Standardized Value of z

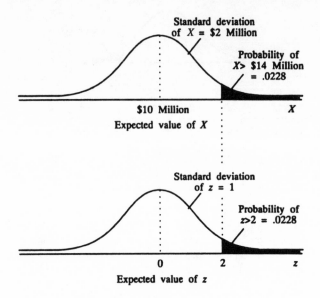

probability of obtaining a value greater than $14 million is .0228, the probability of obtaining a portfolio value less than $14 million is $1 - .0228$, or 97.72%. This is expressed as follows:

$$P(X < \$14 \text{ million}) = P(z < 2) = 1 - P(z > 2) = 1 - .0228 = .9772.$$

Illustration 21-10   Let's look now at how to obtain the probability of obtaining some value between the expected value and a value to the right of the expected value. Suppose the portfolio manager wants to know the probability of obtaining a portfolio value between $10 million (the expected value) and $14 million. From the second property of the normal curve explained above, the probability of obtaining a value greater than the expected value is 50%. Since the shaded area to the right of the standardized value 2, which corresponds to a portfolio value of $14 million, is .0228, the probability of obtaining a portfolio value between $10 million and $14 million must be equal to the difference between the entire area to the right of the expected value, which is .5, and the area to the right of 2, which is .0228. Therefore, the probability of obtaining a value between $10 million and $14 million is .4772 or 47.72%. This is expressed as follows:

$$P(\$10 \text{ million} < X < \$14 \text{ million}) = .5 - .0228 = .4772.$$

Illustration 21-11   Suppose that instead of determining the probability of obtaining a value between the expected value and some value to its right, the probability of obtaining a portfolio value between $11 million and $14 million is desired. This corresponds to the probability of obtaining a standardized value between .5 and 2. Thus, the probability can be found by subtracting the two probabilities. The probability of obtaining a portfolio value between $11 million and $14 million is 30.85% – 2.28% or 28.57%.

Illustration 21-12 The tricky aspect of using the normal distribution table is dealing with values that are less than the expected value; i.e., values that are to the left of the expected value. For example, suppose the probability of obtaining a portfolio value less than $6 million is desired. The standardized value corresponding to $6 million is –2. There is no –2 in Exhibit 21-4; the table gives only positive values for the standardized value, because the distribution is symmetric around the expected value. The symmetric distribution means that the area in the tail of the distribution corresponding to a standardized value of 2 can be used. Hence, the probability of obtaining a portfolio value less than $6 million is 2.28%.

Illustration 21-13 Suppose the portfolio manager wants to know the probability of obtaining a portfolio value between $6 million and $11 million. Note that the expected value ($10 million) is between these two values. The probability can be found as follows (see Exhibit 21-6). First, the probability of obtaining a portfolio value between $10 million and $11 million is calculated by finding the probability of obtaining a portfolio value greater than $11 million and subtracting it from 50%. According to Illustration 21-11, the probability of obtaining a portfolio value

EXHIBIT 21-6

**Illustration of Determining How to Find the Probability of *X*
between $6 Million and $11 Million**

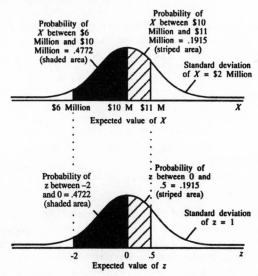

greater than $11 million is 30.85%. Hence, the probability of obtaining a portfolio value between $10 million and $11 million is 19.15% (.5 – .3085). Next, the probability of obtaining a portfolio value between $6 million and $10 million must be determined. This is accomplished by subtracting the probability of obtaining a portfolio value less than $6 million from 50%. Since the probability of obtaining a portfolio value less than $6 million is 2.28% (according to Illustration 21-12), the probability of obtaining a portfolio value between $6 million and $10 million is 47.72% (.5 – .0228). The probability of obtaining a portfolio value between $6 million and $11 million is then the sum of the probabilities of obtaining a value between $6 million and $10 million and $10 million and $11 million: 66.87% (47.72% + 19.15%).

Illustration 21-14   Consider once again the probability distribution for the 1-year total return for a portfolio with an expected value of 7% and a standard deviation of 4% in Illustration 21-5. Suppose that 1-year Treasury bills are offering a total return of 4%. Assuming that the probability distribution is normal, the investor wants to know the probability that the return will be less than the 1-year Treasury bill rate of 4%. If R is a random variable representing the 1-year total return, then

$$E(R) = 7\% \quad \text{and} \quad \text{std}(R) = 4\%.$$

The investor wants to know the probability that R is less than 4%; that is, $P(R < 4\%)$. The standardized value corresponding to R equal to 4% is

$$z = \frac{4\% - 7\%}{4\%} = -.75.$$

Therefore, the investor wants to know

$$P(R < 4\%) = P(z < -.75) = P(z > .75) = 22.66\%.$$

Illustration 21-15   Suppose the portfolio manager in the previous illustration will receive a bonus if the portfolio's 1-year return exceeds the 1-year Treasury return by 500 basis points. The probability that this will occur can be expressed as

$$P(R > 7\% + 5\%) \text{ or } P(R > 12\%).$$

The corresponding standardized value is

$$z = \frac{12\% - 7\%}{4\%} = 1.25.$$

Thus, the probability sought is

$$P(R > 12\%) = P(z > 1.25) = 10.56\%.$$

Illustration 21-16   Suppose that a manager is concerned with extreme losses occurring. More specifically, assume that a manager defines an extreme loss as one occurring with a probability of 5%. What is the amount of the extreme loss if the expected value of the portfolio return is $40,000 and the standard deviation is $100,000? To see how Exhibit 21-4 can be used to answer this question, look at the body of the exhibit, which indicates probabilities. Search for a standardized value where a probability of close to 5% is shown. For a standardized value of 1.65, the probability is 4.95%. Similarly, for a standardized value of –1.65, the probability is 4.95%. This means that a standardized value below –1.65 has a probability of occurring about 5% of the time. We can translate this into an extreme loss value as follows:

$$\frac{\text{Extreme loss value} - \text{Expected value}}{\text{Standard deviation}} = -1.65.$$

For our illustration,

$$\frac{\text{Extreme loss value} - \$40,000}{\$100,000} = -1.65.$$

Solving for the extreme loss value, we get –$125,000.

Thus, if the manager defines an extreme loss as one in which there is a 5% probability of realizing a value equal to that amount or greater, the extreme loss value is –$125,000. Expressed in another way, this means that there is a 95% probability of not realizing a loss on the position greater than $125,000.

Illustration 21-17   Suppose that the manager sets the probability at 1% rather than 5% as in the previous illustration. Searching Exhibit 21-4, we find a standardized value of 2.33. Thus, the probability of getting a standardized value of less than –2.33 is 1%. The extreme loss value is then

$$\frac{\text{Extreme loss value} - \$40,000}{\$100,000} = -2.33.$$

Solving the above equation, we determine that the extreme loss value is –$193,000. Thus, the probability of realizing a loss greater than or equal to $193,000 is 1%. The probability of not realizing a loss greater than $193,000 is 99%.

Confidence Intervals

When a range for the possible values of a random variable and a probability associated with that range are calculated, the range is referred to as a *confidence interval*. In general, for a normal distribution, the confidence interval is calculated as follows:

(Expected value – Standardized value × Standard deviation)

to (Expected value + Standardized value × Standard deviation).

The standardized value indicates the number of standard deviations away from the expected value and corresponds to a particular probability. For example, suppose a manager wants a confidence interval of 95%. This means that there will be 2.5% in each tail. From Exhibit 21-4, we see that a standardized value with a 2.5% probability is 1.96. Thus, a 95% confidence interval is

(Expected value – 1.96 × Standard deviation)

to (Expected value + 1.96 × Standard deviation).

Illustration 21-18   Suppose that a manager wants to construct a confidence interval for the rate of return on a portfolio. Assuming that the rate of return is normally distributed with an expected value of 7% and a standard deviation of 4%, then a 95% confidence interval would be

$$(7\% - 1.96 \times 4\%) \text{ to } (7\% + 1.96 \times 4\%) \text{ or } -0.84\% \text{ to } 14.84\%.$$

Notice that the larger the standard deviation, the wider the confidence interval. For a confidence interval with a smaller probability, the standardized value is smaller and therefore the confidence interval is narrower for a given standard deviation.

NON-NORMAL DISTRIBUTIONS

The normal distribution is only one type of probability distribution. There are statistical tests that can be performed to determine whether a probability distribution can be best characterized as a normal probability distribution. A discussion of these tests is beyond the scope of this chapter.

Similarly, a probability distribution might be best characterized as a non-normal distribution like the two shown in Exhibits 21-7. Such distributions are referred to as *skewed distributions*. The first skewed distribution shown in the exhibit is one which has a long tail on the

EXHIBIT 21-7

Skewed Distributions

(a) Distribution Skewed to the Right (Positively Skewed)

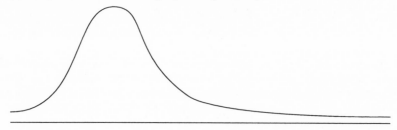

(b) Distribution Skewed to the Left (Negatively Skewed)

right-hand side of the distribution. Such a distribution is referred to as a *positively skewed distribution*. The second skewed distribution in Exhibit 21-7 has a long tail on the left-hand side of the distribution and is called a *negatively skewed distribution*.

The skewness of a distribution can be measured. In the case of a discrete distribution for a random variable X, it is

$$\text{Skewness } (X) = \frac{[X_1 - E(X)]^3 \, P_1 + [X_2 - E(X)]^3 \, P_2 + \cdots + [X_n - E(X)]^3 \, P_n}{[\text{Std}(X)]^3}.$$

A normal distribution has a skewness equal to 0.

A distribution may have a higher peak around the expected value than does the normal distribution. *Kurtosis* is a measure of the peakedness of a probability distribution. Distributions with a high peak are said to be *leptokurtic*; distributions with a flat peak are said to be *platykurtic*. The kurtosis measure for a discrete probability distribution X is

$$\text{Kurtosis } (X) = \frac{[X_1 - E(X)]^4 \, P_1 + [X_2 - E(X)]^4 \, P_2 + \cdots + [X_n - E(X)]^4 \, P_n}{[\text{Std}(X)]^4}.$$

A kurtosis value of 3 means that a distribution is neither leptokurtic (i.e., excessively peaked) or platykurtic (i.e., excessively flat).

RETURN DISTRIBUTIONS FOR BONDS

In many applications in bond portfolio management, the random variable of interest is the rate of return on some bond. For bonds, there is a lower limit on the loss. For Treasury securities, the limit depends on how high rates can rise. Since Treasury rates have never exceeded 15%, this places a lower bound on a negative return from holding a bond. However, there is maximum return. Assuming that negative interest rates are not possible, the maximum price for a bond is the undiscounted value of the cash flow (i.e., the sum of the interest payments and maturity value). In turn, this determines the maximum return. On balance, government bond return distributions are negatively skewed, as JP Morgan reports.[2] Moreover, government bond returns exhibit fat tails and a peakedness greater than predicted by the normal distribution.

One way to overcome the problem of negative skewedness of bond returns is to convert returns into the logarithm of returns. Using logarithms of returns tends to pull in the outlier negative returns resulting in a distribution that is approximately normal. The resulting probability distribution of logarithm returns is said to be *lognormally distributed*.

For any probability distribution, it is important to assess whether the value of a random variable in one period is affected by the value that the random variable took on in a prior period. Casting this in terms of returns, it is important to know whether the return that can be realized today is affected by the return in a prior period. The terms *serial correlation* and *autocorrelation* are used to describe the correlation between the return in different periods. JP Morgan's analysis suggests that there is only a small positive serial correlation for government bond returns.[3]

---

2 *RiskMetrics*™—*Technical Document* (New York: JP Morgan), May 26, 1995, p. 48.
3 Ibid.

CALCULATING HISTORICAL INTEREST-RATE VOLATILITY: AN APPLICATION OF THE STANDARD DEVIATION

The standard deviation is a measure of the variation of a random variable around its mean or expected value. It is commonly used as a measure of the volatility of prices or yields. Because volatility plays such a key role in fixed income portfolio management and the valuation of fixed income options, we discuss how to calculate the standard deviation from historical data.[4]

Calculating Standard Deviation from Historical Data

We have shown already how to calculate the standard deviation and variance of a random variable given a probability distribution. The variance of a random variable using historical data is calculated using the following formula:

$$\text{Variance} = \sum_{t=1}^{T} \frac{(X_t - \overline{X})^2}{T-1}$$

and then

$$\text{Standard deviation} = \sqrt{\text{Variance}},$$

where

    T = The number of observations in the sample;
    X_t = Observation t on variable X;
    $\overline{X}$ = The average sample value for variable X.

Our focus will be on yield volatility. More specifically, we are interested in the percentage change in daily yields. So, X_t will denote the percentage change in yield from day t and the prior day, $t-1$. If we let y_t denote the yield on day t and y_{t-1} denote the yield on day $t-1$, then X_t (which is the natural logarithm of percentage change in yield between 2 days) can be expressed as

$$X_t = 100[Ln(y_t/y_{t-1})].$$

For example, on October 18, 1995, the Treasury 30-year zero-coupon rate was 6.555% and on October 19, 1995, it was 6.593%. Therefore, the natural logarithm of X for October 19, 1995 is

$$X = 100 [Ln(6.592/6.555)] = 0.57804.$$

Illustration 21-19   To illustrate how to calculate a daily standard deviation from historical data, consider the data in Exhibit 21-8 which shows the yield on Treasury 30-year zeros from

---

4   In addition to historical volatility, market participants calculate *implied volatility*. This value is estimated from the observed price of an option which is assumed to be fairly priced according to some assumed option pricing model and the other inputs in an option pricing model.

EXHIBIT 21-8

Calculation of Daily Standard Deviation Based on 25 Daily Observations for Treasury 30-Year Zeros (October 8, 1995 to November 12, 1995)

t	Date	y_t	$X_t =$ $100[Ln(y_t/y_{t-1})]$	$(X_t - \bar{X})^2$
0	08-Oct-95	6.694		
1	09-Oct-95	6.699	0.06720	0.02599
2	10-Oct-95	6.710	0.16407	0.06660
3	11-Oct-95	6.675	−0.52297	0.18401
4	12-Oct-95	6.555	−1.81311	2.95875
5	15-Oct-95	6.583	0.42625	0.27066
6	16-Oct-95	6.569	−0.21290	0.01413
7	17-Oct-95	6.583	0.21290	0.09419
8	18-Oct-95	6.555	−0.42625	0.11038
9	19-Oct-95	6.593	0.57804	0.45164
10	22-Oct-95	6.620	0.40869	0.25270
11	23-Oct-95	6.568	−0.78860	0.48246
12	24-Oct-95	6.575	0.10652	0.04021
13	25-Oct-95	6.646	1.07406	1.36438
14	26-Oct-95	6.607	−0.58855	0.24457
15	29-Oct-95	6.612	0.07565	0.02878
16	30-Oct-95	6.575	−0.56116	0.21823
17	31-Oct-95	6.552	−0.35042	0.06575
18	01-Nov-95	6.515	−0.56631	0.22307
19	02-Nov-95	6.533	0.27590	0.13684
20	05-Nov-95	6.543	0.15295	0.06099
21	06-Nov-95	6.559	0.24424	0.11441
22	07-Nov-95	6.500	−0.90360	0.65543
23	08-Nov-95	6.546	0.70520	0.63873
24	09-Nov-95	6.589	0.65474	0.56063
25	12-Nov-95	6.539	−0.76173	0.44586
	Total		−2.35025	9.7094094

$$\text{Sample mean} = \bar{X} = \frac{-2.35025}{25} = -0.09401.$$

$$\text{Variance} = \frac{9.7094094}{25-1} = 0.4045587.$$

$$\text{Std} = \sqrt{0.4045587} = 0.6360493.$$

October 8, 1995, to November 12, 1995, in the second column.[5] From the 26 observations, 25 days of daily percentage yield changes are calculated in the third column. The fourth column shows the square of the deviations of the observations from the mean. The bottom of Exhibit 21-8 shows the calculation of the daily mean for the 25 observations, the variance, and the standard deviation. The daily standard deviation is 0.6360493%.

The daily standard deviation will vary depending on the 25 days selected. For example, the daily yields from August 20, 1995, to September 24, 1996, were used to generate the 25 daily percentage yield changes. The computed daily standard deviation was 0.8452714%.

In our illustration, we used 25 observations for the daily percentage change in yield. The appropriate number depends on the situation at hand. For example, traders concerned with overnight positions might use the 10 most recent days (i.e., 2 weeks). A fixed income portfolio manager who is concerned with longer term volatility might use 25 days (about 1 month). The selection of the number of observations can have a significant effect on the calculated daily standard deviation.

The daily standard deviation can be annualized by multiplying it by the square root of the number of days in a year. That is,

$$\text{Daily standard deviation} \times \sqrt{\text{Number of days in a year}}.$$

The assumption in going from a daily standard deviation to an annual standard deviation using the above formula is that serial correlation is not a problem.

Market practice varies with respect to the number of days in the year that should be used in the annualizing formula above. Typically, either 250 days, 260 days, or 365 days are used.

Thus, in calculating an annual standard deviation, the manager must decide on (1) the number of daily observations to use and (2) the number of days in the year to use to annualize the daily standard deviation. Exhibit 21-9 shows the difference in the annual standard deviation for the daily standard deviation based on the different number of observations and using 250 days, 260 days, and 365 days to annualize.

Forecasting Yield Volatility

In practice, it is necessary to forecast yield volatility. There are several issues in forecasting this measure in addition to the number of observations that should be used and the number of days for annualizing the daily standard deviation. The first question is what mean should be used in the calculation. In the calculation of historical volatility, the sample mean is used. There are arguments that support the view that a mean value of 0 should be used. In this case, the variance reduces to

$$\text{Variance} = \sum_{t=1}^{T} \frac{X_t^2}{T-1}.$$

---

5   This illustration is taken from Chapter 6 of Frank J. Fabozzi, *Measuring and Controlling Interest Rate Risk* (New Hope, PA: Frank J. Fabozzi Associates, 1996).

EXHIBIT 21-9

Comparison of Daily and Annual Volatility for Different Numbers of Observations (ending date November 12, 1995) for Treasury 30-Year Zeros

No. of Observations	Daily std. (%)	Annualized std. (%)		
		250 days	260 days	365 days
683	0.4901505%	7.75%	7.90%	9.36%
60	0.6282858	9.93	10.13	12.00
25	0.6360493	10.06	10.26	12.15
10	0.6242041	9.87	10.06	11.93

The second question is whether each observation should be given the same weight. There is reason to suspect that market participants give greater weight to recent movements in yield or price when determining volatility. To give greater importance to more recent information, observations further in the past should be given less weight. This can be done by revising the variance (assuming a mean of 0) as follows:

$$\text{Variance} = \sum_{t-1}^{T} \frac{W_t X_t^2}{T - 1},$$

where W_t is the weight assigned to observation t such that the sum of the weights is equal to 1 (i.e., $\sum W_t = 1$) and the further the observation is from today, the lower the weight.

The weights should be assigned so that the forecasted volatility reacts faster to a recent major market movement and declines gradually as we move away from any major market movement. There are possible weighting schemes that would accomplish this. One such possible weighting is to use an *exponential moving average*. This is the approach employed by JP Morgan in RiskMetrics™. The formula for the weight W_t in an exponential moving average is

$$W_t = (1 - \beta) \, \beta^t,$$

where β is a value between 0 and 1. The observations are arrayed so that the closest observation is $t = 1$, the second closest is $t = 2$, etc.

For example, if β is 0.90, then the weight for the closest observation ($t = 1$) is

$$W_1 = (1 - 0.90)(0.90)^1 = 0.09.$$

For $t = 5$ and $\beta = 0.90$, the weight is

$$W_5 = (1 - 0.90)(0.90)^5 = 0.05905.$$

Recently, a popular method for forecasting yield volatility is using a statistical model called an *a*uto*r*egressive *c*onditional *h*eteroscedasticity or ARCH model. The term "conditional" means that the value of the variance depends on or is conditional on some random variable. The term "heteroscedasticity" means that the variance is not equal for a given random variable. A discussion of the ARCH models and its variants is beyond the scope of this chapter.[6]

Interpreting the Annualized Standard Deviation

What does it mean if the annual standard deviation or annual yield volatility for long-term bonds is, say, 15%? It means that if the prevailing yield on long-term bonds is 7%, the standard deviation of long-term yields in 1 year is 105 basis points (7% times 15%).

Assuming that the yield volatility is approximately normally distributed, this means there is a 68.3% probability that the yield on long-term bonds 1 year from now will be within one standard deviation below and above 7%. Thus, there is a 68.3% probability that the yield on long-term bonds 1 year from now will be between 5.95% and 8.05%. Similarly, from the properties of a normal distribution, we know that there is a 95.5% probability that the yield level on long-term bonds 1 year from now will be within a range of two standard deviations (between 4.9% and 9.10%); there is a 99.7% probability it will be within a range of three standard deviations (3.85% and 10.15%).

Notice that the higher the yield volatility is, the wider is the range of the yield level in the future. This means there is greater uncertainty about the future yield level. For example, if the yield volatility is 20% rather than 15%, this translates into a yield volatility of 140 basis points (20% times 7%). Assuming a normal distribution, there is a 68.3% probability that the yield 1 year from now will be between 5.6% and 8.4%; a 95.5% probability that it will be between 4.2% and 9.8%; and a 99.7% probability that it will be between 2.8% and 11.2%.

Empirical evidence suggests that daily percentage yield changes are approximately normally distributed. This can be seen in Exhibit 21-10, which shows the distribution of daily percentage yield changes for the 30-year Constant Maturity Treasury between January 1982 and January 1988.

VALUE-AT-RISK FRAMEWORK

An application of normal probability theory and the concepts of duration and yield volatility can be tied together to provide insight into the risk of a portfolio or position. Specifically, suppose that a manager wants to make the following statement: "There is a $Y\%$ probability that the loss in value from a position will be less than $\$A$ in the next T days." The $\$A$ in this statement are popularly referred to as the *value at risk* (VaR). The VaR can be determined from probability theory assuming a normal distribution, the expected value and standard deviation of the distribution, the specified probability ($Y\%$), and the number of days (T).

The VaR can be exhibited graphically. Exhibit 21-11 shows a normal probability distribution for the change in the value of a position over the next T days. The VaR is the loss of $\$A$

---

6 For an excellent overview of the ARCH model and its extensions, see Robert F. Engle, "Statistical Models for Financial Volatility," *Financial Analysts Journal* (January–February 1993), pp. 72–78. A summary is also provided in Fabozzi, *Measuring and Controlling Interest Rate Risk*, Chapter 6.

EXHIBIT 21–10

30-Year Constant Maturity Treasury, Distribution of 1-Day Percentage Yield Changes (1/82–1/88)

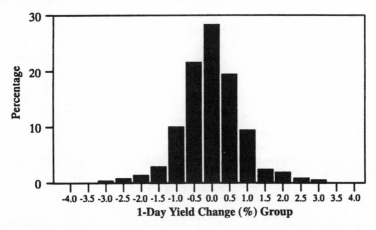

Source: This illustration originally appeared as Figure 5 in William J. Curtin, Nicholas C. Letica, and Andrew Lawrence, "Mortgage-Backed Securities Volatility Risk Management," in Frank J. Fabozzi (ed.), *Managing Institutional Assets* (New York: Harper & Row, 1990).

EXHIBIT 21–11

Graphical Depiction of Value at Risk

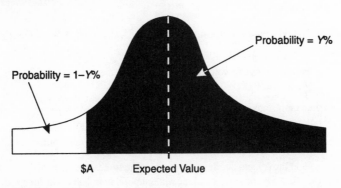

$A = Value at risk

where the probability to the right of that value is $Y\%$; equivalently, the VaR is where the probability to the left of that value (i.e., the probability in the tail) is equal to $1 - Y\%$.

Let's see how we obtain the VaR using a numerical example. Suppose that the probability distribution for the change in value of a position over the next 4 days is normally distributed with an expected value of 0 and a standard deviation of $20,000. Assume also that the probability specified by the manager is 95%. From the normal distribution table (Exhibit 21-4), the standardized value that will give a probability in the tail of 5% can be found. This is done by searching the table for where the probability is 5%. From Exhibit 21-4, this is where the standardized value is about 1.65.

The standardized value indicates the number of standard deviations above or below the expected value. The VaR is the value which is 1.65 standard deviations *below* the expected value. Since the expected value of the change in value of a position over the next 4 days is 0 and the standard deviation is $20,000, then the VaR is $33,000. Therefore, there is a 95% probability that the loss in value from a position will be less than $33,000 in the next 4 days.

Alternatively, the VaR can be expressed as follows: "There is a 1 − *Y*% probability that the maximum loss in value over the next *T* days will be greater than $*A*." In our example, there is a 5% probability that the maximum loss in value over the next 4 days will be greater than $33,000.

VaR begins with measuring the *daily earnings at risk* (DEaR). This is simply the value at risk for a day. For a single position in a bond, DEaR is measured as follows:

   DEaR = Market value of position
              × Sensitivity of the value of position to a 1-basis-point adverse change in yield
              × Adverse yield movement per day (in basis points).

Since the duration of a position is the approximate percentage change for a 100-basis-point change in yield, dividing the duration by 100 gives the percentage change in value for a 100-basis-point change in yield. That is,

   Percentage change in value for a 100-basis-point change in yield
      = Duration/100

Dividing by 10,000 gives the percentage change in value for a 1-basis-point change in yield. That is,

   Percentage change in value for a 1-basis-point change in yield
      = Duration/10,000.

DEaR can then be restated as follows:
   DEaR = Market value of position × Duration/10,000
              × Adverse yield movement per day (in basis points)

The adverse yield movement per day is a based on the forecasted daily yield volatility and the probability specified. The adverse yield movement per day is 100 times the product of the forecasted daily standard deviation of yield changes and the standardized value from the normal distribution. That is,

   Adverse yield movement per day (in basis points)
      = Forecasted daily standard deviation
         × Standardized value from normal distribution × 100.

Illustration 21-20   Suppose that the forecasted daily standard deviation for the yield change of the Treasury 30-year zero-coupon bond is 0.63%. Assuming a normal probability distribution, then the standardized value is 1.65 if a probability of 95% is sought for the VaR. Therefore, the adverse yield movement per day is

$$\text{Adverse yield movement per day} = 0.0063 \times 1.65 \times 100$$

$$= 10.395 \text{ basis points}$$

If the market value of a position of Treasury 30-year zero-coupon bonds is $5,000,000 and its duration is 4, then the DEaR is

$$\text{DEaR} = \$5,000,000 \times 4/10,000 \times 10.395$$

$$= \$20,790.$$

Given the DEaR, the VaR is calculated as follows:

$$\text{VaR} = \text{DEaR} \times \sqrt{\text{Days expected until position can be neutralized}}.$$

where "days expected until position can be neutralized" are the number of days expected necessary to neutralize the risk of the position. Thus, for a trading position which can be neutralized within 1 day, the VaR is the same as the DEaR.

SUMMARY

In this chapter the fundamentals of probability theory are explained and applied. A random variable is a variable that can take on more than one possible value in the future. A probability distribution gives the probability of obtaining the values that the random variable can realize. One particular type of probability distribution is the normal distribution.

For all probability distributions, an expected value and a standard deviation (variance) can be computed. The expected value is the weighted average of the distribution. The standard deviation measures the dispersion of the possible outcomes around the expected value. When using a normal distribution, the random variable must be normalized so that the expected value is 0 and the standard deviation is 1.

Using probability theory, a confidence interval for an outcome can be computed. A confidence interval gives a range for possible values of a random variable and a probability associated with that range.

Not all distributions are normal distributions. A skewed distribution is a probability distribution which is not symmetric around the expected value. A positively skewed distribution is one in which there is a long tail to the right; a negatively skewed distribution is one in which there is a long tail to the left.

The standard deviation is used to measure yield volatility from historical data. Typically, volatility is measured as the percentage change in daily yields. The daily standard deviation is then annualized. There are various market conventions used to annualize the daily standard deviation. When forecasting yield volatility there are several issues that must be addressed.

An application of probability theory is the value-at-risk framework. The value at risk is the amount that a loss is not expected to exceed over some time period with a specified probability. The value at risk is determined from probability theory assuming a normal distribution, the expected value and standard deviation of the distribution, a specified probability, and the number of days.

22

⑥ SIMULATION

The performance of a fixed-income portfolio depends on the outcome of many variables. These influences include the magnitude of the change in Treasury rates, the spread between non-Treasury and Treasury securities, changes in the shape of the yield curve, changes in the quality rating of individual corporate bond issues, and actual prepayment speeds in the case of mortgage-backed securities. Moreover, changes in every random variable may proceed along a substantial number of possible paths. These eventualities make it impractical to evaluate all possible combinations of outcomes in order to assess the risks associated with a portfolio.

In this chapter, we explain a technique called *simulation* for tackling such situations. We describe the steps in a simulation and use a hypothetical bond portfolio management example to illustrate the procedure. We also demonstrate an actual application to a mortgage-backed security problem.

MONTE CARLO SIMULATION

Suppose that a portfolio manager wants to assess the performance of a portfolio over a 1-year investment horizon. Suppose further that the portfolio's performance will be determined by the actual outcome for each of nine random variables and that each of the nine random variables has seven possible outcomes. There are thus 4,782,969 (9^7) possible outcomes, representing all possible combinations of the nine random variables. Furthermore, each of the 4,782,969 outcomes has a different probability of occurrence.

One approach for a portfolio manager is to take the "best guess" for each random variable and determine the impact on performance. The best-guess value for each random variable is usually the expected value of the random variable.[1] There are serious problems with this short-cut approach. To understand its shortcomings, suppose the probability associated with the

---

1 The expected value of a random variable is explained in Chapter 21.

best guess for each random variable is 75%. If the probability distribution for each random variable is independently distributed, the probability of occurrence for the best-guess result would be only 7.5%. At this level of probability, no portfolio manager would have a great deal of confidence in this best-guess result.

Between the extremes of enumerating and evaluating all possible combinations and the best-guess approach is the simulation approach. Simulation is less a model than a procedure or algorithm. The solutions obtained do not represent an optimal solution to a problem. Rather, simulation provides information about a problem so that a portfolio manager can assess the risks of a particular course of action. Because it offers a flexible approach to dealing with business problems, simulation is probably one of the tools most often used.

There are many types of simulation techniques. When probability distributions are assigned to the random variables, the simulation technique is known as a *Monte Carlo simulation*—named after the famous gambling spot on the French Riviera. Monte Carlo simulation enables portfolio managers to determine the statistical properties of a problem that they face. Armed with this information, a portfolio manager can select the most prudent course of action. Monte Carlo simulation is also used in the pricing of bonds with embedded options.

STEPS FOR MONTE CARLO SIMULATION

There are 12 steps in a Monte Carlo simulation:

Step 1   The performance measure must be specified. The performance measure may be, for example, total return over some investment horizon or net interest (spread) income.

Step 2   The problem under investigation must be expressed mathematically, including all important variables and their interactions. The variables in the mathematical model will be either *deterministic* or *random*. A deterministic variable can take on only one value; a random variable can take on more than one value.

Step 3   For those variables that are random variables, a probability distribution for each must be specified.

Step 4   For each variable whose probability distribution must be specified, the probability distribution must be converted into a cumulative probability distribution.

Step 5   For each random variable, representative numbers must be assigned on the basis of the cumulative probability distribution to each possible outcome specified.

Step 6   A random number must be obtained for each random variable.

Step 7   For each random number, the corresponding value of the random variable must be determined.

Step 8   The corresponding value of each random variable found in the previous step must be used to determine the value of the performance measure developed in Step 2.

Step 9   The value of the performance measure found in Step 8 must be recorded.

Step 10   Steps 6 through 9 must be repeated many times, say, 100 to 1,000 times. The repetition of Steps 6 through 9 is known as a *trial*.

Step 11   The values for the performance measure for each trial recorded in Step 9 become the basis for construction of a probability distribution and cumulative probability distribution.

Step 12   The cumulative probability distribution constructed in Step 11 is analyzed. This is done by calculating summary statistics such as the mean, standard deviation, and the range.

Generating Random Numbers

Before we illustrate these steps, we need to explain how random numbers are obtained in Step 6. Any procedure used must have the following property: for each number that may possibly be selected, the probability of selection must be equal.

There are several procedures that can be used to generate random numbers. First, suppose that two-digit random numbers from 00 to 99 are wanted. The portfolio manager could write each number on a piece of paper of equal size, put it in a bag, shake the bag, and then pick out one piece of paper. The number that turns up on that pick is the random number for the random variable. As long as each piece of paper has an equal chance of being selected, the procedure is acceptable for generating random numbers. For each trial, however, the paper picked in the previous trial must be put back into the bag. If it is not, each piece of paper would no longer have an equal chance of being selected in a subsequent trial.

Because there are many instances where random numbers are needed, *random number tables* have been prepared that provide them. Exhibit 22-1 is an example. To obtain random numbers from this table, the portfolio manager can start anywhere in the table (providing the starting point is selected at random) and move in any direction to obtain a subsequent number. Start right at the beginning of the table and select numbers moving down the rows. Suppose that the portfolio manager wants to select five two-digit random numbers between 0 and 99. The random numbers from Exhibit 22-1 would be 23, 5, 14, 38, and 97. If five four-digit random numbers between 0 and 8000 are sought, the following random numbers would be selected from Exhibit 22-1: 2315, 554, 1487, 3897, and 1174. Notice that we skip the fifth random number in the table—9731—because this number is more than the upper limit of 8000.

Spreadsheets and other software include add-on features that can be used to generate random numbers. The function *@RAND*, for example, in LOTUS 123, will generate a random number between 0 and 1. To get a two-digit number, the value generated by *@RAND* can be multiplied by 100.

ILLUSTRATION OF THE STEPS OF MONTE CARLO SIMULATION

Consider a portfolio manager who has invested $15 million in three bonds. Exhibit 22-2 specifies the three hypothetical bonds and the relevant information about each issue. For purposes of our illustration, each bond is assumed to pay its next coupon 6 months from now. The portfolio manager wants to simulate the 6-month period total return assuming that the only

E X H I B I T 22–1

Random Number Table (First and Second Thousands)

First Thousand

	1–4	5–8	9–12	13–16	17–20	21–24	25–28	29–32	33–36	37–40
1	23 15	75 48	50 01	83 72	59 93	76 24	97 08	86 95	23 03	67 44
2	05 54	55 50	43 10	53 74	35 08	90 61	18 37	44 10	96 22	13 43
3	14 87	16 03	50 32	40 43	62 23	50 05	10 03	22 11	54 38	08 34
4	38 97	67 49	51 94	05 17	58 53	78 80	59 01	94 32	42 87	16 95
5	97 31	26 17	18 99	75 53	08 70	94 25	12 58	41 54	88 21	05 13
6	11 74	26 93	81 44	33 93	08 72	32 79	73 31	18 22	64 70	68 50
7	43 36	12 88	59 11	01 64	56 23	93 00	90 04	99 43	64 07	40 36
8	93 80	62 04	78 38	26 80	44 91	55 75	11 89	32 58	47 55	25 71
9	49 54	01 31	81 08	42 98	41 87	69 53	83 96	61 77	73 80	95 27
10	36 76	87 26	33 37	94 82	15 69	41 95	96 86	70 45	27 48	38 80
11	07 09	25 23	92 24	62 71	26 07	06 55	84 53	44 67	33 84	53 20
12	43 31	00 10	81 44	86 38	03 07	52 55	51 61	48 89	74 29	46 47
13	61 57	00 63	60 06	17 36	37 75	63 14	89 51	23 35	01 74	69 93
14	31 35	28 37	99 10	77 91	89 41	31 57	97 64	48 62	58 48	69 19
15	57 04	88 65	26 27	79 59	36 82	90 52	95 65	46 35	06 53	22 54
16	09 24	34 42	00 68	72 10	71 37	30 72	97 57	56 09	29 82	76 50
17	97 95	53 50	18 40	89 48	83 29	52 23	08 25	21 22	53 26	15 87
18	93 73	25 95	70 43	78 19	88 85	56 67	16 68	26 95	99 64	45 69
19	72 62	11 12	25 00	92 26	82 64	35 66	65 94	34 71	68 75	18 67
20	61 02	07 44	18 45	37 12	07 94	95 91	73 78	66 99	53 61	93 78
21	97 83	98 54	74 33	05 59	17 18	45 47	35 41	44 22	03 42	30 00
22	89 16	09 71	92 22	23 29	06 37	35 05	54 54	89 88	43 81	63 61
23	25 96	68 82	20 62	87 17	92 65	02 82	35 28	62 84	91 95	48 83
24	81 44	33 17	19 05	04 95	48 06	74 69	00 75	67 65	01 71	65 45
25	11 32	25 49	31 42	36 23	43 86	08 62	49 76	67 42	24 52	32 45

Second Thousand

	1–4	5–8	9–12	13–16	17–20	21–24	25–28	29–32	33–36	37–40
1	64 75	58 38	85 84	12 22	59 20	17 69	61 56	55 95	04 59	59 47
2	10 30	25 22	89 77	43 63	44 30	38 11	24 90	67 07	34 82	33 28
3	71 01	79 84	95 51	30 85	03 74	66 59	10 28	87 53	76 56	91 49
4	60 01	25 56	05 88	41 03	48 79	79 65	59 01	69 78	80 00	36 66
5	37 33	09 46	56 49	16 14	28 02	48 27	45 47	55 44	55 36	50 90

Continued

EXHIBIT 22-1

Concluded

				Second Thousand (continued)					
1–4	*5–8*	*9–12*	*13–16*	*17–20*	*21–24*	*25–28*	*29–32*	*33–36*	*37–40*
6 47 86	98 70	01 31	59 11	22 73	60 62	61 28	22 34	69 16	12 12
7 38 04	04 27	37 64	16 78	95 78	39 32	34 93	24 88	43 43	87 06
8 73 50	83 09	03 83	05 48	00 78	36 66	93 02	95 56	46 04	53 36
9 32 62	34 64	74 84	06 10	43 24	20 62	83 73	19 32	35 64	39 69
10 97 59	19 95	49 36	63 03	51 06	62 06	99 29	75 95	32 05	77 34
11 74 01	23 19	55 59	79 09	69 82	66 22	42 40	15 96	74 90	75 89
12 56 75	42 64	57 13	35 10	50 14	90 96	63 36	74 69	09 63	34 88
13 49 80	04 99	08 54	83 12	19 98	08 52	82 63	72 92	92 36	50 26
14 43 58	48 96	47 24	87 85	66 70	00 22	15 01	93 99	59 16	23 77
15 16 65	37 96	64 60	32 57	13 01	35 74	28 36	36 73	05 88	72 29
16 48 50	26 90	55 65	32 25	87 48	31 44	68 02	37 31	25 29	63 67
17 96.76	55 46	92 36	31 68	62 30	48 29	63 83	52 23	81 66	40 94
18 38 92	36 15	50 80	35 78	17 84	23 44	41 24	63 33	99 22	81 28
19 77 95	88 16	94 25	22 50	55 87	51 07	30 10	70 60	21 86	19 61
20 17 92	82 80	65 25	58 60	87 71	02 64	18 50	64 65	79 64	81 70
21 94 03	68 59	78 02	31 80	44 99	41 05	41 05	31 87	43 12	15 96
22 47 46	06 04	79 56	23 04	84 17	14 37	28 51	67 27	55 80	03 68
23 47 85	65 60	88 51	99 28	34 39	40 64	41 71	70 13	46 31	82 88
24 57 61	63 46	53 92	29 86	20 18	10 37	57 65	15 62	98 69	07 56
25 08 30	09 27	04 66	75 26	66 10	57 18	87 91	07 54	22 22	20 13

EXHIBIT 22-2

Hypothetical Three-Bond Portfolio for Simulation Illustration

Bond	Maturity (years)	Coupon (%)	Price ($)	Par ($)	YTM (%)
Treasury	5.5	6.0%	$100	$5 million	6.0%
BBB-corporate	15.5	9.0	100	4 million	9.0
BBB-corporate	25.5	10.5	100	6 million	10.5

EXHIBIT 22–3

Information for Monte Carlo Simulation of a Three-Bond Portfolio–Random Variable: Treasury Yield Curve

Treasury Yield Curve			Probability Distribution	Cumulative Probability Distribution	Representative Numbers Assigned
5 yr.	15 yr.	25 yr.			
4%	6%	7%	.20	.20	0 – 19
5	8	9	.15	.35	20 – 34
6	7	7	.10	.45	35 – 44
7	8	8	.10	.55	45 – 54
9	9	9	.20	.25	55 – 74
10	8	8	.25	1.00	75 – 99

EXHIBIT 22–4

Information for Monte Carlo Simulation of a Three-Bond Portfolio–Random Variable: BBB Corporate/Treasury Yield Spread

BBB/Treasury Yield Spread (in basis points)	Probability Distribution	Cumulative Probability Distribution	Representative Numbers Assigned
75	.10	.10	0 – 9
100	.20	.30	10 – 29
125	.25	.55	30 – 54
150	.25	.80	55 – 79
175	.15	.95	80 – 94
200	.05	1.00	95 – 99

two random variables are (1) the change in the level and shape of the Treasury yield curve and (2) the change in the quality spread between Treasuries and BBB-corporates.

Exhibit 22-3 gives six possible Treasury yield curves 6 months from now that the portfolio manager believes may occur. Exhibit 22-4 gives six possible Treasury/corporate spreads (i.e., quality spreads) assuming that spread is the same regardless of maturity.

We use all this information to describe each of the 12 steps of the Monte Carlo simulation technique.

Step 1 The performance measure must be specified. The performance measure is the annualized 6-month total return for the three-bond portfolio.

Step 2 The problem under investigation must be expressed mathematically. The 6-month total return can be expressed as follows:

Let

V_i = Value of bond i at the end of 6 months (i = 1, 2, and 3, where 1 is the Treasury, 2 is the shorter BBB-corporate bond, and 3 is the longer BBB corporate bond);

c_i = 6-month coupon payment for bond i.

The total future dollars from each bond at the end of the 6-month horizon is then $p_i + c_i$. The 6-month total return for the three-bond portfolio whose initial portfolio value is $15 million is then

$$\text{Total return} = \frac{(V_1 + c_1) + (V_2 + c_2) + (V_3 + c_3)}{\$15,000,000} - 1.$$

Doubling the total return gives an annualized total return on a bond equivalent yield basis.

Step 3 For those variables that are random variables, a probability distribution for each must be specified. In this case there are two random variables—the Treasury yield curve and the yield spread—and a probability distribution must be specified for both. Assume that the probability distributions for these two random variables are as shown in Exhibits 22-3 and 22-4. The coupon payment is a deterministic variable.

Step 4 For each random variable whose probability distribution must be specified, the probability distribution must be converted into a cumulative probability distribution. As we explain in Chapter 21, the cumulative probability of attaining a value less than or equal to a specified value is computed by summing the probabilities over the range of outcomes up to the specified value. The cumulative probability distribution for the two random variables in this case is shown in Exhibits 22-3 and 22-4.

Step 5 For each random variable, representative numbers must be assigned on the basis of the cumulative probability distribution to each possible outcome specified by the probability distribution. The representative numbers assigned for the two random variables in this case are shown in the last column of Exhibits 22-3 and 22-4.

Note that there are 100 assigned two-digit numbers ranging from 0 to 99. Each possible outcome (value for the random variable) is assigned enough numbers so that the ratio of the total numbers assigned to 100 will equal the probability of the outcome. For example, for the Treasury yield curve (the first random variable), the first yield curve outcome in Exhibit 22-3 is assigned numbers from 0 to 19. There are 20 numbers in the range of 0 to 19, so 20 of the 100 numbers, or 20%, are assigned to the first possible Treasury yield curve shape to equal its probability of 20%. A similar choice applies for the fifth possible Treasury yield curve, which also has a probability of 20%. Here the 20 numbers assigned are 55 to 74; the numbers 0 to 19 are not assigned to this outcome because they were assigned at the outset to the first Treasury yield curve.

Step 6: First Trial   Obtain a random number for each random variable. We can obtain a random number for a random variable either from a random number table or by computer generation. Here we use the random number function available in LOTUS 123.

The first random number selected in Steps 6 through 9 will be for the random variable representing the Treasury yield curve. The second will be for the random variable representing the quality spread. The second and sixth columns of Exhibit 22-5 indicate the random numbers for these two random variables. In the first trial, the first random number is 91, and the second random number is 12.

Step 7: First Trial   For each random number, determine the corresponding value of the random variable. Given the random number of 91 for the Treasury yield curve and 12 for the quality spread, the corresponding outcome for the two random variables can be determined with the information in Exhibits 22-3 and 22-4. The Treasury yield curve in this trial would be

> 5-year Treasury = 10%;
> 15-year Treasury = 8%;
> 25-year Treasury = 8%.

The quality spread in this trial would be 100 basis points. Therefore, the horizon yield for the three bonds in this trial is

> 5-year Treasury = 10%;
> 15-year BBB corporate bond = 9%;
> 25-year BBB corporate bond = 9%.

Step 8: First Trial   Use the corresponding value of each random variable found in the previous step to determine the value of the performance measure developed in Step 1. The total future dollars from each bond for the first trial are shown in the eighth, ninth, and tenth columns in Exhibit 22-5. The next-to-last column shows the total future dollars for the portfolio, and the last column shows the total return percentage for the first trial.

Step 9: First Trial   Record the value for the performance measure found in Step 8. The value of the performance measure for the first trial is 10.16%.

Step 10: First Trial   Repeat Steps 6 through 9. Here we describe repeating Steps 6 through 9 for only one more trial.

Step 6: Second Trial   Obtain a random number for each random variable. Exhibit 22-5 shows the next two random numbers to be generated are 64 and 18.

EXHIBIT 22-5

Results of First 20 Trials for Total Return Simulation Illustration

Trial	Rand. No.	Treasury Yield Curve			Rand. No.	Quality Spread (in basis points)	5.5-yr. Treasury ($)	15.5-yr. BBB-Corp. ($)	25.5-yr. BBB-Corp. ($)	Portfolio ($)	Total Return (%)
		5-yr	15-yr	25-yr							
1	91	10%	8%	8%	12	100	$4,377,827	$4,180,000	$7,204,290	$15,762,117	10.16%
2	64	9	9	9	18	100	4,556,546	3,872,551	6,588,839	15,017,936	0.24
3	48	7	8	8	54	125	4,942,085	4,099,740	7,041,255	16,083,079	14.44
4	44	6	7	7	20	100	5,150,000	4,525,841	7,926,164	17,602,005	34.69
5	85	10	8	8	84	175	4,377,827	3,946,091	6,733,821	15,057,738	0.77
6	10	4	6	7	76	150	5,599,129	4,714,877	7,550,584	17,864,590	38.19
7	66	9	9	9	53	125	4,556,546	3,801,105	6,449,317	14,806,968	-2.57
8	38	6	7	7	64	150	5,150,000	4,347,790	7,550,584	17,048,374	27.31
9	42	6	7	7	14	100	5,150,000	4,525,841	7,926,164	17,602,005	34.69
10	23	5	8	9	81	175	5,368,802	3,946,091	6,185,646	15,500,539	6.67
11	61	9	9	9	62	150	4,556,546	3,731,683	6,315,000	14,603,229	-5.29
12	90	10	8	8	5	75	4,377,827	4,262,656	7,373,955	16,014,438	13.53
13	57	9	9	9	51	125	4,556,546	3,801,105	6,449,317	14,806,968	-2.57
14	29	5	8	9	49	125	5,368,802	4,099,740	6,449,317	15,917,858	12.24
15	6	4	6	7	18	100	5,599,129	4,915,682	7,926,164	18,440,975	45.88
16	67	9	9	9	81	175	4,556,546	3,664,220	6,185,646	14,406,412	-7.91
17	38	6	7	7	40	125	5,150,000	4,435,489	7,734,529	17,320,018	30.93
18	42	6	7	7	8	75	5,150,000	4,618,938	8,125,883	17,894,822	38.60
19	68	9	9	9	86	175	4,556,546	3,664,220	6,185,646	14,406,412	-7.91
20	86	10	8	8	71	150	4,377,827	4,021,796	6,884,531	15,284,154	3.79

Step 7: Second Trial For each random number, determine the corresponding value of the random variable. Given the random number of 64 for the Treasury yield curve and 18 for the quality spread, we can determine the corresponding outcome for the two random variables with the information in Exhibits 22-3 and 22-4. The Treasury yield curve in this trial would be

    5-year Treasury = 9%;
    15-year Treasury = 9%;
    25-year Treasury = 9%.

The quality spread in this trial would be 100 basis points. Therefore, the horizon yield for the three bonds in this trial is

    5-year Treasury = 9%;
    15-year BBB corporate bond = 10%;
    25-year BBB corporate bond = 10%.

Step 8: Second Trial Use the corresponding value of each random variable found in the previous step to determine the value of the performance measure. Future dollars for the portfolio produce the value shown in the last column of Exhibit 22-5, .24%.

Step 9: Second Trial Record the .24% value for the performance measure found in Step 8.
    Steps 6 through 9 are then repeated 98 more times. The results of the first 20 trials are shown in Exhibit 22-5.

Step 11 On the basis of the value for the performance measure for each trial recorded in Step 9, construct a probability distribution and a cumulative probability distribution. From the results of the 100 trials shown in Exhibit 22-5, we construct the probability distribution for the total return according to some arbitrary intervals as shown in Exhibit 22-6. The mean and standard deviation are indicated at the bottom of the exhibit.

Step 12   Analyze the Cumulative Probability Distribution Constructed in Step 11
Exhibit 22-6 indicates that the cumulative probability of realizing a negative total return is 19%. Additional outcomes can be found using this information. A portfolio manager can determine, for example, the probability of realizing a total return greater than the 6-month Treasury bill rate (on an annual basis). Suppose that the 6-month Treasury bill yield (on an annual basis) is 4.99%. The probability of realizing a total return of 5% is equal to one minus the probability of realizing a total return less than 5%. From Exhibit 22-6, the probability is thus 65%.

APPLICATION TO A MORTGAGE-BACKED SECURITIES PORTFOLIO
In Part VI of this book, we discuss mortgage-backed securities and the complexities of valuing those securities. Simulation is one technique available to identify the potential performance of a portfolio of mortgage-backed securities. We provide two illustrations to demonstrate this application of simulation.

EXHIBIT 22–6

Probability Distribution for Total Return Simulation Illustration

Range		Number	Probability	Cumulative Prob.
Lower	Upper	of Trials	Distribution (%)	Distribution (%)
–7.91%	–3.99%	11	11%	11%
–4.00	–0.01	8	8	19
0.00	2.99	12	12	31
3.00	4.99	4	4	35
5.00	6.99	6	6	41
7.00	9.99	6	6	47
10.00	14.99	19	19	66
15.00	19.99	7	7	73
20.00	24.99	1	1	74
25.00	29.99	2	2	76
30.00	34.99	5	5	81
35.00	39.99	3	3	84
40.00	44.99	7	7	91
45.00	49.94	9	9	100

Summary Statistics for Portfolio

	Total Future Dollars ($)	Total Return (%)
Mean	$16,091,200	14.55%
Standard deviation	1,290,702	17.21
Minimum	14,406,412	–7.91
Maximum	18,745,770	49.94

The first illustration is based on an example developed by Lakhbir Hayre, Charles Huang, and Vincent Pica to show assessment of the 6-month performance (as measured by total return) of an interest-only (IO) trust under various yield curve scenarios.[2] The IO examined is FNMA Trust 2 based on closing prices on August 11, 1992. Simulation of the yield curve requires that assumptions be made about

---

2 Lakhbir Hayre, Charles Huang, and Vincent Pica, *Realistic Holding-Period Analysis: Technology and Its Impact on Valuation Metrics*, Study #14, Financial Strategies Group, Prudential Securities, August 13, 1992.

* The volatility of short-term Treasury rates;
* The volatility of long-term Treasury rates;
* The correlation between the movement in short-term and long-term Treasury rates.

The projection of prepayments and therefore the interest from the IO requires assumptions about

* A prepayment model;
* The relationship between long-term Treasury rates and mortgage rates.

Finally, the total return calculation requires assumptions about the horizon price of the IO, which is based on an assumed option-adjusted spread.

The specific assumptions for this simulation are as follows:

* The annual volatility (standard deviation) for the 6-month Treasury bill rate is 15%;
* The annual volatility for the 10-year Treasury rate is 10%;
* The correlation between the 6-month Treasury rate and the 10-year Treasury rate is 75%;
* Mortgage rates and the 10-year Treasury rate move together.

The prepayment model used is the Prudential Securities Inc. Prepayment Model.

Exhibit 22-7 shows possible 6-month total returns on the basis of 2000 randomly generated yield curves. The first four columns give information about the possible outcomes for the yield curve. The first column shows the probability of a particular yield curve (as defined by the yield on the 6-month Treasury bill and the 10-year Treasury rate).

The center five columns show the results for the Trust 2 IO. The assumed OAS at the horizon is 939 basis points. The horizon balance is the percentage of the collateral outstanding after 6 months, given the yield curve. Note that the horizon balance is not sensitive to the change in the level or shape of the yield curve. The 6-month total return rate, shown in the last of the five columns reporting the outcome for the IO, varies from a low of –6.64% to a high of 58.45%. The average total return for the Trust 2 IO is 14.31%. The standard deviation is 10.10%, indicating the substantial risk associated with the position.

The next-to-last column shows the total return for a 10-year Treasury for each yield curve environment. The last column shows the total return of a portfolio consisting of the Trust 2 IO and 10-year Treasuries. The amount of each security in the portfolio is such that the initial portfolio duration is zero (i.e., the portfolio is hedged).

Summary statistics for the three portfolios are

	Trust 2 IO (%)	10-year Treasury (%)	Zero-Duration Combination (%)
Average total return	14.31%	6.70%	9.44%
Standard deviation	10.10	5.54	1.11
Low total return	–6.64	–14.26	6.81
High total return	58.45	21.05	12.83

EXHIBIT 22-7

6-Month Total Returns Based on 2000 Randomly Generated Yield Curves

Trust 2 IO: Current price = 21-00; Current OAS = 939 basis points

10-year Treasury: Current price = 107-08; Effective Duration = 6.9

Initial Yield Curve (%) 6-Month 3.31; 1-Year 3.42; 2-Year 4.11; 3-Year 4.66; 5-Year 4.48; 7-Year 5.97; 10-Year 6.48; 30-Year 7.33

Hedged Combination: $100 Par Value of Trust 2 IO, $34.70 Par Value of 10-Year Treasury

Horizon Yield Curves				Trust 2 IO						Tot. Return on Zero-Duration Tsy./IO Combo (%)
Probability (%)	6-Month Tsy. (%)	10-Year Tsy. (%)	10-Yr./6-Mo. Spread (%)	Assumed Horizon OAS (BPs.)	Horizon Price	Horizon Balance	% Price Gain	6-Mo. Total Return	Total Return on 10-Yr. Tsy (%)	
0.70%	2.70%	5.45%	2.75%	939	22.258	0.7235	−22.40%	−3.52%	21.05%	12.19%
3.00	2.78	5.76	2.98	939	23.254	0.7250	−19.78	1.67	16.83	11.36
3.40	2.83	6.12	3.29	939	24.496	0.7281	−15.23	10.69	12.10	11.59
0.80	2.84	6.46	3.62	939	26.035	0.7312	−9.61	21.81	7.77	12.83
0.15	3.07	5.48	2.40	939	21.920	0.7278	−24.00	−6.64	20.48	10.70
4.90	3.07	5.81	2.74	939	22.703	0.7264	−21.50	−1.69	15.93	9.57
14.65	3.12	6.14	3.02	939	23.673	0.7289	−17.93	5.39	11.61	9.37
16.40	3.15	6.49	3.34	939	25.016	0.7316	−13.04	15.07	7.18	10.03
3.85	3.22	6.85	3.63	939	26.406	0.7365	−7.69	25.68	2.71	10.99
0.25	3.25	7.19	3.94	939	27.911	0.7393	−2.15	36.62	−1.39	12.32
0.30	3.40	5.88	2.48	939	22.407	0.7261	−22.53	−3.70	14.78	8.11
5.45	3.42	6.19	2.77	939	23.300	0.7288	−19.20	2.89	10.74	7.91
17.00	3.49	6.54	3.05	939	24.507	0.7324	−14.69	11.85	6.31	8.37
11.85	3.51	6.89	3.38	939	25.916	0.7355	−9.50	22.12	2.01	9.27

Continued

EXHIBIT 22-7

Concluded

	Horizon Yield Curves			Trust 2 IO						
Probability (%)	6-Month Tsy. (%)	10-Year Tsy. (%)	10-Yr./6-Mo. Spread (%)	Assumed Horizon OAS (BPs.)	Horizon Price	Horizon Balance	% Price Gain	6-Mo. Total Return	Total Return on 10-Yr. Tsy (%)	Tot. Return on Zero-Duration Tsy./IO Combo (%)
3.45%	3.55%	7.23%	3.68%	939	27.362	0.7379	-4.22%	32.55%	-2.07%	10.42%
0.30	3.60	7.58	3.98	939	28.916	0.7423	1.73	44.34	-6.14	12.07
0.10	3.78	6.15	2.37	939	22.877	0.7260	-20.95	-0.56	10.97	6.81
2.30	3.84	6.59	2.75	939	24.366	0.7337	-15.02	11.23	5.43	7.52
4.55	3.87	6.91	3.04	939	25.599	0.7359	-10.53	20.11	1.50	8.22
3.55	3.89	7.26	3.37	939	27.070	0.7394	-5.04	30.98	-2.66	9.48
1.40	3.95	7.63	3.68	939	28.686	0.7440	1.16	43.25	-6.95	11.16
0.10	3.97	7.95	3.98	939	30.118	0.7454	6.34	53.46	-10.56	12.54
0.25	4.20	6.90	2.70	939	25.352	0.7342	-11.58	18.06	1.39	7.40
0.75	4.28	7.32	3.04	939	27.055	0.7404	-4.95	31.19	-3.62	8.94
0.50	4.32	7.70	3.38	939	28.713	0.7433	1.16	43.28	-7.98	10.51
0.05	4.49	6.26	3.77	939	30.999	0.7417	8.85	58.45	-14.26	11.97

Note: 1. Based on closing prices on August 11,, 1992.

2. For the IO, the "%Price Gain" factors in the decline in the principal balance.

Source: Lakhbir Hayre, Charles Huang and Vincent Pica, *Realistic Holding Period Analysis, Technology and Its Impact on Valuation Metrics*, Study #14, Financial Strategies Group, Prudential Securities, August 13, 1992, p. 3.

This simulation procedure allows assessment of the risks and rewards of the three portfolios. While the summary statistics clearly indicate that the Trust 2 IO and 10-year Treasury as stand-alone investments have considerable risk as measured by the standard deviation, the combination produces an average total return below that of the Trust 2 IO but higher than the 10-year Treasury, at considerably reduced standard deviation (risk).

Our second illustration uses a real-world application provided by David Canuel of Aeltus Bond Investors. The simulation involves assessing the potential performance of a current portfolio of discount and current coupon pass-throughs over a 1-year investment horizon. The performance is compared to a similar portfolio after addition of an interest-only (IO) stripped MBS position equivalent to about 3.5% of the fund on a market value basis. The IO position is composed of three trusts backed by 8.5%, 9.0%, and 9.5% collateral.

Generating the total returns requires a set of techniques to (1) model a large number of interest rate paths over the 1-year investment horizon and (2) compare individual returns over the horizon. The modeling of interest-rate paths uses historical data on interest rate volatilities and correlations between movements of different points along the yield curve. This is necessary in order to constrain the range of allowable rate levels and yield curve shapes.

Computation of total returns requires models for generating cash flows over the course of the horizon, an assumption on reinvestment of those cash flows to the end of the horizon, and a technique to compute the horizon price. The horizon price and intrahorizon cash flows are sensitive to interest-rate levels. For the pass-throughs, a prepayment function must be specified. As in the previous illustration, the prepayment function is typically "path sensitive": prepayments reflect not only the present level of interest rates, but also the path that rates have followed over time. The total returns for individual securities are weighted and aggregated to compute total returns for portfolios of securities and synthetic securities.

Exhibit 22-8 shows the relative frequency for the current portfolio and the same portfolio with IOs added. Statistics for the return distributions are as follows:

Distribution	Current (%)	3.5% IO (%)
Mean	5.28%	6.41%
Standard deviation	1.27	1.99
Range	−0.90 to 8.63	−3.56 to 10.07

Adding the IOs to the current portfolio shifts the distribution to the right. As the mean for the distribution increases, the riskiness measured in terms of the standard deviation and range also increases. The longer "tail" to the left of the distribution in Exhibit 22-8 reflects the negative convexity of the IO position.

SUMMARY

Simulation analysis is a valuable technique in fixed-income portfolio management. Where there are a substantial number of random variables that will affect the total return of a portfolio, it is generally impractical to evaluate each possible outcome in order to determine the optimal solution or assess the risks associated with a portfolio. Simulation is more of a procedure than a model, and Monte Carlo simulation is a particular type of approach taking the probability distribution for each random variable into consideration.

EXHIBIT 22–8

Simulation of Total Returns for Current Portfolio and Addition of IOs

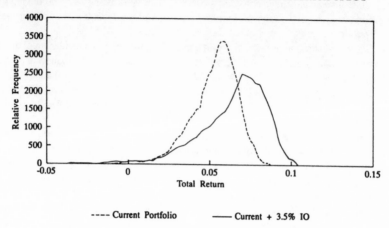

---- Current Portfolio   ——— Current + 3.5% IO

23
⑥ REGRESSION ANALYSIS

Many applications in fixed-income analysis require estimation of a relationship between two or more random variables. In cross-hedging applications, for example, the relationship between the yield on the instrument to be hedged and the instrument being used for hedging (a cash market instrument or a derivative instrument) must be estimated. Evaluation of mortgage-backed securities requires projection of prepayments. A prepayment model requires an analysis of the relationship between prepayment rates and the variables expected to affect prepayments.

This chapter shows how *regression analysis* can be used to estimate relationships between variables. An illustration clarifies the application. At the end of the chapter, a discussion of how regression analysis can be applied to estimate duration is provided.

THE SIMPLE LINEAR REGRESSION MODEL

Suppose that a portfolio manager wants to estimate the relationship between the yield on new single-A rated medium-term industrial bonds and the yield on 10-year Treasuries. Assume that the portfolio manager believes the industrial/Treasury yield relationship can be expressed as

Industrial yield = $a + b$ (Treasury yield).

If the values for a and b can be estimated, the portfolio manager can use the industrial/Treasury yield relationship to estimate the yield on new single-A rated medium-term industrial bonds for a given yield level of 10-year Treasuries. The values a and b are called the *parameters* of the model, and the objective of regression analysis is to estimate the parameters.

There are several points to understand about this relationship. First, there are only two variables in the relationship—the yield on new single-A rated medium-term industrials and the yield on 10-year Treasuries. Because there are only two variables and the relationship is linear, the regression model is called a *simple linear regression*. Because the yield on the industrials is assumed to depend on the yield on 10-year Treasuries, the former variable is referred to as the *dependent* variable. The yield on 10-year Treasuries is referred to as the *explanatory* or *independent* variable because it is what is taken to explain the yield on the industrial bonds. When there is more than one explanatory or independent variable, the regression model is called a *multiple regression model*.

Second, it is highly unlikely that the estimated industrial/Treasury yield relationship above will describe the true relationship between the two yields exactly, because other factors besides the level of 10-year Treasuries may influence the yield on new single-A rated medium-term industrial bonds. Consequently, this industrial/Treasury yield relationship may be described more accurately by adding a random error term to the relationship. That is, the industrial/Treasury yield relationship can be expressed as

Industrial yield = $a + b$ (Treasury yield) + Random error term.

The expression can be simplified as follows:

$$Y = a + bX + e$$

where

Y = Yield on new single-A rated medium-term industrial bonds;
X = Yield on 10-year Treasuries;
e = Random error term.

This expression is referred to as the *simple linear regression model*.

PROCEDURE FOR ESTIMATING THE PARAMETERS OF THE SIMPLE LINEAR REGRESSION

In order to estimate the parameters of the simple linear regression model, historical information is needed on the yield on new single-A rated medium-term industrial bonds and the yield on 10-year Treasuries. The third and fourth columns in Exhibit 23-1 give the yields for 45 months beginning on 11/30/88 and ending on 7/31/92.[1] Each pair of values for the two variables X and Y is referred to as an *observation*. The 45 observations shown in Exhibit 23-1 that are used to estimate the regression are plotted in Exhibit 23-2. When observations are plotted in this fashion, the resulting graph is called a *scatter diagram*.

One way to estimate the industrial/Treasury yield relationship is simply to draw a line through the observations that an observer believes best represent the relationship. Then two points on this line can be used to estimate the relationship. This method, sometimes referred to as the *free-hand method*, is a poor procedure for estimating a relationship. The obvious drawback is that there is no specified criterion for drawing the line; different observers are likely to obtain different estimates of the relationship from the same observations.

Another approach is the *high-low method*, where the two extreme observations for the explanatory variables are selected. These two points are then the basis for the line used to estimate the relationship. This is also a poor procedure, because it ignores all the other observations.

---

1   The data were provided by Ardavan Nozari of Salomon Brothers, Inc.

EXHIBIT 23–1

Worksheet for the Estimation of the Parameters of the Simple Linear Regression: Industrial/Treasury Yield Relationship

Date	Obser. t	Yield on Treasury X	Yield on Industrial Y	XY	X^2	Y^2
11/30/88	1	9.057%	9.900%	89.6643	82.0292	98.0100
12/30/88	2	9.140	10.000	91.4000	83.5396	100.0000
1/31/89	3	8.983	9.800	88.0334	80.6943	96.0400
2/28/89	4	9.298	10.250	95.3045	86.4528	105.0625
3/31/89	5	9.279	10.100	93.7179	86.0998	102.0100
4/28/89	6	9.057	9.950	90.1172	82.0292	99.0025
5/31/89	7	8.598	9.550	82.1109	73.9256	91.2025
6/30/89	8	8.079	9.000	72.7110	65.2702	81.0000
7/31/89	9	7.808	8.700	67.9296	60.9649	75.6900
8/31/89	10	8.256	9.150	75.5424	68.1615	83.7225
9/29/89	11	8.298	9.250	76.7565	68.8568	85.5625
10/31/89	12	7.913	9.000	71.2170	62.6156	81.0000
11/30/89	13	7.833	8.950	70.1054	61.3559	80.1025
12/29/89	14	7.924	9.100	72.1084	62.7898	82.8100
1/31/90	15	8.418	9.380	78.9608	70.8627	87.9844
2/28/90	16	8.518	9.550	81.3469	72.5563	91.2025
3/30/90	17	8.636	9.650	83.3374	74.5805	93.1225
4/30/90	18	9.028	10.050	90.7314	81.5048	101.0025
5/31/90	19	8.599	9.550	82.1205	73.9428	91.2025
6/29/90	20	8.414	9.400	79.0916	70.7954	88.3600
7/31/90	21	8.341	9.200	76.7372	69.5723	84.6400
8/31/90	22	8.854	9.875	87.4333	78.3933	97.5156
9/28/90	23	8.800	10.000	88.0000	77.4400	100.0000
10/31/90	24	8.620	9.850	84.9070	74.3044	97.0225
11/30/90	25	8.252	9.500	78.3940	68.0955	90.2500
12/31/90	26	8.069	9.350	75.4452	65.1088	87.4225
1/31/91	27	8.011	9.200	73.7012	64.1761	84.6400
2/28/91	28	8.036	9.100	73.1276	64.5773	82.8100
3/28/91	29	8.059	9.050	72.9340	64.9475	81.9025
4/30/91	30	8.013	8.900	71.3157	64.2082	79.2100
5/31/91	31	8.059	8.875	71.5236	64.9475	78.7656
6/28/91	32	8.227	9.050	74.4544	67.6835	81.9025
7/31/91	33	8.147	9.000	73.3230	66.3736	81.0000

Continued

EXHIBIT 23–1

Concluded

Date	Obser. t	Yield on Treasury X	Yield on Industrial Y	XY	X^2	Y^2
8/30/91	34	7.814	8.600	67.2004	61.0586	73.9600
9/30/91	35	7.448	8.250	61.4460	55.4727	68.0625
10/31/91	36	7.462	8.250	61.5615	55.6814	68.0625
11/29/91	37	7.378	8.125	59.9463	54.4349	66.0156
12/31/91	38	6.700	7.600	50.9200	44.8900	57.7600
1/31/91	39	7.281	8.000	58.2480	53.0130	64.0000
2/28/92	40	7.257	8.050	58.4189	52.6640	64.8025
3/31/92	41	7.530	8.230	61.9719	56.7009	67.7329
4/30/92	42	7.583	8.300	62.9389	57.5019	68.8900
5/29/92	43	7.325	8.000	58.6000	53.6556	64.0000
6/30/92	44	7.123	7.750	55.2033	50.7371	60.0625
7/31/92	45	6.709	7.300	48.9757	45.0107	53.2900
Total		366.234	407.685	3,339.0338	2,999.6767	3,717.8092

The *regression method*, unlike the free-hand method and the high-low method, does specify a logical criterion for estimating the relationship. To explain this criterion, we first rewrite the simple linear regression so that it shows the estimated relationship for each observation:

$$Y_t = a + bX_t + e_t,$$

where the subscript t denotes the observation for the tth month. For example, for the third observation ($t = 3$), the expression becomes

$$9.800 = a + b\,(8.983) + e_3.$$

For the sixth observation ($t = 6$), the expression is

$$9.950 = a + b\,(9.057) + e_6.$$

The values for e_3 and e_6 are referred to as the *observed error terms for the observation*. Note that the value of the observed error term for both observations will depend on the values selected for a and b. This suggests a criterion for selecting the two parameters: the parameters should be estimated so that the sum of the observed error terms for all observations is as small as possible.

Although this is a good standard, it presents one problem. Some observed error terms will be positive, and others will be negative. Consequently, positive and negative observed error

EXHIBIT 23–2

Graph of Industrial and Treasury Yields

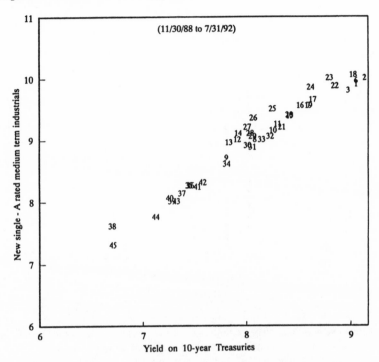

terms will offset each other. To overcome this problem, each error term could be squared. On the basis of that criterion, the objective would then be to select parameters so as to minimize the sum of the square of the observed error terms. This is precisely the criterion used to estimate the parameters in regression analysis. Because of this property, regression analysis is sometimes referred to as the *method of least squares*.

This criterion is portrayed graphically in Exhibit 23-3, a generic scatter diagram with an estimated regression line drawn. Consider point L in Exhibit 23-3, which represents a specific observation. If a line is dropped from point L to the X axis at point N, then the observed value for Y is LN, and the estimated value of Y based on the estimated line is MN. The observed error term is the difference between the observed value for Y and the estimated value for Y. In Exhibit 23-3, the difference is the vertical difference LM.

The estimated line in Exhibit 23-3 overestimates the observed Y for all observed values below the line and underestimates all observed points above the estimated line. Squaring the observed error term removes the possibility that the underestimates and overestimates will offset each other. By squaring and summing the observed errors this cannot occur.

424

EXHIBIT 23-3

Graphical Illustration of Error Term

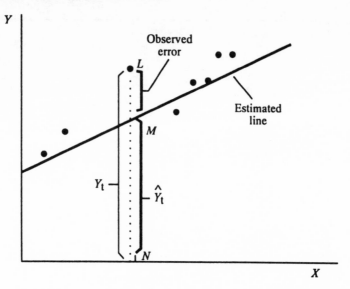

The objective in estimation of the regression line is to select a value for the parameters—*a* and *b*—so as to minimize the sum of the squares of the observed error terms. The formulas used to estimate the parameters on the basis of this criterion are derived using calculus.

If a hat (^) over the parameter denotes the estimated value, and *T* denotes the total number of observations, the estimated parameters for *a* and *b* are computed from the observations using the formulas:

$$\hat{b} = \frac{\sum\limits_{t=1}^{T} X_t Y_t - \frac{1}{T} \sum\limits_{t=1}^{T} X_t \sum\limits_{t=1}^{T} Y_t}{\sum\limits_{t=1}^{T} X_t^2 - \frac{1}{T} \left(\sum\limits_{t=1}^{T} X_t \right)^2}$$

and

$$\hat{a} = \frac{1}{T} \sum\limits_{t=1}^{T} Y_t - \frac{1}{T} (\hat{b}) \sum\limits_{t=1}^{T} X_t$$

where the Greek letter $\sum$ means to sum over the subscripted values.

Although the formulas may look complicated, they are easy to apply in practice. For actual problems with a large number of observations, we can use regression analysis programs that compute the value of the parameters by using the appropriate formulas. Most electronic spread sheets are preprogrammed to perform simple linear regression analysis.

We can use the formulas to compute the estimated parameters on the basis of the observations given in Exhibit 23-1. The worksheet for the sums needed to apply the formula is shown as Exhibit 23-1 and summarized below:

$$\sum_{t=1}^{45} X_t = 366.234; \quad \sum_{t=1}^{45} Y_t = 407.685;$$

$$\sum_{t=1}^{45} X_t Y_t = 3,339.0338; \quad \sum_{t=1}^{45} X_t^2 = 2,999.6767.$$

Substituting into the formula for $\hat{b}$,

$$\hat{b} = \frac{3,339.0338 - \dfrac{1}{45}(366.234)(407.685)}{2,999.6767 - \dfrac{1}{45}(366.234)^2}$$

$$= \frac{3,339.0338 - 3,317.9579}{2,999.6767 - 2,980.6076} = 1.1052.$$

Substituting into the formula for $\hat{a}$,

$$\hat{a} = \frac{1}{45}(407.685) - \frac{1}{45}(1.1052)(366.234)$$

$$= .0649.$$

The industrial/Treasury yield relationship is then

$$Y = .0649 + 1.1052\,X.$$

GOODNESS OF FIT OF THE RELATIONSHIP

A portfolio manager will want to know how "good" an estimated relationship is before relying on it for any investment strategy, so statistical tests are needed to determine in some sense how good the relationship is between the dependent variable and the explanatory variable. A measure of the "goodness of fit" of the relationship is the *coefficient of determination*.

Exhibit 23-4 demonstrates the meaning and measurement of the coefficient of determination. We know that the explanatory or independent variable X is being used to try to explain movements in the dependent variable Y. That is, the variable X is trying to explain why the variable Y would deviate from its mean. If no explanatory variable is used to try to explain movements in Y, the method of least squares would give the mean of Y as its value estimate. Thus the ability of X to explain deviations of Y from its mean is the factor of interest.

In Exhibit 23-4, the observed value of Y at point D deviates from the mean of Y as measured by the vertical distance DF. It is the deviation of Y from its mean, i.e., DF, that the variable X must explain. This DF difference is made up of two components. The first component is EF, which is the difference between the value estimated by the regression line and the mean value

EXHIBIT 23–4

Meaning and Measurement of the Coefficient of Determination

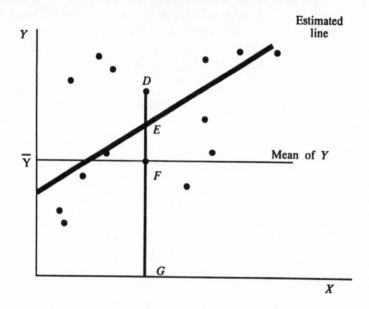

of Y. This distance is the amount of the deviation from the mean of Y explained by X or, equivalently, explained by the regression line.

The second component is DE, which is the deviation of Y from its mean that is still unexplained. Consequently, the deviation of the observed Y from the mean of Y can be expressed as follows:

$$DF = EF + DE,$$

where

    DF = The deviation of the observed Y from the mean of Y;
    EF = The amount of the deviation of the observed Y from the mean of Y explained by X;
    DE = The amount of the deviation of Y from the mean of Y still unexplained.

If the deviations of the observed Y from the mean of Y are squared and all these deviations are summed for each observation, the resulting value indicates the total deviations of the observed Y from the mean of Y. This is referred to as the *total sum of squares*. The second component is the deviations of the observed Y from the mean of Y that are still unexplained. This component is referred to as the *unexplained sum of squares*. Thus,

    Total sum of squares

      = Explained sum of squares + Unexplained sum of squares.

How much of the total sum of squares is explained by X is the factor of interest. One way, therefore, to measure how good the relationship is is to determine what percent of the total sum of squares is explained by X. That is, how good the relationship is can be measured by dividing the explained sum of squares by the total sum of squares. This ratio is the *coefficient of determination*:

$$\text{Coefficient of determination} = \frac{\text{Explained sum of squares}}{\text{Total sum of squares}}.$$

The coefficient of determination can take on a value between 0 and 1. If the total sum of squares is fully explained by X, the coefficient of determination is 1. When none of the total sum of squares is explained by X, the coefficient of determination is 0. Hence, the closer the coefficient of determination is to 1, the stronger the relationship between the variables.

Another interpretation of the coefficient of determination is that it measures how close the observed points are to the regression line. The nearer the observed points are to the regression line, the closer the coefficient of determination will be to 1. The farther the scatter of the observed points from the regression line, the closer the coefficient of determination will be to 0.

The coefficient of determination is commonly referred to as "R-squared" denoted by R^2. Computation of the coefficient of determination proceeds as follows: The total sum of squares is computed as

$$\text{Total sum of squares} = \sum_{t=1}^{T} Y_t^2 - \frac{1}{T}\left(\sum_{t=1}^{T} Y_t\right)^2.$$

The explained sum of squares is computed as

$$\text{Explained sum of squares} = \hat{b}\left(\sum_{t=1}^{T} X_t Y_t - \frac{1}{T}\sum_{t=1}^{T} X_t \sum_{t=1}^{T} Y_t\right).$$

The coefficient of determination is then found by dividing the explained sum of squares by the total sum of squares.

From the worksheet shown as Exhibit 23-1,

$$\sum_{t=1}^{45} Y_t = 407.685; \quad \sum_{t=1}^{45} X_t = 366.234;$$

$$\sum_{t=1}^{45} X_t Y_t = 3{,}339.0338; \quad \sum_{t=1}^{45} Y_t^2 = 3{,}717.8092;$$

then

$$\text{Total sum of squares} = 3{,}717.8092 - \frac{1}{45}(407.685)^2$$

$$= 24.3191$$

and

Explained sum of squares

$$= (1.1052)\left[3{,}339.0338 - \frac{1}{45}(366.234)(407.685)\right]$$

$$= 23.2931.$$

The coefficient of determination is therefore

$$\text{Coefficient of determination} = \frac{23.2931}{24.3191} = .96.$$

A coefficient of determination of .96 indicates that approximately 96% of the total variation in the yield on new single-A rated medium-term industrial bonds is explained by the yield on 10-year Treasuries.

A warning is in order on the topic of the coefficient of determination. A coefficient of determination close to 0 does not necessarily imply that there is no relationship between the two variables. There may in fact be a strong relationship, but it may not be a linear relationship.

CORRELATION COEFFICIENT AND COVARIANCE

The coefficient of determination is related to the correlation coefficient, which measures the association between two variables. No cause and effect are assumed in calculation of a correlation coefficient, so there is no assumption about which of two variables is the dependent variable and which is the explanatory variable. This is different from regression analysis, which assumes one variable is dependent on the other.

The coefficient of determination turns out to be equal to the square of the correlation coefficient. Thus, the square root of the coefficient of determination is the correlation coefficient. As the coefficient of determination can be between 0 and 1, the correlation coefficient will be between -1 and 1. The sign of the correlation coefficient is the same as the sign of the slope of the regression, b. In our illustration, because the coefficient of determination is .96, the correlation coefficient is .98.

The covariance measures how the two random variables vary together. It is related to the correlation coefficient as follows:

$$\text{Covariance} = (\text{std of } X)\,(\text{std of } Y)\,(\text{Correlation coefficient}),$$

where

std = Standard deviation.

STANDARD ERROR OF ESTIMATE AND CONFIDENCE INTERVAL FOR FORECASTED VALUE

Knowing how to assess the strength of the relationship between two variables, we can now show how to use the estimated regression model to obtain a forecasted value for the dependent variable Y. Continuing estimation of the relationship between the yield on 10-year Treasuries (X) and the yield on new single-A rated medium-term industrial bonds (Y), suppose that the portfolio manager believes that the yield on 10-year Treasuries next month will be 7%. X is therefore 7. The forecasted yield for new single-A rated medium-term industrial bonds (Y) is

$$Y = .0649 + 1.1052\,(7) = 7.801.$$

The forecasted value of 7.801% is known as a *point estimate*, because only one value is forecasted. In practice, a portfolio manager would want a range for the dependent variable, along with a probability that the actual value will fall within the range. To accomplish this, it is necessary first to compute the *standard error of the estimate*, which is another measure of how good the regression relationship is. Three steps are required:

Step 1. Compute the unexplained sum of squares, which is just the total sum of squares that is not explained by the regression. The unexplained sum of squares is found as follows:

Unexplained sum of squares
= Total sum of squares – Explained sum of squares.

Step 2. Divide the unexplained sum of squares by the number of observations minus 2. That is, if T represents the number of observations, then compute

$$\frac{\text{Unexplained sum of squares}}{T-2}$$

Step 3. Take the square root of the quantity found in Step 2 to get the standard error of the estimate.

According to the data for the regression estimated earlier:

Step 1. The total sum of squares is 24.3191 and the explained sum of squares is 23.2931, so the unexplained sum of squares is 1.026.

Step 2. There are 45 observations, so the unexplained sum of squares is divided by 43 to give .0239.

Step 3. The square root of .0239 is .1546.

Note that the larger the unexplained sum of squares, the greater the standard error of the estimate. Recall that the larger the unexplained sum of squares, the lower the coefficient of determination, which measures the goodness of fit of the regression relationship. Thus, the greater the standard error of the estimate, the poorer the regression relationship.

Once the standard error of the estimate is found, a range or interval estimate for a forecasted value of Y can be computed, given a value for the explanatory variable X, and a probability can be assigned that the actual value for Y will fall within the range or interval. The interval computed is known as a *confidence interval*, and the probability assigned to this interval is called a *confidence coefficient*.

To compute a confidence interval, nine steps are necessary:[2]

Step 1. Find the difference between the value for the explanatory variable X and the average value for X.

Step 2. Square the value in Step 1.

---

2   This formula is given in J. Johnston, *Econometric Methods* (New York: McGraw-Hill, 1972), p. 41.

Step 3. Divide the amount in Step 2 by the value in the denominator of the formula used to find $\hat{b}$.

Step 4. Add to the amount in Step 3 the value $1/T$.

Step 5. Take the square root of the amount in Step 4.

Step 6. Multiply the amount in Step 5 by the value below that corresponds to the confidence level selected:[3]

Confidence Level (%)	Multiply by this
99%	2.57
95	1.96
90	1.65

Step 7. Multiply the amount in Step 6 by the standard error of the estimate.

Step 8. Add the amount in Step 7 to the forecasted value for Y to obtain the upper range of the confidence interval.

Step 9. Subtract the amount in Step 7 from the forecasted value for Y to obtain the lower range of the confidence interval.

To illustrate this process, we construct a confidence interval with a 95% confidence level for the industrial/Treasury yield relationship, assuming that the yield on 10-year Treasuries is expected to be 7%.

Step 1. Find the difference between the value for the explanatory variable X of 7% and the average value for X of 8.135%. The difference is 1.135%.

Step 2. Squaring 1.135% gives 1.2882.

Step 3. The denominator of the formula used to find $\hat{b}$ is

$$3{,}339.0338 - \frac{1}{45}(366.234)(407.685) = 21.0759.$$

Dividing 1.2882 by 21.0759 gives .0611.

Step 4. Adding .0222 (1 divided by the number of observations, 45) to .0611 gives .0833.

Step 5. The square root of .0833 is .2886.

Step 6. As the confidence level is 95%, multiply .2886 by 1.96. The result is .5657.

Step 7. Multiplying .5657 by the standard error of the estimate, .1546, gives .088.

Step 8. The forecasted value of Y found earlier is 7.801%. Adding .088 to 7.801% gives 7.889%, which is the upper limit of the confidence interval.

---

3 These values are obtained from a normal distribution explained in Chapter 21. Technically, the values given above apply when there are at least 32 observations. For a smaller number of observations used to estimate the regression model, the values to be used are larger.

Step 9. Subtracting .088 from 7.801% gives 7.713%, which is the lower limit of the confidence interval.

Thus a confidence interval for a 95% confidence level is 7.713% to 7.801%. This means there is a 95% probability that the yield on a new single-A rated medium-term industrial bond will be within this interval if the yield on 10-year Treasuries is 7%.

EXTENSION OF THE SIMPLE LINEAR REGRESSION MODEL

In many applications, a dependent variable is best explained by more than one explanatory variable. Estimation of such a relationship is referred to as a *multiple regression*. The parameters of a multiple regression are difficult to compute by hand, but there are numerous commercial multiple regression analysis programs available for estimation.

Interpretation of the coefficient of determination is much the same for multiple regression as in simple linear regression. In the latter case, it is the total sum of squares explained by the explanatory variable X. In multiple regression, the coefficient of determination is the total sum of squares explained by all the explanatory variables. By adding an explanatory variable to a regression model, the belief is that the new explanatory variable will increase the explained sum of squares significantly.

For example, suppose that a simple linear regression is estimated, and that the total sum of squares is 1,000 and the explained sum of squares is 600. Suppose that another explanatory variable is added to the regression model, and that inclusion of this explanatory variable increases the explained sum of squares from 600 to 750. Thus, the coefficient of determination would rise from 60% to 75% (750/1,000). This new explanatory variable would appear to have contributed substantially to explaining the variation in the dependent variable. Had the explained sum of squares increased from 600 to 610, the coefficient of determination would increase from 60% to only 61%, in which case the new explanatory variable would not appear to do much to help explain the dependent variable.

To estimate a relationship, it is not necessary to restrict selection of explanatory variables to quantitative variables, that is, a variable that can be expressed numerically. Qualitative variables, those expressed by a nonnumerical property, can also be used. Suppose that the portfolio manager believes that the industrial/Treasury yield relationship differs in times of economic recession and of economic prosperity. Such an hypothesis can be tested by using a qualitative variable as follows. If the observation occurs in a period of economic recession, the value for the variable for the observation is equal to 1. If the observation occurs in a period of economic prosperity, the value for the variable for the observation is equal to 0. A qualitative variable used in regression analysis is commonly referred to as a *dummy variable*. In general, a dummy variable takes on a value of 1 if the observation has the attribute assumed by the qualitative variable, and a value of 0 otherwise.

We have discussed regression analysis in the form of simple linear regression analysis. A simple linear regression model takes the general form:

$$Y = a + bX + e.$$

Consider the following relationship to be estimated using regression analysis:

$$Y = a + bZ^2 + e.$$

Is the above relationship a simple linear regression model? If we let the variable X equal Z^2, then the relationship can be rewritten as $Y = a + bX + e$. This relationship is expressed in the same format as the simple linear regression model, and the parameters can be estimated using the formulas presented so far.

Consider next the equation:

$$V = cZ^b$$

Can this equation be converted into a simple linear regression model? The answer is that it can. If logarithms are taken of both sides of the equation, and an error term is added, the equation can be rewritten as

$$\log V = \log c + b \log Z + \text{Error term.}$$

If we let Y equal $\log V$, X equal $\log Z$, and a equal $\log c$, then the relationship can be expressed in the format of a simple linear regression. The estimated values of b and a can be obtained using regression analysis. To obtain the estimate of c, the antilog of a can be calculated.

STATISTICAL SIGNIFICANCE OF RELATIONSHIPS

Statistical tests indicate whether a relationship estimated using regression analysis is statistically significant. There are also tests to determine whether an increase in the explained sum of squares attributable to the inclusion of an additional explanatory variable is statistically significant. Such tests are described in textbooks on regression analysis.[4]

Many statistical problems arise in estimating relationships through regression analysis. Some have to do with the assumptions underlying the regression model. Potential problems include *multicollinearity*, *autocorrelation*, and *heteroscedasticity*. Multicollinearity means that the explanatory variables themselves are highly correlated, so it becomes difficult to identify how a particular explanatory variable affects the dependent variable. Autocorrelation and heteroscedasticity have to do with the error term. It is assumed that (1) the error terms will be uncorrelated from observation to observation, and (2) the variance of the error term will be constant for all observations. Violation of the first assumption is referred to as autocorrelation; violation of the second assumption is referred to as heteroscedasticity.

REGRESSION-BASED APPROACH TO ESTIMATING DURATION FOR A MORTGAGE-BACKED SECURITY

In Part IV we discussed how a bond's effective duration can be calculated using a valuation model. In our discussion of mortgage-backed securities in Chapter 20, a completely different approach to the estimation of duration for these securities was mentioned—empirical duration.

Empirical duration, sometimes referred to as implied duration, is the sensitivity of a mortgage-backed security (MBS) as estimated empirically from historical prices.[5] Multiple

---

4 See, for example, J. Johnston, *ibid.*

5 The first attempt to calculate empirical duration was by Scott M. Pinkus and Marie A. Chandoha, "The Relative Price Volatility of Mortgage Securities," *Journal of Portfolio Management* (Summer 1986), pp. 9–22.

regression analysis is used to estimate the relationship. More specifically, the relationship estimated is the percentage change in the price of the MBS of interest to the change in the general level of Treasury yields.

To obtain the empirical duration, Paul DeRossa, Laurie Goodman, and Mike Zazzarino suggest that the following relationship be estimated using multiple regression analysis:[6]

Percentage change in price

$$= c + b_1 \ (\Delta y) + b_2 \ (P - 100) \ (\Delta y)$$

$$+ b_3 \ [(P - 100)^2 \ (\Delta y) \text{ if } P > 100, \text{ otherwise } 0] + \text{error term},$$

where

$$P = \text{Price (with par equal to 100)};$$
$$\Delta y = \text{Change in yield};$$
$$c, b_1, b_2, \text{ and } b_3 = \text{Parameters to be estimated.}$$

The inclusion of the second and third terms in the relationship is to allow for the price sensitivity to vary depending on the price level of the mortgages.

The expectation is that the parameter, c, would be equal to 0 when the relationship is estimated. The expected sign of b_1 is negative. That is, there is an inverse relationship between yield changes and price changes. Finally, the terms b_2 and b_3 are expected to have a positive sign.

DeRossa, Goodman, and Zazzarino estimated the relationship using daily data for the 5-year period (November 19, 1986 to November 18, 1991; 1,264 observations) for Ginnie Mae and Fannie Mae 8s, 9s, 10s, and 11s. The yield used was the 10-year Treasury, although they indicate that nearly identical results were realized if they used the 7-year Treasury. In all of their estimated regressions, all of the parameters had the expected sign. The R^2 for the estimated regressions was not less than 65%.

Given the estimated relationship, the empirical duration for different coupons at different price levels can be found by dividing the estimated relationship by the change in yield. That is

$$\text{Duration} = \frac{\text{Percentage change in price}}{\Delta y}$$

$$= c + b_1 + b_2 \ (P - 100)$$

$$+ b_3 \ [(P - 100)^2 \text{ if } P > 100, \text{ otherwise } 0].$$

For an MBS trading at par, P is 100, and the empirical duration is therefore b_1.

There are three advantages of the empirical duration approach.[7] First, the duration estimate does not rely on any theoretical formulas or analytical assumptions. Second, the estimation of the required parameters are easy to compute using regression analysis. Finally, the only input that is needed is a reliable price series and Treasury yield series.

---

6 Paul DeRosa, Laurie Goodman, and Mike Zazzarino, "Duration Estimates on Mortgage-Backed Securities," *Journal of Portfolio Management* (Winter 1993), pp. 32–37.

7 See Bennett W. Golub, "Towards a New Approach to Measuring Mortgage Duration," in Frank J. Fabozzi (ed.), *The Handbook of Mortgage-Backed Securities* (Chicago: Probus Publishing, 1995), Chapter 32, p. 672.

There are disadvantages.[8] First, a reliable price series for the data may not be available. For example, there may be no price series available for a thinly traded mortgage derivative security or the prices may be matrix priced or model priced rather than actual transaction prices. Second, an empirical relationship does not impose a structure for the options embedded in an MBS and this can distort the empirical duration. Third, the price history may lag current market conditions. This may occur after a sharp and sustained shock to interest rates has been realized. Finally, the volatility of the spread to Treasury yields can distort how the price of an MBS reacts to yield changes.

SUMMARY

Regression analysis is a technique for estimation of the relationship between variables. A simple linear regression includes one explanatory variable and a dependent variable. A multiple regression includes more than one explanatory variable. The method of least squares is used to estimate the parameters of the relationship.

The coefficient of determination is a measure of the goodness of fit of the linear relationship. The coefficient of determination is the ratio of the explained sum of squares to the total sum of squares, and consequently varies between 0 and 1. The larger the coefficient of determination, the better the relationship. The square root of the coefficient of determination is related to the correlation coefficient.

An estimated relationship can be used to forecast a value for the dependent variable. Either a point estimate or a confidence interval can be obtained.

---

8   Ibid.

24

⊚ OPTIMIZATION MODELS

An optimization model prescribes the best course of action to be pursued in order to achieve an objective. The optimization models used in most fixed-income portfolio management applications are mathematical programming models. We describe in this chapter how optimization models can be used in fixed-income portfolio management, without delving into the nuances of these models or the algorithms for solving a mathematical programming problem. Any real-world problem confronting a portfolio manager will be complex enough to require the use of commercially available software to solve.

Optimization models are commonly used in structured portfolio strategies, which do not rely on expectations of interest-rate movements or changes in yield spreads. Instead the objective is design of an optimal portfolio that will achieve the performance of a predetermined benchmark. The target could be (1) the return on a specific benchmark index, (2) sufficient dollars to satisfy a future single liability, or (3) sufficient dollars to satisfy each liability of a future liability stream. The structured bond portfolio strategy used when the target to be achieved is replication of a predetermined benchmark index is called an *indexing strategy*. When the objective is to generate sufficient funds to pay off predetermined future liabilities, the strategy is called a *liability funding strategy*. Optimization models are also used in making asset allocation decisions (i.e., decisions on allocation of funds among major asset classes).

MATHEMATICAL PROGRAMMING

Mathematical programming models are used to solve problems that involve the allocation of limited resources so as to optimize a quantitative goal. An allocation problem assumes there are many acceptable solutions that satisfy the decision maker's constraints or restrictions, but that there may be one best solution that optimizes the value of the specified goal.

Setting Up a Mathematical Programming Model

There are four steps in setting up a mathematical programming or optimization problem.

Step 1   Define the variables on which a decision must be made. These variables are called *decision variables*. In a structured portfolio problem, the decision variables are typically the amount of a security that should be purchased or sold. In an asset allocation problem, the decision variables are the amounts to be allocated to each major asset class.

Step 2   Specify mathematically the objective the decision maker seeks to optimize. This mathematical expression is called the *objective function*. The linear or nonlinear nature of the objective function is what distinguishes the different types of mathematical programming models.

Step 3   Specify mathematically the constraints under which the objective function is to be optimized. One constraint, for example, might be that the portfolio's duration be equal to 4. Or a constraint may specify that the amount allocated to one sector of the market may not exceed a certain percentage of the portfolio, or that the minimum amount allocated to liquid assets be a specified percentage. As with the objective function, the mathematical characterization of the constraints determines the type of mathematical programming problem.

Step 4   Solve for the optimal solution.

TYPES OF MATHEMATICAL PROGRAMMING MODELS

The most common types of mathematical programming models include (1) linear programming; (2) mixed integer programming; (3) quadratic programming; (4) dynamic programming; and (5) goal programming.

Linear Programming

The objective function and all the constraints in a linear programming problem are linear. For example, a structured portfolio strategy may call for construction of a portfolio to satisfy a liability or set of liabilities at a minimum cost. Suppose that the acceptable universe of bonds is 500 issues made up of Treasuries, agencies, and all investment-grade corporate bonds. The decision variables are the percentage of the portfolio to be invested in an issue. There are then 500 decision variables, one representing each of the acceptable issues in the universe.

Let

w_i = Par amount to purchase of a particular issue (i = 1, 2, $\cdots$, 500);
p_i = Price of issue i (as a percent of par value P, e.g., .90, 1.00, 1.05).

Then the total cost of the portfolio is

$$w_1 p_1 + w_2 p_2 + \ldots + w_{500} p_{500}.$$

This expression represents the objective function. The objective function is linear, and the portfolio manager would seek to minimize the objective function subject to the constraints imposed.

Two examples of a linear constraint would be that a minimum of $10 million of the portfolio must be invested in Treasury issues and that no more than $15 million may be invested in BBB-rated corporate bonds. Mathematically, assuming that issues 1, 2, ..., 150 are the Treasury issues, the first constraint can be expressed as follows:

$$w_1 p_1 + w_2 p_2 + \cdots + w_{150} p_{150} \geq \$10,000,000.$$

Assuming that issues 425 to 500 are triple-B-rated corporate bonds, the second constraint can be expressed mathematically as follows:

$$w_{425} p_{425} + w_{426} p_{426} + \cdots + w_{500} p_{500} \leq \$15,000,000.$$

One common linear constraint in structured portfolio strategies is a restriction on portfolio duration. For example, an immunization strategy (discussed in Chapter 14) would constrain portfolio duration to match the duration of the liability. Assuming no short selling, all the decision variables are then constrained to be greater than or equal to zero.

Mixed Integer Programming

Linear programming assumes that the decision variables are divisible and result in whole numbers. Suppose an automobile manufacturer uses a linear programming model to determine the optimal number of various car models to produce, given its resources (capital and labor). The solution might indicate that 555.6 of one type of car be produced and 442.7 of another type. So, is producing 556 of one type and 443 of the other the optimal solution? In fact, (1) the modified (rounded) optimal solution may no longer satisfy all the constraints or (2) there may be another solution that is better than the modified optimal solution. To handle this type of problem, mixed integer programming is used.

Integer programming restricts the decision variables to take on integer values. Integer programming is used in structured portfolio applications when transaction sizes in round lots are sought, or where one of two issues but not both may be part of the optimal solution.

Quadratic Programming

The restriction imposed in employing linear programming is that both the objective function and the constraints be linear. It is common in structured portfolio strategies and asset allocation models, however, to have a quadratic objective function. For example, a common objective in constructing an indexed portfolio is to minimize tracking error. Tracking error is measured by the variance of the indexed portfolio's return from the benchmark (i.e., index) return. Solving this problem requires the use of a mathematical programming model that permits a quadratic objective function. In the case of asset allocation models, the objective is to allocate funds among asset classes to minimize portfolio risk. Portfolio risk is measured by the variance of the portfolio, which is expressed mathematically as a quadratic expression.

Linear programming is inappropriate in these applications. A special type of mathematical programming called quadratic programming does permit a quadratic objective function. Quadratic programming also permits the constraints to be a nonlinear expression.

Dynamic Programming

The mathematical programming models discussed so far deal with solving problems involving a single decision time. Dynamic programming is a mathematical programming model for solving sequential problems where parameters of the model vary from period to period. Although dynamic programming is more powerful than the other models discussed, its computational requirements are very involved and time-consuming, even for small-sized problems.

Goal Programming

A problem with the mathematical programming models discussed above is that they do not permit consideration of multiple objectives. That is, these mathematical programming models can find the optimal solution when a single objective is specified, but for multiple and perhaps conflicting objectives, a special type of mathematical programming model is needed. Goal programming calls for goals instead of constraints. That is, each constraint is expressed as a goal with a priority level specified in ordinal terms. Within a given priority level, there may be several goals.

While goal programming represents a potentially powerful technique for finding optimal solutions to fixed-income portfolio management problems, no applications have been reported at the time of this writing.

APPLICATIONS

Mathematical programming has been used to provide solutions for many types of fixed-income portfolio problems, including immunization, dedicated portfolio strategies, indexing, optimized rebalancing, and asset allocation.

Immunization

Immunization is a structured portfolio strategy designed to protect against interest-rate changes. A single-period immunization addresses one future liability when the objective is to construct a portfolio to minimize the risk that changes in interest rates will result in not satisfying the objective. Life insurance companies use single-period immunization in managing portfolios to satisfy their obligations of guaranteed investment contracts. A requirement for single-period immunization is that the duration of the portfolio be equal to the maturity of the liability.

Multiperiod immunization is used in the case of more than one future liability. Examples of multiple liabilities are liabilities of a pension fund, liabilities of annuity policies issued by life insurance companies, and liabilities resulting from a state-sponsored lottery. Once again, the objective is to construct a minimum-cost portfolio designed to satisfy all the liabilities, however interest rates change. Two requirements of multiperiod immunization are that (1) the duration of the portfolio be equal to the duration of the liabilities and (2) the convexity of the portfolio be greater than or equal to the convexity of the liabilities.

Dedicated Portfolio Strategies

A dedicated portfolio strategy involves construction of a portfolio to satisfy multiple liabilities but without duration or convexity requirements. Instead, a minimum-cost portfolio is constructed so that the portfolio's cash flow matches as closely as possible the amount and the times when the liabilities must be paid. A dedicated portfolio strategy therefore is also referred to as a *cash flow matching strategy.*

A popular variation of the immunization and dedicated portfolio strategies is a *combination strategy,* also called a *horizon-matching strategy.* Here a portfolio is duration-matched, with the added constraint that it be cash-matched in the first few years, usually 5 years. The advantages of combination matching over immunization are that liquidity needs are provided for in the initial cash flow-matched period. Because most of the positive slope or inversion of a yield curve tends to take place in the first few years, cash flow matching the initial portion minimizes the risk associated with nonparallel shifts of a sloped yield curve.

An extension of cash flow-matching is *symmetric cash matching.* It allows the portfolio manager to construct an optimal portfolio that allows for borrowing to meet a particular liability.

Indexing

Indexing involves constructing a portfolio to match the performance of a specified index. There are three popular methodologies for designing a portfolio to replicate an index: (1) the cell approach, (2) the optimization approach, and (3) the variance minimization approach.

The cell approach divides the index into cells, each representing a different characteristic of the index. The most common characteristics used to distinguish a bond index are (1) duration; (2) coupon; (3) maturity; (4) market sector (Treasury, corporate, mortgage-backed); (5) credit rating; (6) call factors; and (7) sinking fund features. The objective is to select from all of the issues in the index one or more issues in each cell that can be used to represent the entire cell. No optimization is involved with this methodology.

The optimization approach requires the portfolio manager to construct a portfolio that will not only match a cell breakdown and satisfy other constraints, but also optimize some objective. An objective could be to maximize the yield to maturity or some other yield measure, to maximize convexity, or to maximize total return.[1] Constraints other than matching the cell breakdown might include not investing more than a specified amount in one issuer or group of issuers and overweighting certain sectors for enhanced indexing. Depending on the mathematical characterization of the objective function and constraints, either linear or quadratic programming is used to solve for the optimal portfolio.

The variance minimization methodology is by far the most complex. It requires the use of historical data to estimate the variance of the tracking error. This is accomplished by statistically estimating a price function for every issue in the index on the basis of two sets of factors: (1) the cash flows from the issue discounted at theoretical spot rates[2] and (2) other characteristics such as those described earlier. Once the price function for each issue is estimated, a variance equation for the tracking error is constructed. The objective then is to minimize the variance of the tracking error in constructing an indexed portfolio. Quadratic programming is used because the variance is a quadratic expression, and the objective is to minimize the variance.

---

1   For a mathematical presentation of this methodology, as well as the variance minimization methodology, see
     Christina Seix and Ravi Akoury, "Bond Indexation: The Optimal Quantitative Approach," *Journal of Portfolio
     Management* (Spring 1986), pp. 50–53.
2   Theoretical spot rates are explained in Chapter 7.

Optimized Portfolio Rebalancing

Once the optimal solution or optimal portfolio is found in any particular application, the optimization process does not end. In most strategies, an initially optimal portfolio must be rebalanced periodically as the characteristics of the portfolio change. For example, in an immunized portfolio, the duration for the individual issues changes over time as the issues approach maturity and as yields in the market change. Therefore the portfolio's duration will change or wander from its target.

Rebalancing requires the purchase of issues (either new issues not in the original optimal portfolio or additional amounts of issues included in the original portfolio) and the sale of some or all of the issues in the original optimal portfolio. An optimization model can be used to minimize the transactions costs associated with rebalancing a portfolio.

Asset Allocation

The objective of an asset allocation model is to divide funds among major asset classes so as either (1) to maximize expected return subject to a certain level of risk or (2) to minimize risk subject to a certain level of expected return. The two are equivalent statements of the asset allocation problem.

The basic inputs for an asset allocation model are expected returns of the major asset classes, risk estimates, and correlations (or covariances) for each major asset class. The portfolio's expected return is simply the weighted average of the expected value of each asset class, where the weight is the proportion of the portfolio devoted to the asset class. That is, if X_i denotes the proportion of the portfolio allocated to asset class i and R_i the expected return for asset class i, the portfolio's expected return, assuming that there are M major asset classes, can be expressed as

$$E(R_p) = X_1 R_1 + X_2 R_2 + \cdots + X_M R_M,$$

where $E(R_p)$ is the expected return for the portfolio.

The expected risk of a portfolio is measured by the variance of the portfolio. Unlike the expected portfolio return, which is a weighted average of the expected return of each asset class, the portfolio variance also depends on the covariance (or correlation) between the asset classes. For example, if there are only two asset classes, the portfolio variance is calculated as follows:

$$\mathrm{Var}(R_p) = X_1^2 \, \mathrm{Var}(R_1) + X_2^2 \, \mathrm{Var}(R_2) + 2 \, X_1 \, X_2 \, \mathrm{Covar}(R_1, R_2),$$

where

$\mathrm{Var}(R_p)$ = Portfolio variance;
$\mathrm{Var}(R_i)$ = Variance of asset class i;
$\mathrm{Covar}(R_1, R_2)$ = Covariance between the returns for asset classes 1 and 2.

Alternatively, the portfolio variance can be expressed as follows:

$$\mathrm{Var}(R_p) = X_1 \mathrm{Var}(R_1) + X_2 \, \mathrm{Var}(R_2)$$
$$+ 2 \, X_1^2 \, X_2^2 \, \mathrm{Std}(R_1) \, \mathrm{Std}(R_2) \, \mathrm{Corr}(R_1, R_2),$$

where

$\mathrm{Std}(R_i)$ = Standard deviation of asset class i;

$\mathrm{Corr}(R_1,R_2)$ = Correlation between the returns for asset classes 1 and 2.

Because the portfolio variance is a quadratic expression (the decision variables—the X_i's—are squared), quadratic programming is used.

Given the portfolio expected return and variance, quadratic programming will yield a set of optimal or efficient portfolios. These are portfolios that will give the minimum portfolio variance for a given level of expected portfolio return.

The asset allocation model can be extended further. Beyond developing a model to minimize portfolio risk, the decision maker can determine the probability of not achieving a portfolio expected return. These probabilities are referred to as *risk-of-loss probabilities*.[3] The model can be extended further to provide an optimal asset allocation when short-term and long-term expectations are different.

SUMMARY

Optimization models indicate the best solution to a problem, given some objective function and one or more constraints. Mathematical programming models are used in problems where an optimal solution is sought. Of the several types of mathematical programming models, the two most commonly used in fixed-income portfolio management are linear programming and quadratic programming.

Optimization models are typically used in structured portfolio strategies, which include indexing and liability funding (immunization and dedicated portfolio strategies). Optimization models are also used in making asset allocation decisions.

---

3 For a further explanation of risk of loss analysis, see H. Gifford Fong and Frank J. Fabozzi, "Asset Allocation Optimization Models," in Robert D. Arnott and Frank J. Fabozzi (eds.), *Active Asset Allocation* (Chicago: Probus Publishing, 1992), Chapter 8.

INDEX